CW00505873

Copyright © 2019 by Binswood Trading Limited

This book is copyright under the Berne Convention

No reproduction without permission

All rights reserved

The right of Dr Hafeez Ahmed to identify as the author of this work has been asserted by him in accordance with the Copyright, Design and Patents Act 1988

This book is dedicated to my next door neighbour
and long-time sweetheart

MR RAY FRENCH

www.thephilosophyfridge.co.uk

THE
PHILOSOPHY
FRIDGE

About the author who never imagined
he'd ever make an appearance on page 3

**Dr Hafeez Ahmed, BDS; DGDP (RCS); FDS (RCS);
MSc perio; Mclin Dent; MRD (RCS); PGCAP.**

Qualified as a Dentist in 1992; then as a Periodontal
Specialist in 2001 and has worked as a part time
clinical teacher throughout the same period. Born in
Birmingham, married with 3 teenage children and no pets.

'Dr Hafeez Ahmed's book
'The Philosophy Fridge' is not just
the story of one man's personal
courage in standing up to the
establishment. It is about turning
negative experiences into a
philosophy of life. What was
initially intended as a useful source
of wisdom for his children is now
available to the public at large. '

Mr Daniel Gysin
Modern Languages teacher
leading London co-educational,
Independent school.

'Under pressure, I'd have
understood if Hafeez had
suffered a complete mental
and physical breakdown.
But the Philosophy Fridge!
Who could have anticipated
that? An essential text
book for HR professionals
about how NOT to do it'

Mrs Jill Faulkner FIPD DMS CertHE.
Retired Director of HR and
Organisational Strategy and
Director of Jill Faulkner Ltd

'Shocking, disturbing, prickly, insightful, inspiring
and laugh out loud. A human tale of the highs and
lows which ultimately make you stronger'

Mr Robert Glinton,
Chartered Accountant

TABLE OF CHAPTERS

INTRODUCTION

As so often happens in life, something good comes out of something bad.

This is a true story depicting resilience being built, and perhaps, the most challenging period of my life thus far. You could call it a bad moment. It describes how after showing the courage to become a whistleblower, substantial deficiencies in my experience and knowledge were exposed. The abstract pain of inexperience quickly became a blood-letting at a medieval abattoir with me thrashing in the hay, short on resilience. You'll learn how instead of allowing myself to continue being indiscriminately beaten, battered and broken, I plugged the deficiencies to clinch the equivalent of a PhD in resilience.

My story took me to the brink of physical and nervous breakdown and back again, and I wanted to write this book for my three children to help them become more courageous and stronger; if it helps others that's also great. I planned not to whinge as nobody likes a whinger and it's easier to like a winner, but in writing realised that some whinging was necessary to portray the dark side of the whistleblower's experience. I aim to give you a glimpse of who I am, why I am, where I'm from and what I've learnt along the way.

My intention is to tell the story authentically and as it happened. Harsh, brutal, primal, shocking and unacceptable. I lay out the blood and guts and then I demonstrate how I transmuted each negative event into a positive self-development opportunity. I let the story unfold as it happened and don't force it. I hope to make clear that, in my opinion, confidence and resilience can only be developed through experience. There is no other way. Its development requires parents to start exposing their children to tailored experiences from a very early age and continue this through the teenage and adolescence years so it can be celebrated in adulthood. The workplace should not be responsible for developing these attributes and nor should it suppress them, if they are present. The problem, as I see it is the vast majority of individuals arrive in the workplace at the age of 16, 19 or 21 not knowing who they are or what drives them to be there.

In my experience, resilience is a characteristic which embodies strength, confidence, tenacity and endurance to impart an individual the ability to cope in any situation, good or bad; allowing them to bounce back favourably. It's usually associated with snatching triumph from adversity. Courage alone was not enough, as it merely got me embroiled in a contrived situation which then required resilience to endure it to its completion. During the experience I repeatedly lost my confidence, my strength and my tenacity but the process of clawing at it and regaining it time after time is how the resilience was built.

A whistleblower is an individual who exposes any kind of information or activity that is deemed illegal, unethical or not correct within an organisation that is either private or public. The whistle can be blown internally or externally. The desired outcome once the whistle has been blown is for the employer to address the concerns, conduct the necessary investigations and rectify the causes. Unfortunately what often happens instead is what happened to me. I became the focus of a vengeful attack by my employer for having raised concerns and exposing failings like a villain or an outcast. Reputational damage and job loss was my preordained punishment, something I attempted tirelessly to prevent.

My former employer was a large university teaching hospital, one in which trainees honed their skills by practising on willing members of the public. To maintain confidentiality I have referred to my former employer as 'The Icon' for its self image. In places I've used, as synonyms; 'The Iconic Machine' or 'The Machine' for its faceless mechanical operations and sometimes: 'The Dental Institute' for its intended function. I was employed by The Icon as a permanent part-time specialist clinical teacher. I'm registered as a specialist periodontist (gum specialist) with the General Dental Council (GDC).

I raised my concerns and simultaneously blew the whistle in **September 2015** because the leadership team at The Icon repeatedly violated their own written professional and ethical policies as well as the policies of multiple regulators.

Truth wasn't the only casualty as my concerns described incidents and provided the evidence of:

- An unnecessary compromise to patient safety.
- Patient harm.

- Negative impact on and compromise to the standards of education of the undergraduate students in respect to integrated restorative care and more specifically periodontal care.
- Concealment of the above.

To make a bad situation worse The Icon ignored patients and students when they complained, something that happened regularly. My confidentiality was compromised within a month of me raising concerns and word got out about how appallingly I was being treated by the leadership team, as they repeatedly scrambled to bury and conceal my concerns. I suffered the professional and personal humiliation of being suspended in **March 2017**. I endured two cycles of disciplinary action and whilst, both were flawed they found the multiple allegations against me unproven. The outcome did not prove any misconduct on my part but despite this I was unfairly dismissed in **January 2018** on the ostensible grounds of a 'breakdown in relationship' by a leadership team who were determined to punish me for having exposed their failings.

I would not encourage anyone to blow the whistle without a serious mental and physical health check, and a significant amount of preparation, especially since, throughout my journey, I didn't feel protected by the law at any stage. There were times when I became deeply anxious and depressed. Constant provocations and the assault on my reputation and self-worth were often overwhelming. However, every time I suffered an extreme episode of doubt, anxiety or depression, a philosophical quotation would somehow 'find me', or be found for me by my very good friend, Dr Ashley Davenport.

I used our kitchen fridge as a whiteboard to gather pertinent philosophical quotations that consoled and inspired me during my experience and they now comprise the theme of this book. Once laden with quotations our fridge took on a new life as **'The Philosophy Fridge'**. Inception over, it serendipitously changed my attitude towards how my wife and I interacted with our three children on matters of education, learning and life in general. I explained to my children how the philosophical quotations became my saviour, empowered me and enabled me to act with greater resilience. I explained my mind's journey, how it became a dark place, and how the quotations brought back the illumination. The words of wisdom provided an organic energy with a whiff of sunrise freshness which lapped gently at the shores of my mind and much like a wave lifts a bronzed surfer-dude they lifted my spirits.

I use philosophy by referring to it in a very general sense rather than as the product of recognised philosophers. My preferred philosophy is practical over abstract; common sense and with minimal complications. The quotes I have included helped me navigate a path and even though some are not from actual 'philosophers' their authors were nevertheless respected iconic individuals. I've presented the quotes purely for the impact the words had on me and exactly how they were preselected to me, and as such the words may not always be how they were originally stated by their respective authors.

I openly admitted to myself that I had fallen and become trapped in a trench of stench, facing painfully tough situations for which I had no experience. These quotes came to me by fate, luck and chance. I'm unable to describe the forces or energies responsible for this remarkable phenomenon but whatever they were proved to be helpful, fulfilling and enlightening. I remain in awe of and am grateful for the experience they have given me, especially since their impact was more than the simple acquisition of knowledge.

I came to realise that the vacuum created by my inexperience and insecurities was instrumental to me becoming receptive of the nuggets of inspirational gold they held. As I received each quote I was no longer working alone but instead, I found myself alongside its author. Their words inspired resilience and a state of mind which changed my thinking altogether. Ultimately, a change in attitude best describes what I've gained from the experience.

I begin each themed chapter by displaying the quotation that broke an impasse where I had no idea of how to proceed; this is followed by a description of the impasse. The quote's author is credited where possible and other key quotes supporting the theme are also liberally spread throughout. Each chapter explains the challenges and the difficulties for which inspiration was required, the moment the inspiration was delivered, my interpretation of the quotation and how the interpretation changed my thinking and my actions.

The Philosophy Fridge has also proven unintentionally, to be my greatest success as a father so far. Once merely our kitchen fridge, it has become the main hub of our house and is now a relaxed, safe environment for us to explore existential ideas with our three children. As they move towards adulthood I am certain they will be grateful for this early exposure to philosophy and that it will have a positive influence on their daily interactions with their world. For now, they've wholeheartedly embraced something that I went through great pain in working out:

'not to question what people do, simply accept that they do it'

Jordan Peterson

During the writing of this book I noted, as a general rule of thumb, that our society has a high degree of discomfort concerning emotions and feelings. One of the consequences of which was my surprise when I realised that it was highly probable that my childhood had left me with higher than average levels of resentment (which I'll explain later). Working this out was an important moment in my life and having done so I have made a conscious effort to minimise resentful tones in my writing to prevent them from undermining the context of the overall experience. I also apologise if in some places it might read like a letter from an angry child to a corrupt cultural cradle.

I hope you enjoy the book!

Progress can be Elusive

'Progress is always driven by an unreasonable man'

George Bernard Shaw

This was the seminal quotation which initiated a fulfilling life-changing adventure, by altering the course of an experience which had unexpectedly come off the rails and turned it into one rich in learning and the one which opened me up to the inexplicable power of words. It snapped me back from the abyss of desperate loneliness.

It was revealed to me on **Friday 6th November 2015** during an alumni dinner hosted at the Palace of Westminster in London. The impasse was a near catatonic mental state which developed in the seven weeks after I blew the whistle. Resulting from a spectrum of anxieties previously unknown, pushing me into an unsolicited courtship with a range of depressions I'd never experienced before. These eight words lifted me out from the anxieties and guided me away from the depressions into something more positive.

In this chapter I will explain why the contradictory behaviour of a leadership team's acts of pretence and sincerity. And other key events resulted in my cradle of self-belief slumping to lowest I had ever experienced. How I had not known that this kind of self-discovery requires - and only occurs during periods of - challenge, uncertainty and change. How it was that luck, fate and chance alone prevented me from missing the quotation. I will talk you through my mind's state during each stage of the journey but especially how the words and wisdom changed it.

The Experience

I raised my concerns and simultaneously blew the whistle by sending an e-mail to my line manager, (my immediate superior) on the **15th September 2015**. He didn't acknowledge it. Not a word. If you've ever been ignored you will already know that it comes as a shock and the wall of silence starts to tear at your core. For those who haven't experienced it, being ignored comes as a shock and tears at your core. I fought off a rising tide of anxieties and submitted a second protected disclosure. In this one, I added to the concerns I had already raised by detailing new ones to the same line manager on the **21st September 2015**. He didn't acknowledge this one either. Again, not a word despite the e-mail being copied to the Head of Department. I was amazed at how lonely I started to feel, (I suspect it was what my line manager intended). Once again, I defeated my negativity and self-criticism and – with Olympic gold standard naivety - I submitted a third disclosure. Again, I added to the concerns I had already raised by listing new ones to the same line manager on the **28th September 2015** again copied to the Head of Department. On this occasion, my line manager acknowledged my concerns and commenced investigations into them. Wrong. He didn't acknowledge this one either nor did the Head of Department.

I'll describe (in chapter 4) in more detail what constitutes a whistle-blow and what makes a disclosure a protected one but for now here are a few excerpts from my first three protected disclosures:

- ....appears to be a complete institutional meltdown....
- ...suffering from a complete widespread institutionalized... incompetence rendering it "not fit for purpose"
- ....is failing to offer the correct level of support for me to do my job....
- ....massively compromised patient safety...
- ....massively compromised student learning....
- ...professional negligence....
- ...circumnavigation of professional responsibility...

I was not reporting minor cock-ups or a small degree of human error. I was spilling the blood and dishing out the shit sandwiches on major failings. The single points of violation of The Icons written professional and ethical polices could no longer be considered as isolated or single, and I had imagined that the leadership team would be murmuring to each other - like high priests - as to how they would respond to my concerns. I had anticipated that I might be faced with a workable degree of conflict, the type which creates some co-operative competition and a 'can do' spirit.

My formal expressions of concern were handled by the most senior members of the leadership team and to respect their privacy I've given each of them a false identity, one which best reflects their role in the story.

Leadership Role	Given Identity
Executive Dean	Professor Awakened
Dean of Education	Professor Honest
Head of Department	Dr Dependable
Clinical Director	Dr Legitimate
Line Manager & Team Lead	Dr Available
Human Resources	Honest Reality
Dean of Undergraduate Education	Dr Comprehensive
Chairman of The Icons Council	Dr Insightful

Having been ignored by both my line manager and the Head of Department, I escalated my concerns to three senior members of the leadership team on the **30th September 2015**; I sent copies of my 3 earlier e-mails to Professor Awakened, Professor Honest and Dr Legitimate. They all sent acknowledgements within an hour or so. (I didn't know at the time but it would be the last time I would hear from Professor Awakened or that she would resign in January 2017 shortly after I'd escalated my concern to the General Dental Council).

I didn't wake up one morning and suddenly decide to blow the whistle, far from it. I did so when all other avenues had been exhausted. I was reluctant to go against a system I belonged to, especially since between 1997 and 2001 I had completed my specialist training at the same place. The decision wasn't an easy one as some of the current leadership team had been consultants during my training and had, by virtue of this become my role models. I was however, a human being with a sense of myself and a heart in the right place. There was a contradictory disconnect between what they were describing as excellent and what was actually taking place on the clinics day to day. This could no longer be ignored and drifting along was not a viable option. I had to contend with the fact my supposed role models were describing the clinics as excellent whilst in reality the very same clinics were dangerous. At this very early stage, I still held respect for them and naturally this made it particularly difficult for me to start to pick apart the potential causes of the problems with the clinics. There seemed to be a bias against relevance; the more important the issue the less it was discussed. But because of it, my teaching colleagues and I were increasingly made to feel as if we were doing something terribly wrong. I could not have known that the verbal sleight-of-hand was deliberate and I hadn't imagined - prior to my experience - that there was a reason for it. It was to prevent us from becoming fully aware of our predicament, as if we did we would demand systemic change and systemic change was very threatening to the business of the university.

Whenever we were given a presentation from any of the above listed individuals they would present The Icon as a beacon of excellence, and speak of all the excellent work they were doing and all the excellent achievements they had presided over. On one occasion during a presentation by Professor Awakened, someone heckled her with 'You obviously haven't been on the clinics recently'. A muffled laugh travelled through the audience like a Mexican wave and although everybody else heard the heckle, Professor Awakened continued unabated as if she hadn't. The Icons excellent performance in the most recent National Student Survey always got a mention as did The Icon's superior position in the world ranking of universities (1) - one of the highest of all the dental schools in Europe. The chorus note to every presentation was the paramount importance of abiding by the General Dental Council's (GDC) published standards which included 'putting patients first'. The importance of abiding by the Care Quality Commission's (CQC) newly introduced 'duty of candour' was always delivered with a seriously stiff and stern face. It would have been impossible to have imagined that this was all just 'lip service'.

(1)   https://www.timeshighereducation.com/world-university-rankings

The teaching was expected to be of an excellent standard and often (in an attempt to keep us distracted) teaching excellence awards and prizes were handed out. What made my colleagues and I uncomfortable was that that none of the above was actually taking place on any of the clinics I attended or managed, or any of the clinics that my teaching colleagues were managing. The students weren't the beneficiaries of any such excellent teaching for which the awards were being handed out.

The need for change in the healthcare world was identified following scandalous failures in care and management at the Mid Staffordshire NHS Foundation Trust. Sir Robert Francis QC had chaired an independent public inquiry into those failings. On 6th February 2013 he produced, at a cost of £13 million to the tax payer an 1800 page report which became known as the 'The Francis Report'. The report spoke of a future of zero tolerance and transparency, it encouraged individuals to 'speak out' and raise concerns. Care providers were to have a whistleblowing policy and were required to encourage their staff to blow it. It said that those who spoke out would be protected against recriminations from the employer. The CQC set up the 'National Guardian's Office' to protect those who spoke out. Off the back of the same report there was a health and social care act reform which resulted in the creation of the current incarnation of the body known as 'NHS Improvement' which also championed and encouraged a culture of speaking out in the name of better care for patients. The regulators published endless glossy brochures announcing what they expected of us. They made it clear they expected 'patients to be put first', 'a duty of candour', excellence in care and excellence in teaching; they wanted individuals to speak out and ultimately for them to 'blow the whistle' when necessary. 'Blow the whistle' incidentally is a term borrowed from the days when police officers carried a whistle and blew them to attract attention to distress.

The leadership team told us that they were 100% behind the drive for excellence and were devoted to making any necessary changes. They implied that they themselves were working to the very highest of standards and they expected the same from the rest of us.

I had returned to The Icon as a Specialist Clinical Teacher in 2013 and immediately found myself in a state of confusion, (looking back I have no doubt that the lack of induction was not accidental). Anyhow, I did what everyone else was doing and adopted The Icon's preferred approach to raising concerns; quietly, discreetly, in doorways, corridors and always 'off the record'. I remained unsure and reluctant for some considerable time but the incongruence of the situation was ever present. I put my feelers out by asking some of the teachers who had been at The Icon for ten years or more. They all reported the same mayhem on clinics. (Wouldn't you be confused if your employer constantly bragged about having one of the highest QS rating's when all the evidence was contradictory?)

In the two years running up to the whistle-blow I raised my concerns verbally about the 'operational peculiarities' with Head of Department, Dr Dependable. Somehow it never seemed like a good time for him to talk. The more important the issue the less likely it was that he would have time to discuss it. On one occasion I expressed my concern to him that 'we were no longer teaching the students how to treat gum disease' and 'we were no longer treating the gum disease in our patients'. His response of 'If we don't make their condition worse over a four year period that's a good outcome' came as a surprise to me at first, but the surprise evaporated when I heard it repeated by another senior member of staff shortly after. On another occasion, during a departmental meeting on performance, when I raised my concerns in front of about six other teachers he silenced me with:

'Can you be quiet; I have to ensure this meeting runs on time.'

Often senior staff lamented, without irony that:

'Our patients get what they deserve, what do they expect for free.'

Only it wasn't free. Whilst nominally free, the costs are hidden, state-funded care via a university teaching hospital is the most expensive option; often more expensive than the local private equivalent. I felt compelled and continued to raise my concerns, and each time I did the Head of Department, Dr Dependable acknowledged them and ascribed them to the leadership team. He told me on several occasions that he had already informed Professor Awakened, Professor Honest, Dr Legitimate and Dr Comprehensive of the problems on the clinics. I had no reason not to so, I kept believing what I was told but kept wondering why there were no improvements.

As the conditions on the clinics didn't improve I continued to wonder why and if, perhaps, I was missing something or if, perhaps, The Icon's preference for incognito communications was because it made it easier to ignore or remove the complainants. In the early days I found it difficult to convince myself of this. But inevitably, I became suspicious – very suspicious - that there was no record of me having raised any concerns. They simply didn't exist - yet the clinics were dangerous. I feared that in the event of a major incident (like a patient having a medical emergency) on the clinics, the burden of responsibility remained mine. It worried me that The Icon recorded major incidents as 'never-events'; for example, if the wrong tooth was removed for a patient it was recorded as a 'never-event', a practice accepted by indemnity insurers. It appeared to me that the leadership team could easily defend themselves against a 'never-event' by claiming that they had not been advised, on record, of any concerns about the clinics, effectively rendering the teacher (me) culpable.

It wasn't long before my suspicions were confirmed when one of my teaching colleagues suffered a bit of a blunder. A patient was dumped on him at short notice. The patient, who came with the trademark woefully inadequate notes, had been dumped on him after an almost standardised sequence of administrative failings and a string of complaints from the patient to The Icon. Upon arrival the patient was already unhappy and this immediately put my colleague on the back foot. In his attempts to protect the consultant and simultaneously appease the already unhappy patient the poor sod provided the treatment even though the consultant had not recorded the patient's consent. He was left to take the fall when, after the treatment was complete, the patient continued to complain stating they had never been informed about some of its implications. My colleague became the scapegoat and was given no alternative but to resign. The incompetent consultant kept his job.

As I thought about it I remembered that I had already raised my concerns 'on record' to Professor Honest back in **January 2015** when I sent him an e-mail detailing them. It could be argued that essentially I blew the whistle in January 2015 but as I hadn't mentioned the compromise to patient safety technically I had not. That said, putting them in writing and 'on record' in this way made no difference as he flicked me off, as one would a flea. As much as the disappointment and curiosity niggled at me I still remained reluctant to go against the system I belonged to but the challenge I faced, and had to the deal with, was that if I continued to raise my concerns I would continue to pit myself against my employer and its leadership team. This started to really worry me and became a challenge I couldn't reconcile or understand. Just as challenging as it would have been to know if it was right or wrong to punch my best friend in the face having caught him kissing my wife. By **September 2015** I had resolved that the only option left available to me was to blow the whistle and that's what I did next.

Blowing the whistle hadn't made a great deal of difference, I got ignored. I started to wonder if my line manager, Dr Available was responsible for some or all the problems on the clinics and perhaps that's why he had ignored me. Bidding against that thought was the fact that I had copied two of the three e-mails to the Head of Department, Dr Dependable and there hadn't been a peep out of him either. I didn't have to contemplate the issues for long as I was swiftly invited to a meeting with the Clinical Director, Dr Legitimate; which took place on **Friday the 2nd October 2015** (two days after I'd escalated my concerns to the senior members of the leadership team). Dr Dependable and Dr Available would be attending the same meeting.

On the morning of the meeting I was tense with trepidation as I wasn't looking forward to a meeting with Dr Legitimate. I didn't really know him personally but had heard some rumours of his unpleasant nature, in addition to which, I knew that one of my colleagues had been cornered by him and given no option but to resign over some blunders. I knew I was frightened but I also knew I wasn't scared. The problem was being created by new anxieties as they were causing blurs in established boundaries. I spent the entire journey rehearsing the possible scenarios that might arise. As hard as I tried, I couldn't relax or stop playing them out in my consciousness; he might say this, I might reply that. You get the idea. I was less worried about the concerns I had raised and more worried about the fact that Dr Available and Dr Dependable might be embarrassed for having failed to acknowledge my concerns. It was possible that if they had, the meeting may have been avoided altogether. Instead, now they would undoubtedly be asked by the Clinical Director, Dr Legitimate for an explanation and that carried with it a potential for recriminations against me. Anyhow I somehow remained optimistic that I might be thanked for raising concerns but bidding against it was a more cautious me; that I might have got it horribly wrong. My expectation remained that the meeting would be used to explore my concerns; to start investigating and addressing them.

By the time I arrived for the actual meeting my emotions were flayed, I felt as if I had already attended twenty meetings, and it was only 8:45 in the morning. I supposed this was how plebs like me felt when they were about to meet with one of The Icon's senior management team. I use the word pleb because to this point I was made to feel I was not good enough but remained confident that I wasn't being treated poorly for reasons of class. I'm not putting myself down unnecessarily as most teaching staff felt the same way. Loaded with jitters I knocked on Dr Legitimates door. He opened it, the look on his face was of a man who desperately needed to take a dump (but had missed his opportunity to do so). His facial expression was tight, firm and forced, warrior-like, and he didn't look pleased to see me. I recognised the look; it was supposed to scare me. With his eyes wide he exhaled heavily as if he was attempting to achieve reverse thrust on his offending torpedo. After one quick look at me he immediately averted his eyes from mine and looked into the distance over my right shoulder. Still looking into the yonder he pointed at the chairs in his waiting room and advised me to take a seat, which I did. He chose his words carefully:

'Ah it's you, you've arrived. I'm busy doing something important right now, take a seat over there; I'll sort you out in a minute.'

His comments crashed into me. Why was he being like this, I hadn't done anything wrong? Had I? I'd only done what I'd been told to do by him and his colleagues at the top. It would have been alright if I had done something wrong, I could have lived with that. I might not have liked it but at least it would have made sense. I searched his face for any sign of compassion, nope just concrete. I'd expected seriousness and resolve but all I got was swagger and impatience. As I took a seat I could feel my heart beating in my temples. Once seated, I closed my eyes and attempted to meditate. I had to try something, anything to calm my nerves. The displeasure in his face gave me butterflies which felt more like moths and I had to keep pausing to take deep breaths. He could have been nominated for an Oscar in the 'aggressive bully boy' category for his use of non-verbal language. His performance didn't help my nerves much, but I doubt it was supposed to.

As I continued to wait, my mind remained tense and only got more tense with time. It simultaneously juggled the past with the present with the future, back and forth; back and forth, it was exhausting. I sat and reflected on how he had deliberately averted his eyes from mine and how he had crafted his words so carefully. And as I did, I sat there repeating to myself, teeth gritted, 'I'm 46 not 4; I'm 46 years old not 4 years old'. He'd chosen his words to portray that he was important and that I was not, and that I was a problem he was going to sort out in a small gap between doing other important things. I sat there and attempted to settle my mind by playing with words:

'It's important for him to be busy, because being busy is what makes him important.'

Oh what fun! My meditation was disturbed when he returned to collect me from the waiting area. He walked over to where I was sat and stood in front and essentially above me. He seemed to miscalculate the distance between us. I had to quickly pull my feet in otherwise he'd have ended up standing on my big toe. Toe-to-retracted toe he growled at me:

'You have got the entire leadership team looking at you right now.'

'Yes? I responded and he felt the need to repeat himself, which he did:

'You have got the entire leadership team looking at you right now, because of the number of e-mails you have sent them all.'

I had only sent one e-mail to each to the 3 most senior members of the leadership team; him, Professor Awakened and Professor Honest. Nevertheless as he had repeated himself I again said 'yes' ever so slightly louder as one would do with someone who they thought might be slightly deaf. I couldn't stop myself from wearing the vacant gaze of a man pretending. It worried me that he had made no effort to conceal that he was rankled, and driven by a subconscious reaction I made no effort to appease him. It was not a good start and my synapses started popping and crackling. He offered no smile, no handshake, no small talk and no team spirit.

I followed Dr Legitimate into his office; Dr Dependable and Dr Available were already seated. Dr Available stood up, greeted me and shook my hand. Dr Dependable remained seated, he had adopted a strange posture for a meeting, leaning back with his one leg crossed over the other forming the figure four, right ankle resting on left knee. His posture made me feel as if I was just a dancing gypsy to him. I didn't know the body language for 'You are starting to worry me'. So I just sat down. I couldn't work out why they looked so pensive, we were only here to roll up our sleeves and figure this thing out but instead it was looking like some great tragedy had occurred. Say what you like about those in leadership roles, I knew they had a tough job on their hands and I'd been on clinics with Dr Dependable and watched him work himself to exhaustion, but we weren't here to discuss that today.

The meeting kicked off - literally - with a firm statement belted out with a tremendous wallop by Dr Legitimate:

'You have accused me of incompetence'

I felt a catch in my throat and acknowledged his statement with a blank gaze of shock and accompanied it with an invisible nod, you know when you feel like you've nodded but you haven't because your brain is in shock. He repeated his statement three more times and each time he repeated it, he did so with a staged increase in aggression. As he continued with a sustained blast of invective it was being confirmed that he had self-anointed himself as chief bully boy. I may have been in disbelief but I still remained thankful there was no arm waving. I couldn't stop myself thinking 'your blouse button has popped open, sweetheart' as I sat looking at him. I imagined myself slowly shaking my head from side to side and saying 'why would you say that, this is not about you it's about the students and the patients.... oh and the institute you fella's have broken'. These were all the wrong sort of noises, it was only about 9.15am but we were already losing daylight. Dr Legitimate had no time for micro-aggressions, he was uptight and getting even more and the only reasonable explanation I could think of was he should've gone for that poo before the meeting started. Whatever he was up to made it surreal for me. He was so manly that he could have been chewing a bullet for all I knew, puce-faced and shouting. Low stress became theoretical and any presumption of my innocence evaporated in the scorching heat. One thing was for sure, the two things I richly deserved were off the menu. I wasn't going to get an apology or a thank you. On the upside my chair was the same height as everyone else's.

There was definitely an air of violence in the room and I didn't feel any love. But why? I hadn't done anything wrong had I? I had only done what I was told to? And whilst I was distracted wondering what was going on I subconsciously (possibly with the assistance of the holy spirit) turned my chair towards Dr Legitimate and pulled myself closer to him, but not close enough for a hug. I was perhaps letting him know that he didn't frighten me with his loud voice (but he did). To maintain some dignity and composure I continued to talk to myself and reassured myself that I hadn't done anything wrong. The hostility replaced any enquiry. It wouldn't be fair to say there was no enquiry because there was one, but it was more a Spanish Inquisition. I wouldn't have minded a thousand questions about my concerns, but I didn't get any. Instead I was criticised for raising each and every one of them. I was asked:

'Why are none of the other teachers complaining?'

I refuted the question with:

'They have been, you have ignored them, or silenced them, just like you are trying to do to me.'

I was asked:

'Why are none of the students complaining?'

I bounced the question back with:

'They have been, you have ignored them, or silenced them, just like you are trying to do to me'.

I was asked:

'What do you want?; "Do you think you are better than the rest of us?'

I just wanted what was best for the students and patients and for doing so I was being mocked and taunted in a threatening way; when all I ever wanted was to do an honest day's work for an honest day's pay. I was being treated like a criminal and not a petty one either. What a wretched state I was in and these weren't the quite mutterings of derision. Murder flashed across Dr Legitimate's eyes. The fury in the room could have lit a bushfire. It could certainly have set my hair on fire. It turned out that the secret prep talk I'd had with myself would come in handy after all. I'd made an agreement with myself:

'Don't behave like a caveman with his hair on fire.'

Irrespective of how I was treated, I was not going to behave like a caveman with his hair on fire. I'd have to show a willingness to be quiet and speak carefully. I'd have to control myself and show some grace under pressure. I achieved this even though I was experiencing confusion, anxiety, fear, shock, anger, realisation and embarrassment simultaneously for the first time ever. I countered my minds chemistry by placing two fingers on my left wrist, under the table, to check my pulse and tried to capture a calm image in my mind. The image I captured was a cuddly, cute, fluffy, white polar bear mauling a man with his bright red blood leaking into the crisp, white snow. I just couldn't seem to access the images of kittens that particular morning. How strange. I supposed what my mind was doing was trying to conceal my terror by thinking of something funny but it kept pinging off the chart.

I cannot believe that throughout the meeting I thought that the hostility would end and we would discuss my concerns. I was wrong. I incorrectly supposed that they would tire of trying to make themselves feel superior by making me feel inferior. By the final whistle the hostility lasted ninety sweaty minutes.

I was gob-smacked, why wouldn't I be? I was sat in a meeting with my peers but felt as if I'd stepped into the arena to take part in a blood sport with some heavyweight confidence tricksters. The Gestapo were shining their torch onto the back of my retina, it was blinding but it was too late; the whistle had been blown and there was no going back. It was not easy on me in any way and given the mental mangle I was being forced through, I felt over exposed, I felt cornered. I held my nerve and responded to all the unreasonable questions. I was honest, I was humble but I was not apologetic. I supposed that it came as a huge relief that no-one cracked their knuckles. We all hope to live a life that doesn't harm us but I was getting the impression that I was about to be harmed. Badly.

Due to the emotional chafing I seemed to develop a sort of gaze of concussion across my eyes which indicated to me that I wanted or needed to be left alone. I started to feel a need for some personal 'me' space away from fellow humans, (I later worked out that this was the first signal that the depression circuit was being tripped). I stared at my peers so intensely and with such an abstract vacancy that I could practically 'see' the oxygen molecules drift past them. I felt distant and dazed as if I'd been hit in the head with a hockey puck; they were starting to make me feel like an absolute horror of a human being. I was left with a hissing thought floating around my head "why are they treating me like I've been unreasonable?'; 'had I been unreasonable?' and with that I caught myself saying to myself: 'I don't want to meet any new humans, there's no point'. I appreciate that my use of the word 'humans' may read as odd, but it's how my mind reacted under pressure when their actions seemed to override my right to be treated like a person. Its use wasn't a conscious one; it came automatically from the deep recesses of my mind; probably as a form of protection.

As I was sat caught in an office with supposed peers feeling like I'd been caught in the villain's lair, it made it impossible for me not to consider if they could potentially have become blinded by a vengeful need to punish me, as if someone had snatched all their other senses. A question blinked in my mind much like a faulty fluorescent street sign: 'Why, oh why do those charged with designing heaven almost always end up delivering hell?' They were definitely holding that bizarre code that criminals hold dear, 'honour among the dishonourable'. The transferable skills on display would have come in handy if the Kray brothers were still recruiting. I wouldn't have dreamt of advising the Krays on how to run their shit or show and it was becoming evident that perhaps I shouldn't have raised my concerns to this crotchety crew either.

I was half expecting Dr Dependable to speak up and express his surprise by saying to Dr Legitimate: 'I've been telling you this and raising the same concerns for years', like he had previously told me he had done. Even if he'd fibbed and hadn't actually raised his concerns previously this was his chance to do so. But no. He proved to be no slouch; he stepped up and behaved equally despicably, with his feral snarling, his huffing and puffing. He put the boot in by asking me a loaded question:

'How is it that I can complete all my duties on the clinic and you cannot?' he asked.

My first thought as I stretched my forehead and raised my eyebrows in surprise was:

'What an absurd question to ask me?'

I supposed that he presumed I would be too shocked or frightened to challenge his statement or question it, but despite the fact that my blood seemed to be leaking into the carpet, he was wrong. I reminded him and the others, that he routinely failed to complete his duties as did everyone else. I went on to present him with a list of recent events in which he had failed to complete his duties. I reminded him of the time when having completed an afternoon clinic he had whinged to me about how it was going to take him two additional hours after the clinic, in his office, to complete his notes. And how I had told him that I wasn't blessed with an office in which to complete my notes.

Flustered by my self-defence Dr Dependable made a lame excuse that he needed to be somewhere else and left the meeting. Before leaving he agreed with Dr Legitimate to report on the clinical concerns I'd raised by speaking to the staff responsible for them prior to referring back to him for further discussions.

Dr Legitimate continued with his criticisms of me and seemed to be of the opinion that the more he treated me like crap the more I would be able to appreciate how important he was. It was having the opposite effect; my subconscious response was to start questioning if he could be trusted. The notion that any of these individuals were remotely interested in putting patients or students first was starting to look like complete and utter nonsense. Anyway Dr Legitimate closed the meeting as if he wanted me to return home like a naughty boy and never disturb him again by telling me that I'd hear from him once Dr Dependable had investigated the patient's notes (I was not to know at the time but he never did).

What troubled me most during the meeting was that my line manager, Dr Available barely spoke at all; he was less than of ornamental value. It was inconceivable that he wasn't aware of what was happening on the clinics, there had been multiple occasions when I raised the alarm, requested help and he'd been the one to help on several of them. This was his chance to help and rectify problems, but instead he let the opportunity drift by. That said, he made a few weak comments to support me and I suppose I should be grateful as he didn't attempt to deny or condemn them like the others had. But he had sat by silently and watched as they treated me like 'shit on their shoe'. They kept up the charade that no-one else had complained when it was inconceivable that they couldn't have known of the complaints made by other teachers. He probably knew that it was inconceivable that, as the head of a team, he hadn't seen the student's written complaints. (I wouldn't see the students' complaints until they were leaked to me and that wouldn't happen until after my dismissal. I was supplied them anonymously by a concerned staff member at The Icon. When I did finally read the students' complaints they mirrored mine closely, it was inconceivable that Drs Available, Dependable and Legitimate hadn't seen them).

After the meeting I returned to a busy treatment clinic and realised that I had underestimated a previous crucial warning and should have anticipated Dr Legitimate would attempt to squash me. The warning came during one of the annual teachers' training days which took place at the beginning of January. It was customary for all the teaching staff to attend these meetings and during one of them a senior teacher (who I shall call Ermentrude), gave a thank you speech for having been appointed 'student liaison officer', I was in the audience for her speech. She told us that she was taking over the role from Dr Legitimate and that he had said to her:

'I am glad you're taking over this role as it allows me to get back to being a bastard.'

The audience reflexively gasped and then after a micro second burst into laughter, leaving Ermentrude blushing. The red-faced Ermentrude was gob-smacked and lost for words but then - with almost perfect comedy timing - she spluttered:

'It's ok, I have his permission to call him a bastard.'

The audience turned and looked at each other in discomfort with raised eyebrows and things like that, but other than a faint hum they remained silent. It was an uncomfortable moment for Dr Legitimate who looked as if he was sinking into a hole. Naturally, the story now took on a whole new meaning, she hadn't been joking and I had no answer for why I'd failed to register the sinister nature of the man. During the meeting he certainly conducted himself in a way that made it clear to me that he rejoiced in his status of being a bully at The Icon, like a badge of honour. There was nothing ordinary or accidental about his behaviour. He was very precise with how he used it to bully me, as if I had no feelings at all.

In the days after the meeting as my adrenaline levels returned to street-level the brutality of it all did eventually catch up with me. It put me on edge for a good while after, and I found it difficult to sleep. My mind would not stop dissecting the meeting, minute-by-minute, over-and-over; I found it difficult to convince myself that they hadn't been tearing at me like hungry dogs. Poor sleep coupled with an overactive mind made me very twitchy. So my doctor kindly supplied 'sleep in a bottle'. Sedatives. I didn't take them for long and still don't understand how those who use them regularly ever get a day's work done.

The meeting had taken place on the morning of Friday 2nd October 2015 and by **Monday 5th October 2015** I had received Dr Legitimate's summary of it. In his summary he had carefully removed all traces of sinister behaviour. He had wiped the crime scene clean. His summary implied that he had conducted some sort of professional business like meeting. All details which may have proved uncomfortable at a later date had been withheld or withdrawn. Under normal circumstances I wouldn't have dreamt of challenging the seniority of the leadership's elite, but as he had me spooked with his bully boy behaviour I did. It was his heavy handed, caricature-like, projections of the non-verbal language that did it. Oh, and the shouting. Oh, and the pre-emptive criticisms. I felt so lucky that he'd treated me like shit. I wouldn't have refuted his summary if he'd taken a 'soft power' approach and 'kept the line' and if he had, he'd have had me snared and convinced me that he gave a damn. Instead, in my spooked state I refuted his summary and sent him my own in which I pointed out everything he had left out of his and pretty much described where all the bodies had been buried. It was lucky that I sent him my summary otherwise no one would have known what had happened; lucky indeed. Imagine if I hadn't refuted his summary; the meeting would've fallen under the radar concealing the bullying, harassment and victimisation.

The meeting had certainly been an unexpectedly difficult and challenging one, a bit 'Krypton Factor' like. At that time I hadn't had time to realise how it would change me. The change in me happened slowly but nothing about it made me feel good. To my strength I remained convinced I hadn't done anything wrong but I remained intimidated and unsure because of the enormity of accepting they that were deliberately engaged in a process of crushing me. Who the 'Oliver Cromwell' does that? We weren't in the 17th century? This wasn't a gangster movie? Was it? The meeting was straight out of 'The Godfather' so I named it the 'Nasty Meeting'.

My mind became preoccupied by The Icon's implications I was being unreasonable. The Nasty Meeting had frazzled my state of mind and I started to wonder if I should have blown the whistle at all. My sense of humour had been replaced with one of emotional spasticity and I lost my perception of time. It wasn't long before I had Ozzy Osbourne tap-dancing on my dura mater. The soundtrack of my mind had been taken over by The Prince of Darkness's hit song Paranoid. Its lyrics and melody resonated with the waves of my mind. The number of times his words yelled at the back of my mind in a single day disturbed me and our shared tragedies started to occupy my mind's sweet spot. The more I tried to distance myself the more it pulled me in. I could not, as much as I tried, convince myself that it didn't connect with me or offer me some sort of perverse comfort. If you haven't heard it, it's worth a listen.

My mind had come to temperature and thoughts popped randomly like pop-corn (one on top of the other). 'Was the meeting all about them protecting their own shit and their prized pay cheques?' They seemed to be using The Icon as some sort of ingenious corporate device; and much like many other corporations this one seemed to have acquired many dubious rights whilst shedding its responsibilities and discarding its obligations. I was unsure then, and still do not have a concrete answer for: 'was their income insufficient to purchase some morals or had their morals been traded for their income?' Anyway, it appeared to me that they were inherently prejudiced against me from the start. They hadn't bothered to portray the illusion of professionalism as their titles enabled them to swing an unprecedented weight. The thoughts kept on popping: 'How many other complainants had been knocked off before me?' I started to suspect that perhaps they had enough previous experience of escaping blame to know how to manipulate the bureaucracy, whilst I didn't.

On **16th October 2015** I attended a strange and awkward meeting with Professor Honest. In the run up to the meeting we exchanged about six e-mails and he said:

'I do not want an official type meeting but I want to chat to you about what works and what doesn't so that we can do better for you and the other teachers. I know what you feel is felt by others and what I want, and I hope all want, is for all teachers to feel valued and able to do the best they can. We do have limitations but we must try and work at the best we can. Don't we?'

I remember being surprised that he did not want an 'official type meeting' but understood that by this he meant he did not want a record of the meeting. I acquiesced to his request and I did not make a record of the meeting but I did send him the e-mail (pasted below) as a summary of it. Its content is self-explanatory and it should give a better understanding of the concerns I had raised and how they were being handled. To reflect that Professor Honest hadn't wanted an official type meeting I named it the 'Incognito Meeting'

Dear Professor Honest

Thank you for meeting with me on Friday 16th October 2015.

You wanted to discuss how best to improve communications between The Icon and the clinical teachers. You were concerned that at this time there was no communication.

I wanted to discuss my recent e-mails of feedback to The Icon and why I had forwarded them to all members of the leadership. We both agreed that we were aware of what I had disclosed in my e-mails. Due to the lack of response I had had to my concerns in the previous two years I had taken a decision to take a more assertive approach. I would continue with my assertive approach as it was clear that it was what was necessary for my concerns to be heard. You felt that it was unfortunate that my team lead had not been available for me to speak with on Fridays. I explained to you that I did not think that it would have made a great difference as I had lost confidence in him on my first day. I explained to you that on my first day at The Icon my team had an induction with our team lead. The meeting took place in the seminar room. He sat and described the screens that we would see when we used the computers. After some time one of the other new teachers suggested that it would be more appropriate for our team lead to locate a computer and simply show us the screens he was attempting to describe. Our team lead responded by saying 'what a great idea'. I thought he cannot be serious, he cannot be impressed by that suggestion, I accepted that perhaps this was the divide between practice and institution. Team lead left the room to locate a computer, he returned some minutes later and advised us that he had been unable to locate a computer on which he could demonstrate what he wanted us to know. He then proceeded to continue to describe the screens that he wanted to talk to us about. The whole morning session with him was a complete waste of time.

You had advised me in one of your earlier e-mails that all problems have a solution. I agree with you. Sadly, during the meeting on Friday 2nd October it was not agreed that there was a problem. The meeting turned out to be a bit of a witch-hunt to establish the validity of my disclosures and feedback. It was agreed at the end of the meeting that Dr Dependable would appraise the patient notes, Dr Available would establish if the other teachers were reading the notes made by the students or if they were indeed simply logging in pressing authorise and logging out.

I told you that it was unfair for Dr Legitimate to question the validity of my disclosures by informing me that in the most recent student survey The Icon had achieved its highest score, ever. The fact is that Professor Honorable had told the students in a meeting that if they underscored The Icon it would affect their chances of employment. I have no doubt that this would have falsely elevated The Icon's rating. You acknowledged this and said it had been a poor choice of words. Now that I have written it down it certainly looks like a poor choice of words.

In respect to your question how to best improve the communication between The Icon and the teachers. I advised you that some of the teachers had had their enthusiasm beaten out of them. They had raised their concerns and they had been effectively silenced. You have always said that feedback was welcome but when the feedback had been offered it had been ignored. The enthusiastic teachers hare become disenfranchised. The rest of the teachers view their day at the dental institute as their day off from proper work.

It was my opinion that if you wanted to get the teachers back onside you would need to be more clear and transparent with your intentions. I could see two ways of achieving such a thing. Admit to the failings and apologise for the effective silencing of the teachers. Secondly, you could send copies of my disclosures to all the teachers. Advise the teachers that you had not realised that things were as bad as I had described and ask them for their feedback. Once the feedback had been collected you could use the January 2016 teacher training day to present the findings and offer a proposal to rectify the same.

I told you that when I returned to The Icon after a break of 12 years it was a different machine. I did not have an induction, I did not get any direction and I did not get any leadership. Most of the teachers I have spoken to are of the same opinion, after securing a teaching post they were left to find their own way.

I told you that the notes for too many patients were inconsistent and woefully inadequate. This had resulted in a very defensive culture where patients who were no longer suited to the students' learning needs were not discharged back to primary care for fear of patient complaints. Should a patient complain the notes are not there to support The Icon's position and as such, students continue to see patients that are not suitable.

The same defensive culture has developed in respect to student complaints.

I told you that the senior clinical teachers that I had spoken to were pointing the finger at your leadership. I also told you that I doubt that the same individuals would have the courage or conviction to tell you personally; I don't know maybe they already have.

I advised you that what needed to be improved was
1. The student experience
2. The patient experience
3. A reduction in clinical teacher stress
4. Rectify the patient notes problem

I also told you that this was a challenge for the leadership, the senior clinical teachers and perhaps the consultants. It was not the remit of a part-time clinical teacher. The teachers want direction and leadership from the leadership team; the students want direction and leadership from the leadership team. It is for The Icon and its leadership to set the standards and goals. The Icon needs to direct its teaching staff and the students how it expects these standards and goals to be achieved. It is disingenuous to continue to ask the teachers and the students what improvements they would like to see.

I advised you that once I had identified the lack of clinical exposure the students had by their 4th Year I had prepared and sent them summaries of almost all their clinical sessions with me. I supplemented the summaries with anonymised essay reports that I had prepared for my patients in practice. This initiative embraced The Icon's objective of blended learning. However I received little or no support or encouragement. I suspect that the reason for this is that the other teachers do not have the time, enthusiasm or inclination to engage in this type of activity. I advised you that in the previous year I had effectively done two day's work for one day's pay. This is not sustainable.

It is recognised that patients require a lot of support to understand the importance of homecare. They need even more support for the learning of the necessary techniques. The Icon has absolute basic home care aids and there are no written or pictorial advice sheets that we can give to them. To address this limitation I started to use my oral hygiene video which I had uploaded to YouTube. After a short period of time the students offered positive feedback in respect to the video. The students were then sent an e-mail by their second year perio teachers to use this video to supplement their training in oral hygiene techniques. The students now routinely give details of this video to their patients on the clinic. Whilst I have accepted that I have been told by Dr Legitimate not to direct any more of The Icon's patients to the site, the students will need to be given the same instruction.

We discussed some of my thoughts and ideas on how best to achieve some of the necessary improvements. I would happily expand on the ideas we discussed but it is not currently part of my remit as a specialist clinical teacher. As a clinical teacher I should benefit from an induction and thereafter I should be given direction and leadership to help The Icon realise its goals. The induction and direction should be formatted and published so that all future appraisals could be used to assess my performance.

I am driven and enthusiastic and I want the problems to be solved. To solve a problem it needs to be accepted that a problem exists. Thereafter if you wish for my further input then time would need to be created for this activity and would need to be agreed how I would be paid for this time.

I am hopeful that things will start to change for the better.

Best regards

Dr Hafeez Ahmed

I had pointed out much the same when I'd written to Professor Honest on the **20th January 2015**. Back then he pretty much told me that his hands were tied but didn't really explain how. (I was not to know at the time but after our meeting on the 16th October 2015 I wouldn't hear from or see Professor Honest again until I would be invited to a meeting with him and HR on 8th April 2016 or that he would open the meeting by stating: 'I am only here because the others couldn't make it; I have no idea what this meeting is about.')

My mind was slowly getting shredded, why wouldn't it have? It was a strange and generally negative experience, one of my roughest experiences in life. I appreciate that some of you might still be wondering why The Icon had such a profoundly negative effect on me so let me explain. I had set out for the greater good of the patients and the students (like I was supposed to), but before doing so I had agonised because I did not want to upset a system that I knew I belonged to. I did however feel strongly about the problems which compromised patient safety and student learning; they needed addressing. The compromises to my day-to-day professional responsibilities had become intolerable and could not continue. My expectations when I blew the whistle were pure and simple; for positive change. Instead, what folded out in front of my eyes made me incredulous, there is no other way to describe it. The early actions taken by the leadership team had not created or been conducive to creating an atmosphere in which to address and resolve the concerns I'd raised. Whilst my mind preoccupied itself with aspects of the wrongful criticisms and The Icon's potential to corrupt future investigations, I had a particularly bad time concentrating on my work and family.

Being knocked about by the leadership team was just the rub that was required to release the self-doubt genie from the bottle. Once out genies are tricky to ignore or stuff back into the bottle. The self-doubt begets self-doubt creating an angst, the neutralisation of which required validation. So to add to my woes I was now on a constant hunt for validation. I hadn't the experience to sustain such a lengthy period of self-validation on a single subject. The process was made a little easier by Imani, my eldest daughter. She played a key role in my validation thoughts as she ticked all the same boxes as the individuals on behalf of whom I had blown the whistle. She had been a patient of mine and she was a student. In my mind my patients and my students were her equals and just like her, they were somebody's children, they deserved the same respect. I didn't want to fail in my responsibility to them as a professional or a teacher – this motivation did not seem unreasonable to me. My self-preservation mantra became:

'I did it for the right reasons and I didn't do anything wrong.'

I hadn't anticipated that each time I'd just about gain a modicum of control over my thoughts and emotions, the wind of doubt would almost immediately blow me off course again. Revalidation became a daily necessity and it became more difficult with each additional week. (It was much later that I would learn that I would have to maintain my resolve with repeated revalidations for over four years). Each time the wind of doubt blew I would invariably ask myself the same questions. 'Am I really being unreasonable?, Can they really not see the horse-shit they are standing in?, What are my odds when faced with the combined tactical manoeuvrings of an entire leadership team?'

Naturally, or rather unnaturally, at times the pressure was overwhelming but bailing out was never an option for me. But, the fact that The Icon and its leadership constantly implied that I was being unreasonable was wearing me down. I had made sound judgments and my actions were supported by the evidence so I couldn't understand how and why it was being implied that I was being unreasonable.

Although it may seem a bit odd as they had nothing to do with my decision to blow the whistle I would still like to explain my personal values and beliefs. They should give you a context which reflects my personality and psychology, and help you understand why I came to feel so crappy.

I believe that when I help others I do it because it makes me feel better about myself. I believe that I am a free agent and that I demonstrate my values through my actions. I believe that other people's values can be accurately judged by their actions or the lack of them. I believe that as I am living in a civilised society I enjoy a host of rights and benefits, but at the same time I also have duties and obligations which include those to my students and patients. I believe that there has never been a delineation of good or bad. Polarising good and bad as it has been in the superhero movies (Superman, Batman, Spiderman, etc, etc....) doesn't help and misrepresents everything in-between. But it does emphasize that it's not easy to prioritise one's duties so I simply act in a - utilitarian - way so as to ensure the greatest good for the greatest number, and treating them all as I would want to be treated myself. I believe that my beliefs are a complex and an inseparable mix of my genetic make-up and my early childhood experiences of how I was treated. All this, in my case, had resulted in my readiness to make the sacrifice for my values; it was impossible for me to sit by and ignore what I witnessed at The Icon.

Towards the beginning of **November 2015** I ended up in the early stages of an unsolicited courtship with depression. She, like any young lover, was attempting to conceal the true nature of her brutal overbearing savagery, masquerading as a somewhat twinkly-eyed coy and kind stranger. Like all new relationships the intrigue was intense but the emotions were impossible to explain. But unlike young love the relationship felt vampish, each time she came round I'd almost always sense a deep-seated urge to pull myself away. She left me feeling guilty and withdrawn, creating more questions than answers but thankfully her ploy to blind me and suck me in didn't work. I seemed to be developing new, morphed and muted versions of anxieties on a daily basis and they pinched and unsettled me in a way that worked negatively against me.

The vast majority of the distress was down to two things, first the implication that I was being unreasonable and second that I couldn't work out what, if anything, I could do about it.

The Inspiration

In **July 2015**, approximately 2 months before I blew the whistle, I had booked some tickets for Imani and myself, as a special treat, for us to attend a dinner party at the Palace of Westminster in November. It was a rare opportunity for some flamboyance and we had booked a fancy hotel, ten minutes from the palace, for the weekend away and were looking forward to spending some quality time together. It was planned as a father-daughter bonding session and a night out to be followed by a day of shopping. The sticking point which was threatening to ruin the event was that I was feeling the lowest I had ever experienced in my life. I just wanted to sit in a dark quiet room and be left all on my own. The last place I wanted to be was at a dinner party with lots of strangers. My mind had fallen under intense and sudden unexpected pressure in just seven weeks, since I had blown the whistle. Seven weeks which felt more like seven months. It was unlike any pressure I'd previously known. There was enough of it to make it feel as if my mind had exploded out of the top of my head and it looked like a colossal aneurysm which I was now wearing like a frilly mohawk style comb as can be seen on the top of a chickens head. Ugh.

Out of sheer fatherly cowardice I hadn't told Imani how bad I was feeling or how I couldn't persuade myself to attend the dinner anymore. I kept putting off telling her in the faint hope that my enthusiasm might return. Imani was 14 years old at the time and I didn't want to upset her or leave an unpleasant imprint on her mind and I didn't think she would understand.

At her age her young mind was in spring season whilst my tortured one was trapped in arctic winter and I knew of no bridges between spring and winter. It certainly didn't feel right for me to tell her that I didn't want to meet any new humans. How would that sound in her head? What would she think of me? What would she think of other humans? Above all, I didn't want her to think of me as a failure. I was certain about that. It was proving impossible to separate my work thoughts from my home thoughts. My mind which didn't feel my own anymore, was caught in a perpetual circle of conscious contemplation which rendered me speechless (most of the time). It couldn't hold a single thought for any meaningful period of time without distraction. It kept dissecting previous criticisms, anticipating future ones and then 'role-played' the whole fucking lot. It played out endless scenarios most of which wouldn't even have taken place in any one's wildest dreams. Telling myself to 'shut-up' – which had worked most of my life so far - wasn't working either.

With my mind coughing, and struggling to cope it was easier for me not to meet any new humans in case I had to talk to them. I had started to find humans frightening and interacting with them had become more of a pain than a pleasure. There were no fun moments. I had stopped talking to my wife, my children and most of the time to my patients. Ironically, they seemed to like the new muted me and treated it like a blessing in disguise. I was home but the lights had gone out. I had morphed into a hedgehog in hibernation, spiky and best left alone. I would – much later - be told by my solicitor that these were all the classical signs of depression. Yes, told by my solicitor because doctors are trained to only express things in a positive way.

Our family home is in Royal Leamington Spa which is approximately an hour and half from London and has a wonky statue of Queen Victoria outside the Town Hall; the wonkiness was caused by a bomb going off not far from her feet during World War Two. The plan was that I would go to work, at The Icon, and Imani would travel to the hotel after school. We would meet at around 8pm. It would be her first time travelling to London alone and she would make her own way to the hotel. Great, the only problem was I spent the whole day trying to convince myself to go and with each attempt the answer came back as a resounding no, no, no, not going. It didn't matter if I tried to persuade myself; ridicule myself or encourage myself no amount of talking worked; the answer remained a definitive: 'Not going'.

I did a full day's work in a state of distraction due to the conversations going on in my head. They went like this:

'Stop being an arse, just go!'

'Not going.'

'Grow up a bit, just go!'

'Not going.'

'Grow up a lot and just go!'

'Not going.'

'Do it for Imani!'

'Not going.'

'You'll ruin Imani's night out!'

'Not going.'

'You're an arsehole!'

'Not going'. etc... etc...etc...

Ordinarily, I was good at negotiating myself out of slumps. Negotiations were usually short and sweet and only required me to say "bugger off" to myself and shah-ding I would get on with things. None of it worked this time. Nothing. I supposed that my failure on this occasion was indicative that I was becoming trapped in a tangled web of depression. Accepting depression – by the way - was not acceptable but my attempts at consciously willing denial didn't seem to work and I was left juggling questions without answers:

Is it worse to accept depression?

Is it worse to deny it?

What would happen if I accepted it?

What would happen if I denied it?

I reluctantly resolved that for the sake of the experience it was best for me to deny it.

After work, at about 6pm, I walked the forty minutes or so from The Icon to The Royal Horse Guards Hotel in Whitehall. It was Friday 6th November; it was drizzling with rain which fell sideways aided by a soft flappy wind. My mood remained stuffy, stifled and shitty. The air just wasn't cold enough nor the wind sharp enough to clear my head. Staying at a 5 star hotel should have been enough to put a smile on my face but instead my mind fussed and focused on the fact that it had been built in 1884 as part of a plan to defraud investors. And how the man who defrauded them was no ordinary street criminal for he was the Liberal MP Jabez Balfour. A member of the establishment. My memory of arriving at the hotel is vague and of low resolution. There could have been a meerkat doing the can-can in the lobby and I probably wouldn't have raised an eyebrow. In stark contrast, when I arrived at our room I was met by a warm gust of air as I pushed the door open. The room was illuminated by Imani who buoyantly announced: "I'm dressed and ready to go, where have you been?"

Thirty minutes later we left the hotel for the short walk to the Palace of Westminster. As Big Ben came into view I could not work out what had happened and was still happening. I'd no previous experience of such a contradiction. Having spent the whole day telling myself I wasn't going, here I was, going. This just bogged my mind down even more; it was never going to clear now. I supposed that for a mind to be a clear one required it to be nourished with healthy food. I appeared to be living out the toxicity of a mind that had been fed nothing but junk. I can honestly say that my mind didn't feel like my own as the cogitation carried on. I couldn't get over it. I had spent the whole day telling myself that I wouldn't be going. I hadn't changed my decision, but here I was walking towards the palace. I couldn't understand what was happening and struggled with the fact that it was happening. I found it plausible that my mind was so clogged up that it was no longer an effective driver and it seemed to me that I was being towed along by Imani. By the virtue of trust I seemed happy to play out Imani's decision; and had simply accepted her lead. I name it the 'The Surrogate Decision'.

Following Imani around allowed me some respite and momentarily made life a bit easier. There are more examples of surrogate decisions later in the book. Looking back, from the thoughts I was having, it certainly sounds as though I might have been having a sort of mental meltdown.

Standing in the courtyard of the palace I continued musing to myself and got the distinct impression that my brain could only make a maximum number of conscious decisions per day. I later came to realise that during my working day most of my work is done subconsciously as I execute numerous sequences of actions. I wondered if I was the only one who did this and if so for what reason. It was becoming evident to me that when I was exposed to prolonged stress, I avoided getting involved in the making of non-essential decisions. In the weeks after the dinner I would read Daniel Kahneman's book: *Think Slow Think Fast*, it helped me understand the mechanics of my brain. The book was his lifelong study of brain functions and brain neuroscience. It outlined many of the mechanisms, short cuts and tricks the mind employs to save energy. Strangely, in some ways, I felt that reading his book changed the way my brain functioned in real time. One thing I was becoming sure was it was overloaded, but I was starting to realise that it was down to me and me alone to neutralise the overload.

I followed Imani through security into the Palace of Westminster and for the rest of the evening behaved like her guest.

It wasn't plain sailing though as I was still left with an outstanding problem, I still didn't want to meet any new humans. Short of standing in a corner with my back to the room I hadn't worked out how to overcome this problem. The riverside bar was heaving and it required some gentle elbow work to negotiate our way across the room to the windows overlooking the Thames. Once at the windows I entertained the idea that we might just stand there and look at the river all night. It would succeed on the not-having-to-meet-new-humans front, but fail on the fun-night-out front. I put on a fake smile and continued to talk to myself behind it. Come to think about it my eyes felt fake as well. Every time I caught someone's eye I pretended I hadn't and gazed straight through them. Imani had to keep repeating most of what she said as I kept losing her mid- sentence.

In the dining room there was a table plan and the seating was organised by name cards. This came in handy as another helpful 'surrogate decision' situation as someone else had done the thinking and made the decision. Sat to my immediate left was Imani, in front of me was a consultant cardiologist and at the table's end to my right was a consultant liver surgeon. They seemed nice enough and had, on the table in front of them, a bottle of claret each. This, I contemplated, could render them harmless or hostile. Both consultants were men in their late sixties and it appeared from their conversation that they had known each other for some time. From the same school, I supposed. I only caught snippets of their conversation as my self-absorbed mind faded in and out. I wanted desperately to talk to them, but my trust in my seniors was at an all time low and I couldn't persuade myself that there was any benefit in socialising with them. I just couldn't stop the constant mental cogitation and the paranoia creeping in at the edges didn't help either. Each time I looked around the table or the room I wondered how many of the assembled individuals worked in institutions just as I did and how many of them would have considered my whistle blowing actions as unreasonable ones. Most of them I supposed.

I willed myself to stop talking to myself and to pick someone else to talk to. The willing didn't work! My mind kept wondering back to what unpleasantness lay ahead for me at The Icon. I was less bothered about the actual unpleasantness and more bothered about the uncertainty of when it would take place. It would've been nice if the uncertainty could've been lifted, perhaps by an act of clairvoyance preferably in chronological order, then my mind would've rested. But as it was highly unlikely I'd be getting any such list, I'd have to 'suck-it-up' and do the best I could in those circumstances. I had no option but to resist the discouragement I was feeling.

I stared pretty blankly at the two consultants entertaining the thought that perhaps one of them may have some experience I could learn from. However, for this to happen I would first have to tell them that I was a whistleblower, something I felt very uneasy about, it felt too risky. They might be part of the anti-whistleblower fraternity and might turn on me. I already felt worthless and on the inside the criticising is all I could hear. My upper limit of being criticised had already been exceeded, I couldn't cope with any more of it. As an aside, I had had a bad relationship with criticism in my other day job, as a dentist. Patients do a very good job of shifting the blame from themselves onto their dentist, all day long. They take very little responsibility for their own behaviours, habits or actions; instead passing the buck seems to come naturally to them. It had taken me most of my adult life so far to reconcile my scathing childhood and then the reasonably unreasonable criticism that comes with serving patients. I hadn't had time to put strategies in place to deal with the barrage of wholly unjustified criticism The Icon was bombarding me with. Unjustified criticism made my blood boil and I needed, as a matter of urgency, to control this natural but unhelpful feeling.

It helped that the dinner was hosted in the trappings of such a grand palace. It meant that I could pretend to be preoccupied marvel at the ornamental carvings, the wood panels and the artwork with a mature reflective look on my face. I pulled off pretending to be an aloof, art critic type very well and managed to keep conversations down to very minor small talk. I hadn't thought to pretend I couldn't speak English. I did manage to make some small and polite chit-chat with Imani, mainly about the menu and the things on it that we hadn't eaten before, but it was far from the night I had planned in my mind when I booked the tickets.

Before long the consultants had empty wine bottles on the table in front of them and warm distant light-hearted facial expressions to match. I took the plunge and told them my story. I gave them the abridged version taking only five minutes of their time.

'Don't you know what George Bernard Shaw said?' asked the liver surgeon.

'Who's George Bernard Shaw?' I asked looking apologetically inquisitive.

The surgeon bellowed over my apology:
"George Bernard Shaw said: 'Progress is always driven by the unreasonable man.' "

Without being asked to do so but having acknowledged the expression on my face, the surgeon repeated softly and slowly: 'George - Bernard - Shaw – said; 'Progress - is always - driven - by - the - unreasonable - man' '.

The expression on my face must have been so incredulous that he'd felt the need to repeat himself. My eyes expressed the gratitude my mind felt, as they welled up. But two soft blinks re-dispersed the fluid and I managed to stop them from leaking. My chest bone lifted effortlessly as if it was attached by strings to a hot air balloon and my head seemed to do an Indian wobble as my neck muscles immediately softened.

Hearing the quote for the first time was more than just a pleasant surprise. It had the most immediate and profound effect that I can ever remember having in my whole life. My mood lifted from a dense crackling grey blue thunderstorm to reveal a smiling sunny yellow Saharan desert, as if it had been flipped by a flick of a switch. This was definitely a new experience, perhaps because I hadn't previously experienced such a prolonged episode of low mood. The peak of the elation exceeded the depressing lows. Actually it was the most elated I'd ever been on account of a single moment of personal discovery and development. More elated than when I got my A level results, when I got accepted into university or even when I became a specialist. A different kind of elation to the one I got when I bought my first house. Joy surged to all corners of my mind. My brain glowed and I imagined it radiated light and gave off different colours like I had seen in research studies into different brain states (MRI images). Above all and undeniably I could hear, in my mind, first from afar, then becoming louder and louder the opening riff of Beethoven's 5th Symphony (the Saturday Night Fever version). I flexed the hunch out of my back; my feet checked where the floor was. I felt like strutting around just as John Travolta had done in the movie. During the epic elation a train of fast flowing thoughts ran like a newsreel across the back of my eyes.

The first phase of thoughts was questions:

Really, does it really take an unreasonable man to drive progress?

When did he say this?

What did he mean?

How come I never knew about this?

How come no one had thought of telling me this before?

Am I the only person who hasn't heard this quote before?

The second phase of thoughts was statements:

Of course it takes an unreasonable man!

I've been treated like an unreasonable man because I was forced to become one!

To achieve progress I had to act in an unreasonable way!

The way to achieve progress was always going to involve some unreasonable behaviour!

Being nice would have been great but it wouldn't have achieved progress!

The amount of 'progress' being achieved could potentially be measured by the forcefulness with which The Icon told me I was being unreasonable!

The third phase of thoughts was celebrations:

I am proud of the fact that I have been unreasonable!

I am proud of the fact that I had acted unreasonably before I had even learnt that it was required!

I am so lucky that I held my nerve before this quotation came along!

Today is a good day!

Thank god I had invited Imani to the alumni dinner!

As the pace of my thoughts slowed down I realised that the corners of my eyes had lifted and I was smiling. My pulse felt higher than Big Ben. For the first time that evening I could clearly hear the other diners talking to each other, they seemed to be enjoying themselves. I noticed the clinking of wine glasses and the clattering of cutlery. I noticed the glitter and the glamour, the colours and vibrancy that the people around me had made a great effort and really dressed up for the occasion. I even noticed some cleavage. It seems to have become frowned upon to make such a statement but I find that when cleavage has deliberately been dressed up for exhibition my eyes cannot pixilate it out. I noticed the name card of the lady sitting opposite Imani and I wanted to know more about her. I was itching to talk to people. I glanced at Imani and she smiled at me as if somehow she knew what I had just experienced, perhaps it's a genetic connection, I supposed with my eyes welling up for the second time. This time I had to tend to them with a finger flick.

The impact the words had on my mind (and body) was a new phenomenon which left me in awe. I was intrigued and I naturally wanted to know more but for now I had a father-daughter event to enjoy and we enjoyed the rest of the weekend traipsing through the shops with short stops in coffee shops.

In the weeks after the dinner I remembered having previously read the book *Words Can Change Your Brain: 12 Conversation Strategies to Build Trust* by Andrew Newberg and Mark Waldman so I went back and read it again. My second reading of it was distinctly different to the first and I found it really helpful as it seemed to speak directly to my mind. It helped me get a deeper understanding of and reinforced the notion of the mind being a funny 'olde' place.

I researched George Bernard Shaw and visited his former home, Shaw House, in Newbury Berkshire, now a museum to his legacy. He may not have been a philosopher but he was a respected playwright, critic, polemicist and political activist of his time. It became apparent that the liver surgeon had taken 'Progress is always driven by the unreasonable man' from:

'The reasonable man adapts himself to the world: the unreasonable one persists in trying to adapt the world to himself. Therefore all progress depends on the unreasonable man.'

It continued to offer me encouragement by disrupting my mind's stagnated chemicals. This was true life-long learning. My spirit and energy were lifted in the knowledge that he, wiser and older than me, had previously questioned the concept of progress. It gave me the confidence to step out from under the shadow cast by the criticisms levied against me by The Icon and to revaluate the concept of progress. I started with a reflection on the lingering questions in my mind:

'Why had it been necessary for me to blow the whistle at all?

'Why was the leadership trying so hard to not identify with the concerns I had raised?'

'Why did the leadership team seem determined to bury my concerns?'

'Why had they been paralysed from taking some positive action to rectify the problems?'

These questions had floated around in the background of my mind; left to right, right to left and back again, like a creaky see-saw. With a renewed vigour I was able to scrutinise them extra critically as a result of which I identified three potential elements The three elements seemed like a reasonable explanation for the mess The Icon was in and which the leadership were attempting to conceal. The elements were:

1. Spin.
2. Progress
3. Feedback.

What was your first experience of spin? Mine was back at junior school when I read the Hans Christian Anderson tale the *Emperor's New Clothes*; we all know the moral of that story, don't we? The emperor was fooled by his tailors marketing. I remember it next when it made media headlines in the mid-nineties during Tony Blair's Labour government. 'Spin doctors' were employed to present information, good or bad, in the most positive manner possible; even if the most positive manner of presentation was misleading, or left the truth behind. Spin appears to be another word to describe lying or not telling the truth and has been with us since the dawn of time. It has become indoctrinated into the fabric of our everyday lives, affecting organisations both public and private. Its utility has stifled the democratic process and having recognised this I started to suspect, and became sure, that The Icon's leadership team had hypnotised themselves into believing that their 'all-mouth-no-trousers' approach would not be revealed.

A couple of synonyms for spin are: 'polishing a turd' or 'putting lipstick on a pig' and everyone knows that's just ridiculous, you can't polish a turd. But, hold on a minute, you can: 'roll it in glitter'. If you haven't come across the expression before you can probably figure out what it means: shit is shit, and you can't do anything about it, but you can sprinkle some shiny stuff on it and try to pretend that it's something else. This is not entirely vulgar as there's a pretty good set of neurological and evolutionary reasons for some people's tendency to roll turds in glitter. Humans are highly resistant to change. We evolved to reduce the amount of variability in our environment – a trait that helped us to stabilise the immediate risk to ourselves and our tribe. We learnt that by keeping to set routines, we could reduce the likelihood of the unexpected, limiting the chance of catastrophe. Consequently, we resist the notion that our preset worldview might be faulty, incomplete, or dangerous.

It seems to me that the students need to go into the working world with their eyes wide open; and in my experience that way they have more fruitful lives.

The Icon was not alone and later it would be demonstrated that turds were being rolled in glitter by a host of organisations positioned to protect the patients, the students and me but as you will learn they all failed to do so. I got to experience (ahem) the General Dental Council, the Care Quality Commission, the Professional Standards Authority, NHS Improvement and the Chief Dental Officer - a man called 'Baza'. (I mentioned previously that as a whistleblower I felt unprotected by the law and now I worry that should this book be published the afore-mentioned organisations might also attempt to punish me for doing so). I worry because I'm human and I've got three children to feed and children need to eat.

The Chief Dental Officer, 'Baza' is what they call the highest dentist in the country and I'm not sure what his poison was but he was definitely high. He came to The Icon in January 2015 to share his wisdom with the teaching staff and told us:

'Treating gum disease is not a priority for the NHS'

and that:

'The NHS does not have the funds to treat gum disease'

because:

'People were living too fucking long.'

And it's time to trust you all with truth because then he smiled like a cheap edentulous whore in an Amsterdam window when I asked him when he would be making the same announcement to the nation. Edentulous if you're wondering means no teeth. I wanted to ask him if his explanation accounted for why Liverpool Dental School no longer had a gum department but enigmatically and in a puff of white smoke he was gone.

My next question was to a senior teaching colleague who seemed to be smoking his turd like a spliff whilst bigging up The Icon. I asked him:

"Has anyone told the students that we are no longer treating gum disease?"

His response was one of a man who couldn't possibly have any children (I don't know if he does or doesn't).

'You don't need to tell them, they are far smarter than you think, they will work it out for themselves.'

Yep. That was about the extent of it. It's what I call the 'no shit Einstein lets fuck-up their careers before they even start' approach. Fair enough I thought but if that's what we are doing surely we should introduce them to Philip Larkin's parents at the same time (you might need to google a poem called *This Be The Verse* by Philip Larkin). In his poem he artistically expressed how parents fuck-up their children. Somehow some of my work-shy colleagues continued to pretend that they couldn't see the link between their own poor performance, the complaints being made by the students and the epidemic of mental health issues amongst them. It seemed a contradiction, in light of their seniority, that they hadn't realised the students were at a stage of biological development during which they could naturally experience lengthy episodes of being unhappy without knowing why. They really didn't need adult deceit to be loaded on top but my colleagues seemed to find it easy to treat the students as if they had no feelings. I supposed that their comfort came from the most recent Law Society Gazette in which an article announced that there was to be no new punishment for suicide.

Whilst the leadership team were preoccupied spinning truth into fantasy I can recall one consultant at The Icon who was happy to describe shit as shit. He gave us a presentation which he titled: 'The Daughter Test'. During his presentation he put up coloured slides of poor quality 'cosmetic' dentistry for the three hundred or so dentists in attendance to marvel at. He asked the question, 'Would you do this to your daughter?' Occasionally he leaned into the audience and called out the names of some of the dentists who had knackered these teeth by cutting them with their dental drills and then bellowed:

"Where are you, you little shit, I didn't teach you to do this shit!"

It was like watching one of those intermittently paused, slow-motion car crash videos. The audience gasped with each new slide and then burst into fits of laughter if the name of the dentist was called out. The consultant concluded his lecture with a summary and he glared into the audience to show us he was speaking to us all

"If all you are interested in is the patients money, then lean forward and ask them for it, leave their fucking teeth alone."

Once I'd identified that 'spin' was inextricably connected to the way 'progress' was being perceived, reported and projected I was able to make even more sense of things. Once I had separated 'progress' further into the three aspects below it made even more sense:

1. The desire to make progress.
2. The making of progress.
3. The claim that progress had been made.

The desire to make progress underpinned virtually every presentation made by the leadership team; it was their mission statement. In the annual teachers training meetings The Icon celebrated statements of positive achievement, with great fanfare, the progress that it claimed to have made. I remember sitting through some of those celebratory meetings and almost always caught myself asking myself "What progress are they talking about? I'd often wondered how many of my assembled colleagues were asking themselves the same question.

That was the problem. The Icon wasn't actually making any progress and progress hadn't been made for a long time. Continuing with the spin was madness. Looking back, by **September 2015,** I had resolved that the magnitude of The Iconic Machine's denial, deceit and reliance upon its own spin could only be addressed by blowing the whistle. The problem wasn't about to sort itself out as the situation had become immune to reason. This validation allowed me a momentary flicker of the possibility that my reputation and my dignity might still be salvageable. It was a 'bring - it - on' moment; of which I had a few of along the way. (However it would become evident that the highs were closely matched by the lows).

Feedback had been crippled and dismantled, but at this early stage I couldn't work out why. It had been replaced by selectively edited versions of itself with the only obvious motive being propping up the 'spin'. The published feedback never reflected the day-to-day clinical activities or the complaints from the staff (or the students and patients). It was carefully selected (from the overall body of feedback) and was invariably incomplete or biased towards the positive. Any negative feedback was deliberately suppressed. To an outsider it would have appeared that The Icon was perfect in all its functionality. The reality was it was only perfect in one way; it was the perfect Ivory Tower. It seems to me that it was highly unethical to suppress valid feedback and correcting this was essential to The Icon's recovery, if there was to be one.

As my contemplations continued, The Icon was starting to reveal itself as The Iconic Machine. It became apparent the leadership team was attempting to distance their identity from the actions they had taken as a collective. They started to pretend they were not the ones operating The Machine's levers. They had hypnotised themselves with their own proclamations and were now incapable of action against the spin's momentum and the magic of their self-hypnosis. Looking back, I believe that the leadership team had resigned themselves to the fact that only a scandal could shake their paralysis. They had been sapped by their own poison. On the one hand they had spun themselves into a position to boast a falsely elevated QS world ranking; but on the other, behind the curtains, they were swamped by an extremely high number of complaints from their students. The students were constantly complaining about poor educational practices, standards which even the Victorians would have been embarrassed about. It seems right to me that it is highly unethical to portray something in a more favourable light than it actually is.

Student complaints, including inadequate preparation for computer use and treating patients, were ignored and consequently the students were losing their incentives, initiatives and confidence. On a particular occasion, during a lecture, a student stood up and protested it was unacceptable for the lecture to have commenced twenty five minutes late and even more unacceptable for the lecturer to be blatantly reading directly from a text book. The student was frogmarched into a meeting with Professor Honest whereupon he was told:

'If you don't change your attitude you might not do so well here.'

Growth in revenue seemed to be the only measure by which The Iconic Machine judged its progress and its huge marketing apparatus was successfully dressing up its educational products. Spin had allowed The Icon to successfully seize control over a sizable proportion of the training sector, mainly by being big and unfortunately not by being good. Some of the students (most of them) were disappointed as they were not enjoying their educational experience. The experience was not the one they had been promised by the marketing and it had failed to live up to the expectations set by The Icon. The students regularly complained of the course being poorly structured, poorly organised and poorly administered. They often spent hours on clinics, twiddling their thumbs as teachers haplessly fumbled around trying to figure out what to teach them. They felt fooled and let down by The Iconic Machine's marketing. The compound effect was much worse than that. Their educational experience was comparable to a sexually transmitted disease where the initial pleasure was very quickly replaced by pain and regret. The disparity between the expectation and the reality traumatised them and left them in a state of confused despair. What made things worse was that The Iconic Machine continued to obfuscate their complaints away. I supposed the trauma The Iconic Machine was inflicting on them was similar to what it was inflicting on me. Even though I was a seasoned professional I was struggling to maintain confidence when reading the poorly written notes in front of the students or the patients.

One of my biggest dilemmas at the time remained unresolved. Should I put my trust in the words of George Bernard Shaw, a man long dead or in my senior peers who were a reality? George or Mr Shaw's words of wisdom offered me a comfort in knowing my so-called unreasonableness was a necessity and I should maintain my conviction. It didn't, however, feel right to me to continue trusting the leadership team. Its endless proclamation that my concerns were invalid and my behaviour unreasonable was nonsense. One thing was for sure, standing against my senior peers, decorated with their academic ranking, would be the most difficult thing I would ever do and I supposed that most of my self- doubt resulted from the perceived relative inferiority of my undeserving position.

I was learning……..

I was learning even before the true learning started. I had already made two of the most important decisions of my experience, without which there would have been zero learning. The first decision was to: 'blow the whistle' and the second one was: 'not to bail out'. The former initiated the experience and it embodied how I wanted to, and did, proceed. The latter meant me having to understand and control my negative feelings to prevent them from causing an implosion. I continued to respond to the challenges by how I knew best. I woke up every morning and, as difficult as it was, ventured back out into my working world to learn some more. I was left wearing a pleasant smile when I read the words of **Friedrich Nietzsche** a German philosopher from the nineteenth century who said:

'That which does not kill us makes us stronger'

I received a sense of validation from this quotation which encouraged me to believe that I had done the right thing. It put me at ease a little, and allowed me to pat myself on the back for not bailing out. From it, I realised that if I hadn't taken the plunge I wouldn't have developed a deeper understanding of my neurological responses.

I was learning how painfully difficult it was for me to accept that my experience, from start to finish, was the opposite of the expectations published by a number of professional regulators and set out during my professional training. (Especially since the same regulators failed to uphold their published standards with any consistent objectivity).

I was learning that it's a monstrously bad start when an experience begins with being ignored. It's a very effective way of knocking someone off their feet. The emotional upheaval is all subconscious and escalates at a blistering pace. It tested my patience with its persistent talk, talk, talking to myself. The silence led me to unnecessarily revaluate my expectations: was I wrong to have expected my line manager to acknowledge my concerns? Was I wrong to expect him to address them? Looking back I had no idea that he was carefully avoiding any collision with the powerful interests of the leadership or The Icon. Anyway, being ignored made my mind dark, creepy and suspicious and to make things worse when I saw him on the clinics he uncharacteristically kept his distance. We spoke many times but he did not mention the concerns I'd raised. My mind boggled at his brazen ability to ignore the fact that he was ignoring my concerns. On the rare occasions we spoke I would be tense but ready to discuss my concerns, but they never got a look in. He seemed content to engage in pitiful chit-chat along the lines of: 'Are you going away this weekend?' or 'Have you been on holiday recently? 'Are the family well?' I found it really absurd and confusing that he could ask me personal questions, particularly ones about my family's health, whilst knowing full well how much harm his inaction was doing to me.

I was learning that 'being ignored' should be recognised as an act of bullying. If I were to write a book on bullying I'd put 'being ignored' right up there alongside being punched in the face or being spat on. I know that both examples sound extreme but I cannot overstate the power of being ignored to destabilise and the strength of its insult. It really was a strange and challenging experience. It suggested and implied that my position relative to his was undeservingly inferior like I was some sort of pleb. There he was, a senior member of The Icon's staff, and there I was, a mere pleb. Yep, and when I looked in the mirror I was still there.

I was learning that 'being ignored' had provoked insecurity and put me in state of shock. My line manager's silence bewildered me in a way that I couldn't even ask him why. I had no idea what had paralysed me and prevented me from simply saying to him 'you haven't mentioned the e-mails I sent you'. I convinced myself that he had done it on purpose and that he must have had some previous experience of its effects on the ignored person and how they fall into an automatic cycle of self-doubt. Looking back, I sort of knew that I was experimenting with fire and my inner human had been telling me: 'you could get burnt.' What I hadn't realised at the time was that I was going to get burnt on two fronts. First I was going to get burnt by the actions of The Icon but much worse, I was going to get burnt by my own mental inexperience and insecurity. All of this kept me awake and was comparable to trying to get off to sleep shortly after you've just seen a big hairy spider fall off the bedside table and crawl under the bed; you don't fall asleep.

I was learning that whistle blowing is a neat way to accelerate the rate of one's eventual death. I use the word accelerate loosely as at times it felt as if I'd thrown a stick of dynamite into my own life.

I was learning that anxiety is a meaningless word. It is used by doctors and therapists to collectively label a range of perceived states of mind. If I wanted, I too could use it to label a feeling within me (which I couldn't because I didn't know which feelings to ascribe to it).

I was learning that if I wanted to see the experience through to its conclusion I would have to maintain an almost constant state of evaluation over the impact my feelings and emotions were having on me. The evaluation would mostly be conscious and require a massive amount of energy with a high potential for exhaustion. (I started to be able to put words and meaning to some of my emotions and feelings by chapter four).

I was learning that provocation is the elementary unit of challenge which acts as a stimulant to create an experience which provides the building blocks without which courage, strength, tenacity and resilience fail to develop. I was never the sort to 'coast' through life and was realising that resilience was a necessary part of making it a more fulfilling, rewarding one and without it, life can feel a bit underwhelming. Resilience cannot be learnt from books or the experience of others. It only develops when we engage in our own challenging experiences. One's experiences which, ironically, make us feel anything but resilient at the time. These provocations can be relatively mundane such as 'I need to get to work but it's raining' or 'the buses are running behind'. That said, it transpired the provocations I experienced after I blew the whistle were not of the everyday type. These provocations were unexpected, shocking, explosive and severe. It really did feel as if I was attempting to climb Mount Everest during a storm, without oxygen, dressed in nothing more than a thong when the most I'd done previously was walk to the local newsagents for a chocolate bar. Yet, as much as I'd realised the gravity of what I had done I had no option but to keep responding to the provocations as they arrived in the faint hope that I might continue to grow 'the philosophy of my life' and 'my way of thinking'. If I did, it would be more than likely that I might match the demands of the never-ending nature of my new experience.

I was learning that 'life is provocation and provocation is life'. By which I mean that I hadn't fully appreciated how the world has always been full of provocation, or that the present moment is full of provocation, or that the future is always going to be full of provocation or that the opportunities of my life would be in those provocations. I started to work out that I should view provocations as a celebrated ingredient of my work and home life and that without them I would not survive let alone thrive. Provocations are what makes life, life. The fundamental mistake I'd made was my assumption that life was supposed to 'treat you kind' and anything other than that was extraordinarily undesirable, (oh how Millennial I behaved). I now knew it was the other way round and one requires provocation on a daily basis for a fulfilling life and expecting anything other than that is somewhat foolish and childish. In my experience it was the uncertainty that came with the provocation which acted as the trigger, prompting me to ask myself the burning questions which fuelled my desire for a better understanding. It was down to me, and me alone, to somehow make some order of the uncertainty and chaos.

I was learning pretty quickly that prior to blowing the whistle I had little or no experience of any prolonged or extreme periods of uncertainty or chaos. I hadn't been required to manage my mind in such circumstances. To the contrary my previous experiences had been heavily regulated and controlled, so not helpful. Almost all aspects of my education; school, college and university were based around a sequence of structured lists and plans (there was no real thinking required). I'd experienced some of the more usual challenges like getting married, buying a house and having children but there were always lots of people offering advice and telling me what to do next and sharing lots of examples. I can honestly say that blowing the whistle was my first big - almost crippling – endurance adventure with uncertainty and chaos. Keeping my mind steady wasn't in any way easy and I will, periodically throughout the chapters, continue to share with you how I managed it.

I was learning that once the anguish struck me it became a constant in the background of my every activity. There were times when I could be sat looking at flowers in bloom or listening to my children play or even be lying on my back watching crisp white clouds float across the most serene of skies yet all I could feel was 'anguish, anguish, anguish'. So much so that I wondered if the texture of my brain would merely change or if it would be damaged and if so would the damage be reversible. I found a book *The Big Questions: How Philosophy Can Change Your Life* by Lou Marrinoff and it offered me some help, advice, solace and sanctuary. As I was a newbie to philosophy it wasn't the easiest book to read but I became reassured from it that I was suffering from a form of mental DIS-EASE and not from a mental DISEASE. The reassurance allowed me to break through the constant anguish to then only suffer smaller intermittent intervals of it.

I was learning that as a novice, reading books on psychology and philosophy was very difficult and confusing. It was a whole new language. On my first read I would be completely lost, on the second I was less lost but it still came across as complete gobbledygook. Often I had to supplement my reading by checking things on Wikipedia or watching a video on YouTube. But I persevered because I wanted to understand my responses to see if there was anything I could do to control or change them. I will have a go at telling you what I learnt but please don't be surprised if its lost on you, or you have to read the next three paragraphs a few times or even if it comes across as gobbledygook.

I was learning about the neurological processes underlying my, and everybody else's, response to provocation. I couldn't believe that I was taught some of this during A-level Biology but I hadn't found myself needing a deeper understanding of its mechanics till now, when I needed it most and had forgotten practically all of it. It is well-accepted amongst the scientists that our response to a provocation would always occur along the same neural pathway. The response would occur in three well recognised stages. The first stage would be the inception and core of the response and is described as the biological response. The response then passes onto the second stage which is the psychological response before passing into the third and last stage the philosophical one. Each stage of the pathway would have formed uniquely by virtue of my genes, my previous exposure and my experiences. My response would always be a culmination of the individual contributions (or lack of them) of each of the three stages.

The first stage, my biological response, is genetically inherited and one which is an automatic, innate, subconscious one based on the genetic fabric of my organic being. In slang it's called my 'animal instinct'. The second stage, my psychological response, is more emotional and based on aspects of my psyche and born out of my early life experiences. It embodies my personality, habits, likes, dislikes, ambitions and aversions. The third stage, my philosophical response is based on my 'point of view' or 'way of thinking' and the theory is that 'my point of view' could be continually enhanced by studying the 'good ideas' of a range of philosophers. I was left with the impression that my biological responses were my strongest, most barbaric and practically irreversible ones. It's the one that makes first impression feel guttural, it's accurate and near impossible to change. It was starting to appear to me that my courage to blow the whistle was most probably from my biological response. Once my biological response had been formed, my more civilised psychological responses were sprinkled over it to create a seamless blended response. I was starting to suspect that responding to the events that occurred after I blew the whistle was not a courage thing but a strength, tenacity and endurance thing, and those attributes most probably came from my psychological responses. In my case as I had not read any philosophy earlier in life my 'points of view' and 'way of thinking' was somewhat limited to my morals, beliefs and values. I realised I'd now have to chase hard and play 'catch-up' to enhance 'my philosophical view' if I wanted to change my responses. The philosophy I could choose from could be as variable as the topic because different philosophers offer a different (acceptable) perspective to the same situation. Essentially, when faced with a new provocation I had the option to select the most appropriate philosopher for help. Of course I would have had to read widely before I could find the correct philosophy to fit each situation. However, I started to appreciate that it would become easier for me to select the correct philosophy as my knowledge of it grew.

I was learning that I found it helpful to accept the fundamental basis of the widely accepted theories of how we form our responses. I accepted that my biological responses would be formed in my ancient primal center known as 'fight or flight' responses. They would be bold and strong enough to match the intensity of the stimulus and would offer an option of violence to any potential offence. I accepted that biological responses alone are considered to lack the sophistication required for today's work environments and we use our secondary psychological responses to temper them. Thus my psychological responses act by honing my primal ones using aspects of my environmental development and personality. Lastly at the philosophical level, the one I had developed least, I would supposedly use reason, intellect and interpretation combined with my will and imagination to rein in my biological response and rule over my psychological one. I accepted that philosophy apparently trains the higher powers of our mind to enable us to deflect offense when we encounter it. I was ready to embrace philosophy with a view to make it my mind's supreme leader!

I was learning that 'control' was more important to my peace of mind than I had previously anticipated. In its absence there were times, when the stress peaked, that I would need to sit in the corner of the room like a statue. It was important (necessary) for me, when at home, to rest and 'switch off' my mind. I found it easier to 'switch off' if I was not asked questions, even simple ones like: 'what do you want for dinner?' or 'would you like a coffee?' because I could never find the answer. At times of stress statements like: 'Its lamb for dinner tonight' or 'Here's your coffee' helped a lot. I just didn't have the bandwidth to process questions unrelated to work and I got some respite when others made the decision for me. This is another example of the 'surrogate decision'. The theory was that: if I were to enhance my philosophical 'point of view' by looking for the answers to my questions in how others had dealt with similar situations, I might be able appease the angst and torture and gain some much needed control by making some internal adjustments and not relying on external ones.

I was learning that 'wisdom comes with age' and it can't be forced. What I mean by this is that the only experience you'll gain from reading this book is one of reading. It's most likely you will be able to appreciate only some of my experience. It's doubtful that you'll be able relate to it in all its glory until you end up in a similar situation, yourself. I am, however, certain that when you end up in a similar experience, aspects of mine will come flooding back to you and you'll pick up this book again to remind yourself what I did when I struggled. As I've previously said, I will continue to periodically through the chapters, show you how and why I struggled and the strategies I used to see the experience to its conclusion.

I was learning that 'QS World University Rankings' which The Icon uses to boost its marketability is an annual publication of university rankings by Quacquarelli Symonds. QS Ranking has been criticized for using a paid survey site to collect responses. Ben Sowter, head of the Intelligence Unit for the London-based company QS confirmed this to be true. Brian Leiter, a professor and director of the Centre for Law, Philosophy, and Human Values at the University of Chicago called the QS rankings 'a fraud on the public.' The QS rankings along with the two others; the Times Higher Education's World University Rankings and the Shanghai Ranking Consultancy's Academic Ranking of World Universities (ARWU), are regularly criticized. Many educators question the value of rankings and argue that they can only measure a narrow slice of what quality higher education is about. There are many other flaws in the ranking system. Most of the common ones are listed on the internet*.

*https://www.insidehighered.com/news/2013/05/29/met hodology-qs-rankings-comes-under-scrutiny

Incompetence trumps Malice

'Never assign to malice that which can be
adequately explained by incompetence'

Hanlon's Razor

What makes quotes so interesting and magical is everyone develops their own views of them based on personal experiences, and as no two experiences are ever the same, nor are the interpretations. I hope my interpretation of this one offers you a context of how it influenced me yet doesn't take away any of its magic for your own.

This one melted onto and dissolved its way into my mind on **Saturday 12th December 2015** (approximately ten weeks after The Nasty Meeting) whilst I was hosting a dinner party at home. The impasse was, as a consequence of anger and tension, most of the muscles around my head, neck and shoulders had frozen resulting in a painful distraction which reduced my ability to think straight. It helped me deconstruct the provocations to identify the blatant attempts to conceal the incompetence whilst simultaneously tarnishing and assailing my reputation. The revelations reduced the anger provoking power of the ongoing injustice.

In this chapter you'll see why the unfolding events causing me to feel angry and have a whole host of other associated undesirable emotions. You will see why I needed to control them. I'll explain how my interpretation of this quote resulted in a pleasant change in my attitude enabling me to interpret the same emotions in a context which suited the situation better. My better understanding of them allowed me to manipulate and adapt my mind's state more favourably to ultimately tame the anger and thus reduce the harm it was causing.

The Experience

Cast in this Chapter

Leadership Role	Given Identity
Dean of Education	Professor Honest
Head of Department	Dr Dependable
Clinical Director	Dr Legitimate

The story so far........

1. 15th September 2015; whistle blown.
2. 2nd October 2015; Nasty Meeting.
3. 16th October 2015; Incognito Meeting with Professor Honest.

I may have been the only member of staff who had pointed out that I had made 'protected disclosures' but I was not the only one raising serious concerns. I have pasted below a copy of a complaint submitted by one of the other teachers. The letter is self-explanatory and describes the problems the teachers were having and openly discussing with each other during most tea-breaks and lunchtimes. I have not altered the letter other than to anonymise it. I have copies of many other letters.

Dear Director of Undergraduate Education.

Dr Watt has recently shown me the letter of concern e-mailed to you from Dr First. My experiences mirror those that are described by Dr First.

We rely on The Icon, it's team of directors and team leaders to help us deliver a teaching/learning experience to the students. However our work concerns/expressions of concern / and in many cases our opinions about how The Icon is falling to support us in this are not being respected or taken into consideration.

I was on a clinic with the new 2nd year students on 1st May 2015. I was very disappointed that the curriculum has failed them at this stage of their education. The students were not as informed and confident as the students I have taken on to clinics in the previous years. The current students have never had hands-on training on the computers and have not even seen any patients as they have done with the periodontal team. In the morning the students had an induction from the nurses, followed by a 2 hour wait, followed by their first hands-on training on the computers. They then had their first patients on whom they had to perform a history and formulate a treatment plan. Once the patients arrived on clinic it was chaos as the students had no idea how to operate the computers with confidence and required more of my time helping them in front of the patients. It was obvious and a big concern to me that the students had had no time to appreciate and practice using the computers. In the 10 years that I have been a teacher at The Icon the state of chaos was the worst I have experienced. It is impossible to see how the students benefited from the chaos and confusion.

It was impossible for me to teach the students because of this – I could not concentrate on what I needed to; preparing the treatment bay, the cross infection control requirements, simple patient communication, simple chair positioning, radiography, history taking. It is to be expected that the students are nervous on their first clinical session. I have seen it for 10 years. Dr Temple and I struggled to offer the students the expected level of clinical teaching. We both felt we had been let down by The Icon.

My biggest concern is that the year 2 students this year have not been given a full pre-clinical course and education and are not at a stage of understanding to see patients on the clinic. In addition to this their preclinical exam has also been bought forward and as teachers examining them we have been instructed to lower our expectations and pass them on a lower capacity than previous years. I cannot agree with this as the students are already failing to meet the standards required by the 3rd year teachers.

I look forward to your considered comments; guidance and reassurance that *The Icon* needs to do more to support the teachers and the students.

Dr Unimpressed

Another teacher raised concerns and complained that students had been allowed to progress to the next academic year without having to retake the competency exams they had failed. She questioned the value of having exams if students are being allowed to progress even when they fail them. She also questioned the associated safety issues and pointed out previous episodes of harm. This was a clear violation of The Icon's written professional and ethical policies as well as those of numerous regulators.

Before going any further I'd like to explain my role at The Icon. I was employed as a permanent part-time specialist clinical teacher; I'm registered as a specialist periodontist with the General Dental Council (GDC). I worked there on Friday, which was a nice change to end the week on. Typically for three Fridays in the month I would supervise the third and fourth year undergraduate students simultaneously and teach them about gum care. The third year students would typically have partially completed some very simple cleaning and polishing on one or two patients in their second year (the nature of that previous training was described in the letter of complaint above). For the fourth year students it was the last of their gum care training as they didn't get any in the final year of the course. I would teach 'chair-side' and the training was vocational consisting of hands-on gum care to willing members of the public. On the fourth Friday, once a month, I would assist on the new patient-consultant clinic during which I would train the students in techniques of consultation, examination, assimilation, diagnosis, discussion, treatment planning and most importantly the role of non-verbal communication. The training entailed supervising and assisting students whilst they conducted consultations with patients who were new to the gum department. The objective of the consultant clinic was to create a treatment plan for each patient prior to feeding them into the Dental Institute's treatment pathway. The failures I had described in my disclosures, more often than not, started at the very beginning of the patient's journey as a consequence of chaotic and slapdash consultant clinics. This resulting in poorly written and woefully inadequate sets of patient notes. Thereafter the students were left juggling a hot potato from the very start.

The expectation for all clinics was for the students to work in pairs with one of them assuming the role of the dentist and the other the role of the chair-side assistant or nurse. This would provide an opportunity for them to understand the requirements of both roles. Both sets of students (third and fourth year) had very little experience of gum care. In their time with me they were scheduled to receive the entirety of their training in gum care. This would take place one day a week for three terms (thirty weeks). On a typical treatment clinic, I would be responsible for supervising sixteen students working in eight pairs of two. The clinic was one of many and had more than forty dental chairs in it; a block of eight chairs would be assigned to me and my students. The serenity would be broken at about 9.00am as students started to arrive on the clinic to set up the treatment bays and start revving up the drills. It often became operatic as harmonies of high-pitched drills came from the far end of the clinic where the students doing fillings were located. Patients were booked to arrive at 10.00am and eight patients would arrive simultaneously; a further eight patients would arrive at 11:15am. It was expected that all patients would have left the clinic by 12:30pm. Lunchtime was at 1.00pm with the afternoon session starting at 2.00pm with the arrival of eight patients at 2.00pm; a further eight patients at 3:15pm and all the patients would have left the clinic by 4:30pm.

Looking closer look at the morning session; if all went to plan sixteen patients would have arrived, received treatment and left between 10am and 12:30 pm. That's sixteen patients in one hundred and fifty minutes, giving me approximately 9.3 minutes per patient. Each pair of students were expected to read the patient's notes, understand what treatment the patient was to receive prior to preparing the treatment bay. Once the bay was ready they would then bring their patient onto the clinic, get them settled and have a brief conversation with them. Prior to commencing any treatment, they were required to introduce their patient to me and offer me a brief presentation of their patient's condition including the diagnosis and the overall treatment plan; up to this stage it would almost always be straight forward. Part of my responsibility was to ensure the patients knew what treatment they were having done and the students knew what they were providing. This is where the problems began.

When I would ask students: 'what is your patient's understanding of their gum disease?' or 'what are your patient's expectations of the treatment? or 'does your patient understand the consequences of having this treatment done?' or 'what does your patient understand about the limitations of the treatment?' or 'your patient has gaps between their front teeth, what do they think is going to happen to those?' Almost always, this information was missing from the notes and I would have to repeat this part of the consultation to ensure the patients were able to give me their informed consent prior to proceeding (or not) with the treatment. A lot of times it would be a complete repeat of what should have been asked and recorded during the initial consultation. I had to check all the data previously collected and reappraise the radiographs. Patients diagnosed with gum disease are usually already aggrieved and having to have the consultation repeated aggravates them more especially since this would take 20-40 minutes per patient and sometimes their whole appointment. In addition to which other students waiting (twitching and tut-tuting) in a yet-to-explode-cruise-missile length queue would become impatient too.

Some impatient students would commence treatment without presenting their patient to me and without any supervision. Their argument for doing so was they had to complete a minimum number of treatments to be eligible to progress to the following academic year and they only had a limited amount of clinic time in which to complete them. They bitterly resented having their clinical time squandered by the poorly written notes. There was always inadequate time for me to perform what was required and my clinics (which were supposed to finish at 5.00pm) would often finish at 7.00pm; something the students complained about even more bitterly. Some patients understandably had other commitments and would leave before I got the chance to check the treatment they had received. I would leave around 7.00pm, my eyes feeling as though fresh onions had been squeezed into them, NOT because I had got all the jobs done, nope. That would have required a major salvage job and I wasn't employed for any salvage work. I'd leave after attempting and failing to do a single day's work during which I had often missed my lunch and feeling knackered.

It was amid the chaos and confusion resulting from the poorly written notes that the environment in which patient safety was compromised and on some occasions harm was done (I would later learn it was at the same time, the same students had been complaining to the leadership team that they felt poorly prepared to be on the clinics).

The piss-poor notes from the consultant clinic jolted the rest of the patient's journey out of whack and sorting out the same woefully inadequate notes became the responsibility of the overworked teachers like me. The catch-up had to be done alongside the poorly prepared students, working on overly booked treatment clinics. Why did the self indulgent, self important consultants expect the teachers and students to mop up their negligence? Especially since the mop-up had to happen without any regard for the absence of suitable time in which to do it. The teaching staff, me included, could be found performing the increasingly onerous tasks which were made worse by the false hope transmitted to the patients by the aforementioned obsequious consultants. False hope almost always resulted in patient's developing unreasonably high expectations, ones which made managing them more awkward and difficult for the junior staff and students.

To add insult to injury there was a professional (written) code: that it is not (and was not) acceptable or professional behaviour for me or anyone else to ridicule the pathetic notes made by the consultants, especially in front of the students or the patients. It feels right to me that it's time for the professionals to have a good hard look at themselves; in the meantime I'll settle for being described as an expert or simply Hafeez.

It became increasingly apparent that most of the consultants knew the system had become dysfunctional but they had found by taking short cuts, clinics could be run on time. I should point out that in the health care profession the synonym for cutting corners is negligence. In their conditioned state they had also worked out that they were more likely to get away with negligence if they concealed it behind the razzle-dazzle of a smile. Most of them, worn-out, burnt-out and disinterested had got the consultation process honed down to a tee. They listened, nodded, ummed and ahhed in all the right places whilst asking questions to elicit how badly the patient might react if they were told the full extent of their gum disease and at the same time identifying the patients other insecurities and expectations. They then managed their time by pandering to the patient's insecurities by making optimistic statements (or at least very few negative ones) about the extent of their condition and any necessary treatment. They often emptily indulged the misapprehensions the patient held about gum disease and the limitations of its care. Then later on, if the same patient complained that their expectations had not been met the pandering and optimism would be defended as 'respecting the patients' right of choice'. All this allowed them to hop, skip and jump to lunch on time, leaving a trail of inadequacy behind them.

I discussed my concerns with numerous consultants and to my surprise they expressed their own concerns and frustrations about how some of the clinics had become unfit for purpose. What remained inexplicable to me was the blockage in communication between them and the leadership team. Why were they no longer on the same side? Had they ever been on the same side? That is, until I worked out that they had willingly assisted in their own redundancy. One of their many frustrations was the realisation that an earlier decision had proved to be a particularly poor one. They had happily turned a blind eye to the failures at The Icon to secure the all important promotion and a foot up the ladder. They had pocketed promotions, from successive management teams, at the expense of their integrity, professional responsibilities and perhaps even their morals and beliefs. Now, in the autumn of their careers they weren't treated with any respect by the same management structures. Somehow they hadn't seen it coming. Their plight seemed comparable to the disappointment experienced by the man who leaves his wife to marry his mistress only to find she has multiple other married lovers. It's pretty nauseating to watch them fake surprise.

Everyone ignored the fact that the poor example set by the consultants would become ingrained in the students and they would enter their careers upside down. They would join the gravy train and become like so many other dentists who poach patients from each other by playing to the patient's insecurities, each one presenting the patient with more optimistic outcomes than the last one; or at least not mentioning the negative ones. Patients fall prey to this because they are busy playing their own game. On their part they are often looking for cheaper deals and have a tendency to tweak their symptoms as they shop around. It all becomes a vicious circle of lies and it's no wonder the regulators can't regulate.

It became increasingly obvious to me that the leadership team had (at some stage) become the front men for big business and big business didn't care much for the teachers, the students or the patients. Instead, they had taken to playing dumb, shaking their head and denying the undeniable to a whole new level. The Peter Principle was self-evident as the competence of the leadership was being judged by the employer and not by the customers. In addition to which far too many of my work-shy colleagues were practicing in a shady way. Having learnt from the consultants they too offered diagnoses and suggested treatment which sounded less negative. They routinely gave patients less bad news, even this was misleading. This pragmatic time management strategy worked well and went some way to ensure the overbooked consultant clinics ran on time; but it didn't do anyone any favours in the long term. Those of my colleagues who weren't engaged in these pragmatic practices were frustrated enough to whinge about it but not frustrated enough to do anything about it.

Given that several consultants openly lamented that the patients 'get what they deserve and what do they expect for free' the reality needs explaining. The NHS created a fund for the treatment of gum disease, which 35% of adults suffer with. The Icon had secured a regional contract to supply the required treatment like all the other dental schools by submitting a bid to a NHS tender. In the bid they stated that they are best placed to provide specialist gum treatment because they employ a large number of consultants and specialists. This is misleading because once the contracts are secured the vast majority of treatments are provided by poorly trained undergraduate students, who are often unsupervised and on overbooked clinics. It's much like battery chicken farming; stack them high, treat them badly. It's about as misleading as how they attract students, in bidding one against another to attract them, the dental schools are supposed to become more competitive. Instead they undermine each other's standards and expose their students, staff and patients to poor quality practices.

Some of my colleagues were very nice people but that doesn't forgive them for shying away from giving the patients the correct information; it wasn't in any way helpful. Patients were often left in tears when they eventually learnt the reality. Patient choice is very important and I'm all for it but the way those choices were being offered served to ease the journey of the caregiver by allowing them to take the path of least resistance. It often allowed patients to make the wrong decisions for themselves. This conveniently made it easier to neutralise the same patients if they later complained. They would be neutralised with 'this was your choice'. If any of them persisted with their complaint they could very effectively be silenced with a well-heeled passive aggressive statement 'have you considered dentures?' This statement effectively covered for all manner of ineptitudes.

The students weren't immune to the work-shy teachers but had themselves become conditioned not to complain; complaining only resulted in being ignored and being ignored was hurtful and upsetting; something I'd got first-hand experience of. The conditioning was comparable to what Pavlov described in his dog studies. Only Pavlov demonstrated positive conditioning whilst the students were being exposed to negative conditioning which went like this:

The students complained,
they were ignored,
they suffered the embarrassment of being ignored (very powerful)
they recovered.

The students complained a second time,
they were ignored again,
they suffered the embarrassment of being ignored again,
they recovered slower than first time round.

The students complained a third time,
they were ignored again,
they suffered the embarrassment of being ignored a third time,
they recovered slower than on the previous occasions.

On the fourth occasion the students didn't complain. The negative impact of the conditioning manifests itself in two broad ways. The students become disorientated and appear muted as if they are 'living in a fog' or are deliberately 'cruising' through the course. They are set up for a poor long-term relationship with complaint and mistake management. It seemed obvious to me that the way they were being conditioned would result in them, one day, treating their own patients with the same contempt. It's pretty obvious how this failure ultimately elevates the risk of future mental health problems.

One of the students' biggest gripes was that the way patients were being managed and how the notes were recorded was nothing like what's described in the textbooks or their lectures. The students do a lot of self-directed studying without any help, and naturally they are left in a state of confusion when the clinics don't compliment or match the expectations that are set during their formal and self-directed study. The Iconic Machine's unwillingness to accept any responsibility for its contribution to the unnecessary mental trauma was an act of deliberate cruelty. Instead, ignoring their complaints was setting a bad example and the students were being shown that it was acceptable to ignore complaints from patients and simultaneously cover-up mistakes.

The student's belief systems were being eroded away by the fact that it was impossible for them to establish the correct context in which they could learn and understand patient care. As part of his elective project, one of the students studied burn-out in dentists and found it happened in the fourth year of the undergraduate course; nice to know. My students complained a lot to me and most of the time their complaints were valid. I never ignored or silenced their grievances. The students had my empathy, as their experience wasn't one rich in science, or educational practices and this is one of the reasons why I supported them by escalating their complaints to the leadership team. Generally, their experience was one of business and not just any old business, it was bad business. They felt 'fobbed off' by the teachers. One student described how, in his opinion, most teachers had become desensitised by the unending number of complaints from them and patients alike. I felt a sense of personal shame and embarrassment for failing to persuade The Iconic Machine to reconsider the harm it was doing. (The lengths it went to defeat me was absurd). It was focused on satisfying a different metric, the delivery of the cheapest possible product to meet specifications. It was not concerned (other than lip-service) about the mental well-being of its students.

Another student's view was that the teachers simply performed a well-rehearsed generic 'appeasement dance'. Whatever it was, the teachers should not have 'fobbed off' the students, it made them complicit to the havoc being wreaked on their training. The leadership team's stranglehold on power was an artefact of the teacher's acquiescence. No one seemed to appreciate that if more individuals were open about the mistakes we are all prone to making, without contrition, The Icon (and perhaps the world) would be a better place.

It wasn't just the students who had to put up with the poor training at The Icon, the staff did too. There was so much of it on display that I'd jokingly convinced myself it was going to make my eyes bleed. At the risk of being judged neurotic it wasn't slightly poor, it wasn't moderately poor, it really was piss-poor. My induction was a great example of how poor it was. As part of it I was trained to use The Icon's computer software or the patient data recording system to give its correct name. I was one of nine new teachers and we sat in a room huddled around the Associate Dean of Postgraduate Studies. The blinds were down, the lights were dimmed and the thermostat had been set to dreamy bedroom. The Associate Dean of Postgraduate Studies sat and described the screens we'd encounter once the computers had been booted-up. He continued to describe in a flat monotone for each screen, what we would see, what we needed to do and some tips on what to avoid, you get the idea. I was having difficulty imagining the screens being described; this was specialist software and not Microsoft Word. I sat quietly and dumbfounded like a hamster with a nosebleed, my eyes swirling as I felt the irresistible hypnotic call of an irreversible trance-like stupor. My head lolled forwards and just as my neck snapped it back with a jolt one of the other teachers asked,

'Would it be an idea to wheel-in a computer and show us the screens you're attempting to describe, it's really difficult to imagine them?'

Everyone murmured in agreement. I was beside myself when the Associate Dean of Postgraduate Studies replied:

'What a great idea!'

Was he joking? He didn't seem the laughing type but I couldn't be sure. I sat in abject disbelief as he left the room to fetch a computer. I asked one of the others if I'd missed a joke but didn't get an answer, just a flick of the forehead and a roll of the eyes. My eyes did almost bleed when he returned ten minutes later and announced that he couldn't find a computer before he sat down and continued to describe screens to us; from which I learned the sum total of fuck-all squared. Some of the other inductions I attended were given by junior staff and they weren't half as good as this one. (I would later, after my dismissal, receive anonymously by post, copies of large numbers of student complaints in which they expressed concerns about poor educational standards. I could clearly identify with their frustrations. I supposed that their training was as bad as, if not worse than mine).

Why did the other teachers find it acceptable to look the other way? I lost count of the number of times I asked myself 'what is wrong with these people?' Their performance was a contradiction to the multiple professional qualifications they decorated their names with. Although I thought about it I never worked out if they were severely deluded or mildly insane. I mean, did they really not realise that their own children would be subjected to the same poor educational standards one day? Is that what they really wanted? Of course not, because in their minds it only happens to others.

It was as if their prized income streams and credentials had overruled their professional and moral duties. I knew some of my colleagues well enough for us to have danced all night and we often did. I knew the others well enough for them to express their frustrations to me but it pained me that so few of them followed up with a written complaint to The Icon. If more of them had done so, change would have been more likely. Instead they sat back and confirmed that 'the bigger the group, the more silent it remains'. It's all part of the 'fuck-it and let some other arsehole deal with it' syndrome. It became increasingly obvious to me that many of them were avoiding the glare of the spotlight in the fear that their own misdemeanors and flaws might be exposed. On the occasions when I discussed my concerns with them they would be in one of two modes, self-defence or self-protection. They'd either describe how the Dental Institute was an impossible place to get anything right or alternatively how they had never done anything wrong and were the epitome of the perfect teacher. It was remarkable how 'group-think' and 'group-act' had ubiquitously pervaded most of them.

They really did surprise me. On the one hand they had told me openly how they were frustrated by the vicious circle of inefficiency yet on the other they continued to contribute to the creation of the inefficiency. I'd taken their expressions of frustration seriously in my decision to blow the whistle. They, on the other hand had become part of a self fulfilling prophecy with no material gains like hamsters on a wheel. The faster they ran the faster they had to run. None of them seemed to understand that their effort was wasted as the wheel wasn't connected to anything. They pretended not to realise that Professor Honest had effectively dismantled the curriculum and infrastructure in a way it was no longer harnessing the efforts of the hard-working hamsters. Some individuals were running flat out but not getting anywhere under his regime.

I remained certain the leadership team's approach of denial and burial would continue making a bad situation worse. They seemed incapacitated by their wounded pride and couldn't seem to get past the embarrassment and pain my concerns could potentially cause them if they became public. They seemed incapable of understanding that the pain was being caused not by me but by the amount of time they'd ignored and buried concerns. They didn't seem to understand that the pain wasn't necessarily a bad thing; but that it was an opportunity for improvement. Instead of taking the opportunity to embrace improvement they had started attacking me personally as if I were a felon. No one seemed to appreciate that it was crucial to fix the feedback chain; the role of which should have been:

Feedback, correction; feedback, correction; feedback, correction; feedback, correction.

The leadership understood it more like this:

Feedback, kill messenger, bury concerns; feedback, kill messenger, bury concerns; feedback, kill messenger, bury concerns.

I was still in the very early days of my enlightenment and was starting to understand some of the reasons preventing the leadership from responding in a positive or objective way. In spite of which, I somehow remained optimistic that they would come to their senses, and address the concerns. If the leadership team were besieged by the fact that they needed to process more patients, more quickly with fewer resources, this was not something they had made anyone aware of. The teachers were fed a diet of propaganda, that the terms of our employment at The Icon required us to comply with the regulators standards, provide excellent teaching and uphold The Icons excellent QS world rating.

Time to get back to the whistleblow, it was **9th October 2015** one week after the Nasty Meeting and a consultant colleague, a good friend, crept up behind me and whispered into my earlobe as I waited in the ground floor coffee shop queue'

'I've been banned from talking to you.'

'So don't talk to me then', I said feeling uncharacteristically playful that morning. I was intrigued and kept the mood light by asking him,

'Whilst you're not talking to me, who has banned you from talking to me?'

'Not me, I really like you" he stated endearingly,

'Who, then, who has banned you?" I asked.

'My boss' he replied, (his boss was the Head of a Department).

'What's it got to do with him?' I wanted to know.

'Well, you know your meeting with Dr Legitimate?' he asked, and went on to tell me that because Dr Legitimate had wanted to get me in urgently he'd cancelled a meeting with his boss at short notice. His boss' ego had been so sufficiently trumped and trampled by the late cancellation that he'd returned to a clinic and thrown a hissy-fit tantrum. He had gone and told everyone who would listen that I was a troublemaker and it was best if everyone stopped talking to me.

'A troublemaker?' I asked.

'Yes', he replied,

'And what do you think? I asked.

He mumbled something that I didn't hear.

'What?', I wanted to know.

'You should take back your complaints, you are being an arse' he said. He then delivered his last words before slipping away, 'I might like you but if anything comes of this I will side with the leadership'.

I deliberately distracted myself for the rest of the morning by gleefully pinching my brain, did he mean to call me an ass or an arse. The distraction kept me from mauling myself or anyone else for that matter.

My confidentiality had been compromised and the word was out: 'I was a troublemaker'. First it travelled around The Icon, then London and then the whole of Warwickshire. Some of my colleagues stayed away from me, others approached me with their collapsed faces. They stopped me in doorways tentatively or offsite for incognito chats. Their eyes darted pensively in case anyone might see them talking to the informer, they acted as if they'd watched too many spy movies. These were the same individuals who'd at some stage in the preceding six months complained bitterly and shared their frustrations about The Icon's unwillingness to support them better. There was a theme to what I was being told, their comments, which were delivered with a defensive sensitivity, included:

'If you find that you need some support, please don't ask me I don't want to rock the boat, my priority is to pay my mortgage.'

'I know it's good what you've done but I don't want to be any part of it I view my day at The Icon as my day off real-work, I only come in for a social and a beer.'

'You're going to lose your job I don't want to lose mine plus I don't have the stomach for this kind of trouble I don't fancy the grief.'

'I hope things get sorted soon, it would be great to have a decent place to work. I'm rooting for you. Please don't mention my name or anything I've told you.'

Their utterances surprised me. These were people I knew. People I had been friends with, people I had lunch with. Before I raised my concerns my relationships with my teaching colleagues were good and my plan was to maintain it that way. Their decisions were their own and if they were happy to sidle away from their responsibilities that was a deeply personal one, and one for which only they could hold themselves responsible. I wasn't there to make their decisions for them and hadn't the time to worry about it on their behalf. I did however, point out to them how their contribution to the poorly written notes impacted upon my responsibilities. Unsurprisingly a sense of separation started to open up between us, just like it had already done with the leadership.

They didn't just want to bury their heads in the sand and ignore the problem; these chicken-shits actually wanted to distance themselves from me whilst I sought necessary improvements. My mind became a touch edgy as I couldn't work out what morals, beliefs and values they held, especially since I was always tolerant of other people's beliefs. In reality I was only interested in their beliefs about their professional standards. As their beliefs remained elusive my engagement with them started to strain. The sheer scale of their cowardice, if that's what it was, scalded the back of my mind. As it blistered and peeled I found it easier to depersonalise my relations with them and view them as humans instead of colleagues. The depersonalisation happened subconsciously and I suspected that this was my reaction to being ostracised and an attempt to stifle my disappointment in them. I couldn't work out what business or profession these humans were in, or how they envisaged that their lives (or those of the students and patients), were going to be made better. They wanted to enjoy the harvest without the effort of sowing any seeds. But, it remains a possibility that they weren't intelligent enough to have known that ignoring problems doesn't resolve them. In the curiosity of the moment I started to ask myself: 'Had the staff broken The Icon or had The Icon broken the staff?' (I later resolved that it was most probable that The Icons leadership team had broken the staff and the Dental Institute).

I had listened to my colleague's whinge and whine about the problems at The Icon for just under two years but when the time came they all sidled (in early defeat) out of sight one by one. Still, I somehow respected them for the honesty with which they stepped up and bravely displayed their cowardice. It was impossible for me to get upset, when they were openly and honestly telling me that they were going to keep their mouths shut and remain silent. I wasn't upset I was disappointed. I held my nerve and informed each one of them that I was going to continue to seek improvements. I invited them to join me and become part of the solution. I attempted to persuade them that their inaction was making them part of the problem. It didn't bother them in the slightest that their inaction was being used by The Icon's leadership to vindicate its statement: 'nobody else is complaining', enabling them to continue to bury my concerns. I found it weird that my colleagues demonstrated, with ease, their will to hide away. They felt it acceptable that I alone was to risk everything in an attempt to seek improvements for us all. The vast number of teaching staff had become an inert mute apathetic blob, making them the perfect accomplices to the tyrannical misfits in the leadership team.

We were all professionals and professional rightness was not relative to our individual beliefs. Professional rightness was provided to us all and laid out as standards produced by a number of regulators, and we were all required to abide by them. The standards had been deemed necessary due to the fact we all have our own individual point of view. They had been designed carefully to allow each one of us to retain our point of view with the underlying concept being if everyone adheres to the standards, the effectiveness of professional dialogue would be improved and make multidisciplinary co-operation easier thus improving the patient experience. However, widespread failures at The Icon to abide by the standards had created an uneven playing field and it often was the most senior staff, the example setters, who were the worst offenders.

I continued to work alongside the Head of Department, Dr Dependable, on the clinics and we spoke on numerous occasions. I remained hopeful that he would take the opportunity to resolve the problems. That is of course until this one time when he stopped me in the corridor. Dr Dependable (D) attempted conspiratorially to test my ethical boundaries, a bit like trying to work out if one could get away with asking an electrician if he'd do a cash deal to avoid paying VAT.

D: 'Stop writing to the leadership, stop raising concerns.'
Me: 'That's not going to happen.'
D: 'Then write your letters more succinctly.'
Me: 'I tried that, it didn't work.'
D: 'Well stop antagonising them.'
Me: 'I'm not; I'm pointing out some problems.'

Eventually in an exasperated tone he growled at me:

'There is a hierarchy around here and those who stick to it do much better.'

As he had made no effort to conceal his threat, I subconsciously made no effort to conceal my indignation for having been threatened. It just made me think about a friend of mine who wore his trousers round his collarbone because he had an unfortunate rash on his arse and needed to keep his unbearably itchy butt cheeks apart. Annoyingly a question kept plopping into my mind as well much like a cowpat hitting the grass, on a hot humid day: 'Have I done something wrong?' This was the same Dr Dependable who interviewed me and selected me for the job in 2013; this was the same man I had known (or as I was realising, hadn't known) since 1997 when I did my specialist training at The Icon. The same man who one day lost his cool on the clinic and barked:

'Why are dentists so shit?'

I waited to see if any of the other assembled teachers would respond but they remained silent so I replied:

'Because we train them so badly!'

Injustice is a creepy character the word alone makes me cringe. It gives the impression of a wispy greenish-yellow mist rising from a grated sewer with a sulphuric smell that's sharp on the nose and makes one's eyes leak. With the smell of slow death in the air it melted its way into my mind more pervasively than Japanese knotweed. I was unable to prevent it from slowly suffocating my mind of its senses. It transformed my mind's playful ambient rays of sunlit hope into marshy woodland during a dark moody thunderstorm. I was staggered by the enormity of its corrosive and debilitating effects. It had only been infiltrating my mind for approximately eight weeks but it had blocked all the exits and drains and I just couldn't clear my head. It wasn't any old eight weeks, it was eight weeks of almost no good sleep. I was feeling as good (or as bad) as the characters in 'Lord of the Flies'; the moral of which could succinctly be described as 'Mankind is only ever three meals away from anarchy'. They craved food, I craved sleep.

On the **19th October 2015,** Dr Legitimate informed me (by e-mail) that he had arranged a meeting between me and The Icon's IT team. I declined the meeting and sent him the following e-mail:

Dear Dr Legitimate,

Thank you for your e-mail. It is not appropriate for me to be meeting with the IT team at this time.

During our last meeting there was a lot of doubt over the concerns that I had raised. Nevertheless they are my concerns. I have offered you the feedback as to what is possible during a consultant clinic at this time and I have also highlighted to you what information should be available in the patient's notes when the patients are seen on a student treatment clinic.

The clinical information and the patient discussions which should be recorded in the patient's records and are necessary for informed consent is nothing new. My concern is that the information was not available in the patient notes. My feedback to you relates specifically to the dates I have listed. We could start looking at some of the cases I supervised last year where the information was also missing. In my feedback to you I have not detailed anything extraordinary. I have only detailed things that we are all required to record for our patients.

The most appropriate course of action is for you as the Clinical Director working with the Head of Department, the senior teaching staff and the relevant consultants to consider my concerns and decide which of the concerns that I have raised are important to the Dental Institute. I am certain that when you have appraised the patient records for the sessions I have described, the evidence will remove the doubt that you had during our meeting on the 2nd October.

Once you have collectively agreed which of my concerns is a concern for the Dental Institute, it needs to be agreed what you want to include in the patient records at each stage of the patient journey through the Institute. That decision can only be taken by you as the Clinical

Director working with the Head of Department, the senior teaching staff and the relevant consultants.

Once it has been decided what information is necessary at each stage of the patient journey, it then needs to be decided how this information can be collected most efficiently using the software. Once the dental institute has an agreement in place of what information should be collected and how it wishes the information to be collected, then a meeting should be arranged with the IT Manager and/or the software company to assess what modifications are possible. The responsibility for meeting with the IT manager or Software Company should be that of the Head of Department or at least one of the full time senior teaching staff.

The agreed model should then be tested and timed to confirm that it is indeed efficient and that all aspects can be completed within the allocated time slots.

Once the model has been tested the part time clinical teaching staff should be instructed as to what the Dental Institute expects from them and they should be instructed by the Dental Institute how it expects them to achieve what is expected.

During our meeting on the 2nd October I was left in some doubt as to the purpose of the periodontal consultant clinics. Previous to the meeting I had understood that as part of the new curriculum the students would attend these clinics to learn the periodontal management of patients in an integrated care setting. My e-mail of feedback dated 18-09-15 demonstrates that this is what I was doing. The feedback also demonstrated a shortage of allotted time to do this. I do feel that the periodontal consultant clinic is the perfect environment for the students to gain their training and exposure about patient periodontal needs in an integrated setting. For this to happen, effectively, there will need to be more periodontal teaching staff on the consultant clinics.

Having considered my feedback Dr Dependable indicated that the consultant clinic was a triage clinic. This part of the discussion was brief and no direction was given. Further direction is required here as to what you want to include in the patient's records at each stage of the patient journey through the Institute.

Best Regards Dr Hafeez Ahmed

I became increasingly suspicious that Dr Legitimate knew full well that my concerns were regarding the woefully inadequate notes, and not the clunky slow software. I came to the belief that this invitation was his deliberate attempt to drown me by embroiling me in the ongoing IT problems. That led from previous management decisions and were now proving to be somewhat of an insurmountable irritant to the current leadership. I'll be referring to this event as 'Dr Legitimates attempt to drown me in IT'. Whatever he was up to he acknowledged my e-mail and informed me that he was in the process of doing almost exactly what I had described. (I had no way of knowing it at the time but this topic would be absent from all future discussions and reports).

The bus hit me head-on, on the **4th December 2015** when I was told by a close colleague that he and three others were sat in the secretary's office talking about me when the Head of Department Dr Dependable walked in and having heard their conversation told them:

'Hafeez is a liability, I'll have to get rid of him.'

A dark moment indeed. Was this an act of arrogance from an individual who thought he was part of the aristocracy, or was it just abstract stupidity? I couldn't decide between hubris and lunacy but he had shown his true colours by puncturing my spine. It was wrong of me to call him Dr Dependable; he was Dr Perfidious (deceitful and untrustworthy).

I reported the incident to the Clinical Director Dr Legitimate, who investigated it in a way that left no fingerprints. Dr Legitimate informed me:

'Dr Perfidious does not recall specifically saying this to either secretarial staff or clinical staff. He does, however confirm that as Clinical Lead he is looking into the clinical care that you have provided for a number of patients and that some staff are, by necessity, aware of this activity.'

Denial and threat in one small paragraph. What interested me most was that he didn't say:

'NO, he did not say it'.

Why not? Because he knew he had, but he couldn't be sure if any of the individuals who had heard him would later become witness to the event. Dr Legitimate (who was starting to resemble Dr Dick Dastardly chose not to pursue the matter formally. I spoke again to the four individuals who   Dr Perfidious had blabbed too. Unsurprisingly none of them wanted to be named; they worried that they would end up being treated like me. They didn't want to lose their jobs. What bothered them most, and they really weren't happy about it, was feeling trapped by the failings of a superior whilst having done nothing wrong themselves. They justified their silence on the grounds that   Dr Perfidious should own-up to his own failings.

Despite what I learnt in Chapter One I just couldn't clear my head. My eyes started to feel as if I had started using eye drops made from crushed glass. I had developed a blind spot on the upper outer visual field of each globe (my doctor suspected this was due to a muscle spasm around my shoulders). To stop my eyes crunching, I attempted to restrict the amount of time I spent at the computer. Ironically, I couldn't. Instead the time increased to keep up with my growing workload as well as preparing documents and responding/defending myself from The Icon. All of which had to be done after an ordinary day's work.   The tension pulled my shoulders two inches closer to my head. I daren't tip my head forwards for the feeling of being stabbed between my shoulders. I stopped going out in the car as turning my head sideways to look in the rear view mirrors had become far too painful. My doctor, who I saw with disturbing regularity, gave me stronger painkillers and a muscle relaxant just so the physiotherapist, who I was visiting weekly, could touch my shoulders. I started to avoid opening my letters and e-mails in case they might contain a modicum of criticism.

To date I was left feeling extraordinarily frustrated and resentful. Anger built up within me and with time this only got worse. Its presence became a constant in the immediate background of my every activity. This was not anger in the 'force of conviction' sense, which we all occasionally use to demonstrate a moment of seriousness. I was overreacting, being overly judgmental and hurting myself and those around me. I knew that being angry wasn't helpful but I was failing to diffuse it. Even my subconscious reactions were loaded with a particularly abrasive version of it. My conscious attempts at internalising the anger made me behave in a somewhat defensive paranoid way as I struggled to conceal the deepening rifts in my mind. I often felt like standing in the back garden to pay homage to my new source of warped solace Mr Ozzy Osborne and almost literally.......'Bark At The Moon' (his 1983 track).

Naturally, I struggled to put up with the intensity that comes with being angry and was having to concentrate hard to avoid outbursts of vitriol (the red mist) as they proved destructive; each one leaving me paralysed for approximately three days. Being angry did not mean I lacked other emotions. I did, but it had taken charge, occupying centre stage and constantly being angry was extraordinarily exhausting. As much as I felt justified for being angry, actually being angry wasn't in any way helpful. I may have been given a lot to be angry about but this wasn't a justification for not being able to control it. Being angry became a self-fulfilling prophecy, as anger begets anger. It was like being caught in a raging forest wildfire, where with the heat comes the smoke and with the smoke comes the poisonous gases. With skin burning, eyes watering and lungs spluttering the prospect of defeat is undeniable.

The Inspiration

It was **Saturday 12th December 2015** (approximately ten weeks after the Nasty Meeting and about a week since I'd been stabbed in the back by Dr Perfidious), and I had to find ways of holding myself up. I certainly couldn't have done it without the regular consoling and support of the Davenports; Ashley and Cathy Davenport (a husband-and-wife team). The Davenports are my closest friends after my wife and children. Daddy Davenport is Ashley and Mummy Davenport is Cathy, they have two teenage boys. We'd usually get together for a dinner party every couple of months. Ashley like me is a dentist and Cathy manages their dental practice. Typically, after dinner, Ashley and I would almost always entertain ourselves by discussing and debating our world; its successes, its failures and the somewhat weird behaviour of some of the humans who inhabit it. We often debated into the late hours.

Whenever the pressure became too much I would find any excuse to invite the Davenports for a dinner party. It was a win-win arrangement as they liked homemade curries and Zahida (my wife) enjoys making them; simultaneously bringing the radiant warmth of an Indian village into the house. The only downside being their dusty rain of aromatic spice scents with their steamy amber notes make their way straight to the wardrobes and sit there for weeks on end. The Davenports were at the same stage of life as me and I could 'chew the fat' with them. Talking to my friends in this way helped me get to know my own psychology, personality, likes and dislikes, beliefs and what my drivers were. Getting a deeper understanding of myself was crucial to understanding how I might continue to change my attitudes and responses. Sometimes I just needed someone to talk too about my circumstances in order to make sense of them, sometimes I felt I needed a parent figure and a reassuring hug; sometimes I just needed to be told I wasn't as hated as The Icon made me feel I was. I would sound my thoughts off them and the collaboration reduced my feelings of isolation. They offered me the therapy of the sane, as they were not in the firing line of The Icons vengeance. They were able to take a view from a position of relative mental and emotional stability. They were calm and collected when I was not; they helped me maintain my emotional health.

It was late in the afternoon on a crisply cold but clear day and the Davenports were due any minute. The sky was clear with only the odd wispy grey blue cloud, the sun's light could be seen but its warmth hadn't removed the chill but there remained a hint that its warm rays could still spread to everywhere. During an earlier walk the coldness had spoken to my earlobes and pinched my fingers but there was no Christmassy snow on the ground. It was cold enough to puff out fake smoke rings and far too cold for the birds to bother themselves with singing. I'd had a particularly shitty night's sleep. I had tossed, turned, clenched my teeth, chewed my cheeks and set my eczema on fire.

In times of peace I loved hosting dinner parties and being the entertainer but as things were on this occasion anger had lobotomised me leaving a barren open pit. I was in no state to be hosting one, I'd forgotten how to smile but I couldn't accept defeat. As much as I'd wanted to cancel it, something deep – the deepest glow plug of my mind - prevented me from doing so. Disappointment was a pill I'd always struggled to swallow at the best of times and but here I was forcing denial upon myself in an attempt to avoid dealing with it. I was holding my own head under water and trying desperately not to behave as if I was drowning. I didn't want my friends to see me being a victim or a failure. But, I was severely wounded and it had nothing to do with pride. I don't consider myself to be better than the next guy. I just think honesty is the key to long-term mental health plus it makes society and the workplace more rewarding. I'm sure I've made as many mistakes as the next guy. I just don't deny them. But as long as the culture favours their denial, life will just remain that little bit more difficult.

The Nasty Meeting had trespassed across my senses like having a near miss at a crossing with a high speed train but it hadn't killed me. But it had been severe enough for me to vomit my self-worth onto the tracks and left my brain cells bouncing about to the fading beat of my severed heart (just like it was supposed to). It was impossible not to think about it and the more I did, the crueller I became. Fuck, fuck and.... fuck, I was in my conscious brain 24/7 exhausting mental energy recklessly. I was fast becoming the twitchiest twitch monster on the planet. I cannot overemphasize the destructive power of anger, like arsenic, it is one of the causes of accelerated death. Not as fast as failing to pay a pimp or drug dealer but faster than the 'grass roots' of nature intended.

Ten minutes after they'd arrived Ashley cornered me in the kitchen and confided in me

'You are being strange, I don't know what's going on here but you are making me feel really uncomfortable, I am not enjoying this!', he said.

My retort was uncharacteristically razor sharp and acerbic, 'You were supposed to arrive at four, you arrived at four, twenty-three, THIS is what happens when you arrive at four, twenty-three, if I had wanted you to arrive at four, twenty-three I would have asked you to arrive at four, twenty-three; not four' I barked in a single hallowing breath. Ashley put on his best soft smile and as the corners of his eyes lifted he said

'Never assign to malice that which can be adequately explained by incompetence'

'What the bloody hell does that mean, are you taking the piss?' was the best I could manage.

'No, it means we didn't do it on purpose, our late arrival was an act of our incompetence, we failed to get our act together and that's why we're late. We didn't do it on purpose to wind you up; we are completely to blame; do you want us to leave?' was his immediate response.

I looked at his soft smile, squeezed my peanut-like eyes a tiny wee bit and pondered as my recital of it echoed around my lobotomised pit of a mind:

'Never assign to malice that which can be adequately explained by incompetence'.

Then I asked him to tell me again what it meant, so he did.

The clock slowed, the next two to three minutes felt more like two to three hours as I plunged into deep distracted distant contemplation. I stood there squeezing my eyes, my forehead crumpled then un-crumpled, accompanied by the odd intermittent squint and what felt like an invisible twitchy flicker of the corner of an eyelash. It was as if someone had pressed the reset button for my cranial nerves causing my mind's switchboards to randomly beep, flicker and flash. Something was happening. I don't know what to call it but in and amongst it I began to notice that somehow what was once Ashley's soft smile had transferred itself, in a sleight of hand sort of way, tattoo like onto the outer surface of my brain; from where it was it was now melting into its crevices slowly diffusing in. It was the chemical version of watching blue ink slowly dissolve into water in slow motion against a white background; one drip at a time. My mind started to feel cool and soothed, something I'd normally associate with the calm of teal or light blue but only on this occasion it began as a deep navy blue which slowly morphed into a plump pink which I imagined was my lobotomy repairing itself. Thereafter for what seemed like the longest time other than the odd creaking my mind was silent, it was bliss.

This was the second significant moment when words profoundly changed my mind's state. I was overwhelmed and effortlessly took a never-ending deep breath as my eyes welled up. I used an exaggerated smile to lift the corners of my eyes in an attempt to prevent the tears rolling down my checks but I failed. As my friend watched the tears roll down my face the clamp on my chest pinged off. In those seconds I continued to take breaths so deep a tantric yogi would be shamed. The breaths were broken by the odd sniffle. It's very tricky to explain but my eyes felt as if the were leaking from their central core with the fluid running inwards and outwards at the same time, cleansing everything as they did. Although I've never been trapped under an elephant I was sure this would be how I'd have felt if it ever got off me without killing me; my ribs creaked but they hadn't been crushed.

Each time I repeated the words they trickled and dissolved further into my mind. They created pleasant comforting yellow waves of warmth as they started to speak to me. They told me that the most plausible reason for the Nasty Meeting to have been so nasty was because it was The Icons deliberate attempt to conceal its incompetence. The words broke the mental deadlock and my mind belted out a theatrically disguised primal scream: 'The infantile bastard pieces of shit'. It was so well disguised that I didn't realise it was fury. My self-belief slowly returned like an bouncy castle inflating minus the noise and I'll tell you how it happened in a minute. My first priority was to apologise to my guests and hosting the diner party. The effect the quotation had on me was not as profound as 'Progress is always driven by the unreasonable man' but nevertheless it got me beyond another impasse into the next phase of the experience.

As afternoon became evening I felt my shoulders relinquish their stranglehold on my neck. It was a delight to feel my shoulders un-hunch, my neck lengthen and for my head to ping up like a slow motion jack-in the-box. I make it sound dramatic because it was. I was momentarily offered more pleasure than eleven concubines could have delivered. I stopped being twitchy and edgy. I've never been in prison but I felt this is how a person would feel when they walk out of one, the difference between being in and out is separated by a single footstep, it happens suddenly. At the time it felt like a lifetime but in reality the impact of the words was sudden. One minute my shoulders were around my earlobes and then as sudden as a popping balloon they dropped with a clang. I felt like a demented emu as I experimented cautiously by looking over my right shoulder and then over my left shoulder. I could perform head turning manoeuvers again. I could still feel the pain in my muscles and my spine but overall, things seemed not so bad. I managed a better night's sleep without having The Icon ploughing my brain. My mind didn't totally clear but I managed to get some of my heart and soul back, which is important as it takes heart and soul to manipulate the will. I managed to partially mute the Nasty Meeting but it remained a muted item in forefront of my conscious mind. Naturally, relapses occurred when I returned back to the same building each Friday but as awful as I felt, I continued to do it.

It wasn't easy to accept that my peers and supposed role models at The Icon weren't playing by any of the rules of fair play but I managed to do it. I realised that common sense and reasoned thinking wasn't going to be sufficient to face the challenges and the corruptions which lay ahead. I needed more help. My second call for it went out to my next-door neighbour, Ray. He was one of those quietly special friends a few of us are blessed to have in our lives. He is 84 years old and a retired Royal Air Force fire-fighter. He was experienced in the brutality of the world, he'd recovered 'body parts' from all over it. Yet he retained something of a good nature in his heart and over time he became fiercely protective of me. Ray was a listener, and not a talker, when he spoke his advice was succinct and sage. He always used measured words and a calm tone to diffuse a situation. Secretly he became my 'campaign manager' and although he never said so I got the impression he enjoyed it. He filled lots of roles but seemed to enjoy office boy most, I have no idea why; but I suspect that's what he'd decided I needed most. He offered me a certain mental stability that I hadn't found elsewhere. In his line of work the harm was easier to measure as one lost an arm or a leg or sometimes a life. In my situation the harm was invisible and mental, making it more difficult to measure. I would sit and talk with Ray at least once a week for what became an experience that dragged on for over four years. Often, if not always, my experiences would pale into insignificance in comparison to his. His lament of his horrific experiences was that it was all part of the inner doom of the human condition.

I remembered a book I had read many years previously and when I went back to it, it was very helpful *The Definitive Book of Body Language*; by Allan and Barbara Pease. Its content was far more meaningful and relevant the second time round. It gave me a valuable insight into body language, some aspects of human behaviour and most importantly boardroom tactics. From it I recognised all the bullying tactics that had been employed during the Nasty Meeting. It was a valuable asset for the preparation of things to come. I came to realise that the body language on display suggested that the biggest bastard wasn't the Clinical Director, Dick Legitimate Dastardly; it was in fact Head of Department, Dr Dependable Perfidious whose body spoke of a cover-up. I became certain it was inconceivable for Dr Dependable Perfidious to not have known about the complaints being made by the other teachers or students. He had known all along but his careerist credentials had prevented him from investigating the concerns to find fault in his own department. Either that or he lacked the courage to raise his concerns to the leadership team above him. He was only then to be consumed by jealousy of me and the disappointment in himself once I'd raised them. Oscar Wilde described this as 'The tyranny of the weak over the strong'. Once Dr Dependable was identifiable as Perfidious he truly epitomised a 'sack of shit' and his supreme pettiness rendered him a hilarious yet dangerous clown in my eyes (and the eyes of others).

I found another very helpful book *Bully in Sight: How to predict, resist, challenge and combat workplace bullying - Overcoming the silence and denial by which abuse thrives* by Tim Field. It provided a detailed encyclopedia of the actions of a bully, his victims, potential pitfalls and a guide to the interactions between the parties. It described Dr Perfidious to a tee. That said, I felt my ability to identify with its content was because I'd already been bullied. Someone who hasn't yet been bullied might not be able to appreciate its true significance or meaning. Experience is essential.

My experience was turning out to be something so very different from what I had originally anticipated it would be. It hadn't taken very long at all to make me feel hurt, lost and broken; this was the pain of inexperience. I should make clear that none of it made me see myself as a victim; that said, I openly admit I was behaving like one. I'd had a choice in the matter and I had chosen to become a whistleblower. I did not view my actions as those of a pure altruist either, as I had wanted to make a positive contribution to the society of which I am a member. I do not have the words to express how grateful I am to live in a society which has created an NHS to enable us to look after one another. However, despite reassuring myself that I had made the correct decision to protect it, I was left feeling that I had made a fundamental error in my decision making.

It seemed unfair to describe my decision as an error as no error was obvious. I hadn't rushed to my decision; it hadn't been a subconscious one. I had agonised about it and then agonised some more - I can assure you that there was no shortage of agonising. In the absence of an identifiable error, the agonising continued. As hard as I tried I couldn't identify my error (why would I, no error had been made). One thing was for sure, the over-analytical ruminations had taken over my life and there were no signs of them simmering down. I resolved that the rumination would have to be stopped by my strength of will. The onus was on me to come up with a way of protecting my mind from itself.

I managed to stop the over-analysis, rumination hyperactivity (whatever you call it) by taking one of my first conscious executive decisions, of the experience. I use the phrase 'executive decision' to describe a decision for which there is no published guidance, prescription or topically specific self-help book. I decided that I'd try and trick my brain with a play on words? It was worth a try. I substituted the word ERROR with MISCALCULATION as it was more playful, less harsh and critical. I recited to myself that my MISCALCULATION had been my decision to become something I knew nothing about. I had no experience of what qualifies someone to be a whistleblower; no idea what kind of person chooses to become one. I didn't know any whistleblowers or what makes a good one. I even asked myself; does a good whistleblower even exist? The play on words was partially successful and allowed me to refocus my consciousness in a way which partially reduced my self-criticism; saving me a stash of mental energy.

I was learning........

I was learning that right and wrong meant something to me. Emmanuel Kant (and others) had opined that all religions were valid in the sense that they attempted to challenge us to fight our bipolar nature and swing it to being good.

I was learning that The Icon's actions were incompatible to my rational (everyday) thinking, it dawned on me that relying on rationality wasn't going to be sufficient. As I wasn't in a position to change my circumstances, (and opting out wasn't an option) I'd have to change my style of thinking. This wasn't an easy step as I'd taken my way of thinking for granted and hadn't had to consider 'thinking' for the sake of understanding it or moderating it. I hadn't previously given thinking any real thought and hadn't (really) realised that there were many different ways of doing it. Some trial and error experimenting in my head was required and I'll continue to describe the tinkering process throughout this book.

I was learning about the ten key recognised philosophical belief systems:

Existentialism	Deontology
Providential	Religious Ethics
Teleology	Objectivist Ethics
Virtue Ethics	Buddhist Ethics
Legal Moralism	Sociobiology

With each one offering its own unique perspective. I started to use them to try and make sense of what the leadership might be thinking. Shortly after learning about them I picked and chose the belief system which best aligned with mine and used it to test and re-evaluate past situations. As I did I was able to retrospectively self-validate some of the actions I'd already taken. I gained a broader understanding of my reasoning behind some of those decisions. Then out of curiosity and for educational fun I started to test each of the decisions against the full range of belief systems. This provided me with theoretical explanations into the widest possible way that the same event could potentially have been perceived by different individuals at the same time. It gave me an insight into how each of the individuals in the leadership team might have been thinking and how they might have justified some of their appalling behaviour to themselves. The wider prospective or enhanced prospective (whatever one calls it) allowed me to justify my future goals and with that justification came a sense of validation and relief. For all my research I couldn't find the belief system the leadership seemed to be working to. They'd taken a belief in the philosophy of 'shoot to kill'. My sacrifice was going to be a small price to pay for the protection and survival of their herd.

I was learning that in the minds of some, the act of 'whistleblowing' was synonymous with 'combat' and that Buddha had said 'to be alive and aware is to suffer'. I realised I should never have taken The Icon's provocations personally as I was only experiencing what Buddha had identified approximately two thousand six hundred years earlier with his proposal 'suffering is ubiquitous among humans'. Once I had appreciated that suffering itself was a kind of necessary teacher I was able to change my 'point of view' towards it.

I was learning a great deal from the thirteenth century Japanese philosopher Nichiren Daishonin who applied Buddha's teachings of 'The Ten Worlds' to daily life and proposed a way for me, and others, to evaluate our state of mind. In his application the ten worlds depict ten states of mind which, we all, experience simultaneously. They are all present together but at any given moment one of the states is experienced over the others in a sort of priority depending on what you're thinking or doing and what is going on around you. The priority state becomes foremost in your conscious mind resulting in the others fading into the background. In an ordinary day the states change continually. Buddha named the ten states as hell, hunger, instinct, anger, tranquility, rapture, learning, realisation, helping and awaking. I wasn't surprised that hell and anger were foremost in my mind. If I were to use the ten states to describe my experience so far I'd put it like this: 'I was stuck in hell, losing sleep, experiencing bouts of anger, protecting my senses intuitively whilst continuing to learn and have the occasional realisation in the pursuit of being helpful whilst hungry to return to tranquility with one episode of rapture' (unreasonable man quote). In Buddha's opinion I just needed to change my point of view to one which allowed me to, focus my mind, myself towards the state(s) of mind I wished to inhabit. (It sounds like an early version of Cognitive Behaviour Therapy). He made it possible for me to move out of hell without any change to my outside circumstances and simultaneously enabled me to articulate my feelings to myself more comprehensively. The new found understanding allowed me to moderate and change my attitude and thus my point of view in a more informed way; more intellectual and less primal. Did I mention water? On some days I'd have a glass of water and the anger would disappear; I was dehydrated not angry.

I was learning that my temperament was as genetically acquired as my height. Having carefully assessed my temperament I'd speculate that my blood was more Genghis Khan than it was Buddha. I've given this considerable thought and have come to the conclusion that it's probable that my genes arrived in the northwest frontier of India during the early Mongol invasions in the thirteenth century. Having Genghis blood was just as well, as the world is still ruled by violence. It is still controlled by tyrannical bullies engaged in emotionally manipulating people.

I was learning that human behaviour was as fluid and flexible as the mood of Genghis Khan's 'Eternal Blue Sky' but rarely predictable.

I was learning not to internalise my emotions, feelings or suffering. I understood that broadly speaking I had five ways of potentially managing them:

1. Keep it to myself (suffer in silence)
2. Escape from it
3. Pass it someone else
4. End it myself
5. Transform it into something good.

I realised that at the beginning of my experience I was keeping things to myself, most probably due to the shock, the surprise and the embarrassment of the appalling way I was being treated. It was impossible for me to escape as mine was a self-induced suffering. I had no option but to continue confronting it and relish the occasional respite. It hadn't taken me too long, to realise my limitations before starting to enhance my philosophy. I did however regret that I hadn't read any philosophy earlier in my life. This was my stupidity. I felt hugely encouraged and uplifted when I realised I 'owned' my suffering from the outset. And how after a short period of intense suffering I'd reached out to my friends for help.

I was learning the fundamental difference between OFFENCE and HARM; offence meaning allowing myself to feel insulted by comments made by others whilst harm meant physical injury to my person. I could be harmed, intentionally or accidently, without my consent whilst offence always required my consent. Harm is possible without offence but feeling offended resulted in a victim mentality. I started to appreciate that The Icon had not harmed me and I could chose not to be offended. It was plausible that I'd generated excessive negative feelings due to my inexperience of dealing with being treated unfairly. It was clear I'd have to make a conscious effort to tolerate the offence better, irrespective of how badly The Icon continued to treat me. I'd have to look at everything as another lesson to be absorbed or a mistake to be understood and not an offence, insult or grudge. What was the point of feeling criticised when the malicious proffering was becoming exposed as an obvious cover-up of incompetence? And with that I started opening my mail with greater ease. If my mail contained anything that vaguely resembled a criticism I'd write to the author and simply ask: 'Is this what you meant to say?' The response was almost always an apology for the mistakes in the original communication and once they were removed so was the potentially (accidental) offence. The removal of offence and the use of a higher degree of philosophical mind control and philosophical moral self-defence put me in a better position to temper my 'point of view'. It became clear that I needed to accept a larger share of the responsibility, which came with the decisions I'd taken so far. As a whistleblower it was necessary for me to put my feelings to one side altogether, and there was no scope for me to entertain normal feelings. That said, I remain certain that the mistakes (designed to stimulate offence) were in fact deliberate acts of malice and almost always intended to appear as acts of accidental incompetence.

At about the same time, I developed, accidently, my meditative breathing technique. I think it happened subconsciously. It's nothing new but it felt new to me when I was drowning. I'd avoided opening e-mails and letters in fear of criticism, well that all changed. When mail arrived (paper or electronic) I'd start by slowly breathing in before slowly breathing out, as I breathed in I'd say to myself: NO PROBLEM and as I breathed out I'd say: EXCELLENT. I'd repeat a couple of cycles of breathing before opening the mail. It worked for me. The magic of the words plus the deep slow delivery of air became a win-win combination.

I was learning that my colleagues hadn't meant to, deliberately, criticise me (personally), and they didn't mean to cause me any harm. They were just protecting themselves and that 'protection of self' is a function of the subconscious, automatic part of the brain. They were protecting themselves automatically with no real regard for the merits of the concerns I'd raised. Whilst they were busy automatically protecting themselves, I was supposed to be enjoying another subconscious automatic brain function: 'cathartic relief' through my open expression of my strong morals, beliefs, values and professionalism. How this is supposed to work remains a mystery to me because the experience was not an enjoyable one at any time. (Granted it was ultimately rewarding but it wasn't enjoyable).

I was learning that the same negative feelings are not ubiquitous across all humans, they are inextricably intertwined with one's beliefs, morals and values. For example, if I'd been a delusional power-hungry, credential-seeking, careerist twat I wouldn't have had the negative feelings in the first place. With this realisation I was able to alter my perspective and strengthen my resolve. It was becoming clear that if I were to survive I'd have to be careful, I may need to tip-toe around a bit and there were probably going to be times when I'd have to run for my life. (I would later learn that realisation and resolve don't always make actions any easier).

I was learning that the tampered feedback provided the foundational support for the spin. And how easy it was for The Icon to manipulate the feedback by sneakily playing with its employee's cognitive biases. It's human nature to avoid giving negative feedback because the giver feels negatively judged by their peers for having done so. For example, I'd often say to myself without really knowing why (at the time) 'I'm never going to look good whilst making someone else look bad'. I could see that it had only required a small effort from The Icon to ensure the feedback from its employees was predominantly positive, most of the time. Using simple tricks like making a positively worded presentation immediately prior to requesting the feedback or standing closer to the giver has a remarkably strong effect. The leadership team used the tampered feedback as a cloak to bury a bad situation while satisfying their personal greed to achieve or retain unfettered power.

I was learning that by not treating the students like a number, I was instilling trust and removing insecurity. They deserved a more fulfilling vicarious reinforcement and I hope that one day the same students develop the confidence to hold The Icon and its leadership responsible. In my experience The Icon couldn't have cared less and seemed content exchanging fees for certificates. They just didn't want to understand:

> 'It will never rain roses: when we want to have more roses we must plant more trees.'
>
> George Eliot

I was learning that large organisations bring out the worst of human nature. It allows individuals to go to work and do the 'shits' that they cannot do near their families. Individuals dump on each other all day long, each one deluded that they are the special one who will not get dumped on. This happens all day long in lots of different ways and is born out of the: 'One rule for oneself and another rule for everyone else' syndrome, or:

> 'All animals are equal, but some animals are more equal than others'
>
> George Orwell

The condition is not restricted to the elite upper class but is ubiquitous across all classes, societies and cultures.

I was learning that there are those who say 'The arc of history bends gently towards progress'; I remain unconvinced. It seems more plausible that their statement results from an illusion created by the mass globalisation of 'rolling turds in glitter'. I accept that the tools we use to live our lives have changed for the better and we wear shinier shoes but the revoltingness of human behaviour has changed very little in the last two thousand years; except for the fashions and fads with which it's reported in the media. New scandals emerge almost weekly and are presented as if it's the first of its kind. Each new one typically demonstrating the same sequence of ignorance's leading up to it, the same panic once it's out in the open, the same overreaction during it and the same attempts to conceal bury and conclude it unresolved.

I was learning not to be surprised that so many of my colleagues were work-shy. Humans are undeniably animals and animals prefer to lazily bask in the midday sun displaying short bursts of energy to forage for food and then eat it. Fed and watered they lay on their backs waggling their arms and legs aloft, dreaming of a mating opportunity. They struggle with the mountains of intense, detailed work and general arse ache that working in large institutions requires. It seems right to me that this inherent laziness plays a major role in the incompetence based scandals which are a part of everyday life.

I was learning that my route to depression was not a simple linear one but subject to the laws of compound exponential multiplications. It's a bit like throwing a match into a hay barn after a long hot summer, it's the same hay but it burns harder and faster. The multiplications were occurring not only because of the continual nature of the negative provocations but because of how my mind had started storing them. It started to store each negative provocation as three independent events. Each time I received a negative provocation it was stored as event one, then each time I asked myself if the provocation might be making me feel depressed the thought would be stored as a second event and each time I reflected back on a provocation it would somehow be stored as a whole new event. It all got out of hand pretty quickly but as a problem can't be solved until it been identified I was thankful for having realised that a single event generated at least three potentially depressing memories.

It had taken me a while to work out I'd subconsciously started storing negative memories in high definition but as I had, it became obvious that their amplification had a disproportionate effect. Each additional one invoked a stronger and more profound sadness by virtue of the compound effect of the numbers alone and irrespective of its content or significance. I found a way of consciously tackling this by switching off my mind's default 'automatic memory storage' switch. I did this by starting a hand written list of depressing events. I was very strict about what I included on the list and I purposefully left things off it. Then, I told myself if it's not on the list it can't have been a depressing event. This technique reduced self-absorbing behaviours, rumination and distraction simultaneously. It felt exhilarating, a bit like coming back to the water's surface after narrowly surviving being drowned seeing the sun once again and taking a breath of fresh air. As I continued to develop the technique I was able to delete events which truly belonged on the list. Is that mad or genius?

I was learning that when friends and family make a mistake they simply apologise and things move on. The Icon was not my friend or my family, and when it made a mistake, it was required – by the burden of its own spin, to hush it up. This was all The Iconic Machine knew and those who had risen to its leadership team did so because their morality was loose and flexible. While the inflexibility of mine kept me trapped. The irony was that being trapped gave me worth and having worth is what fuels my personal value and fulfillment. What's the point otherwise? The Iconic Machine on the other hand was attempting to make itself appear superior by relying on the simple virtue of comparison by making me look inferior. Instead of upping its game it engaged in deliberately concealing its acts of incompetence; this was its only way to protect itself. What a crappy coward it had become?

I was learning that friendship, for me, is a relationship in which my flaws don't clash with those of the other person. My friendships are not based on the fact that me and the other person. have lots of things in common and are perfect in every way. They are based on the fact that our stupidities don't clash with each others. I am in no way perfect and nor are my friends but our flaws are in perfect resonance with each other. I work hard to keep mine out of the workplace.

I was learning that the 'executive decision' which I thought I'd invented, for myself, was already a recognised phenomenon and that the 'executive decision' I had made for myself was in the neocortex of my brain, an area of higher function. In this sense, it directly connects with Ludwig Wittgenstein's assertion that philosophy is a form of linguistic therapy. The fact that I had made it and labelled it an executive decision prior to reading about it offered me great encouragement and confidence that I'd been responding reasonably well under pressure.

I learnt to reassure myself that I'd been right all along and it's entirely possible to treat all patients honestly, ethically and correctly - if that's what one wants to do. My sufferance was exclusively for the fact that I was being punished for having highlighted The Icon's failings (how rude). I felt encouraged by a

Winston Churchill jibe:

'The best argument against democracy is a five-minute conversation with the average voter'

This allowed me to ascribe the poorness of my experience to some of the flaws of a democratic system. I mean democracy in the 'control of an organization or group by the majority of its member's' sense. After all in a democratic way The Icons entire staff – bar two of them – made a personal decision and felt compelled to crush me or sit back and allow me to be crushed. I was learning to forgive myself for how naive I'd been in my overly trusting of others. This was my first proper wake-up call to the 'human condition', I honestly hadn't anticipated it before but once Pandora's Box was open, reflections from previous events in my life took on a new meaning; the muted silencer of inexperience was off.

I was learning that resilience is not associated with physical strength, it's not a product of ego, it's not about being shouty or assertive, it's a complex mix of emotions and intelligence; it's an emotional intelligence. It's built on a foundation of emotions which are calm, reflective, considerate and respectful. Without them the notion of resilience evaporates into steam like cold water poured onto a baking hot engine block; often cracking it at the same time.

I was learning a lot from the crazy charterers in my head as I navigated a path across a fraught but never boring rocky road. The take-home message I'd developed for myself at this stage was enlightening and promising, though I wouldn't say there were any breath-taking vistas.

The natural me – the genetic, biological, animal, intuitive, automatic – was born with a preordained 'stand and fight (and not flight)' template already in place; this wasn't likely to change. I'd say it was like one of those join-the-dot puzzles and likely to be one of many of them (I'd guessed that some even have numbered dots).

The nurtured me – the psychological, interactional, rein-in the animal – emerged as my early life experiences initiated or stimulated my cognitive development. Those early life experiences acted as the pencil joining the dots to reveal my underlying nature. Some of the early life experiences acted as the crayons which brought the picture to life. My colours were laid down as ones which would always question the adults (children in wrinkly skin) and their adult authority.

The <u>philosophical me</u> – had been missing. Prior to reading the philosophy I can honestly say I wasn't really dealing with the impact the situation was having on me emotionally. Instead I'd 'just' continued to get on with it in a 'throw the parking tickets on the back seat of the car' sort of way.

My experience was confirming to me that the nature versus nurture debate wasn't really a debate in me, the nature was preordained and the best nurture could ever do was compliment it. Thereafter the nurtured nature was starting to be enhanced by philosophy (if I had the capacity to understand it). It was becoming apparent and seemed right to me that no amount of nurture or philosophy could change my nature; it was by far the strongest of the three.

Lastly I was learning that when you encounter a bully in the workplace or anywhere else for that matter, there are many different approaches that can be taken depending on what you want the outcome to be. I've been told that hitting them over the head with a golf club is by far the most effective. The problem is that if you hit back you become as bad as the bully, and if you do decide to knock them over in this way you have to make sure they don't get up again. That's not always possible. You could kiss them or say thank you and walk away and make it the last time you ever see them, this is not easy if the bully is your line manager which is often the case. In my experience the following sequence of statements are very effective. To achieve maximum liberation as you speak, you should keep a calm relaxed facial tone and a calm relaxed voice. My guide is: 'Say what you need to say, just say it nicely'.

1. 'You are bullying me, did you mean to bully me?'

2. It is unlikely, but if they say yes then proceed to (4), below

3. If they say no, change your statement to: 'You are bullying me and you are doing it on purpose' then proceed.

4. 'It is unacceptable, please stop.'

In my experience the above is the most powerful and assertive and successful way of neutralising a bully. For the best effect, say it to them in person first and then send it to them in writing (e-mail is good) within an hour. Here's a slightly different version of the same statements:

1. 'You have given me seven hours worth of work to complete in three hours, did you mean to overwork me and put me under undue pressure?

2. If they say yes and tell you that you are such a good worker and you should be able to cope with seven hours worth of work in three hours then proceed to (4), below.

3. If they say no change your statement to: 'You have given me seven hours worth of work to complete in three hours. When you do this you put me under undue pressure' then proceed.

4. 'It is unacceptable, please stop.'

Chaos Prevents Destruction

'Antifragile is when something is actually strengthened from the knocks'

Nassim Nicholas Taleb

This quotation was buried deep inside a 423 page book, the text size of which was a teeny-weeny itsy-bitsy six; 480 pages if you include the glossary, appendix and notes.

I extracted it from said book on **Tuesday 5th April 2016** whilst on a family holiday in Rome, Italy. The impasse was an inability to see tasks and jobs to completion due to a lack of focus and persistent low mood, bewildered by the continued injustice and uncertainty. Through it I changed my state of mind as it enabled me to attach my own meanings to the words anxiety, fear, worry, pity, dread, and feeling vulnerable. Once the words had meanings (or emotions) I was better able to understand the effect they were having on me. It created the second bring-it-on moment of my experience.

In this chapter I will explain why the new events at The Icon continued to give rise to an ever-increasing number of negative emotions (or meanings). How those negative emotions made day-to-day life more difficult. The irony of standing next to the once blood thirsty Roman Coliseum full of fear and feeling scared. On this occasion fate, luck and chance felt more like destiny. Realising that emotions are the chemical derivative of meanings and the same emotions lead to feelings enabled me to take them, flip them into positives and ended up replacing weakness with fortitude.

The Experience

...It was **April 2016** and a lot of not a lot had happened at The Icon since Chapter 2. It had been approximately seven months since I had shown some solidarity with the students, joined hands with patients (and linked arms with my work-shy colleagues). The klaxon that sounded shots had been fired and I was left wondering if I should invest in a stab vest or an axe. The leadership team continued doing a good impression of individuals who should have been pushed back in at birth. Between them, they had done the arse end of nothing in the six month period after I blew the whistle (other than try to squash me). The stench of ineptitude was truly indescribable, less pleasant than human faeces. They were proving that nothing comes out of nothing and their pretence had sufficiently hypnotised them to prevent them from doing any joined-up-thinking.

The cast in this chapter

Leadership Role	Given Identity
Dean of Education	Professor Honest
Head of Department	Dr Perfidious (deceitful &untrustworthy)
Clinical Director	Dick Dastardly (a nasty devious bastard)
Human Resources	Honest Reality

The story so far...

1. 15th September 2015; whistle blown.

2. 2nd October 2015; Nasty Meeting.

3. 16th October 2015; Incognito Meeting with Professor Honest.

4. 19th October 2015; Dick Dastardly's failed attempt to drown me in IT.

5. 1st Week December 2015; Dr Perfidious tells a bunch of staff 'Hafeez is a liability; I'll have to get rid of him' (ouch my shoulder blades).

...**On** the **7th December 2015** I e-mailed Dick Dastardly and expressed a grievance, I've pasted a small excerpt from it below:

The Icon's policy on Information Disclosure (Whistle blowing) is very clear. My earlier Information Disclosures to The Icon are clearly covered by it. There have been several instances of The Icon's staff failing to properly follow the same policy in relation to my disclosures. The matter you are about to investigate represents an escalation of these previous failings and not a new or isolated occurrence.

Dastardly acknowledged my e-mail and informed me:

I am familiar with The Icon's Policy on Information Disclosure (whistleblowing). The version I have on file I downloaded from The Icon's HR website and was approved by the Principal's Central Team on 13th May 2013.

On the **17th December 2015** I was sent a copy of a report prepared by Dr. Perfidious. You'll remember that during the Nasty Meeting he hadn't been able to comment on the clinical concerns I had reported as he hadn't had the opportunity to read the patients notes or speak with the clinicians responsible for the failings. He had agreed to investigate my concerns and then report on them. His report was a big long important one but there was no mention of any investigations into the clinical concerns I'd raised. It was not quite the pentagon papers but it had a nasty whiff to it. What he had included was as in almost all institutional reports, the generic excuses about restrained NHS resources. The contradiction being the restraints he described were the polar opposite of the lofty promises The Icon had made and continued to make to prospective students and patients alike.

In his report he meandered through history and justified the current clinical operations, which were no longer cutting the mustard, if they ever had done. Operations, which were acting more like mustard gas and clogging and choking the students training. Sorry, I meant trainees, mustn't call them stoodents, not PC anymore; being PC requires that they be referred to as trainees. A stoodent is: a person who is stoodying at a university or other place of higher education. A trainee is: a person undergoing training for a particular job or profession (just making a note for the leadership teamo. In all fairness they were stoodent trainees and some of them deserved a refund. Let's get this party started; *Pink 2001.*

I'm all for recycling, we've got a planet to save; but I couldn't even wipe my arse with his report. He side stepped all my concerns and wrote six full pages of absolute garbage. It had all the hallmarks a handsome credential seeking academic fanny magnet careerist twat would include in one. He practically wiped the slate clean and used it to bury my concerns whilst writing it in a way to portray a sincere and genuine effort had been made to address and resolve them. His sincerity was demonstrated by his statement that all staff should be making their notes in accordance with the General Dental Council guidelines. He repeated the same statement three times in the report which indeed listed my concerns and talked over them but did not acknowledge them, address them or suggest credible actions to resolve them.

I would later learn he had also conducted an investigation into the concerns of a particularly upset patient and had produced a separate report, but unfortunately that report wasn't shared with me. The first time I'd get to see it would be in **April 2017** when it was being used as evidence to support my suspension (I would be suspended in **March 2017**). The patient in question was upset because the he didn't receive the treatment he was expecting. Instead the students had complained because they could not understand his notes or work from them. The notes did not record, amongst other things, any of the discussions about the benefits and limitations of the treatment. Whilst addressing the students concerns it was revealed that the patient's expectations were ambitiously high and a contradiction to the advanced nature of his disease, especially since he continued to smoke and wasn't cleaning his teeth very well. His expectations were off-the-chart and if there had been any previous discussions about them they had not been recorded in the notes. I had to repeat the entire consultation and when it became apparent to the patient that insufficient time remained for the provision of any treatment he complained, bitterly. When the student realised that her opportunity to achieve a treatment quota she too complained, bitterly. The patient left unhappy and within a week he had submitted a written complaint, but unfortunately it was not shared with me and Perfidious didn't mention it in his report. (I would only learn of its existence during the investigation stages of my second disciplinary, when I would see a copy of an e-mail the patient sent to the GDC). As part of his aforementioned investigation Perfidious interviewed the consultant responsible and he reported what she told him:

'I do admit I did not write all this down due to lack of time, though I am 100% sure I discussed them'.

He went on to state:

'Dr. Ahmed does often seem to uniquely experience a problem whereby his interpretation of the clinical situation differs from that of various consultants with the DI'.

You might be wondering (just like I was); how was it possible for him to report that the consultant hadn't completed her notes but then in the same report conclude that I was unique for not being able to interpret what she hadn't written. My interpretation of his statement was that all the other staff ignored the woefully inadequate notes and I was unique in that I didn't ignore them. It's a plausible assumption that his statement was his deliberate attempt to implicate me as the cause of the concerns I had raised.

The report opened with Dear Professor Honest and Dr Dastardly so it is inconceivable that they hadn't read it. How unfortunate, for me, the most senior members of the leadership team didn't notice the obvious contradiction. It's really quite simple if the consultant hadn't completed her notes then how was it possible for me to be criticised for being unable to interpret them. There was no rocket science involved at all. In reality, there was no rocket science at any stage in the experience just smoke, mirrors, lies, a lot more lies, a lot more dodgy lies, and lots of pretending.

Dr Perfidious presented another one of his conclusions:

'The consistent pattern emerging with a series of such events would seem to be that Dr. Ahmed feels incapable of managing students in the clinical teaching setting unless everything is completely perfect in all aspects at each and every visit'.

The statement comes across as if it was deliberately intended to poison my reputation and cause me a slow but steady death. He had attached a hosepipe to the cars exhaust and draped it through my window. The problem he created for himself was his first statement contradicted the second one. His second statement correctly identifying that I was working to the very standard of excellence The Icon had set as an expectation to its staff and students.

How crude and rude. His reports were his failed attempt to bury and conceal my disclosures. His success however was in lining me up for a potential allegation of misconduct, somewhere down the line. His reports were part of the evidence that a cover-up was afoot; the rest of the evidence is the patient's notes. This was the moment that made me realise that most things The Icon published about its performance were probably fantasy and far removed from reality. I'd love to see what it submitted to gain its falsely elevated QS world rating.

The same report provided the evidence that I was being discriminated against. Dr Perfidious had stated (three times) the staff at The Icon should be making their notes in accordance with the General Dental Council guidelines. The consultants' notes were not in accordance with them yet she wasn't criticised but whilst mine did, I was heavily criticised. You may think I am harping on and on about the report and the reason I am (if you hadn't noticed) is it reports an investigation into one of my protected disclosures. The reports inclusion in the evidence bundle supporting my suspension was the evidence that linked my suspension to my protected disclosures. Got it?

What makes a disclosure a protected one? The law known as The Public Interest Disclosure Act 1998 defines six characteristics as protected. It states the six characteristics which if included in a disclosure make it a 'protected disclosure'. In other words for a disclosure to be a 'protected' one it must show or describe one of the following:

(a) That a criminal offence has been, is being or is likely to be committed

(b) That a person has failed, is failing or is likely to fail to comply with any legal obligation to which he is subject

(c) That a miscarriage of justice has occurred, is occurring or is likely to occur,

(d) That the health or safety of any individual has been, is being or is likely to be endangered,

(e) That the environment has been, is being or is likely to be damaged, or

(f) That information tending to show any matter falling within any one of the preceding paragraphs has been is being or is likely to be deliberately concealed.

A protected disclosure can be identified by its contents (by reading it). Upon reading, if it includes or describes one of the six characteristics it qualifies as a protected one; for example, if a disclosure reports a compromise to patient safety it automatically qualifies as one as concerns about patient safety is one of the six protected characteristics. Thereafter a protected disclosure is supposed to be a protected characteristic by law, which means there is a law that protects (or is supposed to protect) the individual who made the disclosure from recriminations levied by the employer. It is not supposed to be necessary to write 'protected disclosure' on the top of a disclosure nor does a disclosure become protected just because it has 'protected disclosure' written across the top of it. It becomes protected by what is disclosed in it. Got it? It's chimp proof. (What the law cannot do is stop individuals pretending they didn't realise what the disclosure was describing or that it was protected). One last thing, the disclosure has to have the public interest at its heart for it to be protected.

The common thread running through almost all my disclosures was one of informed consent. There's nothing complicated about it either. There are currently three key organisations that publish guidance on it and the first two also regulate it (or are supposed to regulate it).

1. **The Care Quality Commission**. Who provide the legal guidance in its publication 'Enforcement Policy'; which states that services should only be supplied to individuals once they have consent after having been informed appropriately.

2. **The General Dental Council**. Who provide the ethical guidance in its 98-page publication 'Standards for the Dental Team'.

3. **Faculty of General Dental Practice (UK).** Who provide clinical guidance in their publication 'Clinical Examination and Record-Keeping'; which is a complete reference guide on what should be included in a consultation and also how to record it.

Essentially the Care Quality Commission tells professionals that they can only provide treatment once their patients have agreed to it. The General Dental Council tells professionals what information they should share with patients for them to be considered adequately informed to provide consent for the treatment to proceeded or not. Broadly speaking the discussion needs to include how good or bad their condition is and what the benefits, limitations and consequences of the treatment are. The Faculty of General Dental Practice tells professionals what needs to be written in the notes and how to write it. It sounds so easy.

The GDC are very clear about what they expect from professionals. A copy of their standards can be downloaded from the following website:

https://www.gdc-uk.org/information-standards-guidance/standards-and-guidance

In principle if (and when) a dispute breaks out it should be easy to read the patients notes and check them against the above standard. What could be easier? (Sadly that's not what happened for any of the twenty two or so patients whose concerns I escalated to the GDC, and identified by their hospital number. Not a single case was assessed with any consistent objectivity. Every case was assessed subjectively with lots of supposing, assuming, presuming, excusing, guessing and imagining).

The GDC told me that they have limited powers and they can only regulate individuals, they do not have the powers to regulate organisations. Regulating organisations is the responsibility of the Care Quality Commission. Again, in principle how this is supposed to work is, let's say the GDC find faults with nine dentists who all happen to work in the same organisation. The GDC should alert the CQC for them to investigate at an organisational level. (The reality however was that as the GDC failed to apply its own standards with any consistent objectivity the whole thing fell over at the first hurdle and I have no idea if they raised the alarm to the CQC or not).

In principle the CQC are responsible (or supposed to be responsible) for ensuring that the organisation complies with the law and the law on 'informed consent' changed following a Supreme Court judgment in 2015. The law now states:

'Doctors must now ensure that patients are aware of any 'material risks' involved in a proposed treatment, and of reasonable alternatives'.

This was a marked change from what it replaced which was the 'Bolam Test'. The previous test was whether a doctor's conduct would be supported by a responsible body of medical opinion. The Bolam Test was deemed unsuitable for cases regarding the discussion of risks with patients, as the extent to which a doctor may be inclined to discuss risks with patients is not determined by medical learning or experience, it's usually just a general outline discussion of some general facts and sometimes figures about the intended treatment. The Bolam Test no longer applies to the issue of consent, although it is still used more widely in cases involving other alleged acts of negligence.

The new test moves away from the *reasonable doctor* model to the *reasonable patient* model and is outlined as:

'The test of materiality is whether, in the circumstances of the particular case, a reasonable person in the patient's position would be likely to attach significance to the risk, or the doctor is or should reasonably be aware that the particular patient would be likely to attach significance to it'.

The new test makes it clear that doctors should provide person-centered care. They must work in partnership with their patients, listening to their views and giving them the information they want and need to make decisions.

Back at The Icon... Unfortunately, Dr Perfidious continued with his pretence that he could not get his head around the fact that if the consultant(s) hadn't completed their notes then those notes would need to be completed by the next numpty in the chain (me). I presumed that he expected me to 'tow the party line' and ignore the woefully inadequate notes like so many of my colleagues. There is no way I'd violate the standards published by any of the regulators, especially since he'd specifically stated (three times) that I was required to abide by them.

The week before I received the Dr Perfidious pentagon papers the Nixon administration; sorry I mean Dick Dastardly had sent me another report. This one had been prepared by The Icon's IT team. A committee of four individuals comprising the former Clinical Director who had been responsible for commissioning the software in the first place; the man responsible for maintaining The Icon's computers and two others who Dr Dastardly described as the 'champions' responsible for helping the rest of us use the software. Unfortunately, they completely misunderstood my concerns and, as a collective, managed to only protect themselves. They reported on an entirely different matter, one for which they could find a much happier ending. Their report was a very important one as it was tabulated and in glorious Technicolor. Their unrevealing report did reveal one important finding, which curiously, matched the one reported by Dr Perfidious. They also reported that the cause of the concerns I'd raised was me; yep they too reported that I was uniquely experiencing difficulties using The Icon's computers and that all the other staff found them 'friendly'. The mystery was over, the problem was 'me' and to rectify it I still had the option to get my bumhole waxed. Silky smooth. Their report was yet another failed attempt to conceal and bury my disclosures. They too were successful in shining a light on me to line me up for an allegation of misconduct.

I just couldn't understand the logic behind the cover up, why was a cover-up a good idea? What would it achieve? For whom? For how long?

The investigations and reports and (very carefully) failed to address any of the specific complaints made by patient complainants or the student complainants The evidence of the failings was in the patient notes, and they, along with the students written complaints would have debunked the leadership teams spin, which I suspected is why they were very carefully not reported.

As for my colleagues, they had gone deeper underground; there was too much panic in this town: Jamiroquai 1998. They weren't up to much except moaning and whinging. Still, I had no axe to grind against them though as some of them had confided in me that their priority was to pay their big mortgages (thank God the bankers are an honest bunch). I tried to convince them that if they wanted to stop being oppressed they would need to show some courage. The sharpness of their critique may have reduced but alas their insidious assault on me trickled on. They even started gambling and I had become the sport. How long would I last? Was the bet. The work-shy's would sidle up to me, make farcical remarks and ask:

'Are you still here?'

'Haven't the leadership team managed to get rid of you yet?'

'They are going to throw you out of the top floor window you know'
'Why don't you just leave?'

Who wouldn't struggle under these conditions? Not content with their infantile inability to support me they couldn't stop themselves from sticking the boot in. I hadn't asked for the world. I had only asked them to do what they were supposed to be doing and claimed were doing all along. Which was to treat the patients and the students as they would want to be treated themselves; oh, and to write a half decent set of notes. In exchange for having made such a simple ask I lost my right to relax.

With the dawn of each new month the word around the campus was that I would not last beyond the end of the same month. The sport continued and the work-shy comments indicated that they were certain of my pending doom. I somehow remained unconvinced that me losing my job would be a fitting or desirable way to resolve the concerns. Was I in denial? Had I totally underestimated the corruptibility of humans? Had I been wrong in my presumption that the title of Professor in healthcare and caring meant the same thing? It was becoming plausible that the title Professor was a pronoun being used as a tool which bestowed recipient individuals a stature with which they could potentially produce more money for The Icon. (As my painful experience continued it was proved that my expectations had been wrong and the grand academic pronouns had been corrupted by the pursuit of business)

Like a complete senseless idiot I somehow remained convinced that leadership team would see sense and realise that the right thing to do would be to address the concerns. I maintained hope because it was the right thing to do, wasn't it? With each knock back I got I just thought it required a little bit more effort and perseverance. I convinced myself that the solution was around the next corner, and then the next corner and then the next corner (of the maze). In spite of the difficulties I experienced and due to the leaderships (deliberate) inaction I continued to raise my concerns, here are some of them, take a deep breath and (ahem):

•Students were complaining that they had insufficient training to be providing treatment to the patients.

•Some named students complained because some patient notes were missing.

•Some named students complained because some of the patient's notes were poorly written.

•In some cases patients had not given their informed consent for the treatment, which the students were scheduled to provide.

•Some patients had complicated medical histories, which made them high risk for medical complications and as such unsuitable to receive treatment from students.

•The clinic was overbooked for the students who were poorly prepared to provide treatment for the patients.

•I made a request to improve safety by reducing patient numbers because the students were poorly prepared to provide treatment to the patients.

•I was prevented from completing my statutory professional duties as required by the General Dental Council (GDC) and Care Quality Commission (CQC).

•The report prepared by Perfidious dated December 2015 appeared likely to deliberately conceal what I had reported in my previous disclosures.

•I had not received an update for any (not a single one) of the patients or the named students whose complaints I had escalated to the leadership team and it appeared likely that it was a deliberate omission and an attempt to conceal what I had reported in my previous disclosures.

•The Technicolor report failed to address or resolve any of the concerns I raised and it appeared likely that this was a deliberate attempt to conceal what I had reported in my previous disclosures.

My work-shys colleagues knew they were making poor quality notes; but they covered their tracks by blaming it on the computer software being slow and clunky. They'd realised it could only be used in a time efficient way by implementing short cuts, one of which was not bothering to make good notes at all. They (off-the-record) protested that they had to take short cuts as they weren't given the extra time to compensate for its clunky-ness. The problem with their protest was the evidence demonstrated that long before the invention of the computer they had been making woefully inadequate notes on paper (with their feathered quills). Nevertheless, the leadership team appeared to be under a colossal pressure to hush-hush around the computer system because it was brand spanking new. A brand spanking new slow and clunky system. Awkward.

My nerves jangled less comfortably when one of the work-shys gave me his advice:

'If you are not happy working here you should leave, stop rocking the boat for the rest of us!'

He was a work-shy who couldn't have spelt the word 'work'. Cutting comments along the same lines continued, I was told by other's:

'I like working here, it's easy, I don't really have to work; you should stop complaining.'
and

'The University is a behemoth, do what you like, you will come to an end first, and it won't change; it can't change or be changed.'

Previous comments paled into insignificance when a final year student spat a revelatory saliva sample onto my face:

'I cannot believe you are doing this, you have no idea how much money I have spent to get this far, I am months away from getting my certificate and I need my certificate so I can get out there and start getting money off patients to get my investment back'.

Word-of-mouth has always been a very potent stimulus for me, especially when the mouth was so close that I could feel the halitosis making my hair heavier. I presumed that he wasn't aware of the study conducted by one of his own colleagues, the one that concluded 'burn-out' in dentistry occurred in the fourth year of the five year undergraduate course. I also presumed that he mustn't have known about the audit, which reported that during his training 70% of the computer screens at The Icon had been incorrectly calibrated for examining radiographs, nice to know.

Anyway, as the student's comments trickled down my face they gave me a frightening glimpse of a bigger picture. It was becoming plausible that The Icon I was up against was capitalist society and capitalism itself. The more I thought about it the more I remembered other undesirable experiences that I'd had in my tiny little life and how prior to reading some philosophy I had failed to appreciate anything before the present.

I remembered my experience with the planning department at the Local County Council when I renovated my current house, the one I call home; the council's incompetence added an extra twenty eight thousand pounds to the cost of the renovation. It wasn't a pleasant experience. I remembered the experience I had with NatWest Bank shortly after Sir Fred Goodwin bankrupt it; the bank attempted to save itself by restructuring my lending and increasing my annual interest charge by an additional thirty two thousand pounds, it wasn't a pleasant experience. I remembered the experience I had with Mercedes Benz after the drive belt on my car snapped and knackered the engine as a direct result of their poor workmanship, it cost me one thousand and four hundred pounds to put right, it wasn't a pleasant experience. I remembered the experience I had with the Care Quality Commission when they attempted to cover up an incident after they gave me tons of incorrect advice. Ultimately, we had to rely on the voice recordings of their incompetence in spite of which they still did not accept responsibility; it wasn't a pleasant experience. I remembered the experience I had with British Airways when they bumped us off a flight due to them suffering a catastrophic computer failure at terminal four; they felt comfortable covering it up by falsely assigning the blame to the customers and made us fight for a refund, it wasn't a pleasant experience.

I often asked myself:

'What has the truth got to do with the matter?'
    and
'Do we actually need the truth anyway?'

In my experience the truth does still matter, and it matter's most to a particular group; young adults. Truth is important for their peace of mind and their peace of mind is necessary for their mental wellbeing.

I was prepared to ride out the storm for the sake of young adults and my children.

The anticipation and fear of being crushed was well and truly seated in my upstairs comfy lounge. My mind. Test crash dummy style, with everyone watching for the moment that my head would blow off, in slow motion. I was still in (forced) denial about potential job loss, I hadn't done anything wrong! I couldn't lose my job, it wasn't an option. That said, it would have been less embarrassing to have shat diarrhoea in my pants during a public parade whilst wearing white trousers.

I was working out why my colleagues avoided raising concerns or blowing the whistle but what I couldn't work out is; how could they known what they were avoiding when they had never done it. One plausible answer was cowardice and pusillanimity. The emotional overload had in some ways stupefied me and it often seemed easier and safer to stay in bed, than it did to continue to navigate the challenges. As much as it pains me to say it, I did sometimes stay in bed; sometimes for days on end. I wasn't sleeping though; I just lay there watching my emotions float around my laden mind like bubbles in a lava lamp. I realised that if I wanted to survive I would somehow have to untangle them. Ultimately I was saved by my nature, which compelled me to get out of bed and get on with it.

It was clear that I was turning in on myself and questioning what was going on in what was once my mind. Luckily, I had the sense to make my second significant and deliberate executive decision. This, once again, involved a play on words. This time I substituted the word WHISTLEBLOWER with the word APPRENTICE. I persuaded myself to behave as if when I had blown the whistle I'd done so to learn what would happen next; like an apprentice. I persuaded myself that the course I had enrolled on was a combined apprenticeship in whistleblowing, behavioral characteristics, group behaviour, organisational behaviour, workplace psychology, human resources, sociology of work, management, leadership, and aspects of employment law. Once again, this exchange of nouns and the re-labeling proved to be a successful mind management tool.

My thinking changed and I started to respond to the provocations in a more Socratic way, like a good student would. I behaved less critically, became easier on myself and more inquisitive about the new experiences as they unfolded. In the guise of an apprentice I was able to say to myself "that's different, I wonder what I should do next" or "let's see how this plays out," and this to some extent neutralised some of the pity I felt. Pity would always come as a voice in my head. Always just behind and above my ears on both sides simultaneously. It would always tell me that others had loaded too much onto my plate and it would always point out the injustice. What continued to trouble me however was that ordinarily I never blamed anybody else for anything that happened to me. I was good enough to suffer a little injustice once in a while but this was a whole new ballgame and I have to admit the unjust criticism had got to me. I didn't run my life according to the criticisms of others but on this occasion they were having a deep impact.

If my emotions were to have been plotted on a graph the line would have shown a steep linear progression from uncertainty to anxiety then rising exponentially through fear straight off the top of the chart into and beyond vulnerability. My fear, not meek but stark, was of potential job loss and the associated reputational damage. Vulnerability kicked in on the odd occasion when my mind tuned away from events at The Icon and focused on everyday things like the cost of school uniforms and mortgage payments. I wondered which of my emotions would burn me out first the ones about job loss or the ones about potentially losing our house. As my mind was busy burning itself out I wondered if dis-ease would eventually become disease?

The Inspiration.

Given that my mind had become the closing shoot-out scene from Butch Cassidy and the Sundance kid, Zahida agreed to organise a trip. It was planned as a getaway and an opportunity for some quality family time away from Icon based ruminations. Bags packed, painkillers & muscle relaxants taken, physiotherapist paid, we were good to go. Mobile phone left behind. Check.

Our flight landed in Rome at 8:40am local time. We'd always preferred to arrive in a new city with the sun rising and not setting. Clearing customs was effortless. We were about to take a taxi to our apartment, when my mobile phone ping-pinged. I had received an e-mail. Yep, I had failed to police my earlier executive decision to leave my mobile behind. It had become my blanky or blanket (soother). Failing to follow a previously made definitive decision was a new to me. I faltered not through indecision but through insecurity. As much as I needed some time away from The Icon the thought of not knowing what might be happening behind my back had become an obsession. I craved news; any news but my drug had become good news or at least moderately less bad news.

On arrival at our apartment block I checked my phone, there was an e-mail from The Icon sat in my inbox. I asked myself:

'Do you really want to open the e-mail now, is this the right time to open it?'

It was too late, I'd already opened it; it was a hand, eye, brain malfunction. The e-mail was an invitation to a meeting with Professor Honest who would be accompanied by the Head of Human Resources. The meeting was scheduled to take place three days after we returned home. Bang! An airbag went off and I was cocooned inside it. I was standing in a large inflated plastic bubble, an opaque one at that. I was only aware of it in my peripheral vision. The need for the protection must have come from my sub-conscious. I stood motionless with my eyes pointing at the words "you are invited..." this was a court summons disguised as an invitation and it kept walloping me on my temple. I felt concussed with a sense of mental mutilation. All the strength and courage I thought I had picked up in Chapters 1 and 2 seemed to have evaporated, like a sonic death ray had hit me.

How best to describe the pickle I was in? I'd liken it to a coconut shy at the fairground in that there's lots of different projectiles one can throw at the coconuts to knock them over and there's lots of different directions those projectiles can be thrown from. I was the coconut and different things were thumping into me in different ways from different directions. I'd heard the phrase 'assault on the senses' but hadn't realised how many hidden senses were buried deep in my brain or how ordinarily they remain suppressed.

The apartment owner let us in and showed us round. The apartment was perfect, there was the faintest whiff of newly decorated in the air. The flooring was light oak, the walls were white and the tall shuttered casement windows were dressed with crisp white linen curtains. I felt the same comfort as being in my sanctuary at home, my study. Comfort equals stability but bidding against it was my ears playing up, they felt as if they were plugged with roof insulation. Making me itchy and irritable and partly deaf all at the same time. The landlady spoke perfect English but I hadn't registered a single word she'd said. I heard all of it but registered none of it. It all sounded like a badly tuned radio, high pitched shrills interrupted by hollowed out flat notes all set to a background of hiss noise. I knew the children were running around the apartment but it sounded as if they were in a neighbouring one. It was a strange feeling of distance.

We sat in the piccolo kitchen for some lunch and as I sat eating with my family, we didn't appear to be together. With my mind swamped, it was more like watching a movie of someone else's family having lunch. What was going on? I wanted to be with them but couldn't get anywhere near; it was a very strange disconcerting feeling. My life was continuing to go on around me but I somehow wasn't able to take any part in it. Stress is strange

I needed help, spelt HELP! I needed someone to tell me what to do next. The only person present who could have helped me was Zahida, but I couldn't be entirely sure if she had realised how bad it had gotten. I couldn't even be sure if I knew how badly I was suffering or if given my state of mind I was the right person to be performing the necessary consideration. Anyway, I didn't much fancy sharing my problem with Zahida as hers was a multi-thinking, multi-tasking approach to life, which I found scary. Mine was a single minded, single tasking approach. When we argued about this I'd often say "please do fewer jobs simultaneously, because then I have fewer to re-do". Plus I couldn't take the risk, in case she accused me of having another episode of what she called "less than single tasking". (Ahem, how rude). So I kept my suffering to myself.

I sat on the bed wondering what Professor Honest had in mind and what he had planned for the meeting. Why was the Head HR required? There was a hint of sinister to it. I needed peace and quiet; the children needed noise. I couldn't settle for the noise or hold a train of thought, let alone complete one. When the crunching of interruptions overwhelmed me I asked Zahida if she'd mind me exploring Rome on my own. "That would be great", sounded somewhat jubilant to me, but I sucked-it-up. The children were enjoying the newness of the apartment and weren't ready to venture out anyway. I was desperate to escape the noise.

I'd been out of the apartment for ten minutes before it dawned on me that Rome is full of people. I had already stepped in front of a bus and had my ears blown off and my innards screeched out by a scooter. These lunatics were driving on the wrong side of the road. I decided to make crossing roads safely my new point-of - focus. The last thing I needed was to get run over. I knew it was my own fault, as during periods of vulnerability I coped better if I remained close to home. Navigating feelings of anxiety, fear, worry and vulnerability require a womb. My womb was being at work (earning a living) and here I was, stupidly, one thousand one hundred and ninety four miles from home or work. It was becoming screamingly obvious that my insecurity was causing a mental malfunction and I should never have allowed my mobile to dump shitty news on me whilst I was so far from my cradle. I was absolutely damning myself for having allowed it to happen but I had to accept that I was responsible for (wrongly) pressing the button on it. The sanctuary of my study is where I should've taken the e-mail, and even Stephen Hawing would have struggled to explain how to reverse the effect; I'd have to find a way to neutralise it.

Still no further from the apartment I walked past a bookshop. My thoughts -in slow motion - were:

'That's a bookshop'
'But hold on, you like bookshops, don't you?'
'You'll have to turn round if you're going to go into that one'

It appeared that along with moving 'crossing roads safely' into my conscious control I'd accidently moved all of my decision making into my conscious control center. It wasn't what I had intended to do. I had already learnt my everyday skills operated best when left to my subconscious brain and I needed to get them back there. If I kept over thinking every thought and action I would exhaust myself and make more mistakes. Fracking heightened emotions.

I practiced meditational breathing; N - O   P - R - O – B - L- E- M;   E - X - E – C- E- L- L- E - N - T. The entrance to the bookshop was deceptively small, once inside the shop opened up like Aladdin's cave and was vast; but despite its vastness it was cramped (things always feel closer when I'm anxious). Books were displayed on typical shelves like the ones you get in almost all bookshops. More books were stacked on the floor in the aisles and there were even more books in unopened boxes. There's gotta be a university nearby I supposed. As I walked (tip-toed) around the bookshop, breathing getting slower, I noticed that all the books were in Italian, I'd need to find the foreign language section; but I couldn't find it. 'What kind of bookshop was this with no books in English?' I mused. I pinched my brain and confirmed to myself, Rome is still in Europe isn't it? Yep. I hadn't gone around the world and off the grid. Nope. There must be a section with books in English, nope. I couldn't find any.

As there was no great hurry I slipped into a daydream and somewhere deep in it I had an epiphany. Of course there aren't any foreign language books, the Romans once occupied most of Europe, why would they want any foreign language books. They probably still think that all books should be written in Italian or Latinised Greek.

And then, Sweet baby Jesus, (synonyms Mohammed, Abraham, Krishna, Buddha, Guru Nanak, The Black Hole and red neck Americans) the daydreaming screeched into a wall. I found myself in the used book section, and located at eye level, right in front of me, was a shelf of books in a dialect of Latin. English. These must have been books left behind by other tourists. This section of the bookshop was darker than the rest of it, making it an obvious choice to put the pre-owned, cheap books. There was only one single shelf of English books, divinely placed at eye level. Sweet baby....all of them. The shelves above and below were stacked with Italian books. I started to read the spines of the castaway English books and exactly half way across, right in the middle (to within a millimeter), of the shelf there was a book, the spine of which seemed to read: *Antifragile*. Get the fuck out of here...(my maker was calling to me). I was feeling fragile and the book was called *Antifragile*; who'd have known it. The poor lighting and the small text required me to squeeze my peanuts. I squeezed this way and that way, lightly and then heavy and then lightly again and with the focus-refocus hokey-cokey going on I managed to hold my head

still enough to confirm that book was indeed called: *Antifragile.*
In disbelief I continued to talk to myself:

'How come that book is at eye level?'

'How come that book is in the absolute centre of the shelf?'

'How is it possible that that I am feeling the most fragile I have
ever felt in my whole life and I'm standing opposite a book called
Antifragile?'

The next question was so stupid it bewildered me:

'I wonder what that book is about?'

I didn't even have the confidence to presume the obvious
anymore 'isn't it obvious?' I asked myself and then after the simple
application of science alone, decided that I couldn't possibly know.

I cautiously reversed the book from its parking space and
explored its front cover. Written in the bottom half of the front
cover was the main title; *Antifragile* beneath which in smaller text
was the subtitle; *Things That Gain From Disorder* beneath which
in even smaller text was the tertiary title; *The Ultimate Model To
Aspire To.* Alright... alright... I turned the book over onto its back
cover to find testimonies written by decorated intellectuals and the
mainstream press. Out of the five testimonies one caught my eye
the most, it reported: *Antifragility is the secret to success in a
world full of uncertainty, a system for turning random mutations
to lasting advantage.... highly entertaining...whether you find Mr
Taleb amusing or irritating, you want to read on.* As I repeatedly
poured over this statement my brain slapped itself as my eye
remaining focused on the word *irritating.* Hmmm irritating I
thought as I started to feel a strong sense of connection with the
author and enjoyed some reassurance that some readers may find
the author irritating but even if they did they'd feel compelled to
read on and see what else he had to say. It became wishfully
plausible my colleagues at The Icon wanted to know what I had to
say next, in spite of how I might be irritating them. Shit, I needed a
piss.

As I walked, almost ran, back to the apartment for said piss I
thought to myself, could it be that I was meant to read more than
just the front and back covers of the book. The conversation
continued:

'What do you mean?'...I haven't got the time to read the whole
book.

'Are you really that stupid?'...I'll pretend I'm not offended.

'That book was clearly put there for you?'...what does that even mean?

'Had it been placed at your eye level?'...Yes

'Could it be a coincidence that it was at the exact centre of the shelf?'...Perhaps

'Are you feeling fragile?'...Yes

'Is the book called Antifragile'...Yes

'Could Antifragile be a state opposite to fragile? ...I suppose

'Can't you see that the book was put there for you?'... Who by?

'By him'... Who's him?

'You know him'.... No, I don't know who him is.

'You do know the Vatican is only ten minutes up the road?'.... OH HIM!

I quickly dispensed with the divine train of thought as the archangel of atheism had raised its bow, the arrow aimed at me. My piss evaporated, the hollowness in my ears eased. Seconds later, I found myself back in the bookshop. This time the atmosphere had an eeriness which spoke to me: 'This is a good day to buy a book'. I stood looking at the book soaking up a moment's peace and the now non-hollow silence in the bookshop. In the distance I heard the shop assistant yak-yakking on her phone, as they do; confirming that my ears didn't feel so hollow anymore, and the conversation in my head resumed:

'Perhaps you've got to read that book?'.... I can't, I'm on a family holiday

'Are you happy with how the holiday has turned out so far?'... Nope

'Would you die if you had to read the book?'... Might do.

'So you're going to have to read the book?'... I suppose.

I picked up the book once more and opened it. The text size was six. There were 480 frightening pages in a whole new language, the language of economics. My thoughts consolidated into: 'there's no way I am going to read this book, the writings too small and there is too much of it, it will ruin my already ruined holiday.'

By the end of the first day I was on chapter five; it was a heavy read. The small text was a bitch, to compensate I had to sit directly under a bedside lamp. My once oily light brown peanut eyes were reduced to dried-out wrinkly purple raisins. The chapters were densely packed and the language was all new, but each one created a thirst to press on to the next. The book turned out to be an instruction manual of how I should have been thinking and behaving at this exact moment in my life. It contained exactly what I needed to know and was perfect preparation for my meeting with Professor Honest. There was a problem though, as compelling as it was, the book was based in and on the economics industry. I had no experience of the economics lexicon or reading it. I couldn't think as fast as I could read. So I had to 'read a bit' then 'think a bit' and then go back and 'read a bit' followed by 'think a bit'. Then I would read the whole lot again whilst doing simultaneous joined up reading and thinking. It was almost getting complicated. I had previously taken reading and thinking simultaneously for granted all my life.

As I read on my confidence started to shine again, neat steroids were being massaged into my mind. How can one have an adrenaline rush whilst sitting still? It was like I'd had a cocaine-hit without spending a penny? WHOOOSH. I needed to breathe out ever so heavily every few pages. It was a gymnasium for the mind, I'll never forget the moment, and WHOOOSH.... the high surpassed the preceding lows with ease.

In his book: *Antifragile*, the author, Nassim Taleb laid out his credentials. Please remember this was new language to me and some of it was lost on me, I'll do my best to summarise what he had to say. His twenty-year career in the field of risk assessment lead to his personal realisation that calculating risk was flawed. His view was that the current properties of any 'object', individual or institute, could be used as an assessment to describe it as fragile, robust or antifragile. He described how the properties could be used for an individual or institute (systems) to move from the fragile to the antifragile. His attitude was that the same provocations could affect the same systems resulting in different outcomes depending on their position on the fragile-antifragile spectrum. The example he gave was:

'Wind extinguishes a candle and energises a fire'

He explained that as a strong system 'you would want to be the fire and wish for the wind'.

He defined:

FRAGILE: anything that has more downside than upside from random events.

ROBUST: resists the shocks and stays the same.

ANTIFRAGILE: anything that has more upside than downside from random events.

At The Icon the random event was the feedback but it wasn't entirely that random.

His belief was that our entire existence as a species on the planet had proved successful due to antifragility effects and how acting upon the feedback contained in errors resulted in improvements, adjustments and renewal. He included everything that has changed with time: evolution, culture, ideas, revolutions, political systems, technological innovations, cultural and economic success, corporate survival, chicken soup, legal systems, cities, bacterial resistance. He said the one true test of a system is to use it, assess it, tinker with it and make necessary improvements. Simple.

By the time I had got as far as chapter four my negative feelings had been blunted. They had started to dissolve and I'd been breathing them off. It was still only about 8.oopm on the first day of our holiday and it had been rescued.

With vim, vigour and a renewed sense of purpose I stepped into the kitchen where the rest of my family were getting excited over the freshness of the freshly made local pasta. There was a strong smell of Italian garlic. I checked Zahida's eyes to assess how much damage had been done. They said: handbag, you're going to buy me a handbag. I was relieved that I'd only done handbag damage and not new car type damage. I was also pleased that she hadn't taken the children and left for Cleveland. My eyes were still dry and irritable and most definitely stuck in text size six mode. A small price to pay for the improvement the same text had on my mood. The children were right the freshly made pasta had far more flavour than the dried pasta we had at home, it tasted more Italian; who'd have known. The garlic was garlickier and the olive oil tasted as if the olives had being pressed at the table. I knew the food didn't taste nicer because of its Italian authenticity it tasted nicer because I was in a better mood. I was no longer Bad Mood Bear.

I can't emphasize enough, the impact the first four chapters of *Antifragile* had on my perception and understanding of my negative feelings, especially fear. I was starting to see a vague link between fear and fortitude but would need a bit more time to work things out. In a state of ease and calm I finished the book by the end of the holiday. Each additional chapter enhanced my once dwindling confidence and the event became the third occasion my strength and conviction was regained, perpetuating the third episode of a 'bring-it-on' attitude.

The holiday was made far more exciting by the notion that we were in the ancient and historical home of blood sport and how *Antifragile* was moving my once wilting mind towards something far more gladiatorial. Sitting in the heart of the once mighty Roman Empire my mental strength built day by day, chapter by chapter, I can't think of a better place to have read it. I developed a new prospective, one of blood sport for entertainment. And in comparison to the four hundred thousand individuals who had lost their lives, at the Coliseum, my experience seemed more of a minor inconvenience. The Coliseum momentarily replaced my frown with a smile. My mind had been transformed into one in which the anticipation of meeting Professor Honest and HR became energising.

In the end when the meeting rolled around on **8th April 2016**, the worry really hadn't been worth it because Professor Honest and Head of HR didn't really conduct a meeting. The get-together lasted all of five minutes and was as surreal as a Monty Python sketch. It went like this:

Professor Honest: "I am only here because the others couldn't make it; I have no idea what this meeting is about"

HR: "Can you confirm how you want your complaint to be dealt with? Would you like it to be dealt with as a grievance or would you like it to be processed along the whistleblowing pathway?"

Me: "I would like it to be dealt with as a grievance. My grievance is that the leadership team has not been handling my concerns or disclosures in compliance with The Icon's policy of information disclosure (whistleblowing). I would like the outcome of the grievance procedure to be that the leadership team is compelled to handle my concerns and disclosures in accordance with the whistleblowing policy".

This was the same Professor Honest who only six months earlier had said, "As you know most problems have a solution, and I am sure we can find one together". Professor Honest was turning out to be more of a Professor Honest Pinocchio (prone to telling lies). I couldn't work out if The Icon had broken him or if he had broken The Icon. *Antifragile* presented an interpretation of Greek philosophy, which described him to a tee:

> 'Sissies are born, not made. They stay sissies no matter how much independence you give them, no matter how rich they get'.

This quotation enabled me to hold myself less responsible for the lost and squandered opportunities.

Once again I had prepared myself for a meeting in which I had presumed we would be discussing the concerns I'd raised. Stupid me. They humiliated me and the intensity of my past and present emotions was such that on the train home water poured out of my eyes. I couldn't be sure if I was crying or if this was something completely different. It seemed right to me that it was an outpouring of fury. Fury results from the gradual build-up of the discarded spent emotions generated during episodes of frustration. Like the build-up of silt on the river bed, when the silt levels rise causing the water to back up there is a natural purge. I believe fury is best out than in and I was learning that when it poured out of my eyes, as it did on this occasion, it rips me (and those around me) apart less than when it screams and shouts its way out.

Professor Honest Pinocchio's words confirmed one thing for sure, that The Icon was definitely broken. It also confirmed that he was accepting full ownership for the cover-up.

His handling of the meeting was a calamitous moment which now reminds me of the humour in **Michael Winner's** words:

> 'Teamwork is a group of individuals doing what I tell them to do'

Joking aside, this means a team needs to be lead by a leader; direction is necessary. It should not come as a surprise then, due to his poor leadership; Professor Honest Pinocchio had earned himself the nickname: 'The Idiot' amongst his senior staff. His signature approach being defined by his opening statement: 'I am only here because the others couldn't make it; I have no idea what this meeting is about'.

Professor Honest Pinocchio's actions provided a valuable insight of how his leadership team had become a symbolic notion of a dysfunctional one. Unlike him I was not in denial of my previous experiences of teamwork and leadership. During my interview for the post at The Icon if I had made myself any more transparent I would have become invisible. A panel of four interviewed me. Two of them already knew me (Dr Perfidious and another consultant) the third consultant was one I was aware of but didn't really know. I hadn't met the fourth interviewer before but she (IN) asked some interesting questions, the conversation went like this:

IN: Dr. Ahmed, if we gave you the job here please can you tell me how you work in a team?

Me: I am sorry I don't do teams.

IN: What a ridiculous thing to say, don't you want the job?

Me: I would like the job but I am sorry I don't do teams.

IN: That is the most ridiculous thing I've ever heard in an interview. Don't you want the job?

Me: I would like the job, but I would like to be employed as me and I don't do teams.

IN: This is just nonsense.

Me: Margaret Thatcher wasn't too keen on teams either.

IN: We work in teams here!

Me: I am sure you do, but I have twenty years experience and I have met a lot of individuals who have talked the talk however I have met very few individuals who have then walked the walk. I am sorry I don't do teams.

IN: Do you have any friends?

Me: Yes, I do. But I don't come to work to make friends. I come to work to do a day's work. Whilst I'm doing my job I sometimes meet other people doing their jobs. My friendships develop with those who are doing their jobs well. It's how I've met most of my friends.

In the days after the interview I described it to a friend and he said 'Why did you waste the money to go all that way if that's what you were going to say.'

Anyhow, about eight weeks after my appointment at The Icon I was sat having a coffee (behind a newspaper) in the cupboard we called the coffee room. The one with the fridge that some staff used to ferment their leftover rotting food in and leaving others to remove it; the same others who almost always had their milk stolen by ghosts. The fourth interviewer, who I hadn't bumped into since the interview, came in cursing and went straight to the sink where she continued to curse. She hadn't seen me. She stood at the sink facing the wall washing her cup. Fuming as she did: 'That fucking bastard.... this fucking bastard.... no fucker round here does their job!' The cursing plucked my heart strings and left me smiling. I lowered my paper and chanced my arm by humouring her with: 'Aren't you the person who asked me about teamwork during my interview?' I delivered it with a big fat smile on my face. She attempted to hide her smile but it leaked out and the corners of her eyes lifted for a microsecond. 'You can fuck-off too!' she snapped lovingly, at my open smile, like an edentulous crocodile. She became and remains one of my closest and dearest friends.

I was learning...

I was learning that what I really needed was a holiday away from myself and that wasn't going to be possible.

I was learning that those with the most power at The Icon were disinclined to use it to change the system that had rewarded them so well. The bigger The Icon had gotten the more its students, teachers and patients had shrunk in comparison. As with many other businesses its growth had rendered the power of its students, patients and teachers blunt and diffuse. This diffusion of power had made it easier for The Icon to ignore the dissatisfaction.

I was learning that leadership teams are supposed to develop and support high performing teams and for this to happen the people in them need to be encouraged to raise difficult, risky, or controversial ideas or issues without the fear of being shut down or punished. In my experience mistakes are a part of my everyday life. There is no such a thing as no mistakes. We all make mistakes all day long and those mistakes are necessary as they are the drivers of our life-long learning. It is wrong to attempt to train a whole generation of professionals without giving them an insight into dealing with mistakes, by setting an example of denying the mistakes. The Icon wasn't doing its students any favours by burying its mistakes; they were being denied 'a sense of the real world'. Professional training devoid of mistake management is the perfect recipe for creating more 'millennial snowflakes' and a set up for mental health issues later in life.

I was learning that I'd always been right in my private practice to encourage my staff to point out my mistakes to me as soon as they found them, it is preferable to having my patients point them out to me. It works most of the time but there have been occasions when my mistakes have been missed by my staff and me and have had to be pointed out to me by a patient. Yes, it's embarrassing but I have always apologised and corrected them. My experience is that I manage to make mistakes even when I am convinced that I was 100% concentrating at the time the mistake happened. To learn from a mistake it has to first be recognised as one, it's the easiest way. There is a clear distinction between learning from mistakes and deliberately burying and concealing them. My opinion is that a mistake remains a mistake until you attempt to conceal or bury it, once that happens it becomes negligence and criminal. So the leadership team was dabbling in negligence and criminality.

I was learning my previous perception of the word 'happiness' was over simplified and a somewhat childish one. There is no simple meaning that can be attached to it and I realised that if I was to survive the experience I would have to change my understanding and attitude towards it. My simplistic view failed to appreciate that the leadership team's happiness was driven by their compliance to the role they had accepted for themselves within The Icon. Once I'd understood that happiness, to them, was achieved by climbing The Icon's hierarchy of power I realised that I was dealing with delusional power hungry credential seeking careerists who were protected by The Icon's herd. It's no wonder they are considered to be complete wankers by those who live and work in the real world outside the protection of such a heard. The fruits of my re-think were that I redefined 'happy' and 'happiness' as momentary states of mind, a short period of intense joy and not a measure by which I should judge the overall success of my life.

I was learning which of my emotions and feelings were best ascribed to the word fear and what effect they had on me. This deeper understanding allowed me to exchange my previous perception of fear for one, which allowed me to use it to keep me moving along. Fear was comparable to being chased by a nasty dog, my response was to use its fright to keep me moving forward, sometimes walking, sometimes running but completely satisfied with my new understanding that it was a desirable and powerfully productive emotion. In my world, fear describes a feeling I get deep in my tummy when I experience something different or new, it could be exhilarating or terrifying. It could be the prospect of diving into an ice cold Alaskan lake or riding a roller coaster for the first time or even watching the school bully walk towards me knowing full well he's going to bop me on the nose. Cowardice describes a character of my personality that is the opposite of strong or courageous. I resolved that we all need a measured trickle of fear daily (from an early age) as it's essential for the development of our character and with character comes integrity. The odd acute spike of fear is also good as it acts as a 'soft scare' and a powerful character builder. A world in which there is no fear is a boring, bland and worthless world. A world in which there is no courage is a pathetic, infantile and useless world.

I was learning that The Icon had become pathetic, infantile and useless due to a very childish understanding of fear amongst its staff. Most of whom had side stepped it most of their lives and consequently missed the opportunity to develop into mature useful adults. Courage is what enables me to make a decision to do the right thing, especially when doing the right thing is going to cause me some grief, sufferance and hard work. Strength is what enables me to perform the tasks, which ensue having made the right decision; often performed under pressure. Tenacity is what enables me to continue using my strength until the defined objective of the task is achieved and prevents me from being fobbed off. They merge almost seamlessly to make me resilient. I remember someone once telling me that cowardice ran in his family and how grateful he was that he was the fastest runner in his family.

I was learning which of my emotions and feelings were best ascribed to the word anxiety. It was the ones that made me feel weak, defeated and trapped. The weakness rendered me wraithlike and was similar to a bout of food poisoning where all the nutrients and fluids have been vomited or diarrhoea-ed out. The defeat echoed in my mind as: 'what's the point?' When trapped, I felt as if I was stuck in a faulty elevator in a multi storey car park on the outskirts of town, one in which the help intercom had been vandalised. Anxiety was comparable to a camouflaged hole in the jungle floor, designed to catch me out, trip me up and render me out-of-action. Climbing out of such holes sucked up a lot of my energy whilst not resulting in any forward motion. I don't think I ever managed to understand how anxiety was supposedly designed to be helping me. It seemed right to me that it was a conditioned state fuelled exclusively by inactivity and inexperience. The antithesis of anxiety is experience and my advice to teenagers and adolescents is to get out and get as much experience as you can. I tell my children 'if you're not sleeping, eating or doing homework you shouldn't be in the house'. Get a paper round, go for a bike ride, swim in a stream, go fishing, fly a kite, chase a stray dog, climb a tree, break an arm, break a leg, get them mended, build a den, build a go- cart, camp in the back garden, talk to the neighbours, get used to approaching and walking past strangers, talk to the tramps and then run like crazy. Experience adds up to snuffle, neutralise and eliminate anxiety. My mantra to my children has become: 'life is experience and experience is life'. I'm an advocate of speaking from experience like the author George Gordon Noel Byron as opposed to his rival John Keats whose existence was restricted to his imagination.

I was learning that worry is what I did when I had fallen into a camouflaged hole in the jungle floor and was sat at the bottom, disabled and potential prey. Worry was a state in which I wasted energy considering how much energy would be wasted climbing back out of the hole. Worry acts like a vortex and has a positive pull, to resist it, I had to put up a positive resistance and this required almost as much energy. It sucked me a long way backwards many times along my journey. I don't think I ever managed to understand how worry was supposed to be helping me but I was definitely sure being ignored as I was in chapter one proved to be its greatest exploitation.

I was learning that fear was a good thing and anxiety and worry were best avoided and I found that the best way to avoid them was to keep moving forward. Not just moving but moving at a pace that felt slightly faster than the one which felt intuitively correct. I worked out that the correct pace was the one when I was moving slightly faster than the skills I had or was acquiring. It sounds wrong but it proved to be the best place for me to be. I found that setting the pace correctly helped me keep a truer perception of time, which ultimately allowed me to pitch better.

I was learning which events, emotions and feelings resulted in me feeling vulnerable. For it to happen I would first have had to have fallen into a camouflaged hole in the jungle floor. I would then feel vulnerable if one of two things happened or if both of them happened together. The first was if a nasty predatory animal started circling the hole. The second was realising the hole had a sinking bottom. Examples of nasty predators circling are when Dr Perfidious reported that I was uniquely experiencing the concerns and no one else was, and when the IT team reported that I was the only one struggling to use the software and everyone else found it 'friendly'. An example of a sinking bottom was the stupid professional code that it is unprofessional to say anything disparaging about the woefully inadequate notes in front of students or patients. Which meant if I told the students the notes were a great example of how not to make notes or told patients that half their notes were missing; the individuals who made the woefully inadequate notes were given a valid reason to report me to the GDC for unprofessional conduct. This professional code is a contradiction to putting patients first and any professional training. Other examples of sinking bottom are when I sat reflecting on things I could've been doing but was instead was prevented from doing. Like smiling, I couldn't do that anymore, or talking to Zahida or Imani or Reyaan or Anniyah half as much as I used to. Another sinking bottom was thoughts about the extent of damage being done to my professional reputation or losing the house.

I was learning how to avoid feeling or acting defeated at a time when pity and dread had taken refuge, like squatters, in my mind. Dread was less predictable than pity. Do you know the technique of inflicting pain on someone (discreetly) it involves pinching (between your finger and thumb) the skin just behind and above their elbow and then clamping hard? Dread is comparable to that pinch only it's a pinch of the mind. It immediately shifted my priorities to wanting to break free of the pinch and then keep running to avoid it happening again. I'd experience dread each and every time I was landed in a situation where I'd have to defend myself by writing another ten page rebuttal (in total I wrote more than 40 of them). I managed to neutralise pity by reciting Buddha; I'd say: 'To be alive is to suffer and if you want to carry on living you will have to put up with more suffering.' The more I recited Buddha to change 'my point of view' the easier it got; but the recovery got slower with the passage of time. Dread on the other hand could only be controlled by going for a twenty three minute walk or a semi-hard bike ride. On some days it would take four walks to dredge the dread. Dredging the dread became instrumental to my survival, as it was dread that provided the matrix into which the other emotions would clog. Cardiovascular exercise worked by keeping the sludgy matrix from forming or by pumping it out once it was established.

I was learning to interpret the leadership's actions using a new sense of prospective set by the words of Nassim Taleb:

'The three most harmful addictions are heroin, carbohydrates, and a monthly salary'

I was learning that a large number of my colleagues were cashing in on (in a symbiotic relationship) The Icon's falsified, prestigious, and impressive standing as a credential-building temporary accommodation for private practice. I was under siege because I'd had the courage to say, 'This is unacceptable'. The price I was paying was the smear campaign and the harassment. It's really nasty when a symbiotic relationship develops between two parasites and even less pleasant to watch as they misguide tomorrows adults to do the same.

I was learning that I shouldn't have been surprised Professor Honest Pinocchio's words couldn't be trusted. He was not a free man and he failed to realise that progress comes from a free mind which has a freedom to fail. His loyalty lay with The Icon, as did that of the rest of the leadership team; they weren't of free mind either. The definition of the free man according to Aristotle is one 'who is free with his opinions' or 'he is free who owns his own opinion'. Another helpful definition of a free person is 'someone who cannot be squeezed into doing something he would otherwise never do'. I was behaving like a free man whilst they appeared to be prevented from doing so. Not a single one of them could identify or recognise the concerns I had raised until (after they'd suspended me) the General Dental Council pointed them out to them. (The GDC after reading the very same protected disclosures as the leadership team concluded that my concerns were valid and informed Professor Pinocchio they'd need to be rectified).

I was learning that Seneca and other Greek philosophers in their time had questioned all professionals. There were no Icons back then, but if there had been they would have come under the wider umbrella of professionals and questioned in the same way. They argued that one could rapidly, after a period of indoctrination, become enslaved to a profession (or Icon) to the point where ones opinion on any subject becomes self-serving and as such unreliable for the collective. They supported their arguments with anecdotal examples like, a physician takes not pleasure in the health of his patients and a soldier does not wish for the peace of his country.

I was learning that The Icon was decaying due to the way humans behave in groups. Group stability removes incentive and in the absence of incentives organisations become stagnant like yesterdays news. Icons perform better when the feedback is not suppressed as it keeps them moving. When they are new, organisations tend to be innovative and progressive but without the chaos provided by feedback, they fade away. The feedback acts as a 'Good Shake Up' and is a necessary part to keeping an organisation motivated and functional. Complex systems like The Icon are weakened when deprived of stressors (like feedback), and it is often top down policies which do the harm. Much like a neurotically overprotective parent, those trying to help or pretending to help are often causing the most harm. Whilst bottom up policies thrive under the right amount of stress. Responding to the feedback sooner acts to keep problems small and visible. Nothing is simpler than fixing a problem as soon as it is identified. Ignoring the same feedback makes the problem invisible and far more severe in the long term, and in the process makes progress and evolution far more difficult.

I was learning that being told by several senior members of staff that 'things were much worse at other institutes' did not convince me that inaction was acceptable. It was a weak argument to act as a viable deterrent.

I was learning about my passion and how Ayn Rand in her 1932 novel: **Atlas Shrugged**, touched upon the theme:

> **'There's no surer way to destroy a man than to force him into a spot where he has to aim at not doing his best, where he has to struggle to do a bad job, day after day.'**

It was easy for me to relate to this quotation as it appeared to have been written specifically to describe the dismal work conditions I was exposed to at The Icon. Doing my absolute best was my only option so I would have been destroyed under The Icon's regime even if I hadn't blown the whistle. I felt a sense of honour when doing my best, anything less made me feel fake. My sense of honour was an important driver of my daily enthusiasm and energy; it's what made me get out of bed in the mornings. The Icon's honour was just another staged false sincerity as it was not evidenced in its day-to-day working practices.

I was learning from a range of books by Malcolm Gladwell like **Blink** that my intuitive, naturalistic and ecological instincts were the ones I should rely on first and foremost. His work instilled a reassurance in me to listen to my 'gut feelings' especially since my gut had been telling me I was right and The Iconic Machine was wrong all along. I started to understand organisations behave differently to the individual. Whilst individuals have some natural inhibitions, organisations (machines) lack natural ethics and only obey a balance sheet. Once I'd understood machines have no shame, it was easy for me to accept that shame, has no place to act as a disciplinarian in them, I felt inspired that I'd already identified that my former employers actions were indeed machine like. Unlike the leadership I prefer not to behave like a machine because I'm not one. I didn't have to adapt my ethics or beliefs to put on the pretence of professionalism. Instead it was my ethics and beliefs that defined me as a professional and compelled me to blow the whistle. I did not derive my personal and emotional identity from my work. Instead I relied on my personal and emotional identity to define my work.

I was learning what my colleagues meant when they said: 'The University is a behemoth, do what you like, you will come to an end first, and it won't change; it can't change or be changed.' The great philosophers, Seneca and Montaigne had observed this too. And it has been know since Adam Smith, the eighteenth century Scottish philosopher, that the collective (The Icon) does not require the benevolence of individuals (students & patients), as self interest can become the driver of growth. The Icon had got big enough to afford the ability to ignore the students and the patients as self interest had become its driver. It's 'capitalism without a heart' and I am deeply saddened that the love of money and money alone corrupts the best part of a species. The Icons actions confirmed that patient care and student education had become a capitalist interest only.

I was learning that the aggregate works differently from the individual and when my colleagues made the behemoth comment They were wrong. I prefer George Bernard Shaw's observation:

'People who say it cannot be done should not interrupt those who are doing it'

I resolved that my colleagues' weakness was their problem not mine.

On a final note, the Coliseum has become the symbol against capital punishment. It is recognised that capital punishment is no longer acceptable. It'd be nice if the same could be said for mental punishment, particularly since there is currently an epidemic of mental health illness in society. Some of which is due to millennial snow-flaking (which, and I hate to upset you, on such a lovely evening, has been around since the dawn the species). The worst of which, appears to be in two groups of young adults. The first being entrants to the university population and the second being entrants to the work place. The common feature of both groups is they have little or no experience of workplace culture, group culture and Iconic Machine culture. They lack the experience that experience cannot be taught and it can only be experienced, but for too many of them the experience of getting the experience exceeds their mental tolerance. It's not a smart way forwards.

My experience taught me that only one person could protect me from mental punishment, that one person was me; as only I knew how it was affecting me. The discoveries I made about myself and the workings of my mind were truly remarkable. I had satisfied myself that The Icon's motives were not personal; it lacked the sensitivity to be after me. Due to a well-known glitch in the workings of a machine, The Icon wasn't after me it was after a whistleblower.

Dream Big - Expect little

'If your dreams do not scare you they are not big enough'

Ellen Johnson Sirleaf

This quotation was slipped to me by one of my heroes on his way out. It became the one that confirmed to me that I should indeed be harnessing the freight contained in fear and enabled me to stay calm whilst having bouts of it. It gently soothed away anxieties when I was engaged in doing things I was unsure about. It became the universal extinguisher of emotions commonly associated with both the words anxiety and fear. It taught me that freight and exhilaration are near identical emotions and I'd have to be careful when interpreting them.

I first heard this quotation on the **3rd June 2016** whilst I, like most of the world, was mourning the death of the former world heavyweight boxer and one of the world's greatest sporting figures-Mohammed Ali. The impasse was I kept having emotional relapses through which I was losing track of my goals. This quote inspired me to re-evaluate the methodology behind the way I interpreted my negative emotions and once I'd done so it resulted in positive gain. I realised that what I once perceived as freight was more often than not exhilaration.

In this chapter I'll describe how I managed to keep a cool head (sometimes) despite all odds being against me. How I developed a better understanding of how we develop motivation and drive, and the influence role models offer us in experiences like mine. And how I worked out that harnessing anxiety results in entrepreneurial behaviour whilst fear of the very same anxiety results in cowardice.

The Experience

The cast in this chapter

Leadership Role	Given Identity
Head of Human Resources	Mr Wily.

The story so far...

1. 15th September 2015; whistle blown.
2. 2nd October 2015; Nasty Meeting with Dr. Dastardly.
3. 16th October 2015; Incognito Meeting with Professor Pinocchio.
4. 19th October 2015; Dick Dastardly's failed attempt to drown me in IT.
5. 1st Week December 2015; Dr. Perfidious tells a bunch of staff 'Hafeez is a liability; I'll have to get rid of him'. (Ouch! my shoulder blades)
6. 7th December 2015; my expression of grievance to Dr. Dastardly about the above.
7. 8th December 2015; IT team produces a report, which implicates me as uniquely experiencing the concerns I'd reported. (Ouch!)
8. 17th December 2015; Dr Perfidious produces a report, which implicates me as uniquely experiencing the concerns I'd reported. (Ouch!)
9. 8th April 2016. Professor Pinocchio & Mr Wily failed to re-label my protected disclosures as a grievance.

....I hope you noticed in the previous chapter I successfully side stepped the snare trap laid out by Mr Wily the Head of Human Resources. Given that the leadership teams previous efforts to ignore, silence and squash me had failed they had to come up with a new plan to 'knobble me'. The plan required the assistance and expertise of Mr Wily, a man in his senior years. The wily old gits plan was to attempt to fool me into having my concerns re-labeled, from the protected disclosures they were, to grievances. Had his plan been successful it would have been fatal (more fatal) for me. I only narrowly avoided his nefarious charms thanks to the assistance of a patient of mine from my private practice, Louise. A retired Director of HR and Organisational Strategy and was running her own independent HR consultancy at the time.

I'll come back to how she assisted me in a minute; first let me tell you a bit about her and dentistry in general. Louise had been referred to me ten years earlier (2006) after having been a victim of what is commonly described as 'supervised neglect' (a national problem, known within the profession and the NHS, yet to be shared openly with the public). Her gum disease had been chronic for far too long and had been affected her general health for some time. She had been suffering tension headaches and hot flushes to her face, especially her forehead, for which she had been seeing an acupuncturist but to no avail. By the time she came to me it was too late to save her natural teeth, they had to go. Coincidentally, most of the referrals I receive are of patients whose natural teeth are past their sell-by-date; due to their own supervised neglect or the supervised neglect of a dentist (or a bit of both). Incidentally, in all the professional negligence cases I have been involved in, the fault could be laid squarely at the patient's feet. However despite this the patients often, if not always, won their claims for negligence, not because they had a valid case, but because the dentist had failed by not keeping a comprehensive set of notes.

The neglect itself results from the patient's unwillingness or inability to clean their teeth and gums adequately or failure to make the required changes as instructed by a hygienist or dentist. Scientists call the required change a 'behavioural change' and have studied it extensively to conclude it isn't as straightforward as one might assume or wish for. In my experience its occurrence is exceptional and it happened, meaningfully, in less than 5% of patients I've treated. An added complication is, due to business, competition and greed; dentists find it easier to ignore gum disease than to address it. Their off-the-record defence being: 'I spend my whole day listening to patients who are obviously lying to me'. (I have to concede on this one, as my experience is about the same), but then in a world where everyone is lying to everyone else it shouldn't come as a shock. The notions of innocence, guilt and responsibility bid against each other as neither party is able to give a consistent story. At the start of my career I was troubled by the dishonesty, way before I realised that truth was merely an aspiration not a reality. In the early days I couldn't work out who was worse, patients or dentists. I'd often end up asking myself: 'Who came first, humans or dentists?' over time it was obvious, humans came first and I ended up resolving that dishonesty was an integral part of the 'human condition'. The dentist-patient relationship was just another example of humans dealing with humans and any dishonesty on the dentist's part was by virtue of being human; being a dentist was coincidental.

The worst dentists I have had the displeasure of meeting are the ones who buy themselves awards like the Private Dentistry Awards. What a farce that is. It's a bit like any other shopping channel on the tinternet. You simply fill out a form, select an award, pay for it, and viola you have one. Just to prove it I invested twenty minutes of my time and filled out the application form. My efforts were rewarded. I was shortlisted as a Finalist for Best Referral Practice. But as I wasn't prepared to pay for a table at the awards ceremony I lost my opportunity to receive the award. The organisers put on a good show with the pretence of meritocracy, but it's all a scam. I reported my concern that the awards deliberately mislead the public but the General Dental Council hadn't the time to be interested. (I've worked in many multi-award winning practices and should this book be a success I'd happily include those stories in a sequel. If you would like a sequel please mention it in Amazons feedback section).

It's probably unfair to say behavioural change occurs in less than 5% of patients, because it does occur in the other 95% as well. It happens precisely one second after tooth loss becomes inevitable. It's usually during an acute episode of agony. The pain generates desperation and the series of events leading up to this inevitable moment almost always becomes severely distorted. I describe it to my referring dentists like this: 'You can describe the shit flying across the room towards the whirling fan as many times as you like, patients will not take any action because the shit is not yet on the fan. Then once the shit hits the fan the same patients cannot take any action because they are too busy complaining about the fact the shit is NOW on the fan, their face, the floor, the ceiling and everywhere else'.

It might surprise you but the worst offenders are friends and family. They serve up a double whammy by curiously convincing themselves that their treatment is naturally going to cost less and be far more successful than anyone else's. It's all part of the same human condition. The reality tends to be you spend more time caring for them and their teeth but as a general rule they whinge more afterwards (in your personal time).

The patient-dentist relationship is a precarious one. Knowing a patient could turn on you anytime and blame you for the consequences of their own failings contributes to a feeling of remoteness and vulnerability. Ironically it creates a situation in which both parties become wary of each other. The patient hopes and prays the dentist's drill doesn't hurt whilst the dentist hopes and prays the patient isn't this month's potential conniving scorned complaining litigant. For the record I have worked out those patients who do, do so out of deep disappointment in themselves. However another expression of the human condition is to take it out on someone else and the young newly qualified dentists are the easiest target.

In the background of the constant fretting over potential litigation alienation and frustration set in. I know because I have been a victim of both. In 1993 I was summoned to a full hearing in a wood paneled room at the local council office, which had that strange smell of dry cob webs and stale farts. A 21 year old female I had recently treated had lodged a complaint; she complained that I had failed to do as she had asked. She'd asked me to remove all her natural teeth and replace her picket fence smile with a set of squeaky clean sparkly white dentures. Her father was paying for the treatment as a gift for her 21st birthday. The consultation took over an hour, but alas, I succeeded in persuading her to allow me fix the fixable teeth and remove the rest. For the hour she paid approximately £12.00 from which £6.00 would have been my pre-tax income. The treatment required about 15 appointments and took a few months to complete. I was pleased with the outcome of the salvage operation but had the smile wiped clean of my face when, a few days later, she handed the practice a nine paged complaint. The complaint was handled and botched by the transient organisation known as the FHSA; Family Health Service Association. The hearing was arranged without me being contacted or asked to provide my comments. After months of trepidation, preparation and investment I attended the hearing which lasted all of nine minutes. She lost her case, one of the many reasons being I was the first and only dentist she had visited and as such she had no point of reference. I know other colleagues who have experienced much worse. Year after year, I watch dentists respond to the injustice. Some of them become defensive operators who provide a sort of supervised neglect approach whilst most take to the holy grail of 'fuck the patients' and 'sell hard' to earn a pension whilst the going is good.

What surprised me most about the hearing was what happened after it. The practice owner Dr Giddiup raised her hand to attract the attention of the chairman, and when he entertained her she informed him:

'I don't know why Dr. Ahmed didn't complete the FP17c form-we always keep them in stock at the practice'

The reason for my surprise was the patient had never contested the presence or absence of the FP17c form. In addition to which Dr Giddiup seemed to have forgotten what she had told me at my interview: 'We don't bother with the FP17c forms because they are a waste of time'. And the practice didn't have them anyway. Dr Giddiup's attempt to protect parts of her bacon that hadn't been skinned was stupid and selfish, the natural trait of her breed of (moo-like) madness. As the pretence of chivalry was still in vogue, I refrained from calling her a lying bitch, but instead resigned with immediate. Her husband gave up his attempts to persuade me to change my mind after his first two failed.

I'm not saying that humans are born dishonest, as I do not believe that, and that's probably why I was shocked by the events following the whistleblow. My opinion remains that most humans are born honest and throughout life they try their very best to maintain this honesty whilst simultaneously attempting to survive in a dog-eat-dog, rat-race jungle. When I ask patients a question the answer always starts off as pretty honest but then during its delivery it morphs, meanders, twists and turns. The deceit can always be identified through their facial micro expressions. The easiest place to spot it is in the eyes as their close connection to the brain makes devious manipulation near impossible. I believe the deepest core of everyone's brain is honest (minus pathological liars) and stays that way; always. The outer layers of the brain, however, become conditioned by local environmental factors, with the effects of the conditioning becoming more entrenched with age, exposure and experience of shit-y-ness.

I have met some nice people in a twenty-five year career but sadly I have met many more strange, dishonest, deluded, and nasty (real nasty) ones. I would guestimate the ratio as 1:10. Dentistry, like other professions dealing directly with the public, lends itself to the privilege of a private audience followed by confidentiality. This allows individuals to lie to their hearts content; often subconsciously. I say subconsciously, because they are not all lying but in the same breath they're not telling the truth either. I believe they wouldn't tell the lies or talk the shit they talk if their best friend was sat next to them...thinking about it perhaps they would.

Patients are good at pretending they don't understand tooth decay is irreversible and that gum disease results in loss of bone or that both can result in tooth loss. They pretend to lack the cognitive capacity of understanding the dentist didn't put the tooth decay or gum disease in their mouths. They find it unjust that the blame cannot be laid at someone else's feet. That said, I do understand how some of them become so perplexed, it's created by the way most dental practices use spin to promote their services and generally suggest they have a solution to all eventualities. The spin is usually underpinned by some misleading content designed to suggest sincerity. I audited 100 websites:

• 60% of them claimed that their dentist was some sort of 'teacher' of dentistry.

• 64% of them claimed that their dentist had 'lectured' nationally or internationally in dentistry.

• 63% of them claimed that their dentist had been 'trained' by a renowned expert.

I reported my concerns to the Chief Executive of the General Dental Council, Mrs Evlynne Gilvarry. I suggested it would be less misleading if the dentists list the name of the institute where they teach or taught and include the dates of employment. And to list the national or international lectures they had given to include where and when they had taken place. I proposed it would be less misleading if the dentists listed the name of the expert who trained them and what, when and where the training took place. It's a far more objective (and less deceptive) way of promoting oneself, but Mrs Gilvarry informed me that she was too busy to be interested.

Patients will have to continue to be misguided by the 'I can fix everything and have a solution for every eventuality, trust me govnor, because I teach nationally or internationally and was trained by some profiteering knob-head', websites. Over the years I have attended a number of training sessions on marketing, given by PR and business gurus. The most memorable was given by the maker of profiteers; Mrs Cathy Jameson. She gave a presentation at one of my workplaces and promoted the exploitation of shady ways to empty every American dime out of a patient's pocket. She claimed to be a student of 'success literature', in reality she was just a fleece merchant. During her presentation, I challenged her advice as inappropriate one time; and got away with it. I challenged her advice as inappropriate a second time and still lived. But when I challenged her tripe on a third occasion she stamped on the floor waved her arms in the air, went completely mad and shouted at me: 'Dr Ahmed do you actually want to learn how to make more money'. Her rant lasted a good three to four minutes and exposed all her capitalist motives. It was difficult to not feel sorry for her; the tantrum clearly exhausted her.

I can understand why patients often (if not almost always) ask for guarantees so I always offer them one. I tell them:

'I guarantee that the day I complete a filling or fix a crown is the day it will start to fail and if you're one of the lucky ones it will fail slowly over a twelve year period.'

The same applies to most forms of restorative dentistry. However in my experience the same is not true for gum disease. Gum disease can fully relapse over a three month period if the homecare is not maintained at the highest level. Incidentally, in those who are susceptible to gum disease regular brushing makes little difference. Gum health requires the cuff or crevice of the gum (from which the tooth emerges) to be disturbed and this requires small precise gadgets used painstakingly carefully with patience.

Twelve years may not sound long to some of you but I can assure you it's a good length of service. Back in 1996 the official statistics of the transient organisation known as the DPB; (Dental Practice Board) showed that crowns, on average, lasted a total of twelve months. One reason for this was the NHS would pay for a new crown on the same tooth twelve months after the previous one and at twelve month intervals thereafter. So some dentists, being human, couldn't resist the temptation and replaced crowns as soon as they could claim the next payment. When the NHS stopped shelling-out for a new crown every twelve months almost magically, crowns started lasting longer. This kind of financial abuse is nothing new, it's as old as time, but I'm just pointing it out it hasn't gone away. Nor is it restricted to dentistry, it remains true of all modern professions, like fraudulent prescriptions in pharmacy and lawyers offering shady advice to encourage legal aid applications. The Duplessis Orphans in Quebec gained widespread publicity in March 1999 for having suffered badly because of it, the Canadian government offered subsidies to church groups to care for both orphans and the mentally ill. The payments for the mentally ill were double those of the orphans, so thousands of orphans were falsely diagnosed as mentally ill. It's shameful but the church groups were only human.

What baffles me is how individuals engaged in dishonest acts honestly believe the same bad shit won't happen to them. Most can't comprehend or cope with how it happens. Everyone goes about their own business, each fleecing and shitting on the next guy whilst truly believing they themselves won't be fleeced or shat upon. Their expectations being someone else will pick up the flak in the system a: not-my-problem sort of way. This is clearly the shortsighted view only the plain stupid would take. That said, one look at the government should confirm it is too late to bring back the truth. The nails are well and truly in that coffin. Before it died truth had been wearing a label reading: do-not-resuscitate for as long as I could remember. Change would require a revolution and revolutions require heroes, not the current incarnation of liberals and certainly not the millennial's.

Back to confused patients, in their defence and in the words of

Bob Dylan:

'You can't criticise what you can't understand'.

Patients don't understand gum disease easily and I see two explanations for this. First and foremost they find pretence and ignorance easier to handle than responsibility and secondly, the professionals fail to offer a consistent approach to help them combat this. A good number of my colleagues have told me that they deliberately keep their patients in the dark; it's better for their bank account. I highlighted my concerns on this in a letter (pasted below) to the British Dental Association, which they kindly published in the British Dental Journal (Vol: 222 No5 / March 10 2017)(1).

What is gum disease?

Sir, despite our best efforts the UK prevalence of chronic periodontitis has remained at 45%. I believe that many patients are confused about 'what gum disease is', often using this phrase themselves. They report inconsistency in the information and advice given by different healthcare providers and respond better if they understand the potential seriousness of periodontal infection and the consequent inflammatory reaction.

As a specialist in periodontology, ten years ago I started using these simplified sentences in my discussions with patients:

Gum disease is an infection that irreversibly destroys the bone that holds your teeth in place.

When a significant amount of bone has been destroyed your teeth will feel loose or wobbly.

When insufficient bone remains to support your teeth they will start to drift or fall out.

Consequently, my patients readily appreciate the seriousness of their condition and, almost always, express their gratitude for the unambiguousness of the communication. Whilst the statements have a negative tone, once patients appreciate the seriousness of their condition positive tones can be introduced by discussing the benefits of resolving their condition, for example, avoiding bad breath. There are no studies on topic-specific words and their influence on patient understanding and compliance but I am hopeful that this letter might encourage this.

(1) **https://www.nature.com/articles/sj.bdj.2017.196**

In my experience patients prefer: straight to the point, cut to the chase, a single management plan and an expert opinion. They particularly dislike the tyranny of proffered choice. The direct approach results in the same patients liking me less in the short term, but ultimately ends up with them trusting me more in the long term. Long-term trust works better for me than does being immediately liked by patients. Once the trust develops the liking part comes naturally and sustains itself better. I am certain patients (humans) can't change from how they were born. That said, it's a weak argument for poor professional services. It's difficult to recall, when I was a general dentist, a single patient who didn't whinge about their previous dentist. When I became a specialist this all stopped, now they whinge about their current dentist which is usually the one who referred them to me. I say to them: 'I have never met a dentist I trusted', they usually smile and then after a long pause I finish my sentence with: 'nor a patient'. Actually it's unfair to say I've never met a dentist I could trust; I have met at least eight. It's about the same for patients.

My trust in dentists went up in smoke back in 1992; my first year in dentistry after I qualified. I attended a postgraduate training event at the Royal College of Surgeons in London. It was a masterclass on how to do root fillings. A root filling is one of the options to deal with a tooth when it has rotted through to the nerve that lies at its core. There were approximately 300 dentists attending the event. The event kicked things off with the presenter taking a straw poll. He asked us to raise our hand if we were still using a material called *endomethazone.* The material was in routine use back then although some concerns had been raised that it might be a bit toxic. Suggestions were made that perhaps it might be an idea that we possibly think about considering thinking about stopping using it (nothing vague). I sill was so I raised my hand. To my surprise out of the three hundred dentists I was the only one to put my hand up. Naughty me. It appeared that all the others had stopped using it. The presenter then extended his open palm down at me and invited the audience to offer me a round of applause:

'Let's put our hands together, our colleague here has purchased 8600 bottles of this stuff, so far this year'

The audience erupted into laughter. Not shy meek embarrassed laughter but boisterous, throw you head back, Kaiser Wilhelm laughter. They literally fell about in the isles laughing. My experience of dentists never really got any better. The irony is that some ten years later in 2002 it would be a root filling specialist, Dr Richard Kahan, who would become my most influential role model in dentistry.

I am not saying that dishonesty started in 1992; we all know that shits being going on ever since Eve took a bite of the serpent's juicy apple. 1992 is when the stage lights came on and I started having my professional experience of it, the vast majority of which wasn't good. Dishonesty wafts around in endless circles, here's an example of one of its cycles. In 1770 Captain James Cook claimed New South Wales in Australia for Britain. By 1788 Commodore Arthur Philips had turned it into a penal colony by depositing 162,000 English convicts on it. The convicts were put to work and told to clear the forests and dig trenches. By the 1950's (about the same time the high pitched whizzy drills were introduced) their descendants were back in England digging their trenches in patient's mouths for money. The Australian trench became the term which described the technique of cutting a cavity in a back tooth using a whizzy drill and then drawing it forwards cutting its way through each of the teeth in front, one after the other, to end at a front one; the trench would then be back filled with a mercury based metal filling effectively joining all the teeth together with one big slab of a filling. It's all in the genes.

It wasn't much later in 1994 that I worked as a Regional Dental Officer (RDO) in North West London. Back then if an NHS patient required a course of treatment which was going to exceed two hundred and fifty pounds in value, the proposed treatment would first have to be approved by an RDO. My role was to assess the patient and ensure that the proposed treatment was appropriate and in the patients best interest. I did this at a community clinic in the evenings and my remuneration was below the national minimum wage (introduced in 1999). An absolute requirement for any complicated costly treatment was that the patient's gums should be healthy. If they weren't the treatment would be declined. One particular dentist who ran a successful NHS factory in North West London would turn up and hover over me whilst I performed the assessments on patients. If I declined a request (which was most of time) he'd say: 'Come on Dr. Ahmed, you're not god and the moneys not coming out of your pocket'. Ho-Hum. Other NHS factories circumnavigated the approval process altogether. Let's say the factory had six dentists, the patient would arrive and be assessed by one of them and treatment amounting to just short of two hundred and fifty pounds would be supplied to one corner of the mouth. Then the same patient would be passed round another three of them and each would take it in turn to do just less than two hundred and fifty pounds worth of treatment in each of the four quarters of the patient's mouth.

I have met tons of dentists who've told me that they love teeth, love dentistry and love all their patients (they are good) and then after two small glasses of wine.... dandandanhhhh...............the same dentists hate everyone and everything (2). They should get a grip of themselves and only hate people as much as they deserve to be hated. I am often reminded of what a consultant once told me, 'I took a decision early in my career that I wasn't going to let dentistry get me'...I didn't really understand what he meant but I'll finish the story in Chapter 6.

**(2) https://www.theguardian.com/society/2000/sep/10/fut
ureofthenhs.health**

I've often wondered if it is the training pathway or the business of dentistry which turns dentists into what they became, or whether they were actually born that way. And have never reached a definitive conclusion as I've had experiences which support both arguments. This one stands out; loud and proud. It's how a student reacted when I mirrored his behaviour and treated him the same way he was treating me:

Student: I don't like how you're talking to me!

Me: I am sorry; I find it difficult to work out how to talk to someone. When that happens, I simply mirror back how I am being spoken to. I am sorry that you don't like being talked to the same way you were talking to me.

Student: Do you know I am a qualified doctor?

Me: No.

Student: I am a qualified doctor!

Me: Oh, I would never have worked that out from your performance on this clinic.

Student: I have already been offered a job at a specialist implant practice in West Sussex. I will be banging in implants all day long. To do so I've worked out it's better for me to be double qualified (medicine& dentistry).

Me: I have never banged in an implant in my entire career!

He was unable to comprehend the principle: 'treat someone like a bitch and they respond like a bitch'. Nevertheless I was shocked by the arrogant pride with which he announced his capitalist motivations. For him it was all money, money, money; his qualification was going to be his license to print it. He'd obviously not heard Denis Brown lamenting in his 1979 song: 'Money in my pocket, but I just can't get no love'. I often shared this story with some of my patients and they would ask me: 'What makes you different, Dr. Ahmed?' and to my surprise the first time I was asked, I didn't have an answer. I'll have worked it out by the end of this chapter though.

I remembered the time when I worked in a practice in Cheltenham. I was the in-house gum specialist. One of the big boy dentists had purchased a dental laser (to offset his taxes). He used to sidle up behind me and say: 'I'm going to refer you a patient with gum disease. I want you to tell them it needs to treated by laser and then send them back to me for it'. He had a nasty grey complexion. The new dentist in the same practice had a novel way of relaxing in his lunch break, his willing nurse would strip to her underwear and he would give her a massage. I supposed that the unlocked door was some sort of invitation to like minds.

Enough stories for now! Back to Louise (my patient) the human resources expert. I had cared for her for around ten years and at the time of writing was still doing so. When she first came to me I found it difficult to not feel saddened by where she and the professionals had landed her. I extended myself beyond the normal call of professional duty. At one point I needed to refer her for some complex restorative work which was beyond my then skill-set. My faith in my senior colleagues was poor so I accompanied her to the consultations. It was lucky I did. The first consultation was at the Tatum Clinic and Institute in Birmingham. I sat through the entire consultation with Dr. Tatum thinking: 'the clinical conversation will start any minute now', but nope there was very minimal clinical discussion. Nothing about limitations, and consent didn't get a look in either. When Dr. Tatum's report arrived, surprise surprise, it contained very minimal clinical discussion. There was very little to be impressed or happy about.

During my visit, the Clinic Directors, Dr Hilt Tatum and Dr Ben Aghabeigi offered me a teaching job at their Institute and invited me to stay and observe for the rest of day. I took up their kind offer and stayed and I'm glad I did, as it proved crucial, for Louise; that I witnessed the poor standard of care taking place. More specifically there was a last minute, keystone-cops style scramble, immediately before a patient was to receive an *inferior dental bundle relocation*. It's one of the most complex and risky operations, which a very small number of specialists provide. The patient hadn't been consented and no one knew who was to administer the sedation. Dr. Tatum nominated, by waggling a finger, one of the course delegates (dentist) to consent the patient and another to administer the sedation. I have no idea what discussions took place for the patient to give her consent as Dr Tatum and I left the room for a tour round the institute. This was weird to me as I always consent my own patients.

Following a bit of fuss and confusion, the nominated delegate administered the sedation with a look of reluctance and trepidation. At the end of the procedure Dr Tatum placed the first suture before standing up and announcing: 'I have a train to catch, can you finish this off' leaving Dr Aghabeigi to complete wound closure. This was weird to me as I always close my own surgical sites. The Clinical Directors were clearly happy with their standards otherwise they wouldn't have asked me to stay. In my experience the benchmark in dentistry is low, very low; except on websites. What made the situation even more horrific was that the poor standard of care was being demonstrated to the dozen or so course delegates as if it were the gold standard. It was shocking. The same dentists would go on to pick up a certificate of postgraduate training and make the claim: 'trained by the world renowned'.

Anyway, I declined the opportunity to join the Tatum Clinic and Institute as a clinical teacher. I had seen enough to be concerned and remain concerned that those who were being trained are now most probably engaged in providing equally poor standards of care. I would later learn how close a shave it had been for Louise and me. The Tatum clinics educational director Dr Benham Aghabeigi, who simultaneously held the post of consultant oral surgeon at the Birmingham Dental Hospital, a few years later, pleaded guilty to twelve charges of fraud at Birmingham magistrates' court (3).

(3) https://www.birminghammail.co.uk/news/local-news/birmingham-dentist-admits-defrauding-nhs-160374

My concerns about dentists were validated once again when, sometime later, I received the referral of a patient who wanted a second opinion. She was not happy with the one provided by Dr. Mende Slabbert. Dr. Slabbert had some sort of link to the Tatum clinic, the full extent of which was not clear. The patient brought with her a report prepared by him and it was the work of a seasoned profiteer. Dr. Slabbert lost his licence to practice and was erased from the dental register (4). I continue to see reports of the same ilk at least once a month.

(4) https://www.coventrytelegraph.net/news/coventry-news/struck-off-dentist-carries-on-working-3136423

I was equally lucky to be turned down by Dr Surinder Hundle for a job at his Knightsbridge practice, Lund Osler. I generally prefer to keep a distance from those who engage in professional misconduct especially those who sleep with their patients (5). It raises too many questions about their attitude towards their professional responsibilities especially since my experience is they are invariably flawed.

(5) https://www.telegraph.co.uk/news/uknews/8382175/TV-dentist-with-a-roving-eye-met-patient-for-sex-sessions.html

In the end Louise accepted my earlier recommendation and had her treatment provided by a specialist friend of mine in London. For my own ongoing training I accompanied her for the larger stages of treatment and assisted by being the nurse. I did for her what I would have done for my wife and in return when the time came she shared her HR expertise with me and taught me some of the tricks often (always) played by Human Resource departments. How naive I was.

Louise taught me (in my own words):

Grievance is: A personal matter, it relates to me and not my patients. It's a concern that I might have about aspects of my employment. Examples of which may be: How I am being treated, what I have been asked to do or being asked to complete eight hours worth of work in two hours. Essentially, any discrimination or breach of contract.

Whistleblowing is: Made in the public interest. It is not a personal matter and not about me. It is about my patients and the wrong doings of my employer.

Louise warned that when staff 'grieve' too much or too often they are tagged: 'high risk' and, in the hands of a competent leadership, they are told: 'we no longer need you'. In the hands of an incompetent leadership they are sacked at the earliest possible convenience and there's not much that can be done about it. Since I had 'blown the whistle' or made a 'protected disclosure' there was a law in place (Public Interest Disclosure Act; PIDA), which would protect me.

Louise worried me to shit with her question: 'What has your solicitor advised you'. My immediate thought was: 'I don't need a solicitor; all will be sorted in the next few months'. Anyhow, she made it plain and clear: 'You have had made a protected disclosure and if you get fired for having done so, and you can prove it, the law will protect me'. (Thank god lawyers and barristers are an honest bunch).

Blowing the whistle certainly blew a lot of stress my way and the effect it had was a deep one. Some of my patients noticed me struggle and a number of them asked me: 'is everything OK?' I simply and truthfully told them it wasn't. When I shared my story with them, guts and all, they felt compelled to share their own of their own workplaces. Their comments went along the lines of: 'my work place is a shitty place' and 'the people I work with are shitty!' and 'what is wrong with the individuals I work with?' and 'where have all the heroes gone?' In my struggle I had started to find adult humans frightening and I later learnt that the authors of Peter Pan, Alice in Wonderland and Wind in the Willows; JM Barrie, Lewis Carroll and Kenneth Grahame all refused to engage in the adult world.

Dentistry is hard enough under the best of circumstances as it is by virtue a bad news industry. Teaching students in the best of settings and the perfect environment is difficult enough due to the never ending array of behavioural characteristics they bring to the party. It shouldn't be difficult to understand then that both jobs, if done well, stimulate a certain level of negative emotions on a daily basis. The load at The Icon became excessive and if at any time I give you the impression or you assume that I was carrying on with my life normally, I was not. If at any time I give you the impression that the irreverence was intentional or easy, it was not. In addition to which, I have never found it easy to express negative emotions. So writing this book is not proving to be easy at all. Managing negative emotions is just as difficult as trying to express them. It's near impossible especially since the brain is designed to automatically delete them as soon as possible after they appear. The leadership team had pressed a whole row of buttons with each one triggering cascades of emotional landmines. Each one detonating indiscriminately.

Negative emotions are complex (at the best of times) and I remember being told: 'only one thing ever comes from an argument and that is the desire to apologise' I didn't understand what this meant at the time but it started to develop meaning during my experience. My desire to apologise occurred irrespective of me having had a valid reason for arguing my point in the first place. I lost count of the number of times I felt it would be in my best interests to apologise to the leadership team for having pointed out all the problems they had created and get on with my life; in peace. I wanted mercy. (I would not understand the desire to apologise until after the experience was over). Bidding against it was the other constant thought, the one that haunted me more: if I bailed out I would have failed to keep my promise to the students and patients. The conflicting thoughts continued to tap dance, in high heels, over my mind as I trundled on. Guilt and shame are complex and weird.

My mind continued in automatic operation, deleting or altering my negative emotions whilst I developed a sixth sense not to avoid them. It was telling me, that to ignore them, would lead to a potential backfire. I had already experienced several episodes of the 'red-mist' which had torn me raw and rendered me useless for three to four days whilst it screamed and shouted its way out. Stopping my brain from performing its defensive functions wasn't easy; it created a massive conflict in me and became a complex negotiation. My mind knew it couldn't let the negative emotions upset me day after day because that would destroy me in a different way (by increasing the rate at which I'd stumble and fall into camouflaged holes in the jungle floor). I resolved the conflict and controlled the exhaustion by taking my third executive decision; all emotions were to be labeled as mere 'generic messages', nothing more, nothing less. I started to deal with them as I did the mail; I left them in the inbox until I was ready to open them and when I did open them I'd ask myself: 'I wonder what I'm being told?' This encouraged a belief in me that negative emotions weren't essentially bad and my problem was due to me having little experience of the sheer number of them.

I had already started to work out that anxiety and worry were avoidable as long as I used the freight of fear to keep me moving forward. When I did so, using my will to change my minds state, shifting it back in the direction of strength and tenacity, was more successful. But there remained a trio of linked emotions, which kept knocking me off course: anger, resentment, and frustration. In chapter two I thought the injustice created frustration fuelling resentment and resulting in anger. As I looked at them again I realised I had been wrong and that frustration was the end product (pouring out as fury) of the spent emotions generated by resentment. I had also worked out the interesting role anger was supposed to be playing. I would explain it this way, to keep move forward required a lot of energy, to produce the energy my metabolism needed elevating, anger did just that. I concluded (for now) that anger was necessary as without it there would be insufficient energy. I knew too much of it was causing the house would go up in flames bit I'd need a bit more time to master controlling it better. Especially since it was a derivative of my temperament and that was as genetically inherited as my height.

Resentment, anger and frustration kept catching me off guard due to the contradiction between feeling the pain of being whipped and beaten whilst around me all I could only see was my peers and role models. Each of their provocations initiated two contradictory chemical themes in my mind. The first theme was the response to being whipped and beaten which was generating defence and battle chemistry. In the mindfully respectful chemistry was generated. The opposing nature of the chemicals made the resulting emotions difficult to decipher. I found it near impossible to reconcile the phenomenon. How was it possible for the same provocation to create two opposing themes? The only way I can explain it is by getting you to imagine a scenario. Imagine three buckets of water. In the first bucket (on the left) you have steaming hot water, in the last bucket (on the right) you have ice-cold water and in the middle bucket the water is at room temperature. Now imagine plunging your left hand into the left bucket and simultaneously your right hand in to the right bucket and hold them under water for 90 seconds. Then simultaneously plunge both hands into the middle bucket to find that the same water has a different effect on your two hands. The same water makes one hand feel hot and the other feel cold. It's complicated (and easy) but it what happens.

In search for the answers, I continued to reflect on a thought that repeated in my mind:

'There must be a reason why my emotions had been designed to make me feel uncomfortable.'

I would say to myself:

'I'm sure that I should listen to them before I throw them out.'

This was around the time I had started to question my own motives and remained uncertain of what I wanted to do next. I wasn't sure if I wanted to continue being a catalyst for change. In and amongst the nonsense I couldn't sure what my motivation was anymore. I was on a very different journey to the one I had set off on. I had grossly underestimated the detriment I might suffer. I hadn't wanted any sort of reward for my efforts but the detriment was such that I wasn't so sure anymore. All I could hear was 'the heckling' coming from the leadership team, making me jealous of people who weren't miserably sad like me. If life was truly a stage, I was failing to put on a confident performance in my day job or at home.

I had started to work out the relationship between the rate of expression of negative emotions and time and it was not only an exponential one, it was the most intense and compounding of all the relationships in my experience, I'd describe it as:

LARGE NUMBER OF INTENSE NEGATIVE EMOTIONS + TIME = PANIC

Panic always resulted in memory lapse, my memory cells defaulted to a pre-experience state. I'd have to regroup and remind myself of what I'd previously learnt. The impact of which exacerbated a state in which I continued to question my mental wellbeing.

There was no doubt the steady stream of 'but how's' were making life uncomfortable. But back then I hadn't realised I couldn't become stronger without the discomfort. There were times when I became desperate to get away from the discomfort. It was creating colossal pain in my mind, my body - and my arse. I mean literally, irritable bowel is like shitting a starfish, whole! Ask anyone who has suffered with it. I had to dig deep and often revisited my beliefs, morals and motivations. I was 46 years old when I decided enough was enough. I wanted my students and patients to get the same as what I expected for my family. My motivations were driven by the fact I wanted my family to be able to visit the local doctors and get the correct advice and best treatment and for that to stand a chance of becoming reality my patients would have to get the same from me. I wanted my children to have the best possible schooling and education and for that to stand a chance of becoming reality my students would have to get the same from me.

I wanted to make a positive contribution to the society I belonged to and did not want to be like so many other 'burnout' doctors. After we married in 1997, Zahida moved to London from Yorkshire and joined my doctor's practice. She had gone to the doctor with a head cold. When she (ZA) returned the conversation went like so:

ZA: Your doctor is rubbish

Me: Why'd you say that?

ZA: She had already written a prescription for antibiotics, before I had even sat down.

Me: Ah yes, that'll be because most patients' will give her grief if she doesn't give them antibiotics and she, no longer able to cope with the whinging, just hands out what the herd wants, antibiotics. It's not perfect but she's a product of a bad system

ZA: Well she is only making the bad system worse

Me: The question is: how would you have reacted if she had not given you some antibiotics, what would've you said if she'd sent you home to rest, drink lots of water and balance a lemon on your head?"

ZA: That's exactly what I would have done"

I upset my wife by failing to stop the next few sentences falling out of my mouth:

'Rubbish, no you wouldn't, you would have done the same as all the others. You would have whinged about not being given antibiotics. It's called the Human-Condition and it generally revolves around saying one thing and doing another'.

'It's a well known fact that the doctor was simply taking the path of least resistance, largely to minimise the mental trauma being caused to her by patients ignorance, arrogance, unreasonable behaviours and snide comments. She was protecting her own mental wellbeing.

'I don't agree with it as it sets our kids up for a fall, but I do recognise the human condition nature of it'.

Patients are no angels, far from it. I have had enough of my own bad experiences; too many to list here but here's a particularly good - bad one. Deep scar. A female patient, a freelance journalist, in her forties complained bitterly about suffering pain and discomfort after some gum surgery I'd provided. "What have you done wrong?, was her opening question when she returned for the review appointment; and then followed this up with a statement delivered firmly and bluntly: 'I've been in agony'. Two weeks earlier I had cracked on with treatment after she'd arrived twenty minutes late for her appointment. Once I had anaesthetised her gums she waved her hand aloft and announced that she needed to make an urgent phone call. Whereupon she made her way to the back garden and proceeded to chain smoke two cigarettes immediately before the treatment and then continued to smoke during the healing period. Her ignorance knew no bounds and she dug her heels in with a four-page letter of complaint. It's not difficult to dislike some patients.

The Inspiration.

I was only 5 years old when Mohammed Ali 'rumbled in the jungle' with George Foreman. I was too young to have understood their lives, had no idea about colonial history, the slave trade, or the legacy of the black man. I sure do now. Shame on you white European man! Past, not present. Thank god today's European is an honest one.

It seemed right to me and I naturally liked Mohammed Ali but I had no understanding of why, it was just instinct. Earlier in my career I remembered watching an interview he gave back in 1974. I heard it around 1994, about the same time almost every one of my patients was telling me: 'I had no idea that sugar causes tooth decay, no idea at all, no one has ever told me'. In his interview Ali said 'I have to educate my people, I have to tell them to stop eating that candy, because that candy is making holes in their teeth'. It made me think that twenty years had passed and my patients still hadn't got the message. It would be much later that

I'd learn that they knew all along but lacked the ability to be truthful.

How is it possible to be so connected with someone you've never met? , How is it possible to get so emotional and reflective when someone you've never met dies? As I rummaged through YouTube clips (for more than three weeks) there was not a lot to 'not like' about the man. He was brave and courageous and used divisive techniques to get himself noticed and heard. He refused to serve in the Vietnam War and sacrificed his crown and money for his principles. Yet his bravest and most divisive move of all was his decision to appear on international television with his new girlfriend. That's the bravest way I've seen a man communicate with his wife; it was no accident.

I became entranced by his courage and confidence. Of all his achievements I was struck most by his endurance and stamina. I watched his three fights against Joe Frazier and I witnessed an artist at work. I realised that professional boxing is much more than two blokes thumping the shit out of each other. It was much more. It required preparation, mental and physical, tact, cunning, courage, strength and conviction. Once committed the fight was on, he had to fight and fight to the end. Once committed a change of mind wasn't an option, bailing out was not an option. Once committed he didn't suffer offence, he only suffered harm. He knew that catching his opponent on either side of the chin button, twisting their head abruptly about their neck produces a far more devastating effect than does brute strength, although that works as well. The winner was often the man who out maneuvered his opponent, mentally and physically. Studying Ali became my endurance training and my perception of what was required of me changed. I needed to get used to being thumped.

For all the psychology books I read none connected with me as much as the book *Soul of a Butterfly* which he had co-authored with his daughter: Reading it was an uplifting experience and his words resonated with me because he was describing his personal experiences. He had done all the things he was talking about and was therefore able to express himself in a way that the psychologists and psychology books could not. Psychology books didn't connect with me because they were one individual's (bad) account of another person's experience. To make things worse the persons experience was often twisted and presented (badly) in a way which supported the psychologist's ideology. That just didn't do it for me.

I sat back and slumped in sheer delight when I read his quotation:

'If your dreams do not scare you they are not big enough.'

His words embodied and expressed the differentiation between the manifestations of anxiety when it is coupled with fear versus the manifestations of the same anxiety when it is coupled with ambition. The way he used them made me realise that my experience was offering me the potential for positive growth and gain. He made me realise that by engaging in the sort of combat I'd gotten embroiled in, falling into the odd camouflaged hole in the jungle floor was to be expected. Tears to hope.

Reading these words for the first time was one of the 'Top Ten' moments of my experience. This was my second moment of rapture. The way the words were strung together spoke to me in a way that others on the same theme had not. This quotation confirmed to me it was perfectly normal of me to feel anxious and scared .... It gave me permission to feel scared! It told me I shouldn't feel scared about feeling scared. It made feeling scared sacred. You might never understand its importance or the impact it had on me until you pluck up the courage to stand up for something and see what happens next. It told me if I didn't do things that resulted in me feeling scared I was not working to my full potential. I realised that if I wasn't feeling scared I was most probably doing something crap or useless or worthless with my life.

In chapter three, I said: 'in my world 'fear' describes a feeling I get deep in my tummy when I experience something different or new, it could be exhilarating or freighting. It could be the prospect of diving into an ice cold Alaskan lake or riding a roller coaster for the first time or even watching the school bully walk towards me knowing full well he's going to bop me on the nose'. I might have said it back then but I didn't really understand it. I was now certain that it was when fear was coupled with anxiety that it resulted in me feeling frightened. However when (and most importantly) the very same fear was coupled with ambition it made me feel exhilarated. I got the sense that I'd have to be more careful not to confuse the two feelings, especially since they are inseparable whilst the outcomes are at opposite ends of the spectrum.

This quotation held my hand like a parent holds a toddlers. Quite often a single recital of it would neutralise an entire rainbow of anxieties which helped me endure time better. When time was controlled panic was less likely. It helped me mend my wounds to stay afloat even though I had lost sight of the shoreline. It helped me retain a notion of partial emotional health at a time when it was very difficult for me to tell my wife and children how appallingly I was being treated at work. It prevented me from screaming out 'I'm not a savage'.

My research continued and as it did I came across an article in which Ellen Johnson Sirleaf was quoted as having said: 'If your dreams do not scare you they are not big enough'. Naughty-naughty I thought. She had stolen or at least appeared to be taking credit for Ali's words. I was wrong, it turned out that Ali had borrowed her words (she was much older). I noticed that she'd written an autobiography: *This Child Will Be Great*. How do you not read a book with that title? I wanted to know how a child becomes great. I finished it in two days. Ellen Johnson Sirleaf was the first black female president of an African nation, Liberia. She was married to a military man who would don his full dress uniform as a sign to let her know he wanted to row something out (Note-to-self). In her book she presented the darkest, chillingly dark, acts of men. She used the most sublime beauty and prose to describe horrific satanic acts as she told the stories of two coup d'état in her nation. It was a gripping read and about ten pages from the end I started to feel sad. Ellen had become my new parent and the book was soon to finish. She soothed me and I had enjoyed her company, and I was about to lose it. I wasn't looking forward to being on my own again, lost and lonely. What would I do or read next? Almost as if she'd heard my thoughts, on the very next page Ellen praised a book from which she had gained great benefit. *A Personal History* by Catherine Graham, which I immediately ordered a second-hand copy of on Amazon and it arrived two days later, which is just as well because I was holding my breath.

Wow… what a sucker punch, Catherine Graham was a great writer and her story is one of the most compelling I have read, so far. I was far too young to have appreciated it when it happened back in the early 1970's. Catherine was the owner of the Washington Post newspaper when Richards Nixon's administration tried to destroy her for having reported the Pentagon Papers and the Watergate Scandal. What an extraordinary life she led. I practically sucked the words right off the six hundred and forty two pages in five days. Given my eyes, neck, head and shoulders were already extremely sore; the price I paid for the pleasure of her words was high. It was raw pain. This was endurance reading. I loved it.

I was learning...

I was learning to feel a sense of worth from feeling scared and there was a lot for me to be scared about. The leadership team had deliberately structured themselves to be blind to any of the concerns I'd raised and I had initiated a process of peeling away their camouflage. I hadn't anticipated they would show a complete abandonment of personal responsibility and hunt me in an organised way; whilst they protected their coterie. Demonstrating, as they did, the classical sign of careerists with little or no interest in the advancement of the many. By blowing the whistle I had made myself identifiable and was left wondering somewhat loosely what the value of being identifiable was? I was learning that in most parts of the animal kingdom being identifiable carries a higher target value than weakness does. It's a myth that predators exclusively take down the weaker animals. Making myself identifiable and putting my head above the parapet positioned me front and centre as the predators prime target. The weak ones are merely identified and tagged as potential scapegoats to be used strategically.

I was learning that when my endurance and stamina was put to the test, my beliefs and morals were not enough. I needed a different kind of support. I needed the support of role models; something **Friedrich Nietzsche** neatly touched upon:

'When one had not had a good father, one must create one'

I was learning that some behavioural characteristics are easier to learn from examples set by role models. Learning through the experiences of others (as part of my overall experience) laid down a more powerful mind print than books did. The role models had experienced their own adversity and I learnt to appreciate the behaviours they demonstrated during the adversity. They'd had to navigate their way through some very tough situations, tougher than mine. They had been forced into corners and were required to make some seriously important decisions for themselves, much tougher than mine. They had been terrified in their own way in their own time. It taught me tough decisions were never easy, not for anyone, not even for the toughest of people. It made me think of the time when a friend of mine introduced me to a friend of hers: 'this is Hafeez, he thinks no one else has any problems'. She got my vote and made me smile.

I was learning that one of the fundamental characteristics of a resilient person is they can take a decision and move on. They do not linger, they manage to switch off the rumination. They 'compartmentalise' and periodically lock things away by using their mind as if it were made of separate compartments. I started to practice the technique and enjoyed some partial success. I was held back a little because I was working with a mind that had already become too twitchy due to the fretting. I couldn't always compartmentalise, it only required a small distraction and doors would fly open all over the place. The concentration required was intense. And then I found a more reliable way for me to compartmentalise, I simply scheduled ruminating and put it in my diary. I would put it in for say between 4 and 5 pm. If I caught myself ruminating outside this time I would talk myself out of it by saying: 'not now, it's in the diary for 4'. This worked wonders for me and is based on similar principles to mindfulness.

I was learning that when we select role models for ourselves we do so depending on our motivation and drive, and John Finch expressed some cautious words about selecting motivations in his book *The Father Effect*:

'Money, sex, drugs, fame, or power will never be enough'

John was eleven years old when his father committed suicide and his book offered me a valuable glimpse into his life. He explained the degree of care necessary when developing ones motivations and drivers.

I was learning what made me different. Previously, when my patients had asked: 'what makes you different?' I didn't have an answer; I did now. I realised that my childhood dentist had been my role model. She was the reason I decided to become a dentist. I hadn't worked it out back then because as a child I was a dingbat. It had taken this experience and forty odd years before I unraveled the mystery behind some of my early life decisions. Shocker. Once I had got it, I could see it clearly. She was one of the only adults in my life who wasn't routinely engaged in attempting to beat the devil out of me (things were different back then). I don't think she ever spoke to me, ever. She was not my friend she was a role model.

I was learning that logic or reason was evading all the players in this story. The leadership team was certainly incapable of it. Their hoity toity intellectual narrative alongside their high and mighty aristocracy was just a cover-up to conceal their poor standards. As they went about their business of being bad role models whilst swatting the students with the unforgivable turgid arrogance held dear by childish adults. They continued to pretend to have solidarity with the work force despite having nothing to do with them. Suppressing them with a certain snobby elitist attitude and generally having contempt for them. My early life experiences of similarly aggressive techniques plus the simply horrendous experiences described by Ali, Ellen, Catherine and John made it easier for me to accept that perhaps human behaviours had been ubiquitously appalling since the dawn of modern mankind. I decided that the fewer expectations I held the less upset I would get. Thus my expectations of my fellows shriveled up to the size of a stinky rabbit dropping. It's not normal for me to hold such low expectations but it was in a 'needs must' situation. That was that.

I was learning that all emotions come about in the same way, whether positive or negative. They have the same pathways in the brain but with different outcomes. A stimulus provokes a chemical change; the chemical change makes you feel the way you do. With some chemicals you feel one way with others you feel a different way. The composition of chemicals is as unique as the moment. Somehow the release of the chemicals is associated with the linguistics centers of the mind as they are only initiated once they get meaning to do so and that meaning is contained in the words used to describe the situation. Thereafter it really starts to get heavy because the meanings contained in the words is as unique as the individual, which essentially means each word could potentially have 8 billion meanings. But for me removing the pronouns happy and sad from the equation made a big difference as it allowed me an understanding the process and enabled me to use it more mechanically, as a tool, which offered me great positive benefit.

I was learning to manage my negative emotions whilst avoiding the shame created by them to instead embrace them. It was plausible the shame was a result of indoctrination or conditioning so I challenged it. I re-programmed myself to avoid denial of them. It enabled me to sit and listen to them, which wasn't quick or easy. On some occasions the process felt like soothing a molested child and on others it was like stroking the mane of a nasty predator. As I experienced each one or each episode I questioned why I was feeling what I was feeling. I extracted the message from each emotion, one by one, as soon after it arose before moving onto the next one. I would say to myself 'there's a good reason you're having this feeling, what is it?, what is it?' I viewed them as 'states of mind' and 'signals' designed to force me to pay more attention to the events creating them. The buggers were rarely pleasant but they existed for a reason. It turned out that, for me, feeling bad became the fertiliser that nourished my growth. I dismantled and threw out the notion that feeling bad should be frowned upon or that it was politically incorrect. At the same time I realised that the millennial's created by oedipal parenting would require similar reprogramming if they were ever to be useful. I now spend a lot more time talking to my children about the power of bad feelings and how to use them for their advantage. (I'd later learn that the way I deconstructed my emotions into messages shared some similarities with Jacques Derrida's philosophy on deconstruction).

I was learning that maintaining some stability over my negative emotions was like preventing a tower of cards from collapsing in the wind. The tower once it's up is fragile pretty much by default of design and construction and blows over easily. Invariably, especially at the beginning of my experience, a new provocation from the leadership team would act like a gust of wind and blow my emotions all over the place; the tower of cards would collapse. I would have to rebuild it from scratch but with practice I got faster and faster at the re-build. I never really came to understand why my tower of emotions would almost always be blown over and have to be rebuilt from scratch. But thankfully I managed to accept it and stopped standing about and got on with the rebuild sooner and quicker.

I was learning to accept that the word happy had been one of the most misunderstood words of my life, so far. Previously I'd accidently been using the feeling of pleasure to measure the success of my life. I've since learnt the benefits of the dark side of happiness; are much stronger. I've since revisited some of my childhood memories and my perceptions of the happiness I thought I'd seen in Disney movies. At second glance they weren't actually as happy as I remembered them to be. Most of them contained moralistic warnings. Warnings of evil people, engaged in evil deeds. Nothing being darker than 'Rumpelstiltskin' and that shit was happening four thousand years ago. I must have been part mental cabbage when I first watched them; it's also possible they were a relative joy compared to my childhood. I no longer use feelings of pleasure to measure the success of my life. I now use the lack of pain or disease as the measure. Unlike Peter Pan, I don't need a 'happy thought' most probably because in Pan Story, Peter had already lost his way. He'd already become an asset stripping corporate pirate. Having lost touch with humanity he needed a happy thought to rescue himself to become a more content and satisfied person, one who could reconnect with his children. Anyway as I reflected over the private inner thoughts that patients and students had shared with me I became convinced that they too had a misunderstanding of happiness.

I was learning why I was constantly exhausted. I was dragging emotions I'd been programmed to process in my subconscious (lazy) brain into my conscious brain. I was working against the design of my neurological system and forcefully attempting to challenge my programming. Being able to explain my exhaustion allowed me to enjoy my afternoon naps more.

I was learning that my inability to control my anger was telling me something needed to change. I guess the reason for this was the sustained nature of the threat of danger. I was being warned to distance myself somehow from the threat. I sensed that I could potentially control both anger and frustration simultaneously by addressing resentment. Resentment was telling me I needed to change my perception of my relationship with the leadership team and if I did it would put more distance between me and them and the danger. I had to step out from under their shadow. I changed my perception in two ways. First, I recited: 'progress is always driven by the unreasonable man', more often and it taught me I should have expected things to get nasty all along and I was currently experiencing the 'justice' that comes with going against the leadership team of an Iconic Machine. In essence I changed my perspective by replacing the word injustice with the word justice (the power of words again). I found that expecting to be treated badly reduced my feelings of resentment. Second, I stopped holding the leadership team aloft as some sort of role models and instead demoted them to the garbage can; as shit on my shoe. The actions I took eliminated resentment almost in its entirety, the same events, which once made me angry, started to make me smile. Each time I sensed some anger brewing I'd flip my mind to imagining how annoyed the leadership team would be from learning they still hadn't crushed me and 'I was still standing'.

I was learning that it wasn't just me who found humans frightening. In her book: *Mind of a Survivor* Megan Hind would have rather met a wild animal in the jungle over a human. Her experience was humans are far more unpredictable.

I was learning that Ali's fans were in awe of him because of his ability to predict which round he would knockout his opponents. They thought he had some sort of higher 'witchcraft' power. Ali explained that by predicting the round he was simply setting himself a goal to chase. The goal setting was necessary for him to will, focus, his mind and it gave him a sense of determination. If he was going to realise the goal he had set himself he'd have to work harder. No voodoo, just ambition and attitude.

Freddie Mercury certainly demonstrated his ambition when he showed an interest and asked if he could be the lead singer of Queen. Brian May the guitarist let him down softly: 'not with those teeth mate'. Given that Freddie had a big dream to realise and an ambition to fulfill, he made the most of it. 'I have four extra incisors which means more space, which means more range' and then smiled hard. Ambition appears to have a healthy disregard for upset.

I was learning that uncertainty was indeed uncertain and too much of it plays tricks with one's mind as communicated by

Friedrich Nietzsche:

'If you stare into the abyss, the abyss stares back at you'

Communication and Blurred lines

'The single biggest problem in communication is the illusion that it has taken place'
George Bernard Shaw

This quotation instantly put a soft smile on my mind shortly after which I laughed out loud (introspectively) whilst the leadership team continued with their childish campaign to punish me. Its effect enabled me to better identify the corruptions of communication hidden within the provocations and profferings. Through it I began to sidestep their power to blatantly invoke anxiety and worry.

I received it in **August 2016** at a time when I had been stunned by The Icon's brazen audacity. The impasse was my disbelief that they could have and had reverse engineered an investigation so as to conclude that I had been communicating poorly. Thus allowing them to make the claim that they could not have known I had blown the whistle. The quote helped me reveal the reality and transform more of the uncertain into the certain. It helped me take the deliberately elusive and turn it into something I could understand and do something with.

In this chapter I will explain the sleight-of-hand being employed and how it was being loaded into communications, alongside other trickery and how it all came together to deceive, corrupt, conceal and cover-up. I'll also explain the moment I realised my actual form of communication was causing the leadership team some discomfort.

The Experience

The cast in this chapter

Leadership team	Given name
Head of Human Resources	Mr Wily
Chairman of Council	Mr Insightful
Head of Department	Dr Perfidious (deceitful& dishonest)
Dean of Education	Dr Comprehensive
Line Manager & Team Lead	Dr Available

The story so far........

1. 15th September 2015; whistle blown.

2. 2nd October 2015; nasty meeting with Dr Dick Dastardly.

3. 6th October 2015; incognito meeting with Professor Pinocchio.

4. 19th October 2015; Dick Dastardly's failed attempt to drown me in IT.

5. 1st Week December 2015; Dr Perfidious tells a bunch of staff 'Hafeez is a liability; I'll have to get rid of him'. (ouch my shoulder blades)

6. 7th December 2015; my expression of grievance to Dr Dastardly about the above.

7. 8th December 2015; IT team produces a report which implicates me as uniquely experiencing the concerns I'd reported. (ouch)

8. 17th December 2015; Dr Perfidious produces a report which implicates me as uniquely experiencing the concerns I'd reported. (ouch)

9. 8th April 2016. Professor Pinocchio & Mr Wily failed to re-label my protected disclosures a grievance. (phew)

.....In the nine month period since I blew the whistle I received no feedback whatsoever on the patients whose concerns I'd escalated to the leadership team. On the clinics, the students continued to express ongoing concerns and asking what, if anything, I had done about the previous ones. Even though it was getting repetitive and embarrassing, I continued to reassure them the leadership team would be in touch to address their concerns.

The leadership team however kept their hands in their pockets and did the square root of fuck-all. In light of which I continued to make further disclosures. Each time a patient or a student made a complaint I'd record it and escalate it to them. The overall theme of the concerns remained almost the same as before:

Here are some of the concerns I raised.... take a deep breath:

•Students were poorly prepared to provide treatment to the patients.

•Some named students complained because some patient notes were missing.

•Some of the patient's notes were poorly written.

•In some cases patients hadn't given their informed consent for the treatment which the students were scheduled to provide.

•Some patients had complicated medical histories which made them high risk for medical complications and as such unsuitable to receive treatment from students.

•The clinic was overbooked and students were poorly prepared to provide treatment to the patients. I made a request to reduce patient numbers to improve safety

•I was prevented from completing my statutory professional duties as required by the General Dental Council (GDC) and Care Quality Commission (CQC).

•The Perfidious report dated December 2015 appeared likely to be deliberately concealing what I'd reported in my previous disclosures.

•I hadn't received an update on any of the complaints to date and it appeared likely to be a deliberate action to conceal what I had reported in my previous disclosures.

•The IT teams report failed to address or resolve any of the concerns I had raised and again seemed likely to be a deliberate attempt to conceal my previous disclosures.

After the Monty Python Sketch meeting on **8th April 2016** Head of Human Resources, Wily, e-mailed me on the **17th May 2016**. He had arranged a grievance hearing for me with someone high-up in the University. Mr High-up was called the investigating officer (IO). I was expecting some sort of fancy Poirot like detective, but instead I got a man who wasn't medically or dentally trained. The hearing took place on **25th May 2016.** It seemed a bit odd for The Icon to appoint an investigating officer who had no experience of dentistry. Wasn't it obvious he would struggle to contextualize the content of the concerns he had to address? How naive I was. I hadn't realised at the time but this was one of the defining moments when The Icon was shedding a dry scaly skin to reveal the underlying mechanics of an Iconic Machine which had been set on a deliberate course to exhaust me. On the upside I could tell the investigating officer was a 'high-up' because he had the radiant reddish glow of a man who'd recently been basking in the French Riviera but more so because he kept his wrap-round sunglasses on his head for the entire hearing.

The hearing turned out to be one big tedious and frustrating exhaustion exercise, everything I uttered I then had to define and explain. Despite the tedium I accepted that if this was what was necessary for improvement to happen, then so be it. (Silly me). After I'd spent longer than Dr. Johnson defining words Wily made some summary remarks to bring the hearing to a close. He then made a flinty eyed promise that I'd receive an outcome letter after Mr High-up had completed his investigation and no later than the **1st June 2016.** What interested me most at the time is that this would give high-up exactly 4 working days to conduct all his investigations and interview all the individuals who were involved. How efficient is that.

Nothing arrived, so on the **26th June 2016** I requested a copy of the minutes to the meeting. When I got them, unfortunately, any mention of The Iconic Machines failings had been removed; the minutes had been wiped clean. I had the sense to contact Wily immediately and I supplied him with a copy of the notes I had made during the meeting. It was lucky that I had made those otherwise no one would have known what had happened. Throughout June and the beginning of July I contacted the Wily on a further five occasions to remind him I was still waiting for the outcome letter. He acknowledged my correspondence and reassured me he was not ignoring me. By ignoring me.

Once again, nothing arrived; so on the **18th July 2016** I wrote to Mr High-up directly and informed him I still hadn't received the outcome of the investigation into my grievance. Whereupon I was told by a new HR officer that Wily had retired and had somehow forgotten to send me the outcome letter. The new HR supplied me with a copy of it, at my request. It was indeed dated **1st June 2016**. It letter informed me that Mr High-up had decided the words I had used in raising my concerns were ambiguous and as such the leadership team could not have known that I had blown the whistle. Really. The outcome letter also informed me I hadn't complied with the strict terms of communication required by the universities whistleblowing policy. I had not copied my disclosures to the Chairman of the Council; Mr Insightful. So I did what I was advised and escalated my concerns to him on **26th July 2016** and at the same time copied him all the disclosures I had previously made to the leadership team.

Mr Insightful acknowledged my concerns on **4th August 2016** and I received the following e-mail from him:

Dear Dr Ahmed

Information Disclosure (Whistleblowing)

I am writing further to your email of 26th July 2016, in which you raise the issue of whistleblowing and name a number of staff within the Dental Institute in relation to an information disclosure.

As the Designated Officer, I have decided to appoint a reviewer to investigate the matters you have raised under the College's Whistleblowing Procedures.   In order to assist the conduct of an investigation I would be grateful if you could provide a concise written statement of your specific and outstanding concerns to augment the folder of documents you have sent me.   This statement should capture the key points of concern ideally in no more than 350 words.   Your statement should aim to focus the investigation on the key issues about which you are concerned, so it is important that you are as direct and specific as possible in the way in which you characterise these concerns.   It is also important that you frame your statement in a way that is consistent with the provisions of the Information Disclosure (Whistleblowing) procedure. I have attached a copy of the Procedure for ease of reference.

As you have already provided a lot of relevant written material in the folder of documents, it would be helpful if your written statement referenced specific incidents, as well as dates, times, names of witnesses etc. in relation to specific documents contained in the folder of documents. In this way the reviewer may investigate your concerns efficiently and accurately. I would be grateful if you could send this short statement to me by the 31st of August 2016.

I have commenced the process of appointing a reviewer to conduct the investigation. I will contact you as soon as possible after I am in a position to confirm this appointment.

Thank you for your earlier messages and the documentation I received yesterday. I can assure you that the matters you have raised will be treated with great care under the Whistleblowing Procedure. If you have any further queries please don't hesitate to contact XX in HR who is performing the role of case manager.

Yours sincerely

Mr Insightful

In accordance with his request I sent him the following summary on **20th August 2016**:

Dr Hafeez Ahmed   Outstanding Concerns 19-08-2016.

The concerns I have raised describe illegal, dangerous, unacceptable, corrupt, not fit for purpose, incompetent, professionally negligent and bullying activity. Sadly none of the concerns that I have raised and presented in the bundle of documents has been addressed or resolved.

Patient management and treatment was compromised and the patients who attended clinics dated 11-09-2015, 18-09-2015, 25-09-2015 plus patients listed in (60-78) need to have their case notes formally investigated, amended and formally reported as there was insufficient time for me to validate what the inexperienced students had written; (1-13). In all cases the patient notes made prior to these clinics were woefully inadequate.

Student learning has been compromised and students continue to observe and be taught poor quality patient management. I have identified staff members, these cases need to be formally investigated and formally reported. (1-13 & 60-78).

As a consequence of the poorly managed clinics the students have developed very little knowledge of self management and very little experience of patient management; (3). Several teaching staff have complained that students who they have failed in exams have been allowed to proceed to successive years without resisting the exams. In 2016 this has resulted in an incident where a tooth was wrongly extracted. Over the same time 3rd and 4th year students have complained about the poor quality of the end of year exams.

Student's remains dissatisfied with the poor quality of teaching, lack of support and the confusing feedback they receive when they identify irregularities in patient care on the clinics. The students have expressed that some of their mental health issues are caused by these events. The students identified (60-78) have not been contacted. This failure in engagement has resulted in further negative self belief and self confidence in the students.

The staff to student ratio remains inadequate for patient management or student teaching. (29-30).

Improvements have not been made to the software as suggested by me (31-33) and acknowledged by Mr Dastardly (30).

The curriculum remains unsuited to the training "safe beginners" as defined by the GDC. (79-80).

Thereafter Mr Insightful remained silent as HR managed the whistleblowing investigation. They got in touch with me on **12th August 2016** to inform me that Mr Insightful had appointed Dr Comprehensive (Dean of Education) as the whistleblowing investigation officer. I contested his appointment on the grounds of him being a member of the leadership team and as such not independent. I pointed out he had previous knowledge in spite of which he had remained silent so far. I was overruled and Dr Comprehensive remained the whistleblowing investigation office.

I only had one meeting with Dr Comprehensive and it took place on **30th September 2016**. My distrust of the leadership team had evolved from a mere suspicion to a resolute maybe perhaps. I was the first to arrive for the meeting and took a seat at the nest of four square tables that had been pushed together to make a larger square in the middle of the room, creating seating for twelve, comfortably. The room had the look, feel and smell of the back office at the local independently run car garage. There were sheets of A4 plain paper covering the small quarter window in the door, with the dry edges of the sellotape peeling at its edges. The wall of venetian blinds was up in places, down in others and somewhere in between in the rest of them. The Human Resources officer arrived next. We sat making polite chit chat about polite people doing polite things in a polite way. Then we chatted politely about how polite people always do polite things in the politest of ways and how other polite people appreciate being treated politely. The politeness continued until Dr Comprehensive arrived. On his arrival the first thing he did was ask the HR officer to step outside for a brief chat. As they left the room he turned back to me and said:

Don't worry, nothing sinister'.

Which I had the sense to translate into:

'Do be so kind to excuse us whilst we have a rather sinister chat about you outside'.

I had become far more confident of my new found ability to translate the language of leadership. Far more confident than I was when I first blew the whistle. During the meeting which lasted approximately forty minutes Dr Comprehensive told me (more than ten times) that I could trust him. I told him that all the evidence was contained in each of the patient's notes and he'd have to report on each of them individually to reveal it. I also told him that the students were still waiting for their concerns to be addressed and that I'd told them someone from the leadership team would contact them to do so.

The meeting carried on with the same pretence of sincerity and when it was over I had developed a very clear understanding of what I had been told by Dr Comprehensive. He had informed me he wasn't independent, he couldn't be trusted, he was going to be sinister and that I should get my armbands on if I wished to avoid being drowned. He was an extraordinarily obsequious piece of work but I felt I had got a good measure of him. His actions reminded me of a joke (I've altered the original):

Question: How do you stop Hafeez from drowning?
Answer: By taking your foot off his head!.......boom boom
*(I had no idea that I'd be left treading water until **31st January 2017** for the outcome of his investigation or that he'd apply such a*

firm foot to my head whilst shielding himself with the use of championship grade ambiguity)

I'll come back to his whistleblowing report (in which he'd reveal he was Dr Comprehensively Delphic) in a few chapters.

The challenge remained extreme and required more than a surfeit of optimism as I continued to face an entire leadership team. Who stood proudly in front of a silent grazing heard engaged in accidently (or intentionally) crushing the corpses of the student's futures under their hooves. I hadn't anticipated the experience would become so intense and personal but as it had I found myself attempting to maintain my sense of balance (sanity) by leaning in the direction of my faith. I have a strong faith but do not align myself with any religion. My faith, a bit like Genghis Khan, had become the 'Eternal Blue Sky'. I was leaning on my faith because I couldn't find any reasonable argument for or a rational way out of the situation. Could faith help me? Did it hold any answers? Might it calm my mind? It was worth a try.

I was born into a British Muslim family. One which had inadvertently adopted the Christian Catholic doctrine: 'all children are born with the devil inside them and there it stays until it is beaten out'. Not many days passed when my siblings and I weren't having the devil beaten out of us. Thank god for that. In keeping with the rest of the animal kingdom sexual abuse was ripe and rife. Thank trusted uncles – if that's what they were - for that. No surprise then that the shattering disgrace resulted in me being a guest at the local police station (for the first time) when I was only thirteen years old. Nothing serious: drunk, disorderly and a bit of honest – primal scream - vandalism. So there you have it my trust in adults went up in smoke and as it later became evident that is how it would remain for the rest of my life. It sometimes felt as though I was born into the world backwards. Awesome. It appeared to me that 'blowing the whistle' happened when I could no longer tolerate the deceit of adults (wrinkly children).

What I have wondered throughout my life is how and why did the Christian Catholics come up with the doctrine. It seems right to me that they were onto something important and that there was indeed a need for a doctrine. I just don't think that it had anything to do with any devils though. It feels right to me that their observations indicated and suggested that children need a firm (guiding) hand in early life. In my experience the firmness required is slightly more than that which feels intuitively correct. It feels right to me that boys should have their parenting (from birth) provided exclusively by their father at least 40% of the time, by both parents acting together 40% of the time and by their mother alone for the remaining 20%. It feels right to me that girls should have parenting (from birth) provided exclusively by their mother 40% of the time, by both parents acting together 40% of the time and their father alone for the remaining 20%.

It feels right to me if one adopts an alternative approach like let's say the: 'if it moves, fuck it and if it gets pregnant it's time to escape approach' then one should accept what comes ones ways more stoically.

It feels right to me that life starts at birth and if you squander the opportunity to nurture your newborn in the first 'any' number of years you can't claw it back in later years. Children are not born with habits, they form them. They maintain the ones that are not frowned upon or restricted, they become addicted to the ones they associate with pleasure and avoid the ones they associate with pain. For the most, concentration is a pain, practical work is a pain, and responsibility is a pain. As wisdom only comes with age they require the firm hand of a sage until they reach age. In my experience the early years are the most important and parents only have until their children are 14 years old to have any influence at all. It works best if parents do firm parenting until the child reaches 14 and then for them to slowly slip into the supportive friendship role.

It feels right to me that the three waves of feminism we have had as far, along with the Athena Swann initiative combined with the current #me too movement should be used to create the environment in which mothers and fathers can better realise their children's needs.

It feels right to me that nobody should be compelled to adopt any given doctrine or regime as it defies the organic nature of independent existence. That said, whatever doctrine or regime one selects for oneself one should be far more stoic about the outcomes of one's choice(s). What has always surprised me and continues to surprise me are the reactions of parents when their children reach adolescence. They behave as though they have no idea how their child could possibly have turned out as useless as they have. They immediately start describing a list of possible reasons; looking in the mirror is almost always missing from the list.

My early life experiences resulted in me describing myself, at about the age of 44, using the word atheist. Yep it takes a long time to step out from under the shadow of indoctrination. Atheism lasted for about two years before I realised I needed more than pure science and knowledge. It seemed too sterile and inorganic, so I swapped to using the word agnostic for a while until ultimately I replaced it (for the final time) with 'Eternal Blue Sky'. I believe in the entity of a creator but do not believe in any of the creator's worldly manifestations, when the need arises I look to the sky and remain comfortable with the support it provides. I ended up relying on that part of my faith which tells me 'what goes around comes around'. It worked for me as it holds a potential for a happy ending and prospects of happy endings offered me respite and provided some assistance with which I continued to endure aspects of the ongoing injustice, frustration and resentment. Each time I recited: 'what goes around comes around' I entered a short period in which I successfully dismissed my unhappy thoughts and experiences.

Whilst we are on the subject of communication there is one which sticks in my mind. It happened eleven years ago in 2008, and is still as sharp as a butcher's cleaver between my shoulders (which happened to be on my back). Nothing to do with The Icon. This one had to do with an entirely different almost identical Icon in another part of the country. Professor Iain Chapple, then Head of the gum department at the Birmingham Dental Hospital slandered me to Dr Ashley Davenport by telling him:

'Hafeez is dangerous you should stop referring patients to him'

Wowza.....back in 2008, Dr Davenport, whom I had only known professionally for approximately two years at the time, had referred a patient to me. He asked me to assess his patient and consider taking over the periodontal treatment. He had become concerned that despite his patient having been under the care of the gum department at the Dental Hospital since 2003 there had been little improvement in his condition. The patient's symptoms were on the increase and tooth loss appeared inevitable.

I assessed his patient and he did indeed have an advanced form of gum disease with extensive bone loss. Some teeth were going to fall out soon. The patient told me he was disappointed with the Dental Hospital because its staff at had informed him his gum disease had been resolved. He repeatedly asked me why after more than 5 years of professional care his condition remained so advanced. I wrote a report in which I made my recommendations for further treatment and in it, to address his concerns, I listed the sequence of appointments he told me he had attended at the Dental Hospital. I was careful to leave out any observations or judgments about the previous care as I didn't know what had been said or done. I couldn't have made any judgments as I had no idea what the patient's original presentation had been five years earlier. However the dates didn't look right so I included them. In the weeks after his appointment with me the patient returned to the Dental Hospital and shared the report with Professor Chapple and used it to support his expression of dissatisfaction in the advice and care he had received from his department.

I was unhappy that Professor Chapple had slandered me so I arranged to meet with him. The following week I was sat opposite him in his office. I had known him since 1992. I had to respect the fact that he'd sworn Dr Davenport to secrecy so I didn't mention we had spoken. Professor Chapple told me my report had resulted in the patient complaining to him and how it had taken him some considerable time to calm him down. He told me he disapproved of the fact that I had inserted the dates of the patient's previous appointments at the Dental Hospital into my report. I explained that during my assessment the patient had repeatedly expressed significant dissatisfaction and was difficult to appease. In addition to which his gums looked untreated and there was no indication whatsoever he had been the beneficiary of any care. In light of the patients dissatisfaction it required significant effort on my part to justify the additional treatment making the inclusion of the dates a necessity. And with that I left.

Sometime after our meeting Professor Chapple wrote a report of his own having reassessed the patient. As if by magic the majority of the gum disease had gone away. It appeared that the patient had finally got the message and had made massive improvements to his homecare. Gum disease can resolve spontaneously, it is possible and I've seen it happen. It happens when patients get the homecare spot-on. Spot-on homecare takes 12-15 minutes of detailed disturbance of the gum margins using fine gadgets after a roughly performed clean using a regular toothbrush. Getting patients to change their homecare to the desirable one is hard work and often requires a team of professionals singing from the same hymn sheet. Sadly in my experience most professionals are singing from different hymn sheets plus 'less bad news' opens wallets.

Anyhow it's pretty obvious he knew what he was doing when he slandered me and what he was attempting to cover-up with the distraction of it.

I had an equally shitty experience at a private university called BPP in Birmingham City Centre from which some staff were simultaneously supplying their incompetence to the Birmingham Dental Hospital. I managed a stint of around eight days in 2017 before I could no longer cope with their incompetence or stupidity. Within two days of being there I called for a meeting of the senior staff and informed them alongside the Head of Faculty, what I had witnessed on their clinics was dangerous, illegal and unacceptable. I told their students what I would have told Imani:

'Ask for a refund, try and learn from the experience and move on'

The Head of Faculty was another one of those educationalists who had decided not to register with the GDC and he hadn't treated a living human for over ten years. He was another individual who didn't look inside patient's mouths- he only taught other's how to do it. It wasn't long before I realised he had only employed me to help his department 'get through' a forthcoming GDC inspection-I was to be the mouthpiece and communicator. I wasn't going to sell my soul, or lie, or be involved in of their shit and resigned. The GDC inspection was critical enough for BPP to terminate their hygiene and therapy course. I have no idea what happened to the students. The closure was publicised in The Times Higher Education supplement.*

*https://www.timeshighereducation.com/news/bpp-shuts-dental-course-regulator-raises-safety-concerns

Communication is fundamental to patient care and along the way I have made my own contribution to it as published in the BDJ(Vol: 222 No5 / March 10 2017). The problem with my way of explaining things is it's the polar opposite of what I was told early in my career by a senior warhorse. His advice was: 'things work best if you keep patients in the grey' in my experience his message had travelled further and wider in the profession than mine was likely to.

Imprecise communications are precisely that and some dentists use them with great focus and effect. I'm reminded of this one time when I had to offer some moral support to a dental hygienist who had got herself into a bit of a pickle with a dentist. I was working at a private practice in central London and was sat writing a letter at the computer in my surgery when the practice owner (PO) strolled in, crowing: 'he's in here, let's see if he can help you' the hygienist followed him in looking grief stricken. Head hanging low. The conversation went like this:

PO: She needs your help

Me: Sure, I'm happy to help her

PO: I've got this patient booked in a couple of days for 20 veneers

Me: Yes

PO: The seditionist is already booked

Me: Yes

PO: The patient wants to cancel her appointment, because this one has gone and told her that her gums are bleeding and veneers should be done once the gums stop bleeding. I can't believe she's gone and said that. She's made such a mess.

Me: What do you want from me?

PO: I've spoken to the patient and told her she needs to get on and have the veneers done because the appointment is already booked.

Me: But what do you want from me?

PO: The patient has worried me. She's gone and said, she thinks I have given her bad advice so she's told me she's going for a second opinion.

Me: What do you want from me?

PO: I've told her that I agree with her and that the second opinion should be from a gum specialist.

Me: But what do you want from me?

PO: I've booked her in with you for a consultation and I want you to do a thorough examination.

Me: I always do a thorough examination

PO: I mean a proper thorough examination

Me: I always do

PO: I want you to do a careful proper thorough examination

Me: I will

PO: A proper careful thorough examination

Me: I get the feeling you are trying to say something to me

PO: Yes I said a properly careful thorough examination

Me: I will

PO: What will you say do you think?

Me: I'll tell her that it's best to do the veneers if and when her gums stop bleeding

PO: Why?

Me: It's the correct way of doing it

PO: Is that how they are doing it nowadays?

Me: No, it's how they've always been doing it.

PO: Well, I need you to be careful

Me: I will

PO: Are you listening to me?

Me: Yes, I heard every word you said, you want me to do a careful proper thorough examination.

PO: I said, are you listening to me?

Me: Yes, is there something else you want to say to me?

PO: Why are you still standing here, haven't you got work to do?

And with that the hygienist sidled out of the surgery. Head still hanging low.

PO: Do you understand me?

Me: Yes, you want me to do a careful proper thorough examination, if there is something else you want to say to me, please can you use some different words?

After a long strained pause....

PO: I have dug a big hole for myself and all I ask is you don't make it any bigger

Me: I can do that.

I examined the patient and told her that her cosmetic concerns could be addressed with one small white filling on a lower front tooth and it was best done once her gums had stopped bleeding. That's the last I saw of the patient, the incident was never mentioned to me again and I have no idea what she did next. The hygienist remains a friend of mine. I would later learn an adage that drives treatment planning in elite central London practices 'empty the patients wallet before someone else dose'

I've shared the veneer story (and others like) and I remain surprised by the number of people who've shrugged their shoulders and said: 'I'm not surprised; we live in a capitalist world'. Some say it whilst displaying a confident stare but most cannot stop their eyes darting all over the place as they speak, so why the darty eyes? Two reasons come readily to mind. The first is they are probably reminded and embarrassed by something they do in their own line of work which is similar. Secondly (and equally probably) they have convinced themselves they are immune to the same sort of shit happening to them or their loved ones. They rationalise their own behaviour (and that of the veneer dentists) as being the actions of some sort of shrewd businessman. I find it impossible to work out what is wrong with these people? I am not saying that we should sit around in a circle holding hands singing Kum-ba-yah but things aren't going to get any better until a larger number of people stand up for treating others in a way they would wish to being treated themselves. If everyone were to start saying what needs to be said and saying it nicely, there would be a powerful positive change and a revolution in the work place and its markets. The problem at the moment is as soon as one person speaks up, everyone else hides in a cupboard and allows the former to be dismissed only to be replaced from the never ending stream of the moral-free version of the human.

The Inspiration.

I was struggling, of that there was no doubt. My perceptions of The Icon had changed and I had started seeing it for The Iconic Machine it was. The Machine was determined to bury my concerns. Its leadership had intensified the scramble for their survival and it was becoming increasingly apparent that their survival was dependent on my sacrifice. Having failed to investigate or rectify any of my concerns, they committed themselves to a full blown cover-up in the guise of a whistleblowing investigation.

On **Saturday 15th October 2016** (15 days after my meeting with Dr Comprehensively Delphic) Ashley Davenport popped around for a coffee and to see how I was coping. I had already given him a four minute summary of how the meeting had gone on the day it happened. He had come around for the long version. As we sat chatting he said:

The single biggest problem in communication is the illusion that it has taken place.

I was intrigued and I wanted to know where he had found it. He told me after our previous conversation he was just sat twiddling on Google and came across it. There is no denying that I hate being beholden and was disappointed that the quote had gone to Ashley and not come to me. He might be my best friend but that doesn't change my animalistic reactions.

Of all the quotes in this book this one makes me smile the hardest every time I hear it. By drawing my attention to the topic of communication it compelled me to go back and reflect upon all the previous ones; on and off the record. I went back and looked at them again; I rewound and re-played them again and again. Going back over the old footage with a renewed prospective highlighted and illuminated the various corruptions of communication which had occurred before my enlightenment. It was ironic that the leadership teams accusation was I had communicated badly when all along my concerns were about the poor communication the woefully inadequate provide.

Despite having researched George Bernard Shaw back in Chapter 1 I did some more. This time I ended up discovering the 1964 movie version of the musical 'My Fair lady' which was inspired or perhaps based on George Bernard Shaw's play Pygmalion. I watched the movie 4-5 times in as many weeks. It became my number 1 movie of all time because it offered me my second connection with Ludwig Wittgenstein's assertion that philosophy is a form of linguistic therapy. It offered me more than just linguistic therapy; it offered me......... a whole new book.

Back at The Icon the diction couldn't have been more contra; as in contradiction. The concerns I had raised were basic and elementary. They were pure and simple yet the most senior members of the leadership team claimed they couldn't have known I'd blown the whistle. Really. Perhaps they might reflect on that in their retirement years. For now, if true, their approach implies that perhaps the adult human brain lacks full development and requires the constant assistance of a sign language person. Something I didn't believe for a minute as the pretence had become as obvious as a whole bunch of other millennial pretences. It was as obvious as the pretence of 'oh my god' you're kidding me there's really a hole at the top back of my legs from which brown stinky stuff pours out of. My parents never told me that hole was called my arsehole. My parents only told me to spray it with flowers from a can. My parents never told me the brown stuff was called shit or that I was biologically engineered to take the goodness out of everything I consumed to turn it into shit. My parents never told me I was the processing plant that turned goodness into shit. My parents certainly never told me not to flick my shit onto others. My parents only ever told me I was 'an angel' and that's why I now live in the clouds.

I had (since the beginning of the experience) become suspicious of a peculiar strangeness in the writing style adopted by the leadership team of The Icon, now my senses had been alerted so I continued to research. It appears harmless and twee but it's downright sinister. I came to describe the technique as 'hiding in plain sight'. There's two ways turd rollers apply the technique, both are corruptions of the fact that seeing or reading a chunk of text is not the same thing as understanding it.

G K Chesterton's literary character father Brown offered me a valuable insight into some crafty writing techniques; father Brown asked:

"Where does a wise man hide a leaf? In the forest. But what does he do if there is no forest? He grows a forest to hide it in."

Their writing was particular in places, precise in others but overall managed to create an effect similar to a dog chasing its tail; it travelled round in a circle and went nowhere.

The In the forest part involves stating the facts and the truth –honestly – in a continuous sequence of four or five sentences and then in the sixth sentence making a statement of conclusion which contradicts the aforementioned facts. This works because invariably during the early stages of internal disciplinary investigations the reader only reads and acts upon the conclusion. The reader who is almost always from an unrelated discipline relies on the conclusion for two reasons. The first of which is laziness which results in them speed reading and the second is they are not clinically trained. Thus the reader comes to the wrong conclusion in plain sight of the truth; as intended by the writer by which the whistleblower is neutralised. The technique offers protection to the wrongdoer as should the same document end up in experienced hands (as happens when the employer fails to dispose of the whistleblower internally and the case gets referred to an external regulator) it allows the employer to state: 'but I gave you the facts'. Genius. It all gets even more cloudy because most of, if not all the staff working for the regulator are not clinically trained and have no experience of working on clinics or treating patients.

The He grows a forest to hide it in is when a report is deliberately padded out with unnecessary information (by using a hundred words when one would suffice) so that the reader misses the important facts. Or simply by obfuscating or writing in a way that makes it difficult to understand what is being said. In my case the obfuscation used by The Icon portrayed it as having acted carefully, caringly and thoroughly whilst distracting the reader from the key hard points.

It would later become apparent that the peculiar writing style had not only been adopted by the leadership team of The Icon but by practically all the staff at all the other 'turd rolling' organisations. They all seemed to have attended the same writing school, which I seemed to have missed out on. They'd adopted the written version of rolling turds in glitter.

The corruptions of communication are not new their existence was recorded by **Winston Churchill** in his statement:

'The English never draw a line without blurring it'

There was nothing I could do about the information being 'blurred' and 'hidden in plain sight' but being able to recognise it taking place allowed me to change my point of view and attitude.

I don't think for a minute that I had communicated badly but now that we are on topic, communication difficulties are well known in sufferers of autism (and in my opinion in one way or another we are all on what is called the autistic spectrum). They too, just like the students at The Icon, are being let down badly by the educational system; actually they suffer more. Something which was highlighted to me by: **The Reason I Jump: One Boy's Voice From The Silence Of Autism** by Naoki Higashida who offered me an insight into his version of the condition. His depiction and the words he used to tell his story allowed me to improve my previous thoughts, views and understanding. He described a true neurological disorder in a way I could connect with it. His conviction to be heard could easily be measured by the fact that he wrote a whole book describing it. The book was more meaningful to me than the comments of the psycho-social scientists (who consider themselves as the experts to understand the condition). To me their classification of the assumed Autistic/ Aspergic situation appeared more of a fashionable classification (see Duplessis Orphans).

Some groups have pointed the finger at the contraceptive pill, others at the caesarean delivery, others at the amount of antibiotics being pumped into the food chain. Some becoming convinced that it's linked to vaccinations. They seem incapable of doing the 'joined-up-thinking' required to realise that the condition is most probably a combined effect of today's culture on a genetically driven characteristic which has been with the race since its inception. One reason I'm not convinced with their speculations is because human madness and oddness has stretched throughout history from the dawn of time to the present day and that's exactly how it's likely to remain in our life-time. Nothing has changed since time, immemorial and scientists have merely invented more labels to describe things. I would argue that labeling individuals is a great way to lump ones with similar characteristics together but if they are then changed to fit in with everyone else this will result in the loss of large chunks of tomorrows talent. It seems right to me that the Autistic/ Aspergic spectrum attempts to describe madness or oddness which when nurtured brings out specific talents and often geniuses. Both ends of the spectrum offer a different contribution to society with those at the lower end of it offering love, diligence, graft and labour whilst those at the higher (Aspergic) end of it offer a commercially preferential one. Human madness is probably the wrong word but whatever it is it needs to be celebrated more and criticised less. Especially since the man who first identified the high functioning individuals Hans Asperger said:

'It seems that for success in science and art, a dash of autism is essential'

It's clear to me that nowadays instead of nurturing the potential talents of the odd ones they are instead being systematically destroyed by the current educational systems, effectively marginalising them out.

I was learning……..

I was learning that my approach to communication was causing the leadership team some considerable discomfort. They would have preferred it if I had stuck to their unwritten rule by raising my concerns quietly, verbally and off the record to my line manager, Dr Available, or the Head of Department, Dr Perfidious, whilst tucked away in a recess or a corridor. This would have allowed them to identify me as having morals which were incompatible to The Iconic Machines business. If I had done so it would have allowed them to stitch me up – consensually – and turf me out preventing a whistle blow. As it was I had slipped past their first radar and now they'd have to catch me in other traps. Trap 2 was to discredit me. Trap 3 was to exhaust me and trap 4 was to get me dismissed. It's ironic that none of these techniques are taught at school or college or university, unless you've been to the likes of Eton.

I was learning that I had caught the leadership team off-guard by breaking their rule of communication and they might be feeling the pinch like the French army did during the Battle of Agincourt in 1415 when they were caught off-guard by the British army. England secured a major victory over them by breaking the rules of the time. Serfs (regular soldiers) could only fight opposing serfs and noble men could only fight the opposing nobles. If a nobleman was captured by either side he wouldn't be harmed. He would be held and swapped for other captive nobleman at the end of the battle. The English serfs (at the request of their nobles) not only fought French serfs they fought French noblemen and they killed them. The muddy conditions came in handy. Once a nobleman was knocked off his horse the serfs rolled him onto his front and suffocated him in the mud with a helpful foot on the back of the head. This handed the English their victory and the battle is now recorded somewhat differently by the two sides. The French felt so humiliated that they have almost entirely deleted it from their national history whilst the English have attempted to write out their deceit. Having been caught off-guard the likes of Dick Dastardly were attempting to change history with his 'cleaning the scene of the crime scene' (back in chapter 1). These techniques appear to be used exclusively by senior staff who expects a subordinate who they've recently bullied and victimised to be too frightened to challenge their superiority.

I was learning I had been right to follow my gut feelings as they were faster and stronger than any feelings my brain might have in the immediate event. Like when Dr Comprehensively Delphic had said: 'don't worry, nothing sinister', my gut feeling had been rapid, accurate, valid and true; whilst my brain sat chewing it over.

I was learning that gut feelings can only be developed through first-hand experiences and not through reading books.

'The only valuable thing is intuition'

Albert Einstien

For me, anxiety is not a gut feeling. Gut feelings are rapid reactions to immediate situations whilst anxiety is the lingering doubt of inexperience.

'Always trust your gut instinct. It knows what your head has not figured out yet'.

Romie Mushtaq

I was learning we are all blessed (from birth) with intuitive gut feelings (ready to be nurtured) but they are slowly hammered out of us by the 'tin-can' nature of the schooling system. I was in dismay when I read, not too long ago, an advertorial in the Sunday Times promoting a government backed course. The course which was being hailed as a major success was teaching young adults how to 'read a face' and 'shake a hand'. It might be an ingenious, entrepreneurial response to the current situation but my gut feeling was that it's better to design a schooling system which doesn't remove the natural born skills in the first pace.

I was learning humans will soon be described as the cancer of the earth. I am sure of it. The other thing I'm sure of is that tomorrows geniuses are today's odd individual's (the Autistic Aspergic's; or whatever they'll be labeled next). Why wouldn't they be? They have been throughout history. Since the dawn of time the vast majority of inventions and innovations have come about due to odd minded men sat tinkering with their thoughts in a garden shed. That's right odd minded men, not odd minded woman as it has almost always been men. If you don't agree try and look for examples of the inventions made by woman other than Stephanie Kwolek who gave us Kevlar and Hedy Lamar the Austrian born American film actress whose early work resulted in the invention of GPS.

I was learning that I find it impossible to ignore the fact that so many innovations came about as the result of errors. That it was the passion (and not reason) of the innovator that resulted in the deciphering of the errors. Penicillin, insulin, chemotherapy, plastic, the pacemaker, even the slinky; all resulted from errors. Even helicopters are attributed to a Russian man who was trying to improve the performance of his vacuum cleaner. It's impossible for me to ignore (that contrary to the evidence) we have been left with modern universities and pharmaceutical companies by a marketing industry falsely plugging exaggerated virtues of structured science. The British economist **William Stanley Jevons** said in 1874:

'The errors of the great mind exceed in number those of the less vigorous one'

I was learning from about Chapter 2 onwards that I regret not having read any philosophy earlier in my life and how this was my own stupidity. Having read a truck load of it and feeling enlightened I'd formed the following opinion (with some confidence):

'of all the animals in the animal kingdom none is as stupid as the human'

It's only right that some of you will disagree with me but please don't confuse power and greed with lack of stupidity. Based on averages 50% of you are likely to agree with me, of the remainder, 10% of you will be incandescent and stamping your feet. The reason you're stamping your feet is because in your heart of hearts you know I'm right? If you're not convinced, you could Google the comments made by Professor Maciej Henneberg. He has opined that "Animals offer different kinds of intelligences which have been under-rated due to humans' fixation on language and technology."*

*https://phys.org/news/2013-12-humans-smarter-animals-experts.html

I was learning that to maintain confusion the story of World War 1 appeared to be deliberately shrouded in a sense of complexity. My summary of it may help you demystify your understanding of the stupidity as it makes the greed and power more visible. Here's the summary: 'World War One was a family feud'. Kieser Wilhelm in Germany got upset when his two cousins King George in England and Tsar Nicholas in Russia stopped inviting him to the annual family boat race. Wilhelm got his knickers in such a twist that he decided to destroy his cousin's empires. His campaign included his agents inciting the Muslims in each of the empires to turn on their Christian rulers. Then it all kicked off when Franz Ferdinand got assassinated. When you understand the war in these simple terms it's easier to identify the obvious greed, power and stupidity. Here's another stupid thing, one of the biggest satirical questions of modern time still remains, who won World War 2?

I had learnt previously in Chapter 1 that we humans resist the notion that our preset worldview might be faulty, incomplete, or dangerous and due to this trait you may still be unconvinced by my earlier statement. For those who remain unconvinced I would be agreeable to replace the stupidity statement with this one:

'of all the animals in the animal kingdom none fucks things up as much as the human'

I am not saying that stupid animals are not born into the other species, they are, everyday. Whereupon they die. In some ways on the odd occasions when success has been achieved by humans, its debt is most probably fate; occurring not because of lack of stupidity but in spite of it.

I was learning, on the topic of stupidity, that people are far more aware of it than they let on. I overheard a couple of my nurses talking and they were certainly aware of it. One had just returned from maternity leave and her friend asked her the following question 'I've heard that when a woman pushes out a baby she pushes out 10% of her own brain at the same time?' 'Yes' came the reply and continued 'that sounds about right, I felt a bit distant after my first baby was born and now I feel a different sort of distance'. She went on to say 'I'm sure that saying ga-ga to my baby all day long is making me ga-ga myself'. I didn't give it much thought as it all sounded about right to me. It tends to explain the differential in the stupidity between men and woman. It does not however explain the stupidity of men. Unless that is explained by the disproportionate exposure they get to their mothers in their early life. Who knows? Whatever the reasons for it denial appears to be an automatic function of the brain.

Decision Making- the Fabric of Life

'If you are going through hell keep going'
Winston Churchill

This quotation offered me an interpretation of endurance which was better matched to the leadership teams hell bent campaign to exhaust me. It enabled me to facilitate my previous decision to harness the freight contained in fear and anxiety. It made it easier for me to resist the leadership team charismatic approaches and gave me a type of inner strength which I was previously lacking.

This quotation came as pleasant surprise on **Sunday 18th December 2016** during a family trip to Blenheim Palace, Winston Churchill's birthplace and family home. It comforted me when hope was fading fast. The impasse was indecision, I could not decide if I should escalate my concerns to the regulator or not. The indecision was being fuelled by my reluctance to go against a system I belonged to, plus my previous negative experiences of the regulator. It settled my nerves, strengthened my resolve and allowed me to continue doing what was right.

In this chapter I will explain the moment I resolved that I was only feeling depressed because of a thing called hope. How hope had fooled me into believing things would get better. I realised I was less likely to have become depressed if I hadn't had hope in the first place. It became necessary to remove hope from the equation so that I could accept that my actions were unlikely to make any positive change. I dropped my expectations of fellow professionals along with the notion of fair play. I developed a very different appetite for adventure. It was time to dodge bullets. Not time for a picnic. I tweaked the objectives behind my decisions to ones of survival alone. After all I was going through hell and I'd have to keep going until I popped out the other side.

The Experience

The cast in this chapter

Leadership team	Given name
Dean of Education	Dr Comprehensively Delphic.
Clinical Director	Dick Dastardly (a nasty devious bastard)
Chairman of the Council	Dr Insightful
Executive Dean of The Icon	Professor Awakened.
Dean of Education	Professor Pinocchio (prone to telling lies)

The story so far........

1. 15th September 2015; whistle blown.

2. 2nd October 2015; Nasty Meeting with Dr Dick Dastardly.

3. 16th October 2015; Incognito Meeting with Professor Pinocchio.

4. 19th October 2015; Dick Dastardly's failed attempt to drown me in IT.

5. 1st Week December 2015; Dr Perfidious tells a bunch of staff 'Hafeez is a liability; I'll have to get rid of him'. (ouch my shoulder blades)

6. 7th December 2015; my expression of grievance to Dr Dastardly about the above.

7. 8th December 2015; IT team produces a report which implicates me as uniquely experiencing the concerns I'd reported. (ouch)

8. 17th December 2015; Dr Perfidious produces a report which implicates me as uniquely experiencing the concerns I'd reported. (ouch)

9. 8th April 2016. Professor Pinocchio & HR failed to re-label my protected disclosures a grievance. (phew)

10. 18th July 2016; Mr high-up concluded the leadership couldn't have known that I had blown the whistle.

11. 4th August 2016; Dr Insightful initiated a formal investigation into my concerns.

12. 30th September 2016; Sinister meeting with Dr Comprehensive.

.....Making decisions is the fabric of life and I was faced with a colossal one. Was I going to escalate my concerns to the regulator?

My dilemma was built on the carcasses of three themes. Firstly, I had set out in the greater good of the patients and students but I was agonised as I did not want to upset a system I belonged to. I did however feel strongly about the problems compromising patient safety and student learning. These needed addressing and I had achieved very little so far so I was compelled to continue going further down the same route.

Secondly, all the decisions I had made thus far had landed me in the hardest, harshest and darkest experiences of my life. I was regretting having blown the whistle, but the sheer scale of the injustice and insult prevented me from buckling under fire. I was trying so very hard not to lose it.

Thirdly, I had reported rogue dentists to the regulator before and the regulator had failed to protect the patients involved. Not just a bit useless but completely useless. The regulator was as capable of protecting patients as I was of convincing Donald Trump to lose the comb over.

I remembered the time back in 2013 when I had to report the Eastman Dental Hospital to the General Dental Council. A member of Eastman's staff to be precise – a patient I referred to them was treated inappropriately and suffered for it. It's a long story which started when a younger dentist who I had known from a previous place of work rang to inform me he had enrolled on the dental implant course at Eastman. He asked me if I'd be prepared to refer some patients to him so he could practice placing dental implants, the patients would be getting the dental implants on the cheap. He requested simple cases and asked me to reassure my patients his work was to be supervised by the course organisers. Reluctantly, very reluctantly I referred a patient to him. My patient asked me 'do you trust him? I told him 'yes, as a human; yes as a dentist; no, as an implantologist.' I reassured my patient that I was making the referral with the understanding the treatment would be supervised by qualified staff at the Eastman.

The staff at the Eastman unfortunately misread my letter of referral and went to town on my poor patient. They thought I'd asked them to treat him as if he were a Resusci Anne manikin*. I had assessed my patient and he was suitable for a simple straight forward implant and as such I'd decided it was appropriate for me to refer him to a novice working under supervision. My patient ended up with an internal summers lift packed with pixie dust and a simultaneous single stage implant placement with the healing collar poking out into his mouth. I had assessed my patient before I had referred him, all he needed was an implant placed into his own natural bone. PING; and just like that the Eastman's implant fell out. Funny that.

*https://www.laerdal.com/gb/doc/2404/Resusci-Anne-QCPR.

My patient asked me to escalate his concerns to them and when I did the staff member at the Eastman was quick to step forward. He very quickly stated that all the treatment planning had been carried out by the student and not by him. My patient wrote to him and pointed out the contradictions, he reminded him it was he (hospital staff) who had made the treatment plan and provided the treatment; it was not the student.

The General Dental Council took a full three years to completely soil the investigation before they ultimately neutralised my patients compliant. After three years of dicking about they were in no position to criticise the Eastman Dental Institute, so they didn't. My poor patient poured scorn on the GDC's pledge to put patients, anywhere, let alone first. The evidence spoke for itself. I have no idea what went wrong at the GDC as I was deliberately kept in the dark. I can only recount the paperwork I did see to cast a partial judgment based on incomplete information. I supported my patient the best I could and wrote to the CEO, Mrs Gilvarry, on two separate occasions to express my concerns. To no avail. Faced with a patient who had been failed by the GDC I contacted the Professional Standards Authority (the official regulator of the regulators; in which fantasy world) and they showed no interest in establishing why my patient had been failed by the Eastman Dental Institute or the General Dental Council. My patient had become a victim of institutional insensitivity and for all they cared he could swing from the trees and lick his own nuts.

During the experience I'd often reflect on something one of my previous consultants had said to me:

'I took a decision early in my career that I wasn't going to let dentistry get me'. At the time I dint know what he meant and asked him to explain, his story was that shortly after he'd qualified he enjoyed reading the editorial page in the British Dental Journal. The author became a sort of role model to him as he presented himself as a balanced, informed and content individual. Then all of a sudden the editorials stopped. It was announced sometime later that the editor had committed suicide, leaving my consultant shocked, surprised and unable to reconcile why the editor had concealed his emotions and had not felt able to reach out for help. Be careful Hafeez he told me, be very careful. Looking back I hadn't realised he had attempted to point out the dangerous nature of the sharks in the tank with me.

I have never understood something I've seen lots of; people dump on each other all day long and then act surprised when they get dumped on, as if they somehow they can't see the links. I'll also never understand how a convicted rapist gets upset when his daughter is raped. To my mind everything is linked to everything else, I find it's really very easy to see. I remember a discussion I had with a female dentist in her mid during a meeting I had organised. I was the branch secretary for the Warwickshire Section of the British Dental Association and the conversation went like this:

Her: Dr Ahmed, I would really like you to speak to my husband.

Me: Is he here? Do I know him?

Her: No, you don't, but he's a dentist. He's at home.

Me: Oh.

Her: He doesn't go out anymore; I am convinced he is depressed!

Me: Oh, why do you think I'm the right person to speak to him?

Her: You are so confident, Dr Ahmed.

Me: Thank you. It's not easy being me. You should tell him to contact his doctor.

Her: He won't go to his doctor.

Me: He should go speak with his doctor.

Her: He doesn't trust his doctor.

Thank God doctors are an honest bunch, but anyway, perhaps her husband really didn't know it's the very same reason patients avoid going to the dentist. I didn't feel flattered by being described as confident because I really regretted my decision to become the branch secretary. My fellow professionals were driving me to distraction with an almost endless stream of selfish (arsehole) behaviours. Here is an example of one that really got my goat.

I was the branch secretary for three years between 2009 and 2011. It was a voluntary unpaid post and I was required to put on six annual postgraduate professional development meetings for the local dentists. Something I didn't mind as I enjoyed all things educational. I managed to organise six meetings each year – eighteen in total. The most the branch has ever enjoyed in its history. To do this I was required to (in my personal time):

- Contact and lobby potential speakers
- Agree a title for their presentation
- Book a venue
- Make and distribute the marketing flyers for the event
- Field the enquiries from the local dentists
- Collect the booking fee from each dentist
- Book a caterer
- Give the caterer some numbers
- Set up the audio-visuals at the venue
- Make and distribute feedback forms for the meeting
- Make and distribute attendance certificates

Most dentists, precious and important, almost always confirmed their intention to attend in the 24 hour period before the meeting. Making catering a nightmare. One particular dentist who talked about his church passionately attended three consecutive meetings. He never once booked. He never paid, not for a single one. He arrived just as the food was laid out, enjoyed the food and presentation before collecting his attendance certificate and disappearing again. Incensed and with my head on fire I could not work out how to out maneuver this weasely turd. So I phoned a friend, much like who wants to be a millionaire, and this is how the conversation went:

Me: How do I get the turd to pay what he owes without resorting to swearing at him?

Friend: Write him a letter and inform him you have suffered an episode of incompetence. Tell him you have misplaced his three payments. Beg him for forgiveness and request he makes another payment for the full amount.

Job Done. I wrote the letter and sent it to Mr Weasely Turd by e-mail. The turd delivered the payment in person the same evening. Arsehole. He attempted to conceal his embarrassment but it leaked out like diarrhoea. Anyhow he was not embarrassed of what he had done. He was embarrassed for having been out maneuvered.

Back at The Icon...there had been no forward movement. It was **December 2016**; sixteen months since I had blown the whistle and nine weeks after the sinister meeting with Dr Comprehensive. Throughout this period I continued to escalate new complaints made by students and patients alike in the same way as before, each time they were made. As they continued to be ignored I had written to the CEO of the NHS trust on **24th October 2016** and raised the same concerns to her. She had got back to me on **23rd November 2016** and informed me my concerns weren't valid as she had been told as much by Dr Comprehensive. She informed me he had told her there had been no problems with patient consent and he had also confirmed patient safety had not been compromised either. But his report wasn't ready. How bizarre. I spoke to some of the students who had complained and they informed me they hadn't heard anything more about their complaint, I did the same with patients, they hadn't been contacted either. I started to wonder what colour his white wash report would be. Thank god that CEO's are an honest bunch.

Then one Friday morning; **16th December 2016** approximately eleven weeks after Dr Comprehensive had informed me he wasn't independent, he could not be trusted and he was going to be sinister. I clocked him in the distance coming towards me as I entered a clinic. He walked towards me almost cartoonish and was distracted looking sideways so hadn't seen me enter. By the time he saw me it was too late he was upon me and we were practically dancing cheek to cheek. That's when everything went into comedy slow motion. His body crumpled inwards as he tried to stop it colliding with mine, with his elbows shooting out at the sides. As he struggled with the demanding halt process his shocked face failed to conceal the micro expressions of his brain as it leaked out: 'oh my god why didn't I spot him earlier, it's too late for me to duck out now' as he clumsily spluttered 'yes, yes, I am waiting for the report too, it should be ready any day now'. His crumpling body had parp-ed out some back-end air or he was taking part in some sort of halitosis study; you know the ones where participants are required not to clean their teeth for a while. As the gaseous concoction mounted an assault on my senses he stopped trying to halt himself and instead gave himself a wallop of energy up a calf, and skirmished past me turned sideways and shot straight out the door like an out of control Bouncing ball. Ping Ping Ping gone. There was no hello Hafeez and no handshake.

My guts immediately wrapped themselves around the lack of a hello and the missing handshake. That's all it takes for the formation of immediate gut feelings, no hello and no handshake. It isn't rocket science and gut feelings rarely require complexity or difficulty or intricacy to respond. My gut knew something was wrong, but what was it? How bad was it going to be? What did he mean when he said 'I am waiting for the report too.' Why had he assumed that was going to be my first question? Why was he waiting for something he was supposed to be writing? Was it possible he had run out of parchment and was waiting for a cull? Maybe the hawk had taken back its quill? Or could it just be that Human Resources were putting the final touches to it to make it the best possible stitch-up it could be? No surprise that I suspected the latter.

At the end of the very same day the funniest thing of the entire experience happened. I was stood at the lifts waiting for a friend. She was getting changed and we had planned a quick trip to Bombay (code for a trip to the bar). As I stood there the doors to the furthest lift on my left opened. Standing in the back left hand corner of the lift was Dr Dick Dastardly. He was in my direct line of sight. I could see him clearly. Head like a panther, his mouth crowded with teeth, eyes wide in burning disbelief that I was stood looking at him or perhaps just constipated. Whilst I was still looking at him he slowly disappeared out of sight; sideways. I couldn't believe what I was seeing he literally did a crab-walk and moved his upright body sideways to the opposite corner of the lift and moved himself out of my sight. As funny as it was I knew that this meant something super sinister and shitty was happening at that very moment; right at that precise moment. Why else would he be unable to look at me or have me looking at him. His brain had moved him out of my sight because it couldn't cope with his deceit and dishonesty. I was a dead man walking. I can't deny that I found his crab-walk hilarious especially since he was the self anointed bad-ass bastard bully boy; this was the surest confirmation that bullies are hard shelled wimps and I stick to the advice I gave you back in Chapter 2 on dealing with them.

I felt the heat on my arse and knew I had to act before whatever fuse they had lit detonated.

I had made my decision within three days and on **20th December 2016** I informed the leadership team by e-mail; I'd be escalating my concerns to the regulator. Here is an excerpt from it:

No single aspect and no single element of the university's actions, so far, demonstrate they are taking the issue of my whistleblowing seriously.

If the university were taking my whistleblowing seriously:-

1.The investigation would have completed and we would not be in correspondence at this time.

2.The leadership staff at the university/dental institute would not have advised the CEO of the trust that patient safety has not been compromised; prior to concluding their investigations.

3.The leadership staff at the university/dental institute would not have deliberately mislead the CEO of the trust, by advising her that patient safety had not been compromised; prior to concluding their investigations.

4.Some action would have been taken to remedy the causes of the concerns that I have raised. However no actions have been taken and no change has occurred at the clinic level since I first raised my concerns.

5.The Chairman of the Council would have made enquiries when the investigating officer failed to complete his investigation by the given date; that being end of November 2016.

In light of the above and the fact that we still do not have a definitive date for the completion of the investigation there is no option but for me to make contact with the General Dental Council, which I will be doing immediately after the holiday season.

On the **26th of January 2017** I escalated my concerns along with those of the patients and students to the General Dental Council. I have pasted a copy of the letter I sent below; I have made no alterations to it other than to anonymise it:

26th January 2017.

Dear General Dental Council; Fitness to practice & Standards for education Committee.

I have raised some concerns via the whistleblowing pathway at The Icon. The concerns that have been raised are in the accompanying document file. The document file is 182 pages in total.

The areas of concern raised include:-

1. Patient safety
2. Patient harm

3. Negative impact on and compromise to the standards of education of the undergraduate students in respect to integrated restorative care and more specifically periodontal care.

I have attached to this letter 2 documents from the document file. These 2 documents give an overview of the situation so far. The documents are:-

1.   A copy of the summary which I prepared on the 19th August 2016 at the request of Dr Insightful; the Chairman to the council at The Icon.

2.   A copy of an e-mail dated 20th December 2016 to the new Chairman of the council of The Icon; a new Dr Insightful.

Reporting this situation to the GDC has not been an easy decision but the internal investigating officer has been unable and or unwilling to conduct a credible independent investigation. This is now a matter for the GDC to investigate. Please can you investigate. In the document file there are approximately 22 patients identified. Some patients have been managed inappropriately and some have suffered harm. The patients who have suffered greatest harm and need to be contacted as a matter of urgency are:-

1.Hospital Number 5745155S; page 61 of the document file.

2.Hospital Number 5058960J; page 71

3.Hospital Number 5933022Z; page 126

4.Hospital Number 1584057X; page 130

5.Hospital Number 5908102G; page 131

6.Hospital Number 5951085Z; page 133

I remain happy to assist you with your investigations as you feel necessary.

Kind regards

Dr Hafeez Ahmed.

The **31st of January 2017** was particularly cold and harsh. Dr Insightful sent me an outcome letter for the whistleblowing investigation in which he informed me of his decision. He told me he had read the whistleblowing report prepared by Dr Comprehensive and that he agreed with it. He told me my concerns had not been upheld as they were not valid and that I should not raise any more similar ones. That he preferred suspenders over tights. He told me his decision was final and there was no further avenue for me to appeal it within the university. It was unfortunate but Dr Insightful was behaving more like Dr Magoo and as he hadn't sent me a copy of the whistleblowing report I had no idea what was in it, so I requested a copy. (Mr Magoo was a famous 1950's fictional cartoon character who was easily blinded and rarely accountable. His extreme near sightedness was compounded by his stubborn refusal to admit the problem).

I suspected I already knew why I hadn't been sent a copy of the report, because it was sinister and a pack of lies, but I needed to know how sinister and what kind of lies. It's important to remember that there had already been two reports, One by Dr Perfidious and the other by the IT team; this report was the trilogy. Both previous reports had independently reached the same conclusion, that I was uniquely experiencing all the concerns I'd raised. Given that Dastardly had failed to bully me into silence and the previous reports hadn't prevented me submitting new protected disclosures meant Dr Comprehensive would have had to have taken a different approach but what had it been?

Dr Comprehensive's whistleblowing report was whiter than the foam suds one washes ones car with. It was a brazen whitewash so I'll be referring to it as the soap-sud report. He opened with an introductory disclaimer that he didn't know anything about gums. It was not his field; as if gums are not in the mouth. It was important for him to pretend that he had insufficient knowledge or expertise, how else could he avoid being accused of perjury or deceit at some later date. Dr Comprehensive absolutely revealed himself to be Dr Delphic. He had crafted his report using 'hide in plain sight' as described in Chapter 5 and two other techniques I'd experienced before, being:

•Applying a thumb to the scales

•Shining a torch

Applying a thumb to the scales. In the old days - not now – the greengrocer would discreetly apply his thumb to the scales, charging you for more grocery than he was supplying you with. He applied his thumb sufficiently away from your line of vision, whilst keeping you distracted. You left believing you'd been charged correctly for your groceries. He smiled on and bid you farewell like an honest grocer does. Dr Delphic had applied his thumb to the scales and he had tipped them towards 'a potential breakdown' in my relationships with my colleagues. The leadership team needed to make it look as if they'd had to suspend and dismiss me because of a breakdown in their relationship with me and not because I had blown the whistle. Yes ma'am, that's how you do it. So there you have it Delphic's report was structured to implicate me as the potential cause of a breakdown in relationship when the reality was the other way round, they had commenced a personal attack on me and I'd merely defended myself. (How lucky was I that I had escalated to the GDC five days earlier).

Shining the torch. A very different deception technique. Imagine you are in a large dark room, the lights are off and you are armed with a torch. You can only see what your torch illuminates. Homicide detectives would tell you that it's not a clever or efficient way to examine the crime scene. The best way to do that would be to put all the lights on so the whole room becomes fully illuminated enabling you to see everything and allowing you to glance across the whole room. Delphic took the approach of leaving the lights off and shining his torch. He shone his beam on positive statements about The Iconic Machine and suggestively negative statements (nothing too obvious) about me; it's known as calumny.

They neutralised all the concerns by blaming it all on the transition from paper records to electronic ones. His report stated the exact opposite of the previous ones and ignored the fact that Perfidious and the IT team had previously identified me as uniquely experiencing the concerns I'd raised. Delphic reported that whilst other members of staff were struggling to record their notes adequately on the software or paper, I was not. He described my notes as 'very comprehensive'. How can it be possible that the IT team looked at the same material as Delphic and concluded that I was the only staff member struggling to use the software when Delphic concluded the exact opposite? How is it possible for an entire leadership team to somehow fail to identify this contradiction?

Delphic's report staggered around like a drunkard in a poorly light alley with piss on his pants. He acknowledged that making notes using the software was slower than making paper notes. He didn't however do the joined-up-thinking required for him to conclude that this means more time is needed to be allocated for it on the clinics.

Unfortunately, he did not contact or report specifically on any of the patients who had made complaints and were the subjects of my disclosures. (Oversight or convenience).

Unfortunately, he did not contact any of the thirty or so students I'd named in my disclosures; the same students who had complained bitterly about poor educational practices. (Oversight or convenience).

I informed the leadership team on **2nd February 2017** that I'd escalated my concerns to the regulator. Here's an excerpt from the e-mail:

I have a professional obligation and a duty of care to patients and the undergraduate students. I am pleased that I have had the opportunity to fulfill both of these by expressing my detailed concerns and protected disclosures via the whistleblowing pathway; I have fulfilled my professional obligations and duty of care in doing so.

The Chairman of the council has advised me of his decision and he has supplied me with a copy of the investigation report. I accept his decision which he has informed me is final and there is no further way of appeal within the University.

His decision and the investigation report do not change the concerns I have raised. The patient cases that have been identified need to be investigated independently. I have now, reluctantly and with regret, forwarded my concerns to the General Dental Council and requested an independent investigation.

There is a gross inaccuracy in the investigation report. The inaccuracy is on page 8 paragraph 3, which reads....... (this bit of torch shining was covered in chapter 2).

I had anticipated the leadership team might feel embarrassed and maybe even threatened by the serious concerns I'd raised, but I couldn't understand what prevented them from taking positive actions to start turning things around. Once they'd embarked in the direction of obfuscating and burying my concerns it appeared that they couldn't back down. In return for the fact that I had blown the whistle, they'd embarked on a deliberate process to discredit me. I became well aware of being a target of their vengeance. Once rankled they seemed so sure of destroying me by virtue of their seniority that they never really made any kind of effort to address my concerns. (What I hadn't anticipated and would not learn until after my dismissal was they were already aware of the concerns I'd raised because some of the students had raised the same concerns directly to them. Copies of the student's complaints were leaked to me around **April 2018** approximately three months after my dismissal).

So there you have it. I'd shaken the freak tree and the freaks had started to fall out. In two of my disclosures I had named a consultant Professor and highlighted his failings as: 'circumnavigating his professional duties' and 'professional negligence'. To avoid facing justice he resigned his membership with the General Dental Council and became an educationalist. He was no longer a dentist, he was an educationalist. I hadn't realised until this event that dentists are only required to register with the General Dental Council for the purpose of looking inside a patients mouths. It came as a surprise to me that they didn't have to be registered to teach others how to look inside patients mouths. Sounds like pantomime season again. Everyone has their own view of what independence is and his was that he was untouchable. He didn't have to face justice. He was far too important for that. The rules didn't apply to him. How ungallant and a bit like the man who hangs about by the bins round the back of McDonalds wearing his wife's clothes.

The Titanic had hit the iceberg and it was taking on water. Time to get off. First to go was Professor Awakened the Executive Dean. She had revealed herself to be more of a Sleeping Beauty; she opened her eyes, paused to yawn, and resigned. She could no longer muster up the energy required to sustain doing nothing. She called time and stepped off shortly after Delphic had started his deliberately vague and ambiguous investigation. How strange, she'd resigned only months after renewing her contract, having extended it for a further four years. She didn't move a muscle. I learnt later, much later, from information supplied to me that Dastardly had asked her to take responsibility for handling my concerns but she had bounced it back on him. 'Talk about going round in circles' he squawked in his e-mail.

Those who thought we were in some sort of austerity were wrong. The president was alive and well. But he didn't respond to my letter of complaint, or my request for a grievance. He stayed out of site, hiding like a Jessie during a brawl in the roughest pub in Glasgow.

The concerns I had raised seemed to offer some explanation for the findings described in an article I read *'The Standard of Newly Qualified Dental Graduates – Foundation Trainer Perceptions'** which appeared in the British Dental Journal volume 222, pages 391–395 (10 March 2017). I'll be referring to it as the newly qualified's study.

*https://www.nature.com/articles/sj.bdj.2017.226

The studies authors stated:

'There would appear to be a disconnect between the educational processes and outcomes of the undergraduate training programmes and the activities that newly qualified graduates are expected to undertake in the situation they find themselves in on qualification.'

It described the general collapse of dental skills amongst newly qualified dentists but it's hardly surprising that it didn't get wider national coverage. The study refocuses ones perception of the phrase 'practicing dentist' to someone who hasn't got it right yet'.

I should explain the training pathway for dentists. Typically, but not always, undergraduate students complete a 4 to 5 year course at a dental school for which the entry requirements are 3 A's at A-level. Upon completion of the course they are recognised as 'safe beginner' by General Dental Council who coined the same term and enter into a period of vocational or foundation training for two years prior to practicing solo. The newly qualified's study records the comments of the vocational trainers at the point at which the beginners are safe to enter into vocational training.

The aim of the study was to assess the changes in perceived standards of newly qualified graduates as reported by their foundation (vocational) trainers. The study was a cross-sectional survey and was conducted using a self-completed internet-based survey tool sent to all foundation trainers (FTs) in England, Northern Ireland and Wales. The results were that a total of 312 responses were obtained covering all postgraduate deaneries. There were mixed opinions regarding standards of new graduates, with 51% of the vocational trainers reporting that the overall standard of those entering foundation training was 'unsatisfactory'.

Standards in key clinical areas were considered to be unsatisfactory by large proportions of the vocational trainers. 85% considered standards to be unsatisfactory in 'crown and bridge'; 75% in 'extraction of teeth'; 74% in root fillings; 67% in dentures; and 62% in treatment planning. Experienced trainers identified a decline in standards in particular clinical areas. The authors concluding comments were that a large proportion of foundation trainers consider the current standard of new graduates to be unsatisfactory for entering foundation training. What the study doesn't mention is that the foundation training programme doesn't offer a rescue plan to address the unsatisfactory nature of the 'safe beginners'.

Reading the study for the first time came as a breath of fresh air, but it was annoying to know that I had not been able to influence a change at The Icon. Its outcomes described the natural progression based on my experience; it's what I would've expected. It confirmed the consequences of the poor educational standards the students had been complaining about. I was reassured   and received some validation and confirmation that I had been doing the right thing and I hadn't gone mad. It didn't stop me feeling lousy when it dawned on me that my vindication (for the clearance of doubt) would require the leadership teams dispute with me to be tried in a legal court; an employment tribunal. What a palaver.

For the first time in a long time I felt good for having felt bad for the students. I felt even better that the leadership team hadn't succeeded in suppressing me and that I had continued to express my concerns. My regrets were skewed towards those students who had a genuine passion to be dentists and less for the ones with purely self absorbed career motives. The passionate ones got my admiration as they clearly wanted to do well for patients; they wanted to be good practitioners and were driven by a sense of personal value. Most of them displayed a desire to express their ability for individual innovation, some as future dentists, some as future business owners and some as future researchers. The study implicated not just The Icon I worked at but all dental schools which suggests that all of them need to accept some responsibility and ask themselves how and why they had let this happen. Perhaps they all needed to appreciate continuing to bury concerns was not a sustainable way forward; that is if the actual objective was training the dentists of tomorrow. If however the objectives are to make the universities postgraduate courses not just desirable but a necessity then the right thing for them to do would be to continue to bury the concerns being raised by the undergraduates.

The study described a 'disconnect' and one explanation for it is the curriculum may no longer be 'fit for purpose'. It seems to me the curriculum is too heavily skewed towards medicine and away from teeth and gums. The skewing started a long time ago in the days when individuals who dreamt of being doctors didn't get into medical school but instead settled for dental school. They had no real desire to be dentists, they craved being important and busy in a doctory sort of way. They meddled with the curriculum and it started to reflect the needs of important doctory types, they appear to have continued to meddle with it rendering it unsuitable for the vocation of dentistry. If dentistry is to recover itself the curriculum will need a reform to put teeth and gums front and centre. The same goes for the hygienist and nurse courses as currently both are diluted homeopathic versions of the dental one.

The egotism has resulted in the training of patient dental care to be fragmented in a way that the students are no longer taught an accurate narrative of the workings of a dental practice in the 'real world'. Somehow the 'real world' is missing from any curricular considerations. The curriculum is designed to promote feelings of self importance as this makes the inflated fees more acceptable to the self absorbed part of the students, who sign up for them. It's become a credentials heavy market place which has already resulted in the credentials having less value. I can't imagine a dental nurse wanting to pay elevated fees to attend a course which trains her about the importance of putting dental materials back in the same drawer she found them? Or the importance of placing an order for replacements just before a current stock of material runs out? Or the need to clean debris off the instruments with any degree of consistency. Never.

Consequently the sausage factories are pumping out poorly trained dentists and hygienists who have studied far more mediciny stuff than they need to but have very little practical experience of teeth and gums. Poorly trained nurses who know far more mediciny stuff than they need, which gives them just enough information to sit around criticising dentists and hygienists all day long. A close friend of mine who used to nurse for me on Saturdays has just completed the hygiene course at the Eastman Dental Hospital. We often chatted about the course and about what she was and wasn't learning. The picture she painted was a spitting image of what was happening at The Icon; and I, regrettably, wouldn't employ any of the hygienists being trained at The Icon. As part of a survey on patient communication I asked the final year trainee hygienists to answer the following question: what is gum disease? The answers were as depressing as they were hilarious.

One interpretation of the newly qualified's study is that after four or five years of training the 'safe beginners' were ready to treat patients who didn't have any tooth decay or gum disease. The interpretation sounds about right to me because it's around about where I was myself shortly after I qualified in 1992. I realised early in my career that I hadn't been a particularly good student or been on a particularly good course. I undertook a lot of post graduate training to get myself out of that hole and I doubt I would be able to afford it at today's prices. Some of the undergraduate students at The Iconic Machine had become suspicious they were being groomed for its postgraduate courses. Their conspiratorial speculation was that the undergraduate course was purposely starved to drum up demand for the postgraduate courses. The undergraduates were working on the misguided presumption that the postgraduate courses were better organised than the undergraduate ones. What the undergraduates didn't know was the postgraduates were complaining just as much as they were. They were right in their realisation though as The Icon's marketing team could have sold the Eiffel Tower to Victor Lustig.

I reckon those students, who had cottoned on, were right as the gatekeepers had let them down. However there were far too few of them to make a difference. The whole thing about self importance and postgraduate courses reminds me of a question I often asked them, 'what is a specialist?' Invariably they would say: 'someone who has undertaken further training to do complex procedures'. I'd tell them 'a specialist is an individual who creates the time and the space in which to do the simple stuff to the highest standards and if the simple stuff is done with consistency to a high standard the complex stuff sorts itself out. The complex evolves from an ignorance of the simple. The problem (as I see it) in dentistry is that everyone (dentists, nurses and hygienist's) is rushing about wanting to do complex important stuff. Each one of them needing to feel more valued than the last one. The hygienist role only came about because the very important dentists thought they were far too important to clean teeth. They were too busy dreaming about being very important doctors. With far too many professionals living in a daydream it leaves no one to do the simple stuff. It's the 'unbearable lightness of being'. That's why they drink so much coffee, so they can do stupid things faster with more energy.

It's very easy to turn the simplicity problem on its head. The correct patient care model would be the one in which patients pay the correct fee for consultation and advice and the correct fee for simple preventative hygienist treatments, but they just don't and won't. Patients don't like to pay for simple stuff but find it much easier to get their wallets out for something that sounds complex or advanced. Patients talk with their feet and they like to go to practices where the routine examination takes eight seconds and a detailed one takes 8 minutes. For me the simplest of consultations takes approximately 30-45 minutes and I've met very few patients who want to pay that kind of money. Not wanting to pay for the simple stuff results in them getting a lot more of the complex stuff done, resulting in their teeth and gums, the only vaguely complex things in the equation, getting damaged. What makes it even more laughable is (most often) the complex stuff is being provided by individuals who are far too important to respect the simple stuff. Thereafter the layers of nonsense just get deeper and deeper as everyone looks on beguiled and bewildered.

I'd like to mention the newly qualified's study doesn't mention their ability to take a history from a patient or perform an examination to reach a diagnosis. Which in my experience is far more challenging than delivering treatments, it requires the highest order of seasoned expertise to get right. The diagnosis is essentially the professional's interpretation of the patient's story and this has to be carefully teased out of them. Patients need help to understand which information is required and which is not. Some patients cannot respond to the simplest of questions and require expert input. Often a simple question like 'how long have you been in pain?' can produce a response which is longer than war and peace. Patients withhold important information in the misguided hope it will result in a more favourable diagnosis. Some embellish the symptoms in the hope of receiving a recommendation for a type of treatment which they perceive to be more successful, usually because a friend has had it. It's no wonder so many get the wrong treatments.

The newly qualified's study reminded me of the time a colleague of mine raised concerns to the leadership team. She reported an incident in which students had taken patients onto the clinics before she had arrived to supervise the same students. She had another more fundamental concern, she had previously failed some of the same students in an end of year clinical competency exam and they hadn't attended the re-takes. She knew this because she had supervised the re-takes. She asked the students why they hadn't attended the re-takes and was told: 'we were told that so many students failed that some had to be pushed through'. She included, in her two page complaint, a major breach to patient safety. Her complaint was neutralised. I have kept copies of the complaint and the derisory response used to neutralise it.

Other teachers had made complaints listing concerns of similar events. One teacher left on grounds of ill health and another left at short notice after a meeting with Dr Delphic. Staff turnover was high but the human conveyor belt always seemed to provide near identical replicas each time. One reason for this was the leadership team could not risk taking anyone on who had the ability to work out how bad things were as if they did it would be the beginning of the end for them. I've already described the (accidental) nature of my recruitment in Chapter 3.

The students training should have been modeled on a working class style with working class language and working class emotions, with the openness and roughness of speech one finds in the real world. Not in fancy jargon created by the pseudo professionals to conceal the toxic hypersensitive environment they had created by never protesting about The Iconic Machine's business model encroaching upon the educational standards. It's understandable why the leadership team preferred a stuffy, pompous politically correct language. It allowed them to masquerade around as some sort of professional hoi polloi as they pushed a useless curriculum. Offering their superior view of a reality they no longer understood. They had risen to the top not because they were good dentists but because they had become the 'corporate types'. They were in servitude to The Iconic Machine because they, unlike me, had never protested about the poor standards. Under their leadership The Icon had become a behemoth which was likely to collapse under its own weight.

Not only was there a compromise to their training, the students were being set up. Academic degrees can be faked but professional performance cannot. When they are awarded a university degree that says they have mastered a given body of knowledge and therefore qualified to pursue a given career, it needs to be true otherwise we no longer have standards of professional performance. The students were being set up for a fall, ironically by the very people who had been put in place to protect and nurture them. In my experience it takes the newly qualified approximately five years to realise how badly they have been failed.

The knock-on and cascading effects of poor training appear obvious but were beyond the scope of the study and not mentioned. Vocational training is not equipped to rescue the newly qualifieds and most of them struggle to acquire the necessary cognitive or mechanical skills. They float around in a haze of insecurity looking constantly to their senior peers, for what that's worth. Only last week I saw a patient on referral from her dentist. The dentist who had been qualified for approximately 10 years was in the process of providing the patient with a crown on one of her molar teeth.   When the patient arrived at my practice the temporary crown had fallen off allowing me to look at the crown preparation underneath. It reminded me of a fabulous term I have heard far too often in dentistry 'it's not the best I've seen but it's not the worst'. In reality it was shockingly poor.

In my experience dentists lack the ability to accurately calculate their ability. I qualified in 1992 and realised by 1993 that to earn a living under the NHS it required stacking cases higher and higher to complete them cheaper and cheaper. This wasn't the environment to hone any skills. This was the environment to learn the rush job which wasn't why I had trained to be a dentist. I knew I couldn't do it this way and at the time I worked in a succession of practices where the receptionists would cram emergency patients onto my list with apparent disregard for time. I was forever in a pickle and some sort of blunder based bother. To say that quality wasn't a priority would be an understatement as it wasn't even an option or possible.

Looking back I was probably about 50-60% competent in crownwork by 1996. I completed my specialist training in 2001 and became 100% competent in crowns in about 2003. It takes time. Preparing a tooth for a crown is an important dexterous skill. Deciding whether to fit one is necessary (in the first place) and is a very different cognitive skill and sadly in my experience these skills are   inconsistent, irrational and at times ambiguous within the profession and at others plain incompetent.

As well as this, due to the newly qualified's being 'unsatisfactory' it's unlikely they would be able to treat anything but the simplest of patient needs without supervision. It's likely they would need intensive supervision from their trainer. As obvious as it may seem the majority of newly qualified's I have spoken to have told me that this is the opposite of the reality. They struggle with the fact that the training practices do not reduce the workload. The number of patients they are expected to treat on a daily basis, with their acquired skills or lack of them, is excessive. One of the reasons is it would reduce the income generated for the training practice and the trainer themselves if they were to see less patients. Essentially the vast majority of treatment is being rushed with little regard for accuracy or quality.

The impact of the newly qualified's being 'unsatisfactory' is 'doing it right first time' is no longer an option in primary care. It has become a vicious circle with cases (especially those of gum disease) having undergone supervised neglect, being referred onto secondary care where, ironically, they are treated by yet more poorly prepared students.

Looking at it in a bit more detail; let's assume you are one of the 35% of people who are susceptible to gum disease. Let's assume you have neglected your homecare early in life. Let's assume you have lost 50% of the bone that once held your teeth in place. Let's assume they've started to feel wobbly and gaps have started to appear between them. At this stage your case would be described as too complex for a local dentist and they'd refer you to the Dental Institute. When you arrive at said Dental Institute you will be consulted and examined by a poorly prepared undergraduate student or newly qualified dentist in further training on an overly booked clinic. Then a consultant comes along and checks what the student has done. Thereafter, if you are offered any treatment it is on the condition that it will be provided to you by a student or a newly qualified dentist. So in essence, you are agreeing to the provision of treatment, described as too complex for a general dentist, to be provided by a poorly prepared student with limited supervision on an overly booked clinic. This is plainly absurd. The consultants often lament or defend themselves with statements like: 'It's how we've always done it' or the mother of all fabulous statements ever made 'The vast majority of patients are happy with the service they receive'. I promise you they are not and guess what? It's not cheap and it's a complete waste of money.

The Dental Hospitals are not the only ones providing NHS specialist services. There is an alternative and that is specialist care in a high street practice location. I worked in such a practice for a short period of time in 2011. I won't write the full story even though it would probably be a real page turner, suffice to say the sequence went like this:

1. A dentist; let's call him Dr Dodgy had seen an opportunity to make money by offering to supply a specialist service from his practice.

2. Dr Dodgy put in a bid for the local health authority tender for the contract to supply such a service.

3. The local health authority accepted his application and informed the local dentists to refer non smokers with advanced residual gum disease to his practice.

4. Dr Dodgy employed a second dentist to provide the specialist care; only the one he picked wasn't a specialist.

5. The local health authority informed Dr Dodgy that they required specialist services to be provided by (ahem) a specialist.

6. Dr Dodgy recruited me to provide the specialist care and provoked a curiosity in me by asking if I could be relied upon to be a 'team player'.

7. Dr Dodgy denied my request to get into the surgery earlier so that I had time to read case notes and prepare; nope I was only allowed in ten minutes before the first patient of the day.

8.His practice provided me with poor quality everything to include a computer that crashed at least twice a day, eating all the notes I'd made.

9. Dr Dodgy encouraged me to write my notes in a way to give the impression patients arrived with lots of gum disease and left with very little gum disease. I refused and this created tension.

10. His repeat requests for me to write misleading notes coupled with the poor quality everything else was wearing. I resigned and reported him to the Local Health Authority and the Care Quality Commission. They were obviously satisfied with his performance because at the time of writing his practice was still offering specialist services.

The skills and knowledge (or the lack of) held by some dental professionals is really worrying. I was asked, not too long ago, by a female dentist in her forties if I'd have a quick look at some veneers she'd had fitted by a cosmetic dentist. She was experiencing pain and wasn't satisfied with them. I asked her if she had discussed her concerns with the cosmetic dentist. 'I don't trust him, I think he tricked me' was her response. I declined the opportunity to look at her veneers and advised her she could, if she wanted to, express her dissatisfaction to the General Dental Council.

Another time, again not too long ago, a male dentist in his forties asked me if I'd have a quick look at his teeth. He was getting food stuck everywhere after a colleague of his had performed some interdentally striping (cutting teeth to make them thinner) as part of some invisible brace treatment. The food packing was causing a bad smell and starting to give him a bit of pain. I asked him if he had discussed his concerns with the dentist who stripped his teeth. 'He keeps fobbing me off with crap' was his response. I declined the opportunity to look at his teeth and advised him that he could, if he wanted to, express his dissatisfaction to the General Dental Council.

On a final note for this section I found a baffling joint letter titled: Dental education: Potentially damaging disconnect*, the letter appeared in British Dental Journal volume 222, page 909 (23 June 2017).

*https://www.nature.com/articles/sj.bdj.2017.520

The letter was remarkable, offering a strange assistance to the plight of the newly qualified's. It lacked any notion of responsibility but made the hope of improvement look wildly optimistic and unrealistic. Prospects of hope remain effectively extinguished until the regulators protect those who 'speak out' and stop sitting on their hands watching them being squashed. It appears to me that the power which could possibly prompt improvement lies with the teaching staff, the students and the patients. It also appears to me that successive governments have carried forward policies to remove (or tone down) any (and all) regulations which hinder the act of business. Their view is consumer driven or consumer forced self-regulation is more efficient. Sadly, the consumers seem to be unaware the market has been left to self-regulate and largely remain in the grey due to the intentionally accidental confusion.

Students, patients and teaching staff need to appreciate that democracy of a system is not sustained by the system that prescribes it but by the challenges to that system. Any possible improvement requires a chorus of concerns and objections to be maintained. Put another way a teaching hospital is only as good as the capacity of its critics. Its performance can only be fine-tuned by means of an incorruptible feedback mechanism. It may help to consider if the voice of concern and objection managed to break the back of totalitarian state communism, surely, it can force governments and regulators to hold teaching hospitals to account.

The Inspiration.

I had avoided spending time with my kids purely because I couldn't keep a clear mind long enough to find any activity enjoyable, in any meaningful way. Then one Sunday morning,**18th December 2016**, I looked out onto a silvery blue sky set against a crisp yellow sun with not a single bird in sight. For the second Christmas of the experience, once again, there was no snow on the ground. Out of nowhere I conjured a plan which had the potential to strike two birds with one stone; spend time with the kids and research strategies of war planning at the same time. That's right a family trip to Blenheim Palace. As war was threatening to break out I felt it would be a good idea to see if researching one of the most revered wartime leaders the UK has ever had might benefit me. Winston Churchill was liked by some despised by others but remains one of the most iconic leaders and located in Woodstock, Oxfordshire, his former home was only 60 miles from ours.

The kids remained unconvinced as we set off. Reyaan is a foodie who has big dreams of being a chef one day. I'd fibbed and told him the restaurant at the palace had a Michelin star. He was the first in the car. Little did he know it wasn't and I had not been able to make a booking at the non-Michelin star one. I'd told my youngest daughter, Anniyah – 8 years old – that we were going to see sheep. She was the second one in the car, easy peazy lemon squeezy. On the drive I wanted to get them ready for a visit to Blenheim Palace and also wanted to make another point, 'learn to think for yourself and don't be fooled into thinking that others will do it for you'. I captured their interest by asking them to imagine two scenarios. The first one was a herd of wild sheep on a hillside without a shepherd and the second was a herd of sheep on a hillside being tended by a shepherd. I asked them which sheep would last the longest. Tick- tick – tick; Reyaan responded first. He sits in the front passenger seat because like his father he is a pain in the butt (and suffers from travel sickness). "The sheep without the shepherd will last longest"; was his response. How's that? I asked. 'Well you see dad the shepherd will trick his sheep, use them, kill them and sell them. What for? The milk, the wool and the meat'. Never, I thought. My work was already almost done.

I continued to engage them. This time I asked them to imagine (for a minute) that humans were animals just like the sheep. Yes, they said. I then informed them that humans had a shepherd too and the shepherd was called the government. I explained how the government was created by a bully (the King) to collect money from the humans to fund his fights with other bullies. Over time the government stopped working for the King (because he was a greedy bully) and pretended to work directly for the humans instead. It was difficult to convince them the King was a bully so I tried to explain what charisma is and how it works to fool herds of people. They still weren't convinced so I went all the way back to Roman history to try and explain the evolution of Kings and Governments. I explained that the Romans were invaders and invaders often kicked your door down and said 'give me your money' and 'your wife' and 'that food'. And you'd have to point out to them that that's not food; that's my children. I knew I had their attention from the way they said 'ooohhh'. I explained how the Romans wanted to simplify the collection of money so that most money could be gathered with the least amount of effort. I did this by telling them my summarised version of the already abridged version I had picked up from **The Shortest History of Europe** by John Hirst; it went like this:

• The Romans said; we need to work out how we can get the most number of people to just hand over the money, whilst using the least amount of effort.

• They struggled to work out how to do it because they didn't do thinking.

• They decided they might find the answer by looking in one of the places they had previously invaded and looked at what the Greeks might have done because the Greeks were known to be thinkers?

• After a while (and having studied thinking) the Romans decided that the easiest way to get the money from humans with the least effort would be by telling them that up beyond the mountains in the clouds there is someone called God, etc, etc, etc. He is your creator and we work for him. He said we are in charge and you have to hand over your money to us because we work for him. Done

• The Romans then decided it would be an idea to have some local offices in which to collect the money. They struggled to decide what to call the offices and settled with calling them crutches, which is spelt C-H-U-R-C-H and pronounced crotch as-in I'm going to put my hand on yours.

The kids were captivated and enchanted by the Disney like style of my storytelling. They were far too young to understand the full extent of the bullying but seemed to get the idea that Kings, governments and Winston Churchill were a progression from the Roman story yet probably not direct descendants. They were fascinated and enlightened and I was happy with the background scene I had set for them to learn more from the exhibits they would see at Blenheim Palace.

We had a great day at the palace. I guess it was the cold crispness against the bright sunshine which resulted in me enjoying the clearest mind I'd experienced for a while. It was one of those days where I had to keep moving to avoid feeling the cold, but if I stayed out of the wind I could feel the heat of the sun on my cheeks. The grandeur of the palace soon had me daydreaming and into cloud cuckoo land with me crunching through the gravel with my new best friend; Winston. He didn't really speak in traditional sentences so I 'prattled the cackle' with him as we walked. Anniyah kept interrupting because she wanted know when she might see the sheep.

Blenheim Palace was built as a gift to John Churchill, 1st Duke of Marlborough, by Queen Anne to express her gratitude and say thanks for the victory at the battle of Blenheim on the 13th of August 1704. It was home to one of the most important collections in Europe including portraits; furniture, sculptures and tapestries. Yet the kids were disappointed by the lack of sheep. Amongst the treasures were the famous Marlborough Tapestries. I was awed by the library which was not to be missed, its walls lined with ten thousand books, many of them hundreds of years old and of great historical significance; but still the kids wanted to see the sheep. I discretely asked one of the palace staff and then concealed the fact he'd informed me that the estate didn't have any sheep. As my admiration for Winston grew and grew the kids became more and more despondent due to the lack of sheep.

I read as many placards as time would allow and whilst doing so my tortured mind gazed, twinkled eyed at this onebefore succumbing to the charms of a gentle smile:

'If you are going through hell keep going'

I didn't smile for too long as I had been deprived of my mental liberty for far too long and smiling no longer felt appropriate. Smile or no smile it continued to comfort me even though my whole body remained tensed as if it was one big muscle and it seemed as if my existence was in free fall with my right to happiness revoked and overruled.

This quote was endorsing the dark side of reality and enabled me an uplifting reassurance and encouragement from words which felt so perverse and morbid. I had always been told to avoid strife but on this occasion I was being encouraged to plough headlong into it. My perception changed again as I started to reflect on what I had learnt about the dark side of happiness. It simplified what appeared to be a complex situation confirming once again the punishment the leadership team was dishing out was what I should've expected all along. I was realising I had been too generous with my previous admiration of them, now they had been exposed as absurdly overrated. Above all it allowed me to keep looking at them despite my blood on their fingers.

Strain lifted from my wrinkled eyes as I continued to read the placards.My interpretations of which suggested it was best if my response to further criticism be one of mockery as this would deflect the proffered harm or offence:

'You have enemies? Good. That means you've stood up for something, sometime in your life'

And then I had a laugh-out-loud moment as I read his response to Lady Astor who had told him 'Winston, you are a drunk',

And you, madam, are ugly. But I shall be sober in the morning'

As we left the palace, I felt somewhat compelled to express my gratitude, and drove the small distance from the Palace to his burial site to pay my respects for the assistance, and as I did I was reminded of something **Friedrich Nietzsche** had said:

'In heaven, all the interesting people are missing'

It took me a while to explain its meaning to the kids; they were still looking forward to going to heaven. But not as long as it took me to explain Dresden to them. Dresden Germany 1945. It drew my mind to the nature of peoples behaviour and simultaneously endorsed the fact there is no delineation between good and bad, there is no black and white. Anyhow it all paled into insignificance compared to how upset the kids were when I told them the 'take home message' from the day was, they were the sheep.

Over the next few weeks I mulled over how life may have been for Winston and how he had lived in difficult times. How did he know what to do? How had he coped? Difficult times reminded me of a summary I had previously prepared for my students. It was concerning talents and how they are developed, I had written it some years earlier shortly after reading: *Talent Code. Greatness Isn't Born Its Grown* by Daniel Coyle. I had forgotten what I'd written so I decided to find it and surprise myself:

Dear All
From now till the end of the 4th year I anticipate that you will be (knowingly or unknowingly) engaging in 2 types of specific learning activity. The 2 learning activities can be described as:-

1.Desirable difficulty
2.Capitalization learning.

These 2 types of learning work on opposite logic. Desirable difficulty works by making things harder, forcing you to think harder and deeper. Capitalization learning works by you building on your previous skills and talents.

At the beginning of the 4th year it was anticipated that you would be unfamiliar and or anxious to engage in the discussion process that occurs with a clinical teacher in the presence of a patient on the clinic. It was anticipated that you would hesitate for 3 reasons. The 3 reasons are:-
1. You had limited experience of 'the skill / talent development cycle' previously.
2. You had a limited appreciation of what was expected from you during the clinical sessions.

3. You had a fear of getting the answers to the questions wrong (in front of a patient).

You now have a clear set of guidance for what is required from you during a clinical session and you have realized that I am less interested in the answers that you provide and that I am more interested in how and what you are thinking in providing the answers you provide. You have all learnt that you were anxious to engage in a discussion but guess what, you survived. Each time you survived there was a feeling of excitement which was slowly replaced by a flavour of invulnerability. You have all become more sure of yourselves. The way this works is that we are, all of us, not merely liable to fear and anxiety, we are also prone to be afraid of being afraid, but guess what..... the conquering of fear produces exhilaration. When you were afraid that you were going to get the answer to the question wrong, it had to happen. Once it has happened you reflect on your performance and hopefully you find that you exhibit to yourselves and others nothing but a calm exterior (we are now safe) the contrast between the previous apprehension and the present relief and feeling of security promotes a self confidence and is the very cornerstone of experience and learning. Am I wrong??, do you agree?? Give it some thought. This feeling of self confidence that comes from the struggle is what we will be focusing on. A skill and a talent is not something you already have that allows you to treat patients when they arrive on the clinic. A skill and a talent is what you EARN when you have been through the tough times and you discover that they weren't so tough after all. You will need to continue to embrace that fact that the process of skill and talent development is less do to with the answer to the question and more to do with how and what you are thinking. Once I can see how you are thinking I can help you; and I have done. This, process, may have not been a pleasant fact to contemplate at the beginning of your 4th year, but now you have learnt that for each time you engage in the process of discussion with me you become much stronger. There will be a time when you are qualified practicing dentists and that your patients will depend on the fact that you have become hardened by the experiences you are offered during skill and talent development. You have to realise, of course, that skill and talent does not save all the teeth that you want to save.

Desirable difficulty

Conventional wisdom holds that a disadvantage is something that ought to be avoided. That it is a setback or a difficulty that leaves you worse off than you should be otherwise. During training and acquiring a skill / talent this is not the case. You might think that this sounds strange. Normally we think that we are better at solving problems when they are presented clearly and simply. During training and skill / talent development the opposite is true. The fact that you have to read the patients paper notes, check the electronic notes, find the radiographs, appraise the radiographs, realise and appreciate that the patients description of their condition has changed, realise and appreciate that the patients expectations have changed, means that you have to work a lot harder to understand and stay ahead of the situation. In training and skill development all that extra effort pays off, because you are being forced to think more deeply or more carefully about what is going on. If you have a hurdle to overcome, you'll overcome it better when you are forced to think deeper or harder. The difficulty is desirable. When we first met at the beginning of the 4th year you may have been left feeling demoralised and inadequate after a clinical session; that has changed. I can see the confidence and skill developing in each one of you (at very different rates of progression, which is natural). You now have a different appreciation of the science behind clinical periodontal treatment. You are learning through your struggle and it is one of the best ways to learn. What is learned out of necessity is more powerful than the learning that comes easy. Struggle and error are different experiences; learning through error is more powerful than learning through struggle. Struggle and error are a fundamental and important part of developing skill and talent.

You are starting to appreciate (some more than others) that before any clinical activity you need to plan and strategize. You have learnt (some are still to learn) that this planning and strategising takes time. If you have a patient at 10am you need to arrive on clinic at 9am or 915 at the latest to plan and strategize in a logical and consistent manner. It is worth thinking about the kind of personality that characterises innovators and entrepreneurs. They are all essentially micro managers.

Capitalization learning.

Most of us gravitate naturally to the areas in which we excel. Tiger Woods was unusually coordinated for his age and found that the game of golf suited his imagination and so he liked to practice golf. He liked to practice so much he got even better and better, on and on in a vicious circle. In order for you to recognise and build on your strengths please manage each of your clinical sessions as I have prescribed in my summaries. Once you have developed the core skills you will have a better idea of the areas in which you excel. For now, it is the time to learn the cores skills. You have all learnt that when you present your cases to me in the formatted fashion we have more time to enhance and advance your understanding as we have the time to look at the finer details of your patient presentation.

I felt as stupid as a brick when I read my own words back. I was dumbfounded that I'd written about the power of difficulty but hadn't seen a connection or thought to revisit it until this stage in my experience. My failure to make the connection troubled me for a long while but the summary itself states: 'learning through error is more powerful than learning through struggle'. I do have to add one thing; Daniel says in his book 'Greatness isn't born its grown'.My experience is: 'the potential for greatness is born, then grown'. Anyhow I had known for some time that I was having difficulty maintaining concentration. It's difficult enough at the best of time let alone under the type of extraordinary sensual assault I was under. I drew some topical encouragement when I read: Like the Roman, Enoch Powell's biography, namely his words:

'What you start, you must finish'

I should clarify I've included this quote like all others for the impact the words had on me and not for the political ambitions any of their authors may have held. That said I identified with Enoch for two reasons, he was once described as the 'odd man out' (I was certainly feeling like the odd man out) and he was born in Birmingham approximately twenty minutes (as the crow flies) from where I was born. Instead of bailing out or becoming distracted with the instant gratification from the ever present endorphin stimulating pleasures on social media I got my fix from Enoch's biography.

I don't know exactly why (other than respect) but his words inspired me to maintain my resolve, my concentration, my focus and my beliefs. It has been pointed out to me that some individuals have interpreted his words to mean: one should stubbornly maintain a single objective or course of action and pursue it at all costs. This isn't what it meant to me. In my mind, it's always better to reflect and have the courage to stop a course of action if you recognise that you've taken a wrong turn. I had already realised that stubbornness is often considered a virtue amongst leaders but from what I have seen it gets a lot of people into lots of trouble. See Donald Trumps insistence on "building a wall" and Theresa Mays insistence on "delivering Brexit" and see the leadership team at The Icon trying to destroy me. According to Professor (emeritus) Keith Grint, leadership is making others aware of the complexity of the problems they face, not coming up with a simple solution and pursuing it at all costs. In a way, me writing this book about my experience in raising my concerns is a form of leadership according to his definition.

I was learning……..

I was learning ultimately I had to stand on my own two feet, in my own shoes. When faced with adversity there is only one option; step up and deal with it. Others before me had made far more important decisions, in far more difficult circumstances. They hadn't given up when hope had all but faded.

I was learning why I had not thought to connect with what I had previously written: The difficulty is desirable. Chiefly because expressing my concerns wasn't supposed to have been difficult because I was dealing with my peers and doing exactly what they had told me to do. The nature of the shock that the very same peers were the enemy was much worse than having a trusted uncle slip his index finger up my arsehole. My previous perceptions and expectations were skewed and distorted because my professional indoctrination had taken place in the hands of the very same leadership team (and their like) who were now fighting me. Fighting me and treating me roughly as they challenged their own indoctrination. The indoctrination had left me with the expectation that patients come first, notes should be written carefully, patients should be consented prior to receiving treatment, mistakes and errors should be flagged up, learnt from and resolved. I hadn't ever expected I'd have to unwind or deconstruct the entire indoctrination process to make sense of its role in the difficulty of the experience. As a result of the indoctrination my expectations of human behaviours were ambitiously romantic, the polar opposite of reality and way off the mark. They certainly weren't suited to dealing with the reality of the corrupt dishonest behaviours of a cosy establishment.

I learnt that Mumbai is exactly five thousand four hundred and ninety nine miles from my house in Leamington Spa. It holds some of the most glamorous sapphires in the world. Sky blues ones being the most desirable.

I was learning from an experience in our local launderette that the decision making process is generally poorly understood. I was enjoying the therapy that comes with folding warm radiant clothes when I was disturbed by the owners daughter. She asked for my opinion on a dental matter. She had been to three dentists and having received three different opinions was now confused. She was twenty-three years old and wanted to get her crooked teeth straightened. I straightened up her thinking by telling her, in my opinion, all consultations are a two way affair and in this case, between a patient and a dentist, both are equally responsible for any resulting confusion. The inconsistencies in the advice are usually the fault of both parties. I then told her what I tell my own kids all day long:

'You are at an age where you should be able to make your own decision'.

She smiled and told me she couldn't make a decision as the advice was inconsistent. I told her the inconsistency usually occurs for one of two reasons. Patients typically tell each successive dentist a different story and the story is built on their likes and dislikes of the previous dentist's advice. Successive dentists typically take on board the patients likes and dislikes of the previous advice and then offer a less negative alternative in an effort to encourage the patient to invest in their practice. She smiled and asked: 'So, what shall I do?' and I advised her again:

'You are at an age where you should be able to make your own decision'.

Once again she confirmed she could not do so and asked me again what she should do next, to which I smiled hard and responded:

'You are at an age where you should be able to make your own decision'.

Faced with her blank expression I told her I could not make her decision for her because I hadn't attended any of the consultations. I had no idea what she had asked for or how she had asked for it. I had no idea what she'd been advised and how it had been advised. I had no idea what her facial expressions had requested or how the facial expressions of the dentist had responded to her request. I had no idea what her limbs had requested or how the limbs of the dentist had responded to what hers had requested.

It was clear to me she (just like my kids and students) had not appreciated the face and body language (non-verbal language) accounts for approximately 80% of communication. During the decision making process the non-verbal communication needs to be considered as it is far more informative than verbal communication. As she hadn't appreciated this I described the 'decision making cycle' to her and advised her to repeat it for each and every earthly decision she made. Here is the decision making cycle:

1. Let's assume a consultation with a trades person be it with a dentist, doctor, window cleaner, plumber, car dealer, estate agent, lawyer.

2. During it, listen to the advice you are given and carefully observe the facial language of the giver so as to identify sincerity against falsified sincerity.

3. During it, listen to what you are told whilst also carefully observing the body language of the giver so as to identify sincerity against falsified sincerity.

4. Consider the advice you've been given and reach your decision. The required decision is: 'do I trust this person?' If you don't trust the person, thank them and move away from the consultation and start over again with the next person. Continue to do so until you meet a person you trust.

5. Once the decision is made, make a conscious note of the thoughts you had whilst making it and also make a conscious note of the expectations you have developed (of the service) from the discussion and the promises that were made.

6. Request the service and have your experience of it.

7. After the service has been completed decide by comparing the actual experience of the service against the expectations you feel you had been promised.

8. If the service you received matched your expectations pat yourself on the back and try and anticipate how much of 'your good decision' was due to your due diligence and how much of it might have been down to fate alone.

9. If the service you received FAILED to match your expectations decide how far off the experience was.

10. Describe the difference between the expectation and experience back to the service provider and listen to their response. Whilst at the same time carefully watch their face and body language. Compare their face and body language with that which was displayed at 2) & 3), above. If there is no difference then it's likely the fault was your own misguidance in perception and expectation and the service you received was as good as could have been expected. If there is a difference in the face and body language the amount of it should give you a guide to how badly you have been fleeced.

11. Continue to have consultations as necessary with trade people such as a dentists, doctors, window cleaners, plumbers, car dealers, estate agents and lawyers.

12. Repeat the above sequence for every decision you make and realise to get better at it you need to carefully consider the outcomes at items 8), 9) & 10) and carefully use these to fine tune how you develop your expectations and make your decisions.

As I left I advised her it's impossible to accumulate without speculation. Meaning, she would have to make a decision and get on with it. She'd only learn from her mistakes; she would not learn from the mistakes of others. She'd only start to learn how successful decisions are made after she'd made a lot of mistakes and had a shed load of crappy experiences. It's the complete opposite of the millennial situation in which parents make all the decisions for their precious little iddlings forever and ever and ever; just to protect them.

Danger Signs require Rapid Responses

'It is dangerous to be right in matters about which the established authorities are wrong'.

Voltaire

The encouragement I drew from this quotation further endorsed my previous realisation that the manner of The Icon's appalling treatment of me is exactly what I should have expected all along. It offered the reassurance that I hadn't actually made any real mistakes and affirmed that the hard way is the only way something worth learning can be learnt. It also confirmed that the leadership was unlikely to see the sense in a change of direction.

This quotation draped itself over me on **Saturday 22nd April 2017.** It had been peaking at me for a while and then stepped out to me during a shopping trip with, Imani. The Impasse was utter disbelief in The Icon's appetite for propping up its wrong doing. This quote put the wrong doing in perspective and made it easier to not accept.

In this chapter I will give you an insight into the behaviours of the leadership team by describing the nature of the punishment they continued to unleash upon me. How I learnt that most of the same behaviours where not new and had been known to others for longer than I had lived.

The Experience

The cast in this chapter

Leadership team	Given name
New executive Dean	Professor Pinocchio (prone to telling lies)
Head of Department	Dr Perfidious (deceitful & untrustworthy)
Clinical Director	Dick Dastardly (a nasty devious bastard)
Human resources:	Horse Rectum ((defecates bullshit on a regular basis)
Dean of Education	Dr Delphic (deliberately obscure & ambiguous)
Chairman of Council	Dr Insightful

The story so far.......

1. 15th September 2015; whistle blown.

2. 2nd October 2015; nasty meeting with Dr Dick Dastardly.

3. 16th October 2015; incognito meeting with Professor Pinocchio.

4. 19th October 2015; Dick Dastardly's failed attempt to drown me in IT.

5. 1st Week December 2015; Dr Perfidious tells a bunch of staff 'Hafeez is a liability; I'll have to get rid of him'. (ouch my shoulder blades)

6. 7th December 2015; my expression of grievance to Dr Dastardly about the above.

7. 8th December 2015; IT team produces a report which implicates me as uniquely experiencing the concerns I'd reported. (ouch)

8. 17th December 2015; Dr Perfidious produces a report which implicates me as uniquely experiencing the concerns I'd reported. (ouch)

9. 8th April 2016. Professor Pinocchio & Mr Wily failed to re-label my protected disclosures a grievance. (phew)

10. 18th July 2016; Mr high-up concluded the leadership couldn't have known that I had blown the whistle.

11. 4th August 2016; Dr Insightful initiated a formal investigation into my concerns.

12. 30th September 2016; Sinister meeting with Dr Comprehensive.

13. 24th October 2016; I complain to the CEO of the NHS trust.

14. 26th January 2017; I escalate my concerns to the General Dental Council.

15. 31st January 2017; Dr Magoo neutralised my concerns citing Dr Delphic's whiter than white soap-suds report.

.....It had been a typical day for the time of year it had rained and dried; rained a bit more and now the sun was shining blinkeringly bright through the open window. I'd just finished re-sticking a crown for a friend of a friend. If I had been at the bottom of the garden I'm sure I'd have been tilting my head sideways at a rainbow. My surgery window is always kept open; any sort of breeze helps my claustrophobic skin. Not today it wasn't though, there was no breeze and the air was loaded with evaporating moisture carrying with it a low-down fine earthy vapours. It was **Thursday 16th March 2017** at precisely 4:58pm. I had moved to my decontamination room and was busy cleaning cement off my instruments (I often did this because the skill eludes dental nurses) when my receptionist called down to me. She likes to shout at me from a great distance in spite of me pleading (with her) that I can hear her better if she joins me in the room I'm in. The intercom remained an option but my last 5 attempts at showing her how to use it hadn't been successful. Hey-ho, no problem, I washed my hands and walked to her, giving her the opportunity to tell me that if she had known I couldn't hear her, she would have walked down to me. Without moving my lips or eyes I asked: 'what?' Sensing my annoyance she, using her sweetest novelty smile, informed me there was an important sounding person on the phone, 'who?' I asked, she lifted her hand off the receiver and beckoned in a high and mighty pompous tone; 'might I ask whom might be wanting to speak with Dr Ahmed?' before looking back at me she said 'it's Human Resources (HR) from The Icon'. I put my hand out and she once again beckoned down the receiver: 'I'll just put you thorough' (if only).

Human Resources (HR) invited me to a meeting the very following morning. I asked who would be attending and was informed: 'just the 3 of us, you, me and Professor Pinocchio. I confirmed I would attend. Professor Pinocchio had by this stage been appointed Interim Executive Dean shortly after Sleeping Beauty's departure.

The reality was in spite of escalating my concerns to the regulator I had never given up hope (in the practical sense). I'd made every effort to avoid it. The leadership team knew (as much as I did, if not better) that outsiders (of any sort) would introduce their own self serving agenda's and were best avoided, at any cost. I'd convinced myself the leadership would take the opportunity to change their direction. They could, in the eleventh hour, have pawned the whole episode off as a delayed realisation and effectively resolved the concerns and generated an explanation to appease the regulator. It seemed the only sensible way forward so I looked forward to making it happen.

It was **Friday 17th March 2017** and it was going to be a great day, I had bounced out of bed and landed in a slightly too hot shower and sealed the deal with a cold quench. I felt like I had the strength of a thousand tigers.

Professor Pinocchio collected me from the holding bay outside his office and politely asked me to join him in it, whereupon he informed me: 'I have received some concerns and need to conduct some investigations and I don't think it's appropriate for you to be here whilst those investigations are being conducted so I have taken the decision to suspend you'. I wasn't expecting to run headlong into a brick wall, but that's the thing about brick walls; they can be built anywhere and then you can run people into them. He then gestured towards the HR officer and asked her to present me with my suspension certificate. The certificate included the allegations being relied upon to frame me, also included were the conditions of my suspension which were:

• I was not allowed into my normal place of work to include the canteens.
• I was not allowed to contact my work colleagues including my line manager and subordinates.
• My access to documents and e-mails might be restricted.
• I was to remain available to return to work in my normal hours at any time.
• I must remain contactable.

There was no melodrama and Pinocchio seemed to believe what he had said. I was suspended fair enough. The seven allegations seemed insurmountable; this was not a situation I was going to wriggle out of easily. Lucky for me that I had already lost respect for Pinocchio almost a year to the day - April 2016 - in the same office when he made his feeble statement of denial: 'I have no idea what this is about; I'm only here because the others couldn't make it'. Professor Pinocchio still hadn't realised that I was going to take an uncompromised stand because I wasn't afraid to fail. I viewed my suspension as a sabbatical and was going to live out a fantasy in which patients were 'put first' and the education of the students mattered. I thought him and his colleagues might stop trying to outsmart the truth but instead he was making it clear that they were going to continue to run me up a dark alley.

One the train home as I gazed out of the window hypnotised by the green blur of the tree's whizzing past my memory drifted back to the meeting I'd had with Pinocchio on **16th October 2015** in the weeks after I blew the whistle and tried to imagine the mark of a man who would then on the **8th April 2016** say 'I am only here because the others couldn't make it; I have no idea what this meeting is about', and reminded myself: 'Sissies are born, not made. They stay sissies no matter how much independence you give them, no matter how rich they get'.

My suspension created a great emptiness which followed me around where my duties used to be. I was left seeing stars; they were all around my head and memories of previous events continued to compete for centre stage like the flashing of a paparazzo's camera. I eventually settled on a thought that setbacks pave the way for comebacks; it became a potent one. Imaginary flashes over I was left with the real images of the students who had supported me in my attempt to seek improvements and shown an ocean of desire. I'd always been accessible to them and now I had become inaccessible. I had requested their support by e-mail way back on **16th May 2016**. I'd made my request transparently and here it is (unaltered):

Dear P group and a few others.

It is almost the end of your time with me or…………………….. my time with you.

I would really appreciate your comments about the 4th year perio module I have provided you with.

This feedback is not compulsory and you are not obliged to do it however it would be really helpful in my campaign for much needed improvements in the course.

You are all unique individuals and you all have different learning styles. I have tried very hard to understand your individual needs and I have tailored my interactions with you and feedback to you based on my understanding of you over the year. The written summaries were all prepared in my personal time. I appreciate that the summaries have been sent to you as a collective and not as individuals. I did write them carefully to include as many attributes of individualism as I could. On the upside you do now have a practical clinical periodontal handbook.

Your feedback is important to me as it will allow me to moderate my teaching style for future students.

I plan to use your feedback to help improve the periodontal course the best I can. I intent to share your feedback with Dr Available, team lead for P group; Dr Dependable, Head of Department; Professor Pinocchio, Dean of education; Dr Legitimate, Clinical Director and Professor Awakened, Executive Dean of *The Machine*.

Please can I have the feedback, by e-mail, before Friday 27th May 2016.

Kind regards

Dr Hafeez Ahmed

It meant something to me when 100% of the students I was responsible for supplied feedback and it was clear they had given it great thought. Here is one of the feedbacks (it has not been altered).

Teaching Feedback for Dr Hafeez Ahmed Mr VE

Dr Ahmed's teaching methods are unconventional.

One resounding truth that I have found having spent a year with Hafeez Ahmed is that he is highly committed to his subject and more importantly, his teaching. He will stop at nothing to impart his knowledge onto the students. The impact of this is that we have never left clinic on time and have all been subjected to grueling discussions, both with the patient present, and without. However, I feel that the demanding regime that we were subjected to has been highly beneficial. These crucial benefits span not only periodontology but the other disciplines in dentistry.

This passion for education has been exemplified, not only by the disregard for conventional teaching hours, but by the external communication that was delivered as an adjunct to his teaching. Throughout the year we were provided with a "clinical handbook" that explained, in detail, what he expected on clinics. We were urged to print this out and then consult it during patient sessions. The topics varied from "how to carry out an initial consultation or a review" to "how to perform RSD" and were instrumental in improving our clinical experience.

I personally believe that if every student in the year had received the clinical handbook, by Dr Ahmed, the quality of dentistry would be significantly higher than the pathetic state that it currently is languishing at. In an ideal teaching establishment, each tutor would provide this level of detailed feedback each week, as Dr Ahmed has done, to enable the students to reflect on their performance and critically appraise themselves.

Anecdotally, if I was asked to compare the teaching of Dr Ahmed to anything I would like to draw similarity to my A-Level Chemistry teacher. I attended a state school with individuals who had severe range of abilities yet the tutor always tried to inspire each pupil, on their own level. After numerous years of education, on our final lesson with him, he uttered the following statement: "I hope your exams all go well and that the grades you receive reflect what you deserve – by that I mean, I hope some of you pass with an A* and some of you catastrophically fail, as that is what you deserve. Good luck". It was with that proclamation that we embarked on our study leave, sat our exams and I subsequently attended this dental school. I mentioned this because I feel that it exemplifies the mentality of Hafeez Ahmed. He is happy to help any student but when it comes down to it, he wants results. He wants those students that have performed well in the year to accomplish in the exams. I am by no means a model student, far from it, but there is no doubt that the teaching I have received has improved me as a future dentist.

In a warped world where The Icon is filled with replicas of Hafeez Ahmed, the level of stress and overall panic within the Institute would be tremendous but upon exit and onto DF1 I would implore you to find a better set of graduates.

Being suspended and feeling excluded, ostracized and outcast was particularly hard on me. Two questions haunted me the most: 'what is wrong with these people?' and 'what the fuck is wrong with these people?' Ok and a third 'had I let the students who supported me down?' Especially since some had expressed their concerns about possible recriminations. The 3rd year student who wrote the following feedback made very clear to me that her desire to be a good dentist was greater than her fear of recriminations.

Taking time out to reflect at the end of my BDS3, I have come to the conclusion that Dr Ahmed has been the only tutor I've come across at *The Machine* who has got teaching right. Despite overseeing more students than his fair share across both BDS3 and BDS4 during our sessions, Dr Ahmed has found the time and energy to teach us far more than just perio this year.

There is never a moment during our clinical sessions where Dr Ahmed is not actively engaged in teaching students. All my other clinical tutors only come over when asked and can otherwise be found in empty bays on their phones or reading Dental Update! This is not to say that Dr Ahmed doesn't allow us the freedom to treat patients independently. But whilst other tutors only witness the 'end product' of our appointments, Dr Ahmed is aware of how we operate throughout the appointment. To my mind this is the only way in which errors in our methods can be picked up and hence the only way in which real improvement can be made.

Not only does he have an active approach to teaching, Dr Ahmed does his best to tailor his teaching to our individual learning styles. Continuously asking for feedback as to how he could best adapt his methods to support our learning needs. This is something I have not experienced elsewhere, with most tutors adopting a one-size-fits-all approach to teaching.

Dr Ahmed is also the only tutor that I have had that takes the time to teach the student acting as dental nurse how best to support the student acting as dentist. This has been extremely useful because not only does a well-trained dental nurse ensure that appointments are able to run more efficiently, but once we go out into practice we will be better equipped to train our dental nurses how best to support us.

Additionally, Dr Ahmed is the only tutor who advises us how best to write our clinical notes. As I am sure you appreciate, in a world where dento-legal cases are becoming much more common occurrences and clinical notes act as our best defending evidence, this lesson is invaluable. It astounds me that if it were not for his efforts, I would have no formal training in how to write clinical notes.

Something else that I have found invaluable during my time with Dr Ahmed is the weekly summaries that he provides. Each week Dr Ahmed takes time out of his own personal time to write his group a synopsis of that week's session. It is clear that a lot of thought and consideration goes in to preparing these summaries. Looking back through these at the end of the year, I can see that they form a working clinical guide to periodontology for which I am immensely grateful. In this guide he successfully bridges the gap between our scientific knowledge taught in lectures and how to put this information into practice clinically.

He also supplements our clinical learning by recommending books outside the curriculum to support our patient interactions. This really gives the impression that he cares about us all becoming the best dentists we can be. Unfortunately, this is in stark contrast to others, with whom it feels that they treat their one day a week at *The Machine* as an extension of their weekend!

In light of this, it is clear Dr Ahmed goes above and beyond what is expected of tutors at *The Machine*. However, I feel his approach should be the norm and not the exception. I feel it is truly a shame that I will not be taught again by Dr Ahmed during my time at *The Machine*. However, I am just grateful that I had him as a mentor at all.

In case you have ever wondered how the disciplinary process works. It is supposed to go like this:

1. First the employer presents a set of allegations which they believe if proven amount to gross misconduct and the employee is often suspended during an investigation.

2. Then there is an investigation period during which an investigating officer is appointed to gather the evidence to support the same allegations. The investigating officer usually interviews the suspended employee as part of their investigation. They also interview the employer or the author(s) of the allegations.

3. Then the investigating officer makes their decision basing it on the evidence they have collected and if there is sufficient evidence a disciplinary hearing is recommended to test the same evidence. In the absence of evidence the suspension is reversed and the employee is returned to their normal duties.

4. The disciplinary hearing is typically a panel of 3 high-ups from within the employer's hierarchy with the highest-up one taking the role of chairperson. The hearing commences with someone from HR reading out the allegations. The suspended employee is asked if they understand the allegations. At this time the investigating officer is invited into the hearing to present the evidence which they relied upon to recommend the same hearing. Witnesses from the employer's side attend next to present evidence on behalf of the employer. Witnesses on behalf of the suspended employee go next. Finally, the chairperson makes some concluding remakes and then within a fortnight the panel presents their decision to the employer and the employee in writing.

5. Thereafter any appropriate sanctions, if indicated, for any proven transgressions are administered prior to returning the employee back to their normal duties. The sanctions are designed to punish, deter, protect or rehabilitate.

6. If however there are multiple allegations, a substantial number of which are proven with transgressions significant enough for a claim by the panel of gross misconduct then the sanction which is most appropriate is dismissal. The dismissal is usually performed by a high-up in the employer.

I became confident that my suspicion was an indication that the leadership team had planned to use (and abuse) the disciplinary process to have me dismissed by someone other than themselves; they needed to keep the blood off their sticky little fingers, but how would they do it? Who would do what? Would I be able to see who was throwing the bricks? I couldn't do anything more than guess at it. Their plan, I was certain, was to put me through the (pantomime) motions of a process, a process in which they had, no doubt, had plenty of experience. I had none. My suspicion was that their experience was one where a single individual always came to a nasty end when an entire leadership team ganged up them. I had anticipated that with or without evidence, they would abuse every ambiguity and uncertainty of the bureaucracy and I'd be dismissed on the grounds of gross misconduct. That's why it was important for them to raise 7 allegations against me, as the 7 preordained ticks were going to look far more significant than one. Here are the allegations against me:

1. Have expressed a lack of trust and confidence in the Dental Institute and the university in general to students, informing a group who you are responsible for teaching that you have reported the Dental Institute to the General Dental Council for failures in patient management.

2. Have on more than one occasion told patients, in front of students on the clinic, that they have been treated inappropriately and that as a result you have reported the Dental Institute to the General Dental Council.

3. Have been telling patients what to say in the event of a General Dental Council investigation and suggested that patients may receive monetary recompense if they complain in this manner.

4. Have failed to keep students' and patients' interests at the forefront of your teaching practice by refusing access to the use of curettes or ultrasonic equipment, in conflict with accepted teaching practice within the Dental Institute and potentially compromising teaching outcomes.

5. Have failed to check courses of treatment undertaken by students.

6. Have compromised the progress and clinical experience of students through the above.

7. Have breached the trust and confidence of your employer as evidenced by inappropriate communication to a Dental Institute patient using your private practice letterhead.

None of it was true and I wasn't buying it, it was nothing more than hocus-pocus, jiggery- pokey, misrepresentation and a pack of lies. I practically smiled when I first read them, I was so relieved by them that a bit of brain juice leaked out of my left eye and tracked down my cheek. The allegations were all professional ones. My work-shy colleagues had been whispering that I might get stitched up by the leadership paying someone off to claim that I had touched her boobs inappropriately. That's just not me, I don't touch boobs; not in the stairwell, not in the lift and certainly not in the back office where the others do it. How rude. The allegations were heavily suggestive that The Icon considered me as one of its chattels and that they had expected me to be coerced into taking part in their wrongdoing.

As much as I wasn't surprised by it my suspension came as shock and this became a complex contradiction that I had to continue to deal with. The shock was a manifestation of my wounded pride and as much as I hated to admit it I had been snookered. In an effort to make the absence of security more acceptable I took affirmation in the knowledge that I would be paid whilst suspended. In a strange sort of way I was grateful that I'd managed to prevent them from burying their teeth into my neck there and then (or at an earlier stage).

The theatrical performance of the leadership team on the morning of my suspension was symbolic of their biology and hilarious and needs to be told. It was Friday **17th March 2017** and I was sat in the holding area outside Pinocchio's office having arrived at about 8.45am for a meeting scheduled to start at 9am. The holding area was a large square area with doors to 4 offices located at 8, 10, 2, and 4 on a clock face. The entrance to the holding area was at 6. I was sat at 5 looking towards 12. In the centre of the area was an island made up of four desks pushed together for the secretarial staff. When Pinocchio arrived he went straight into his office which was the door at 10. He arrived through the door at 6 and walked around to the left of the island (away from me) taking a straight and the shortest route to his office at 10. You got it. And then Dr Dastardly arrived, he went the long way round. He came in at 6 turning towards me sat at 5, past

4 and 2 and round the island to end up in the Pinocchio's office at 10. Then Dr Delphic arrived and took the same long route to Pinocchio's office. Two other members of the leadership team (non –clinical) arrived and did the same. They each took the long route because I was sat on it and they needed me to see them. Animals; sniffing bums and all that kind of stuff. The animal in them wanted their image to be the last visual in my mind prior to being suspended; this way every time I had a thought related to my suspension immediately behind it would be their image. Its genius how it works.

I wasn't made to wait long but I was intrigued by what was going on. I was slightly perturbed that HR had told me there would only be 3 of us, me, her and Pinocchio but now the whole motley crew were assembled; minus Perfidious. Posturing with their faux furrows. The mystery continued as, one by one, the whole crew left again, each one taking the long route out so I could sniff their bums again. What a pea - cock show, what plumage. What splendour; the thought of it will make me smile forever.

The spanner that cracked the most teeth off the cogs in my mind (pun intended) was the evidence pack which arrived by e-mail (and post) on the **12th April 2017**. The evidence pack contained the documents being used to support my suspension and it containing approximately 12 pages of spurious statements gathered by perfidious from students, some more spurious paperwork crafted from Delphic's office and a 5 page report prepared by perfidious into the concerns I had raised about a patients care (I'll be referring to it as the soil report). The whiff of excrement emanating from the allegations and the evidence pack contained all the earthy keynotes of someone shitting their pants and those soiled pants belonged to perfidious. He was the top pseudo aristocratic dog who had gotten himself into a position to lose the most from my survival.

Fracking hell, war really had broken out. Fair play had evaporated fast and the Geneva Convention became ancient history. The allegations against me didn't worry me one little bit but the evidence pack did, it was a low blow indeed. A whore is a whore but a lying whore is a different prospect. It was clear to me that perfidious had rounded up some students and coerced them to write the statements. This wouldn't have been too difficult as they had already identified his department in their complaints as providing the poorest teaching. They had been complaining since long before I joined it. Anyhow as I worked in the same department it wouldn't have taken much for him to point the students in my direction by implying to them that I was cause of all the problems. *(The leadership became unstuck at a later date as none of the students consented to go on record and as such none of the spurious statements could be used as evidence).*

Pictures look best in frames and to frame this one the arrival of the evidence pack was the lowest point of my entire experience, probably as low as Europe felt in 1349 when the Black Death was wiping it out. I didn't sleep for three straight nights. In and amongst the chemical mist in my mind a question beamed itself (Star Trek style) into it. I had no idea who had sent it or where from but it was: 'what does the phrase quintessentially English mean? I didn't have a clue, so I passed it to my old sage Ray French (next door) and asked him what it meant. It took him over two weeks to come back to me with an answer. He's a slow walker and once the walking was over he sat down to rest his bony behind. Ray told me 'Quintessentially English means the biggest lying bastard on the planet'. His explanation was certainly true of the Englishmen I was experiencing. As I looked back at him his eyes twinkled as his head moved gently side-to-side; in disapproval. Irises floating freely his eyes were locked on me and with his mouth aimed at my eyes he said: 'You do worry me Hafeez, you act is if you were born yesterday and I was born the day before'; his words complimented his laboured face language. 'What?' I asked. 'It's a ubiquitous statement; it's the same all over the world!' he explained and continued. If a middle aged Spaniard was struggling in a similar situation to yours and he'd asked his trusted Spanish sage the same question he would have been told: the Spanish are the biggest lying bastards on the planet. If a middle aged Australian was caught in a similar situation to yours and he'd asked his trusted Australian sage the same question he would have been be told: 'the Australian's are the biggest lying bastards on the planet. I got it.

In the corners of mind I just couldn't seem to find a reason to believe that I could survive this attack, it was another round of bullets piercing my skin. But I had no option but to stand and defend myself in their war. My mind had gained hope, lost hope been forced to reduce hope and I could only wish that it wouldn't implode. This was the moment I (consciously and deliberately) extinguished the small flickering flame of hope that remained in me and replaced it with a candle of remembrance. It felt as if everything that could go wrong all went wrong all at one time, I really did think I would lose my mind. I seriously wondered if I would hold out during these trials. How much ammunition did they still have left? How many more bullets would I have to swallow?

The stakes were high; this was my professional reputation, my career, my livelihood and the potential we could lose our family home. I prepared diligently, my support team were Paracetomol, Ibuprofen and diazepam. (*Would it be so wrong to call the leadership team infantile bastard pieces of shit*).

An investigation officer from high-up in the university was appointed and I was invited to an investigation meeting scheduled to take place on **21st April 2017** (19 months after the whistle blow). Investigating officers are supposed to be disinterested individuals who hold high office and rank. In exchange for the privilege of office and rank they occasionally have to take part in some disciplinary duties.

On the **21st April 2017** the meeting started and after introductions were over we all sat down. The investigating officer was accompanied by a member of team Horse Rectum (HR) and I was accompanied by a union rep. The investigating officer was a stout little fire breathing busy body with piercing eyes and each time she wanted to emphasize her importance she'd momentarily intensify her stare. She had perfected her impression of Jeff Dunham's ventriloquist dummy: 'Achmed the dead terrorist'. The formidable task ahead of her was to get me to my disciplinary hearing on time. It was her job to issue the approval for a hearing irrespective of the evidence or lack of it. She had to put up the pretence of appearing to observe the formalities of and abide by the protocols and guidelines produced by The Icon and those of ACAS (Advisory, Conciliation and Arbitration Service). My suspicions were confirmed almost immediately. I offered 'Achmed the dead terrorist' two written statements I'd prepared for her attention and she refused to accept them. I made three further attempts at getting her to accept them but she politely declined on each occasion. I adroitly got round this by responding to each of her questions by saying:

'I'll just find the answer, bare with me; it's here somewhere in one of these statements I prepared for you'

Then I'd proceed to read her the answer whilst looking down at the statement. She eventually tired of this and with some reluctance accepted my written statements one at a time. The first statement, pasted below, had the desired impact (in the, be careful what you wish for way). She let me know when she'd got to paragraph 3 because she rose from her chair with her fingertips perched on the table like the claws of a wolf ready to pounce. She leaned towards me intensified her stare and roared 'I AM NOT COMPLICIT'; her uvula rattling around like a church bell in a Mexican desert storm. She confirmed two things, she was an accomplice and I had her undivided attention. And for a brief moment I felt the potential wrath I may have to endure if I dared defend myself effectively. It certainly made the meeting more of an interactive one. I was confident that I had made it clear to her that I had no intention of leaving the room without defending myself or without presenting her with the evidence.

WRITTEN STATEMENT No 1 about my suspension (unaltered)

It is clear to me that my suspension and this investigation relating to my suspension is an act of intimidation, harassment and bullying by the leadership team at the *Dental Institute* (DI). I am being intimidated, harassed and bullied for having used the DI's protected disclosure procedure to raise my legitimate and serious concerns, both internally and to the General Dental Council (GDC) about dangerous and illegal practices at the DI.

The leadership team at the DI are using this process of intimidation, harassment and bullying to attempt to silence me and prevent me from continuing to criticise the DI in an attempt to avoid having to face up to and remedy the problems that I am describing.

What is not clear to me is whether you are also complicit to this intimidation, harassment and bullying. This will become evident as your investigation progresses.

I would like to:-

1.   Point out to you as the investigating officer that the Public Interest Disclosure Act 1998 specifically protects whistle blowers like me from being treated unfairly or dismissed as a result of making a disclosure in the public interest.

2.   Point out clause 3.1.1 of *The Machines* Policy on information Disclosure (whistleblowing). Which states workers are also protected against victimisation and harassment by their colleagues for making a protected disclosure.

3.   Two of the patient cases which I reported to the DI and GDC in my protected disclosures and which are currently under investigation by the GDC are listed in the evidence schedule supporting my suspension. The fact they are is evidence that I am being victimised, intimidated and bullied as a direct result of my protected disclosures.

4.   Point out that much of the evidence in the schedule is evidence that originates directly or indirectly from one of the registrants (Perfidious) that the GDC has chosen to investigate as a result of my protected disclosure. I supplied the GDC with exactly the same document folder that I have today supplied to you. It is the same document folder that I previously supplied the DI in support of my protected disclosures to them. On reading the contents of this folder the GDC has decided to commence an investigation against Perfidious and I am sure he is upset and embarrassed about the implications that the investigation may have. As such it is totally inappropriate for him to be in any way involved in this investigation. It is certainly totally inappropriate for him to have been allowed to round up a group of students and coach them to produce questionable and I suspect spurious witness statements against me.

5.   Point out that the terms of my suspension have prevented me from speaking to work colleagues and that I must insist that I am immediately allowed to resume normal communications so I can begin to collect witness statements in my defence.

6.   Point out that I am confident that there is ample evidence that these proceedings represent me being victimised and bullied for whistle blowing internally and to regulators about dangerous and illegal practices at the hospital. I had a Duty of candour which is my legal and ethical duty and I was required to disclose my concerns to the affected patients.

7.   Present my understanding of and my explanations about the allegations against me. I have pre-prepared a summary and make direct reference to evidence in the document folder and I can direct you to further evidence

in the clinical records of patients if required. I have made a copy of the document file for you as the investigating officer. I will point out inaccuracies in the statements by making reference to the evidence in the document file.

8. I will need the ban on communicating with students and work colleagues to be lifted so that I can collect supporting witness statements from them.

9. I must insist that I am afforded the opportunity to question and challenge the author of any witness statements as I have very significant doubts about the authenticity, honesty and accuracy of the statements. I am confident that the authors will change their stories under my cross examination.

Back in the investigation hearing.... Under the table in my bag was a folder containing copies of all the documents I'd planned to submit as evidence; I had prepared it lovingly for her. 180 pages of pure love. Given that 'Achmed the dead terrorist' had already been reluctant to accept my written statements (7 pages) I was certain she wasn't going to accept the evidence bundle with open arms. I'd have to ease its passage, so for the remainder of the meeting I made repeat reference to the evidence bundle and each time I did she'd pretend sincerity by saying:

'Yes, the evidence bundle, it is very important for me to look at the evidence'.

By the end of the meeting I'd managed to mention the evidence bundle seven or eight times, enough times to exhaust her pretence. She concluded the meeting with summary remarks and outlined what would happen next (it all sounded very official). We all blew each other a kiss and I got up to leave. Halfway out the door I turned back and declared with a look of beguiled bewilderment:

'I almost forgot to leave the evidence bundle'.

I removed it from my bag and handed it to Achmed being very careful to ensure she could only see its spine. I will remember (for the rest of my life) the look on her face when she caught a glimpse of its contents. It was comedy gold as her eyes sprang-out before wilting back into their sinkholes as she squealed:

'Dr Ahmed, there's got to be more than 200 pages here!!'

I had to bite back my smile as I reassured her enthusiastically: 'there's only 180 pages' and with that I left. She'd already accepted a copy of my second statement in which I had referenced the evidence bundle by page number.

I have pasted my second statement below; the bold black text after each allegation was my response; I supplemented each of my responses with approximately 2 pages of direct reference to the evidence bundle (which I've left out).

WRITTEN STATEMENT No 2 and my response to the allegations:

Have expressed a lack of trust and confidence in the Dental Institute (DI) to students, informing a group who you are responsible for teaching that you have reported the DI to the General Dental Council (GDC) for failures in patient management.

This allegation is not correct.

I have not directly informed any groups of students that I have reported the DI to the GDC. I have followed my duty of candour and told patients about shortcomings in their care and those discussions have occurred in front of students. Patients have asked me about letters they have received from the GDC in front of students so those students would have heard my response.

Have on more than one occasion told patients, in front of students on the clinic, that they have been treated inappropriately and that as a result you have reported the DI to the GDC.

This allegation is correct, but it is totally inappropriate and illegal for the institute to be citing this as a potential disciplinary matter as it is my duty of candour to act in this way. I have now reported the DI and the registrants on its leadership team to the GDC for failing to follow GDC guidance regarding duty of candour. I will be keeping the GDC advised regarding these proceedings.

Have been telling patients what to say in the event of a GDC investigation and suggested that patients may receive monetary recompense if they complain in this manner.
This allegation is not correct.

Have failed to keep students' and patients' interests at the forefront of your teaching practice by refusing access to the use of curettes or ultrasonic equipment, in conflict with accepted teaching practice within the DI and potentially compromising teaching outcomes.
This allegation is not correct.

Have failed to check courses of treatment undertaken by students.
This allegation is partially correct. I have had very significant concerns about the DI's failure to support me sufficiently for some considerable time. I have raised these concerns with the DI and with the GDC as part of my protected disclosure. It is inappropriate and illegal to victimise me for having made those disclosures.

Have compromised the progress and clinical experience of students through the above.
This allegation is not correct. I was not given any induction whatsoever when I started my teaching post (page 21). I have never been given a written policy on what the DI wants me to teach or how it wants me to teach it. I believe no such written policy exists.

I thought I did a good job of defending myself. Hey.

I was informed by team Horse Rectum (HR) on **13th June 2017** that Achmed had made her decision. She had recommended that a disciplinary hearing was appropriate and necessary. Joy. I'd have to continue to defend my professional reputation and endure having my life ripped apart whilst continuing to attempt to prevent it from being destroyed. What intrigued me most and left my mind on a sort of precipice was what evidence she had found. I'd have to wait the 24 days; 576 hours; 34,560 minutes for her to share it with me (and the panel). What had she conjured up? Attempting to ease my mind with: 'Never assign to malice that that can be adequately explained by incompetence' wasn't working, why would it; her acts were brazen malice.

The disciplinary hearing took place in **7th July 2017** *(22 months after I'd blown the whistle)*. As I entered the room (with my union rep) there was a hint of stale office carpet in the air accompanied by a floaty feeling that this was important. I was ripe to be aggravated so I'd have to concentrate hard to control myself. To open the hearing (a bit like an Olympic ceremony) the investigating officer, Achmed, confirmed to the panel that the allegations against me were serious and could result in my dismissal for gross misconduct. Only on this occasion she was playing a sort of wounded Bambi, fragile, pre-occupied and distant; no sign of the dead puppet anymore. She confirmed that in gross misconduct cases the investigation should be of the highest order. She acknowledged that as part of her investigation she had interviewed potential witnesses and collected the evidence impartially. She confirmed she had interviewed the leadership team but when asked for the minutes of the same interviews she apologised as she had failed to make any. When asked for any notes from the same interviews she apologised as she hadn't made any of those either. When asked for any statements or testimonials from the interviews she apologised as she had failed to request any. She acknowledged that in the absence of minutes, statements or testimonies those interviews could not be included in the hearing. She confirmed that she had not interviewed any other witnesses or collected any other evidence and as such she could not and did not present anything to the hearing.

Let me say that again, she did not present the hearing with a single crumb of evidence; not a single rabbit dropping.

She then admitted to the panel that her investigation had NOT been of the highest order and that she had NOT read a single one of my disclosures. The panel then addressed each of the allegations against me one by one. In the absence of any evidence the chairman put each one aside, one at a time. All allegations expect allegations No 2 & No 6 which I had already partially accepted (but were inappropriate) were put aside.

After a short recess for lunch the hearing resumed. Three witnesses were scheduled to attend; first it would be Professor Pinocchio, followed by Dr Perfidious with Dr Delphic coming last. Professor Pinocchio arrived looking uncharacteristically surly and took a seat. Once he was seated I used his right eye as my fixed focal point and stared into it for most of his presence in the hearing. He was reluctant to answer the questions being asked by my union rep, until the chairman of the panel instructed him that would have to. He too admitted to the panel that he had NOT followed up on a single one of my disclosures. I was more than surprised to hear him admit so and on hearing him say so I took an unexpectedly deep inhale. It was if the planets had purposely lined themselves up to bring about this moment. I asked myself; did Pinocchio really just tell the panel he hadn't followed up any of my disclosures. If he had, I wasn't expecting it. I stopped using his eye as my point of focus and decided to move it to his mouth. Did he just say what I thought he said or was I daydreaming? I leaned my head in as if I was going to catch his words bouncing of the wall, but no. I blinked hard several times but nope that didn't work either. I had to settle for what I had already heard but kept looking around the room at the others to see if they heard it too.

Pinocchio's testimony was so bent and wobbly it's become one of the most unexpected moments of my experience during it he confirmed to the panel that he was aware of the student's having complained bitterly after Professor S attempted to corrupt them by telling them that they should rate The Icon high in the forthcoming National Student Survey; it was extraordinary. He looked irked and his responses displayed a clunky bias, heavy and slow when he felt vulnerable and razor sharp when given any opportunity to assail me. One thing was for sure his testimony left me dazed. Poor Professor Pinocchio didn't know when to quit. At times he seemed confused and unprepared at others he was very animated passionate and precise. I'll come back to him in a minute but for now let me tell you how the rest of hearing played out. Oh and my union rep Claire you'll meet her again in chapter 8, I'll tell you about her then.

After Pinocchio left the hearing the chairman asked me if I had any comments about his testimony. I did and I summarised them as 'Pinocchio has already decided I should be dismissed'.

The Chairman then started to tap his papers on the desk and made what sounded like his concluding remarks which attracted an enquiry from Claire 'Aren't we still expecting two more witnesses?' the Chairman looked in the direction of the member of team Horse Rectum who announced: 'We've been informed that unfortunately they can't make it' and with that the hearing ended.

I couldn't make sense of it, Dr Perfidious and Dr Delphic suddenly couldn't make it. What did this mean? Can you hear Marvin Gaye in the background.... ain't no mountain high enough; ain't no valley low enough.... These fella's were taking 'taking the piss' to a whole new level. I had no option but to rely on my faith and recite: 'what goes around come around'; what else could I do?

I would have expected my mind to feel cleansed and relieved but instead the hearing acted like a gust of air passing over hot sticky tarmac; the stench remained. Whatever their plan had been it had fallen apart; I was impossible for me to know if I should have been in elation or mourning. The leadership were probably standing behind a closed door murmuring 'you were only supposed to blow the doors off'. It appeared to me that each one of the witnesses had planned to attend the hearing and bury axes into my spine. Something they would do by delivering carefully pre-prepared statements crafted in a way to insidiously assail my professionalism and maybe even me personally; acts of pure calumny. It appeared they hadn't anticipated they'd be cross examined by me or my union rep. Professor Pinocchio certainly wasn't wearing a poker face, he wanted the panel to believe what he had said was true. He clearly wanted them to believe what he said otherwise he would not have said it. Looking back I shouldn't have been unnerved by this but I hadn't had any experience of such brazen lying before. Pinocchio was a liar lying about being a liar. He had exposed himself as a mendacious agent of self interest? I don't think he was supposed to say what he said; not out aloud anyway. I believe that the evidence he gave was supposed to have remain a secret amongst the internal mechanics of The Icon but he'd let it slip out in a moment of frustration. His lie was the lie that exposed The Icon's campaign to punish me for having raised my protected disclosures. I guessed that I wasn't supposed to have crawled out or the hearing let alone leave with my head held up high. Poor Mr Khashoggi.

Surely they'd have to bail out. Surely they'd have to remove the shackles off my feet. Surely I'd be allowed to dance again. Anyhow for the time being I got stuck into some more mind zapping rumination. Perfidious and Delphic had bottled it and Pinocchio became exposed as the obvious scapegoat. The pre-prepared statements he made during the hearing are crucial to remainder of the story, so I would like to address them in a bit more detail.

Professor Pinocchio's pre-prepared statements are presented below in bold, my comments follow each one:

'nobody at this institute believes that HA had a valid reason for raising the concerns he has raised, none of the consultants, none of the teaching staff, not even the part time teachers like himself. The students have told us that they do not like HA approach to teaching.'

This would later be proved as a lie. Numerous other staff had raised similar concerns plus I had escalated the complaints of approximately 30 named students who had complained to me and numerous others had complained directly to The Iconic machine. All the students I had been personally responsible for over a two year period had provided written testimonials which I had previously sent to Pinocchio. Every single one of my students had written one, that's 100% of them; the feedback was balanced as it included some negative remarks but overall was very positive and supportive of my teaching. Some eleven months earlier (June 2016) The Dental Institute had completed its formal assessment of my teaching by way of a teaching appraisal. The assessment was very positive and Pinocchio had been sent a copy of it.

'The concerns raised by the GDC had been addressed and fully rectified. There were an extensive number of reports made at the time and the GDC were satisfied that the concerns they had raised had been rectified.'

It would later be demonstrated that the GDC had in fact raised a new set of concerns to Professor Pinocchio in May 2017 (2 months before my disciplinary). They had informed him that their concerns were in response to the disclosures I had sent them. Some of their new concerns overlapped with the previous ones raised in 2013 and at the time of my disciplinary hearing The Icon (headed by Pinocchio) had already agreed with the GDC to address the concerns.

'there is no future between us and HA, we cannot work with him, we have been fighting with HA for 2 years, the relationship is totally untenable,'

This demonstrated that Pinocchio and his leadership team had been fighting me personally rather than addressing my valid concerns. It also demonstrated that they had pre-empted the investigation and had already reached their own conclusion prior to the disciplinary committee completing its investigations. (*The plan was probably hatched about the time that Dr Delphic was preparing his whistleblowing whitewash report*).

No, it's more than that. The Icon needs to move on and it cannot move on with HA as an employee, everything that has happened in the last 2 years has resulted in this lack of trust and confidence.

There was nothing more he could have said to make his position anymore ridiculous. His facial expression looked as if he knew he had damaged himself and that he knew like everyone else in the room that his story was implausible. His plan (if there was one) had started to melt as soon as Claire started her cross examination. He hadn't expected to be cross examined and seemed to answer her questions from his repertoire of pre-prepared ones. If the hearing had been a criminal trial in crown court he'd have blundered his way to convicting himself.

Pinocchio's performance bothered me for a long time, I mean really bothered me. It reeked of an arrogant lack of proficiency which complemented his aimless frivolous attitude. Especially since the previous year he had given a presentation to over 300 members of *The Dental Institutes* alumni. I was in the audience. His presentation compared the students of the 1970's with today's students. He reported student complaints were at the highest level ever. The complaints were nastier than ever. The students were more difficult to appease than ever. Mental health issues amongst them were at their highest level ever. Alcohol and drug abuse was at its highest level ever. I would say that the extent to which these broad concerns have appeared in the literature have placed them in the position of an adage. However they, in my experience, are not a creation of the universities. They are part a broader cultural problem which starts in the home from where they extend into schools. Universities merely contribute to the melee by making their own mess.

What he didn't report was the nature of the complaints being made. In my experience the complainants can be broadly divided into two categories; valid versus Invalid. The valid complaints were generally from students who wanted to be empowered not bullshitted. They despise bouncing bull-shitters who supply a raft of contradictions depending on how they are quizzed. These students wanted to tap the brains of experts not bull-shitters. Above all they want to be shown and taught how to think not what to think. It's entirely possible (and very likely) the students doing most of the invalid complaining were not the same ones who desired the quality training.

It has to be considered that some students are no angels themselves (actually them being angels is part of the problem). They arrive at university ill-equipped to perform the simplest of basic tasks, don't know how to switch on a vacuum cleaner; are unsure if they need to put washing powder in the washing machine. They need to be shown how to identify the top and bottom of an egg and have their hand held as they crack it on to their cornflakes. What's worse they appear to have convinced themselves that they need to keep their vacuous brains as empty as possible for the storage of mathematical formulae and facts falsely hyped as esoteric. The important point to note is this is a consequence of bad parenting.

In my experience there are a substantial and worrying number of parents who send their useless iddlings to universities, having convinced themselves that university will teach them everything (just as they did of the schools and colleges before them). Sadly that's not the role of the universities and universities have been struggling to cope with such individuals for some time. I know that back in the day (at times) mine struggled with me. Universities provide academic input whilst the experience of being at one provides an environment in which to enhance life skills; the key word being enhance. Whilst 'loco parentis' still remains a legal requirement its application started to diminish significantly after 1968 (when Oxford university started to structure it out) onwards in an effort to prevent what might be considered violations of the students civil liberties. Modern universities don't dare tell the iddlings how useless they are (as this would be detrimental to their balance sheet) but instead pander to their millennial needs prior to issuing them a gilded certificate. It would be near impossible to set up a better environment for the perpetuation of the problems Pinocchio was describing; or a better pathway to a mental implosion.

It seems right to me that prior to receiving education in a specific specialised area of academic, industrial or professional interest the basics should be place. It seems right to me that domestic household duties should be embraced as convenient (and cost effective) early opportunities with which to lay down the all important neural pathway template for skills. The home is the children's centre of early development and domestic household skills are the most elementary of the basic ones as they give spawn to the neural pathway upon which all future meaningful talents will be developed. Performing household duties challenges the individual (from an early age) to evaluate a situation and organise its remedy. But instead precious individuals discard them as odious, tedious and demeaning. Another way of looking at the situation is by imagining someone who says: 'I'm going to apply to take part in the Olympics!' who then responds to the question 'what practice have you done?' by saying 'don't be stupid, practice is for amateurs, I'm an Olympian!'

Keeping a bedroom clean or cleaning one demonstrates the presence or absence of the most fundamental and key observational, analytical, organisational and operational skills. It's not about the bedroom it's about the neural pathway. The skills neural pathways ends by triggering a surge of feel good chemicals associated with the feel good factor of 'finishing what was started'. It's a feeling that shapes the approach individuals take in forming their lives and careers in later life. It seems right to me that the state of the bedroom reflects a state of mind, how can it not? (see Maslow's hierarchy of needs). Similarly, using a kitchen to prepare a meal prior to leaving it clean for the use of others demonstrates the presence or absence of the same skills plus ones of integration alongside a healthy respect for the concept of civilisation. The presence or absence of which will most definitely influence how the individual does or does not function in an organised workplace with other team members. Absence exposes a potentially debilitating weakness in concentration or an entrenched disregard for responsibility or both layered with a terribly misguided attitude of self importance.

I would argue that these individuals fail to flourish academically or in the workplace for two main reasons. The basic skills are missing and the idyll attitude which resulted in their shortage. It's inconceivable that their parents didn't contribute to their failure to prepare themselves for the rigours of independent life. I would argue that the parents bare the greatest responsibility for the failure and are (most likely) the same parents who make the work of schools so much more difficult by failing to assist in the development of the basic skills. The backlash of which has been plaguing another community of innocent individuals, those who suffer with a neurological disorder; autism. They suffer more if they do not acquire the basic skills and require a more formal and structured approach to their development.

Autism is a neurological disorder and not the result of bad parenting; however there is an overlap between the characteristics of the child product of bad parenting and some autistic children. In my experience some of children who are the products of bad parenting exaggerate their inability to deliberately mislead others (when it suits them); it's the new 'cry-wolf'. The net result is some children who are the products of bad parenting incorrectly get diagnosed as autistic, it is often deliberately sought. It offers a label behind which their parents and they can hide for the thereafter; breathing heavy fiery scorn on any sceptical onlookers. At the same time children who suffer a genuine neurological disorder get looked upon sceptically as possible products of bad parenting; whilst their parents breathe heavy fiery scorn on any sceptical onlookers. The parents of autistic children often get ground to a pulp amid the bureaucratic and societal scepticism created by bad parents.

Behavioural therapists have reported they spend a substantial amount of time pointing out to bad parents the disparity between the professional assessment of their child versus the parent's 'perception' or 'picture' or 'story' of the same child. I would argue that establishing where an individual falls on the current spectrum is made miasmic and potentially flawed by the inaccuracy (like all things medical) of the 'story telling' by parents and patients alike (most often deliberate). Therapists, of any sort, are challenged and limited as they can only provide a professional interpretation of what they've been told and humans suffer a great difficulty being true to themselves let alone others. This creates the problem that therapists become cynically sceptical that all parents might be delusional and attempting to conceal their bad parenting; which is not fair on those who have a child with a true neurological disorder.

When I went to university I did so with all the basic skills in place. I was, however, poorly prepared for the transition to independent life as the seedlings for some of the more sophisticated skills were missing. The most obvious of which were responsibility and discipline; sadly the tardy inconsistencies of the course didn't do much to encourage a significant improvement in either of them at the time. With the benefit of hindsight I do wish I'd had a more informed childhood.

The general scheme of our cultural and political landscape pays the highest regard for and positions the independence of the individual near its centre. But having workplaces full of individuals (at every level) who lack the basic skills has been affecting workplace performance and the health and happiness of those who have to endure working alongside such individuals for some time (possibly forever). It's a cultural problem which certainly predates the millennial's but needs redress. It seems right to me the basic skills and household duties should be integrated in with other forms of play from the year after diapers come off onwards. It's a clear responsibility of the parents to develop the independence of their individual. Perhaps a deal could done with schools so they might be more involved and by the age of eight the school day could end with the pupils tidying the classroom, wiping down the tables, sweeping and mopping the floor. Once a month they could polish the windows and wash the dining room on a rota. This would encourage children to learn from an early age that life requires the tedious mundane jobs to be done alongside the more interesting ones. It would garner in them the necessity to be able to concentrate in the absence of the cacophony of stimulants they seem to require so much nowadays.

As for mental health problems the **Kevin Hines** story softened my peanuts a bit. Kevin attempted suicide by jumping off the Golden Gate Bridge in San Francisco. He is one of only thirty-six (less than 1%) to survive the fall and he is the only Golden Gate Bridge jump survivor who is actively spreading the message of living mentally healthy around the globe. A great deal of his work is on the internet.

The Inspiration.

I work Saturdays in a Central London practice just around the corner from a fashion shop called 'Zadig and Voltaire' located at number 19 South Molton Street. Imani had seen a dress in the window which she'd wanted for a while, but I couldn't justify the cost so I decided to research why the fashion was so expensive. I typed 'Zadig and Voltaire' into Google and before long found myself teleported into a deep conversation with François-Marie Arouet. We were in a damp smoky coffee shop somewhere in central Paris; it was 1750-ish and François told me that he preferred it if I used his nom de plume; Voltaire. I did as asked, Voltaire it was. We sat chatting for what seemed like days but it was actually only hours (or not really at all). He told me he had written a lot of books on the Enlightenment. How he loved reading history but wasn't so keen on Christianity, especially the Catholic Church. How he was a big fan of freedom of religion, freedom of speech and the separation of the church and the state. I was fascinated. He told me that he knew London well and had lived in Wandsworth as well as Covent Garden. He came across as ambitious and confident telling me that he planned to write twenty thousand letters and two thousands books in his working life. He also knew a thing or two about thugs, especially noble one's who abused their power. He told me about the time he was exiled from France and how whilst in exile he circled English high society. He described having had nasty brushes with authority regularly. He was a good companion and the perfect advocate for me at my stage in my journey.

I shared my story with him and described the struggles I was having. He said it all sounded like old news but nevertheless sympathised with my situation and warned me that I would need to be very careful. His exact words were: It is dangerous to be right in matters about which the established authorities are wrong. As soon as I heard his warning I found myself asking myself: if I had met him prior to the experience and he'd given me the same warning would I have understood what it meant? Would I still have blown the whistle? My experience taught me that I would not have understood it prior to the experience. I also concluded that I probably wouldn't have extracted the same meaning of it from a book either and that the limited experience I could have had from a book was the experience of reading. The only way I could have experienced how dangerous it was to be right on matters which the established authorities were wrong is to have blown the whistle on them..........it's the hard way because it's the only way.

My new friend was certain that I would end up at the gallows unless I started to run (only I wasn't going to run). He tried desperately to get his message across to me and told me:

'It is forbidden to kill; therefore all murderers are punished unless they kill in large numbers and to the sound of trumpets'

I didn't really understand what he meant and asked him to explain it to me again. He told me that in his opinion the existence of God and/or belief in God were beneficial to and necessary for a society to function in a civilised way:

'If God did not exist, it would be necessary to invent him'

He pointed out to me that absent morals or the absence of fair play was nothing new. They were missing back in 1786.

I asked him if his friend Zadig could offer me any advice. He laughed and corrected me. Zadig he explained was not a friend of his, it was the title of a book he had written. The book was a work of fiction in which he had represented his philosophy. He hadn't been overly accurate with some of the history in it but had used the protagonist to make thinly disguised references to social and political problems of his own day.

Having understood that I wasn't going to run he expressed his admiration of me:

'Think for yourself and let others enjoy the privilege of doing so too'

I told him that I had been thinking for myself all along but had struggled to understand why the members of the leadership team had continued with the pretence that my concerns were not valid. Not a single one of them took the opportunity to address or rectify them. His advice was for me to get myself ready for more of the same and to continue to have my mind challenged with even more deceit:

'The more often a stupidity is repeated, the more it gets the appearance of wisdom'

I had already started to understand some of what he meant but asked him why my colleagues had been so shy to offer any support, he described them simply as cowards and fools who had succumbed to the hypnotic charms of a complacent leadership team:

'Those who can make you believe absurdities, can make you commit atrocities'

My frown was replaced with a smile when he told me:

'Common sense is not so common'

What worried me most was how he remained resolutely confident that I would NOT succeed:

'Our wretched species is so made that those who walk on the well-trodden path always throw stones at those who are showing a new road'

He wished me well and told me it would be better for my health if my journey ended sooner rather than later:

'The longer we dwell on our misfortunes, the greater is their power to harm us'

As he got up to leave he paused and sighed heavily before slowly taking in a lung full of air so that he could tell me that if I was not going to run I should prepare myself for more uncertainty:

'Doubt is an uncomfortable condition, but certainty is a ridiculous one'

I was learning........

I was learning more than I had done in the previous 46 years, that when a groups intentions overrule an individual's rights, injustice is rarely far behind. I should never have criticised myself at anytime, not one tiny bit. There hadn't been anything wrong with me; my head had been on straight all along.

I was learning that before civilization began people dreaded a visit from Kings Charles I & II. There men had a tendency to shit everywhere. They would shit in the hallway, in the fireplace, in your pots, they shat everywhere. Later, with the introduction of civilization people sort of stopped shitting everywhere, but somewhere between 1971 and 2019 the pendulum swung a bit too far in the opposite direction allowing the majority of people to start living in denial of their organic nature. For example, the Debrett's

Guide for the Modern Gentleman states: 'it is ruder to point out someone who has farted than it is to have done the fart in the first place'. This degree of denial has allowed some people to disconnect from the fact that the food they put in at the top is turned into the poop coming out at the bottom by them sucking all the goodness out of it and adding their bacteria to it. Which is not a problem because it's another one of the circles in life. The problem starts when the disconnect results in individuals believing that they are evolving at the same rate as the technology around them. Which is just wrong, isn't it? Especially since staying close to nature keeps us happier and healthier and makes disease easier to understand when it develops. Staying in touch with the organic nature of life helps us maintain a better relationship with food as it helps us retain a sense that our body can only extract from it but cannot exceed the goodness it contains.

I learnt a joke which embraced keeping in touch with the organic nature of things and offered an amusing 'point of view'. It goes like this: A man stood looking out from behind the iron bars on his window at the mental asylum. He called out to the estate gardener: 'what's that you are putting on the rhubarb?' Cow shit replied the gardener. 'the doctors think I'm mad, but I put custard on mine' replied the man casually.

I was learning that when the leadership team was busy posturing immediately before my suspension they were at the fight stage:

'First they ignore you, then they laugh at you, then they fight you, then you win'

Mahatma Gandhi

The prospect of a possible win, as improbable as it was, lifted my spirit and left me feeling somewhat sanguine. The optimism contained in Gandhi's words put a smile on my face. Which then removed itself just as fast when I remembered the advice I had received from the first ever consultant I worked for. I had just told him I was thinking of training to be a specialist and his advice was: "Be very careful, the Indian face is the face of cheap NHS dentistry". His statement was fascinating, I didn't really understand what he meant by it but it wasn't racism, he was Indian. Cosmopolitan have since published lists & lists of features, traits and characteristics humans look for in the ones they choose to trust most and invest in. That's far more fascinating.

Will over Skill

'The will has to be stronger than the skill'

Muhammed Ali

This quotation acted as my saviour when all previous inspiration had been exhausted and ran dry. Fate had brought me to this point and was continuing to challenge me, not so softly. This quote offered me some much needed reassurance when the future promised more harshness as every man's hand remained against me.

I first read this quotation back in **July 2016** in the book Muhammed Ali had co authored with his daughter; Soul of a butterfly. The impasse was sheer exhaustion and a total loss in my desire for any human affection. This quote offered me comfort when the prospect of losing everything was the loudest silent echo my mind could hear, whilst I was leading an increasingly lonely life.

In this chapter I'll explain how this quote made it possible for me to make my way back into the same hell I had just fought my way out of. How it made it possible for me to decipher negative emotions with more ease and moved me more swiftly into being subjected to a second disciplinary process. Its effects were weird and wonderful in equal measure. Through it I realised that somehow I was not the sum total of what I had learnt so far because my brain had, against my will, deleted some of the pain (as brains are programmed to do, subconsciously). To my surprise my mind had only part-stored a skeleton of my previous experiences; it had shed the rotting flesh. This quote stopped the heavy criticisms I levied on my conscious self for not 'saving' more of what I had previously learnt. I'll also explain the wonderful part.

The Experience

The cast in this chapter

Leadership team	Given name
New executive Dean	Professor Pinocchio (prone to telling lies)
Head of Department	Dr Perfidious (deceitful & untrustworthy)
Clinical Director	Dick Dastardly (a nasty devious bastard)
Human resources	Horse Rectum ((defecates bullshit on a regular basis)
Dean of Education	Dr Delphic (deliberately obscure & ambiguous)
Chairman of Council	Dr Magoo

The story so far........

1. 15th September 2015; whistle blown.

2. 2nd October 2015; Nasty Meeting with Dr Dick Dastardly.

3. 16th October 2015; Incognito Meeting with Professor Pinocchio.

4. 19th October 2015; Dick Dastardly's failed attempt to drown me in IT.

5. 1st Week December 2015; Dr Perfidious tells a bunch of staff 'Hafeez is a liability; I'll have to get rid of him'. (ouch my shoulder blades)

6. 7th December 2015; my expression of grievance to Dr Dastardly about the above.

7. 8th December 2015; IT team produces a report which implicates me as uniquely experiencing the concerns I'd reported. (ouch)

8. 17th December 2015; Dr Perfidious produces a report which implicates me as uniquely experiencing the concerns I'd reported. (ouch)

9. 8th April 2016. Professor Pinocchio & Mr Wily failed to re-label my protected disclosures a grievance. (phew)

10. 18th July 2016; Mr high-up concluded the leadership couldn't have known that I had blown the whistle.

11. 4th August 2016; Dr Insightful initiated a formal investigation into my concerns.

12. 30th September 2016; Sinister meeting with Dr Comprehensive.

13. 24th October 2016; I complain to the CEO of the NHS trust.

14. 26th January 2017; I escalate my concerns to the General Dental Council.

15. 31st January 2017; Dr Magoo neutralised my concerns citing Dr Delphic's whiter than white soap-suds report.

16. 2nd February 2017; I informed The Iconic Machine that I'd escalated my concerns to the GDC.

17. 17th March 2017; I was suspended on 7 spurious allegations.

18. 12th April 2017; the spurious evidence pack arrived.

19. 21st April 2017; flawed investigation No 1.

20. 7th July 2017; first disciplinary hearing.

.....On the **19th July 2017** I was informed of the outcome of the disciplinary hearing. None of the allegations had been proved. However, the panel expressed their concerns that there may have been a breakdown in my relationship with some of my colleagues; don't figure. I had only defended myself against the allegations and I had taken a measured approach to how serious they were. I hadn't succeeded by fluke, each of the allegations had been tested one by one and one by one they had been set aside in the absence of any supporting evidence. (*Yet I couldn't have known that I hadn't got to the weirdest part yet*).

As none of the allegations against me have been proven there was no case of misconduct. They may have managed to keep it a secret amongst themselves but they had (after all) made concessions with the General Dental Council to remedy the concerns I'd raised. In light of which, I should have received an apology and been returned to my normal duties. I waited patiently for an apology and for the suspension to be lifted. Instead on the **20th August 2017** I received a letter which announced that there was going to be a second disciplinary process. I was, once again, gob-smacked; I thought they might have exhausted themselves and had already tried every trick in the book. Silly me. I asked myself, what other lessons in life was I about to be taught? How would it be approached?

They had come up with a doozy and I have pasted below the letter which started the second round of hunting below:

Dear Dr Ahmed

Re: Disciplinary Investigation

Following my letter of 19th July 2017, my attention has been drawn to a further issue concerning communications with patients which could, if substantiated, amount to very serious misconduct on your part. The issue is whether there are reasonable grounds to believe that you were involved in the preparation and/or sending of one or more letters falsely purporting to be from the General Dental Council ("GDC") to patients of the Dental Institute. I propose to arrange for this to be investigated by an external investigator on behalf of The Icon and either I or the investigator will be in touch with you shortly on this. Pending consideration of this issue and in view of the issues with regard to working relationships between you and key colleagues in the Institute, it will be necessary for your suspension to continue on the same terms as previously notified to you. I attach a copy of the relevant disciplinary procedure for your information.

In the meantime, I am proposing to put on hold any consideration of the broader concerns about a possible breakdown in working relationships between you and key colleagues in the Institute referred to in my letter of 19th July 2017."

  This was no cruel departure; it was a natural escalation of the ongoing cruelty. I had been lumped with the arduous task of preparing for a second disciplinary procedure. Trepidation set in hard and fast as the rules of fair play had already been disregarded, dismantled or willfully breached in round one. Ding-Ding Round 2. Naturally, I wasn't looking forward to the joys that had been pre-planned for me in round two. My reverence for the scale of the audacity was the only thing holding my self control together and I worried that I might lose it. I couldn't remember another time in my life when I had felt like this. Nothing made me feel good anymore. I badly needed someone to hold my hand but my friends were also getting exhausted or exasperated and I was embarrassed to continue to lean on them any longer.

  These fella's were determined to kick the stuffing out of me. I would have loved to refer to the emergence of these letters as a proper handjob but they were printed. It was a sinking moment though, someone had fabricated fraudulent letters with a view to have me referred to Albert Pierrepoint (that's code for 'chop my head off'). FYI Albert Pierrepoint was an English hangman who executed between 435 and 600 people in a 25-year career that ended in 1956. So much for scared being sacred; nothing was sacred anymore. This was a call the cop's moment. (*I would later learn that the GDC escalated the fraudulent letters to the Metropolitan Police fraud squad, only the fraud squad never got back in touch).* Thank god the fraud squad is an honest bunch.

Despite knowing that I had nothing to do with any fraudulent letters I couldn't count on surviving the ambush. Even if I did survive it I could clearly see that I was being lined up for a dismissal on the grounds of breakdown in relationships with key colleagues; it's a well documented technique used by leadership teams to avoid or sidestep the laws designed to protect me as a whistleblower. Anyhow I could have cried but instead by this stage I had developed an appetite for the sport and started to relish what they might conjure up next. It surprised me how pleased I was that they still hadn't paid someone off to claim that I had touched her boobs inappropriately; not in the stairwell and not in the lift and certainly not in the back office.

This time to keep the pretence of sincerity on the go they hired an independent investigator; Brian. Brian was supposed to gather evidence in a disinterested and objective manner. His objective should have been to search for and uncover the truth. I was represented by Claire on behalf of the University and College Union (UCU); she had represented me during the first disciplinary as well. She was the most remarkable woman I have every met in my entire life. Cool, calm, collected, concise, confident, and convivial. She had a kind face and made it clear that she was in control. I knew I was in safe hands the very first time I met her. I think it was the way she pinned me to the floor (metaphorically) during our very first meeting. No wriggle room whatsoever. She managed to pour some sugar on me; that's for sure. It turned out that Claire was very good at asking questions which were designed to only elicit the facts, avoiding hearsay. It was obvious that she was legally trained but I had no idea to what level. One thing was very clear; her questions were all designed to hammer home a point. Which she did very well.

The investigation meeting took place on **18th September 2017** (2 years and 3 days since I'd blown the whistle). Brian opened the meeting by reading out the allegation prior to placing a photocopy of a letter in front of me. He asked me what it looked like to me. I told him it looked like a photocopy of a letter from the GDC.

'It's obviously a fake' was his next statement.
'Why?' I asked.
'It obvious, it's very cutty pasty'.

To which I replied: 'It looks like a photocopy of a letter from the GDC, to me.'

Claire interrupted and asked Brian:
"Have the GDC confirmed that they didn't send these letters?"

Brian confirmed that the GDC had not responded to his enquiry.

Claire told him:
"I'm concerned you have pre-empted your investigation". The meeting ended about 5 minutes later.

Claire wrote on my behalf to Horse Rectum (HR) and Mr Magoo.

Dear *Icon*,

Dr Ahmed has asked me to respond to your email below. As you may know, I attended the investigation meeting conducted by Brian this morning in my capacity as Dr Ahmed's companion.

Please note that it was very clear at the meeting that no information had been provided to *The Machine* which could reasonably be described as "of a potentially serious nature" as stated by you in the email below. The investigation proceeded on the basis that the GDC letters to patients were not genuine GDC letters but did so without any evidence to back up that assertion. Brian told us that he had written to the GDC asking for confirmation of whether the letters were from them but has yet to receive any response. When asked why an investigation had been started when there was no evidence that the letters had not come from the GDC, he replied that "it was very likely" and that they looked like a "cut and paste" job. Clearly these statements are a matter of opinion, not fact and are indicative of the spurious basis upon which this investigation has been launched. As such, we maintain that this is a witch-hunt of our member and a further detriment to him for raising whistleblowing concerns.

We look forward to receiving the transcript of the meeting today as promised (redacted where appropriate). Please note that, until we receive any objective indication that there is genuinely any information "of a potentially serious nature" as asserted by you, Dr Ahmed is unable to determine what evidence (if anything) will be useful to the proper conduct of this particular investigation. Clearly if the GDC confirm that the letters came from them, there will be no case to answer and this investigation should be dropped. Dr Ahmed therefore has no further information to provide at this stage but reserves the right to do so should it become apparent that it is necessary for the proper conduct of a reasonable investigation.

The external investigator has promised to send us a copy of his letter to the GDC and their reply (once received). Please ensure that this is done and kindly expedite Dr Ahmed's grievance as a matter of urgency so that a full and fair investigation of all the facts can be progressed without any further unnecessary delay.

I look forward to hearing from you by return.

Claire

Brian completed his investigation and made the following statement of summary:

'On the balance of probability, I would conclude that Dr Ahmed is a potential author of the letters but the evidence I have seen does not show with a high degree of certainty that he was the author or was involved in sending them'.

Brian made no effort to conceal the bias of his investigation which was that he had only tried to pin the letters on one person – me. He hadn't really given himself the opportunity of a chance of establishing the true author(s) of the letters because the sum total of the people he investigated was one – me. I didn't have any evidence as to who authored them; I only had a list of individuals who had created a real mess and had a lot to lose from my survival.

(I would later learn that the GDC conducted their own independent investigations, they did the same as Brian and instead of looking for evidence to identify the true authors they only looked for evidence to pin them on me and found none).

The lack of evidence didn't deter The Icon from ploughing full steam ahead and swiftly scheduling a second disciplinary hearing to take place on **8th December 2017**. Later in the chapter I have included my response to the new allegation. It is a detailed response and potentially valuable if you ever end up in a similar situation to mine. But for now here's a brief summary: The hearing breached ACAS rules of fair play. I requested permission to make an audio recording, permission was denied. Claire raised something like 8 objections; to include the fact that the New New Executive Dean (no longer Professor Pinocchio) kept deliberately misrepresenting Brian's investigation report. She was shushed.

Dick Dastardly attended to give evidence. His evidence helped me a lot. He had previously told the GDC that none of the patients had made any formal complaints but his own evidence bundle contained a copy of a letter from one of the same patients to the GDC, the patient told the GDC he had written a letter for complaint after which things got better. Dastardly could not explain the whereabouts of the patient's letter of complaint. His evidence bundle also demonstrated that he had spoken with 3 of the patients who's complaints I'd escalated, so I asked him what those patients had told him about the complaints they had made to me.

I have no idea, I didn't ask them! was his response.

He also gave evidence that he had been advised by his indemnity insurer to distance himself from any matters relating to me and the patients but that he had ignored their advice and had continued to be involved.

I prepared two statements for the hearing:
1.   STATEMENT   REGARDING   THE   INVESTIGATION CONDUCTED BY BRIAN.
2.   STATEMENT   REGARDING   THE   DISCILINARY HEARING ON 8-12-17.

STATEMENT REGARDING THE INVESTIGATION CONDUCTED BY BRIAN.

• The General Dental Council (GDC) has not denied sending the letters but I have no explanation for how it could have written to patients prior to being given names and addresses. I accept that the available facts suggest that the letter has probably not originated from the GDC.

• Whilst there is no evidence I accept that it is reasonable to believe that the letters are fake. It is not reasonable to believe that they were sent by me.

• If not sent by the GDC then they could have been sent by anyone with access to the records at The Icon. This could be anyone with an IT system login. All clinical staff, all admin staff, all students, all leadership. Despite the above, Brian restricted his investigation to interviewing only 2 individuals, me and Dick Dastardly.

• The investigation does not question who may have had the motive to author the alleged fraudulent GDC letter. In the context of this case it would be reasonable to consider: Student hi jinx?; A disgruntled student?; A disgruntled staff member? Clinical or secretarial? ; Someone who was aware of my disclosures and who sent the letters as a misguided, inappropriate and naive act of 'support'; Someone at The Icon who was acting for the benefit of the dental law partnership, perhaps on commission for sending them work; Someone wishing to discredit me? The investigation was one sided and only investigated and considered me as the likely author of the letter. All of the above are possible and should all have been investigated and considered as part of a thorough and fair investigation.

• Evidence presented at previous proceedings shows that the IT system keeps a log of who has accessed clinical records and when. Has the investigation checked those IT records to establish a shortlist of individuals who had access to all of the records. Who's names are on that list?; Is Ahmed's name on the list?. If not checked then was Brian informed that this information was available to him?

• Brian fails to consider the possibility that the letters were sent by someone in the leadership team at the DI to discredit me and assist in "getting rid" of me for making protected disclosures as evidenced by the subject access request.

• In his statement Dr Dastardly stated that he ceased line management responsibilities for me in April 2016. In the context of my protected disclosures and the subsequent bullying it is evident that he continued to be involved at all times; this is evidenced in the subject access request.

• Despite a very limited investigation Brian does not come to the conclusion that I was more likely than not to have sent those letters. There is no reasonable reason for this committee to believe that I sent the letter.

STATEMENT REGARDING THIS DISCILINARY HEARING ON 8-12-17

• 2 years ago I noticed some dangerous and illegal practices at the institute.

• I did the right thing and made some protected disclosures to help the institute recognise and improve patient safety and student learning.

• Those protected disclosures are the reason why I am here today.

• Over the last 2 years everything I have done has been entirely correct, entirely professional and entirely in the open. The same cannot be said of the institute or its agents.

• Several other staff members have written letters to the institute detailing exactly the same concerns that I have raised. Those letters appear in the evidence bundle.

• Since raising my protected disclosures it has come to light that the institute was criticised by the regulator for exactly the same failings as I described just two years before my disclosures.

• As a result of my protected disclosures the regulator is actively investigating individual staff members for professional failings including four members of the leadership team. The regulator has already written a statement that it has found failings within the institute in the areas that I highlighted and that the institute has admitted the failings and agreed to necessary improvements. That written statement appears in the evidence bundle.

• At a previous disciplinary hearing in July 2017 Professor Pinocchio stood in front of the committee representing the institute and said 'Dr Ahmed's concerns are not valid and not shared by anyone else at the institute' That statement was a lie. At that point the institute (headed by Professor Pinocchio) had already admitted the failings to the regulator and had already agreed to make improvements.

• Professor Pinocchio told the committee that it was not possible for me to return to the institute because they had spent the last 2 years fighting with me. His choice of words says it all. Instead of properly investigating the protected disclosures as I raised them the institute has instead been fighting me personally. It is still fighting with me because of my protected disclosures.

• When I first raised my concerns they ignored them. Next they invited me into an office and shouted at me. They openly told my colleagues I am a liability and that they need to get rid of me. They emailed each other discussing their plan to suspend me knowing that they had no evidence of wrong doing. They emailed each other agreeing to delay suspending me whilst they found some evidence of wrong doing. They made allegations against me which in a previous disciplinary committee (July 2017) had found to be unsubstantiated.

• Now they have made a new spurious allegation against me with no evidence what so ever.

• The institute has failed to conduct a thorough investigation into these new allegations, failed to properly brief the investigator, failed to provide vital evidence to the investigator, failed to consider other likely explanations other than their continued vendetta against me, blocked me from contacting professional colleagues, students and patients to build my case, blocked me from calling witnesses from the above groups, consistently refused to commence grievance proceedings into the way I am being bullied and harassed.

• The institute and its agents have behaved appallingly towards me and these proceedings represent just the latest episode in that maltreatment. There is no evidence what so ever of any wrong doing on my part and copious evidence of extensive wrong doing on the part of the institute and its agents. There is only one possible explanation for me being here today. My protected disclosures embarrassed the institute and its leadership and as a result the institute wants to silence and get rid of me. There is no other plausible explanation.

• What this committee needs to do now is conclude this disciplinary procedure, throw out this new allegation, return me to my post and recommend a full and formal grievance procedure into the institutes handling of my protected disclosures, the subsequent bullying and victimization and the failings in the university's investigation into my wrongful suspension. This committee is either complicit with me being victimised and bullied or this committee and this process is being used as a weapon by others to victimise and bully me. This needs to stop now as if this committee was not complicit before it certainly becomes complicit if it continues to allow itself to be misused in this fashion.

• On the matter of a breakdown of working relationship my position is unchanged. I love my job and I see no breakdown.

• There must be a proper investigation and a proper grievance process which will identify failings, malpractice and bullying. None of those failings will be mine.

• I have every faith in the process and its ability to identify areas where the institute needs to improve, staff that need retraining, staff that need to be disciplined and appropriate disciplinary outcomes for those staff. The process will identify areas where the institute and its staff owe me an apology. Once the process is complete I will happily put this whole matter behind me and get on with working with whoever remains in post. I love my teaching job at the institute and I am very good at it.

• In time we will all look back on this sequence of events and agree that it was a positive catalyst for necessary improvements.

After the hearing I looked back at the whistleblowing report to confirm to myself that Dr Delphic had indeed 'shone his torch' and lined me up in a way to support a future claim of a possible 'breakdown of relationships' with colleagues. The intention of which was to allow The Icon to claim that I was dismissed for the manner in which I blew the whistle and for not the fact that I'd blown it. I was confident my dismissal was their only objective during the planning of my suspension. Delphic's report was conveniently ambiguous and vague and demonstrated his attempt to fool himself and others with fantasies and delusions instead of what was actually going on. I'm sorry to say but any suggestion that he or any of the other staff could not have known what was going on was, is utter nonsense. Pretty much every qualified staff member at The Icon at the time (specialist or generalist; young or old; male or female; brown, white or yellow; religious or not; under weight, correct weight or over; preferring a fanny or a dick or an arse or all of the options with a cocaine kicker) was fully aware that the patients notes were woefully inadequate in respect to periodontal care in most cases.

Shortly after my suspension I made a SUBJECT ACCESS REQUEST. FYI any employee at any time can request all the information that the employer holds on them. It's made allowable by the Data Protection Act 1998. In accordance with the act I asked to see the information The Icon held on me. The Icon had forty days by law to fulfill my request which unsurprisingly it failed to do. My request was for all documents in which I could be identified. That's emails, letters, memos, meeting agendas and meeting minutes. I had planned to use the information to prepare my defence during the first disciplinary but was prevented from doing so. When the information did finally arrive I used it to prepare a summary for my second disciplinary. Here's the summary:

EXTRACTS FROM A SUBJECT DATA REQUEST PRESENTING A COUNTER ARGUMENT THAT THE ALLEGED FRAUDULENT GDC LETTER WAS AUTHORED BY A MEMBER OF THE LEADERSHIP TEAM OR ONE OF THEIR AGENTS.

• I made a subject data access request for data held by the Dental Institute (DI) in which Dr Hafeez Ahmed could be identified. In total 25 staff member names were listed in the request to include: Pinocchio, Perfidious, Dr Dastardly, Sleeping Beauty, Delphic, Horse Rectum and Dr Magoo.

• These extracts demonstrate that as early as October 2015 it was being stated that Dr Hafeez Ahmed was the only clinical teacher who uniquely experienced the concerns which he had raised. This theme continues throughout the extracts.

• As early as December 2015 Perfidious had stated that 'Dr Ahmed is a liability and I have to get rid of him'

• The extracts demonstrate that several members of staff stated "this has been going on for far too long, we need to come up with a plan to stop him"

• These extracts demonstrate that the activity to "get rid" of Dr Ahmed intensified in the 2 week period after the date on the alleged fraudulent GDC letter; 27th February 2017.

• The final extract is one of many correspondences between the DI and the General Dental Council (GDC) which resulted in the GDC confirming that the concerns raised by me had been valid and that improvements at the DI were necessary. The DI acknowledged this fact and agreed to make the necessary improvements.

• In the overall context of the protected disclosures made by me and the subsequent disciplinary procedures the leadership team had become desperate to silence and discredit me and it is most likely that the alleged fraudulent GDC letter was authored by one of them or by a close associate.

On the day of the hearing, after it was over Clare was as certain as I was that I would be dismissed. Thankfully, UCU arranged an emergency meeting with a legal team comprising a specialist employment solicitor and a specialist employment barrister. The meeting took place on **Wednesday 20th December 2017** (which turned out to be two days before I'd receive the outcome letter for my second disciplinary). Counsel was convinced that I would be dismissed on the grounds of a 'breakdown in relationships'. Not only would laws be side stepped but 'Breakdown in trust' would also benefit The Icon as it would avoid triggering an internal inquiry or recriminations against the leadership team.

One of the main reasons for meeting with the legal team as a matter of urgency was to take their advice as to whether or not (if dismissed) I had a good case for an IR application. They told me I didn't. IR refers to Interim Relief which is an application I was entitled to make to an Employment Tribunal for it to issue an order. If an application was approved and awarded The Icon would be compelled to put me back on the payroll pending a full employment tribunal hearing (whenever that may be). IR is only applicable in a limited number of circumstances; unfair dismissal of a whistleblower is one of them.

The legal team's advice was that my case was far too complex for an application for IR as it had dragged on for so long and the evidence bundle was hefty. This surprised me, as surely a whistle blowing case is a whistleblowing case irrespective of how long it has endured. I understood that should I want to make an application for IR I would have only 7 days from my dismissal to do so. I didn't have a problem with that. The problem, I was informed, was that should I make an application the courts are compelled to list an IR hearing within a 7 day period and courts don't like having to do so. The other problem was that at the IR hearing the judge would be obliged you consider the evidence bundle and judges don't like big ones. But by far the biggest problem was that if a judge were to approve an IR application the dynamics of the case would change dramatically. The focus of The Icon's legal team would shift from me to the Judge's decision. Meaning The Iconic Machine's legal counsel would make criticising and attacking the Judge's decision their first priority. Consequently, judges have a careful look at the size of The Iconic Machine's pockets before they approve any award for IR. In my case The Machine I was up against had the deepest pockets of any university and this made it very unlikely that any Judge was going to put his head on the chopping block next to mine.

Essentially, you can forget about the complaints made by the patients and students where this story started. The focus had previously shifted from them to me and now it could potentially shift from me to the judge. Marvelous.

The Inspiration.

In the weeks running up to my second disciplinary I had started to suffer big long pauses in any given activity. For example if I were frying an egg I could stare blankly at the yolk until the egg eventually went up in smoke. When near the sink I could stare at the congealed fat in an unwashed frying pan for an age admiring the random pattern it had made. I wasn't pre-occupied in deep thought; I was stuck motionless with a vacant mind. I often stirred my coffee for far too long because the tinkling of the spoon was somehow soothing and hypnotic. I could sit and count the oxygen molecules in the air as they drifted past me and on the one day I counted more than 180 before I crashed my car. I would have thought that second time round I'd be more relaxed, I was so wrong. I had even developed a neat ability of counting leaves on the trees which was more fun when they rustled in a blowing wind. I had visited my doctor and behaved a bit mad, it required a visit from the police later that same evening. Thank god doctors and police officers are an honest bunch. On the **5th October 2017** I was taken by ambulance to Warwick Hospital for severe chest pain and a suspected heart attack. Things weren't looking up. I spend the whole day at the hospital connected to machines that wheezed and pinged before being told that I had most probably suffered a muscle spasm in my sternum. I was left with the thought that my heart is a muscle and it's about 2 inches behind my sternum. Phew, a near miss. The suspect the strain was caused by the number of documents I had to prepare for my defence, all of which was being done after a day's normal work. I took a short break from seeing patients.

The hospital told me to take it easy for a few days. In the given opportunity I sat and watched the three heavyweight championship fights between Mohammed Ali and Joe Frasier on youtube, back to back, on a loop, in a trance. I listened to loads of different commentators commenting on different recordings of the same fights. I kept pausing for thoughts prior to repeatedly realising that each pause resulted in me reverting back to mindless gazing. Then it struck me that what was troubling me was the endless and differing faux expert views of the individuals who hadn't the courage to get into the ring themselves. They certainly talked a good talk and postured as if they were the masters, doing the two men in the ring a favour by, bestowing their wisdom on them. Each time either of fighters made a mistake they were belittled as the commentators relished the opportunity for a deluge of criticisms. As I marveled at the endurance of the two men who'd had the courage to get into the ring, I was inspired and the cat's chorus commentary faded into the background. Both fighters had very different styles and skills. During and after the fights the respect they gained for each other was phenomenal and became legendary. For all of Ali's taunting Joe Frazier never gave up his self control, he made 'sucking-it-up' look easy. The insults did get to him but he maintained his dignity. The two men would remain friends for the rest of their lives based on the fact no one else had 'whooped' their arses harder.

The president of America, Barrack Obama explained his thoughts on why Ali was different: 'But what made The Champ the greatest - what truly separated him from everyone else - is that everyone else would tell you pretty much the same thing'.

I watched the Oscar winning movie: When We Were Kings, a documentary of his 1974 fight against George Foreman in Zaire; Again. I then watched the same George Foreman in 1996, by which time Ali was struggling with Parkinson's disease, helping Ali up the steps to receive the Oscar. This was the same George Foreman who'd suffered a massive nervous breakdown after being knocked out by Ali on the world's stage. It appeared to me that some sort of respect comes out of battles even if the opponents don't admit them openly at the time. I must point out the contradiction as I had lost respect for my opponents for all the cheating that was going on.

Ali's words encouraged my endurance:

'My critics make me work harder'

He was over qualified for the job but he managed to keep me upright and walking, he stood by me and whispered in my ear:

'Success is not about winning all the time but how we recover after a fall'

Every few days another whisper:

'We all win sometimes and we all fail sometimes'

Him smiling, me frowning:
'Don't count the days make the days count'

Each time I flayed he'd whisper something:
'Often it isn't the mountains ahead that wear you out, it's the little pebble in your shoe'

Making me grit my teeth:
'You don't lose if you get knocked down; you lose if you stay down'

Encouraging me that I'd been doing alright all along:
'The will has to be stronger than the skill'

And if you're wondering, yep I did cry. Many times but on this occasion it wasn't fury it was exhaustion.

I was learning........

I was learning that I wasn't made of steel or stone but despite my life's lens becoming distorted I had, all along, demonstrated a will stronger than my skill. Being pushed into an experience beyond my comfort zone, for which I had no strategies, exposed my inner being.

I was learning that it was because of my biological responses that I would always stand and fight. They formed the fabric of my being. They were my strongest and the most inflexible ones. On closer scrutiny, however, the secret to my success (given the environment) was my psychological response. My courage to stand and fight may well have come from my biological responses but the resilience definitely came from my psychological response. My early life experiences had shaped me into a free thinking fiercely independent individual with a non-conformist personality. Adults were not to be trusted and the ones in my story rarely demonstrated the characteristics to gain my trust.

I was learning that at the beginning of the experience I had lacked the philosophical range or sophistication to temper my point of view. As I started to find the inspiration it was very helpful and essential. I could not have survived without it but its usefulness had limitations, as hard as I tried to use it to rein in my psychology or rule over my biology, I failed. The reason being the nature of nature is natural; imagine a sink full of water; once the plug is pulled the water doesn't need to be told what to do next. It flows naturally. Whilst the philosophy trained the higher powers of my mind and enabled me to deflect some of the offense, it was not going to be the supreme leader of my mind. It would remain a good personal assistant and that's because enhancing my philosophical view allows me to look at the same plate of shit from different angles; it doesn't remove the plate. Philosophy offered me some helpful filters but it wasn't capable of changing my colours. I am not in any way denouncing philosophy like Karl Marx did as it was crucial to my survival. I am just saying that it didn't help me in the way some scholars have described its utility.

I was learning that my will did not come from me focusing my mind or my consciousness. The main source of my will was my biological, primal, automatic, intuitive processes and I would summarise the evolution of my mental identity as:

BORN, SHAPED, STIMULATED.

I was learning that some individuals lack the confidence or experience to stand or fight and due to an understandable vulnerability have no option but to watch on helplessly as their futures are squandered. In addition to which the students struggle to cope with the high price of university education whilst enduring the frustration of picking up very few practical skills offered by the piss poor educational standards provided by corrupt, corrupted or weak adults. I am not saying that we should sit round in a circle holding hands singing Kum- ba- yah but things aren't going to get any better until (and I repeat) a larger number of individuals stand up for the published professional and ethical standards. If more people were to start saying what needs to be said and said it nicely, there would be a powerful positive move towards a revolution in the work place. The problem at the moment is as soon a one person speaks-up they are silenced, squashed and dismissed to be replaced from the never ending supply of the moral-free version of the human.

I was learning that I fundamentally don't like being dishonest. The leadership team probably didn't either. They were just defending the bad choices they had previously made right at the beginning. Foolishly, they had planned to use their seniority and not ability to destroy me. They misunderstood my politeness for weakness. They were almost smart enough to conceal their criminality. They had definitely succumbed to a thing called 'choice supportive bias', which basically means that once committed to a course of action, we cling onto the choice for dear life becoming ever more convinced that it was the right choice. The memory of the decision making process and why it was taken tends to be re-played repeatedly to back up the decision. There's even some evidence that, the act of telling someone they are wrong, even if you show them all the evidence which demonstrates why this is the case, can actually make them believe the wrong thing more. It's one of the reasons we get groupthink, when the dominant idea in a group overwhelms all the others. The very act of seeing other people do or believe a thing increases a desire to match them. All the classical signs of groupthink were in action at The Icon, as was a convenient collective amnesia. The groupthink was much like that demonstrated in Martin Sixsmith's telling of '**The Lost Child of Philomena Lee'.**

I was learning that groupthink coupled with a modicum of hubris and arrogance allowed the leadership team to believe that continuing to bury my concerns was the correct thing to do; either that or they had truly overestimated their own competence. If they had its not difficult to understand given how people often act in a desperate situation where they are hungry for social standing, or morale, or just need self reassurance that they haven't made a terrible mistake. If you want to read more about this phenomenon I would strongly suggest a paper titled '**Unskilled and Unaware of it: How Difficulties in Recognising One's Own Incompetence Lead to Inflated Self Assessment',** written by psychologists David Dunning and Justin Kruger.

I was learning that greed and promotional incentives had pushed individuals at every level to suppress the negative and spin the positive, creating mass delusion which became a crucial component of the disaster. A perfect storm had been whipped up on the back of terrible decisions, demonstrating that the leadership's capacity to learn from their mistakes remained as tenuous as ever as they missed every opportunity. Unfortunately they had blown the perfect opportunity for reform with a classical bit of delusional super villain style overreach. They simply ignored the bigger picture, instead when setbacks and pitfalls emerged; they ended up believing their own hype and convinced themselves ever more strongly that they'd been right all along. It's hard to escape the feeling that the leadership team were just replaying mistakes of the past at an ever increasing rate. Their failure to see the 'warning signs' would have been relatively excusable if it wasn't for their sustained active campaign to bury them.

Education and Personality

'Education is a process designed to help the individual become what they were meant to be and to hinder them from becoming what they were not meant to be'

Sir Chris Woodhead

My interest in education is as deep as an enchanted wishing well as it stems from the fact that it was my escape route from my Christian Catholic Muslim family who were engaged in practicing misguided doctrines which they seemed to have formed in their poverty stricken post colonial hangover.

I first read this quote somewhere between 2015 and 2016 and the newspaper article attributed it to Sir Chris Woodward but I have been unable to verify if they are his actual words or if indeed he said them. The impasse was my inability to accept how much of a mess the Icon was making of training its students and more generally the mess so many make of educating their own children and those of others. The words accurately represent my views on education which have been formed by observations of my own and that of my children as well as by listening to the recollections of my students and my patients.

In this chapter I aim to explain how I distilled my approach to matters of education and how in my experience each individual's journey or pathway is directly linked to their personality.

The Experience

The cast in this chapter

Leadership team	Given name
New executive Dean	Professor Pinocchio (prone to telling lies)
Head of Department	Dr Perfidious (deceitful & untrustworthy)
Clinical Director	Dick Dastardly (a nasty devious bastard)
Human resources	Horse Rectum ((defecates bullshit on a regular basis)
Dean of Education	Dr Delphic (deliberately obscure & ambiguous)
Chairman of Council	Dr Magoo (easily blinded and rarely accountable)

The story so far.......

1. 15th September 2015; whistle blown.

2. 2nd October 2015; Nasty Meeting with Dr Dick Dastardly.

3. 16th October 2015; Incognito Meeting with Professor Pinocchio.

4. 19th October 2015; Dick Dastardly's failed attempt to drown me in IT.

5. 1st Week December 2015; Dr Perfidious tells a bunch of staff 'Hafeez is a liability; I'll have to get rid of him'. (ouch my shoulder blades)

6. 7th December 2015; my expression of grievance to Dr Dastardly about the above.

7. 8th December 2015; IT team produces a report which implicates me as uniquely experiencing the concerns I'd reported. (ouch)

8. 17th December 2015; Dr Perfidious produces a report which implicates me as uniquely experiencing the concerns I'd reported. (ouch)

9. 8th April 2016. Professor Pinocchio & Mr Wily failed to re-label my protected disclosures a grievance. (phew)

10. 18th July 2016; Mr high-up concluded the leadership couldn't have known that I had blown the whistle.

11. 4th August 2016; Dr Insightful initiated a formal investigation into my concerns.

12. 30th September 2016; Sinister meeting with Dr Comprehensive.

13. 24th October 2016; I complain to the CEO of the NHS trust.

14. 26th January 2017; I escalate my concerns & those of 22 patients to the General Dental Council.

15. 31st January 2017; Dr Magoo neutralised my concerns citing Dr Delphic's whiter than white soap-suds report.

16. 2nd February 2017; I informed the Iconic machine that I'd escalated my concerns to the GDC.

17. 17th March 2017; I was suspended on 7 spurious allegations.

18. 12th April 2017; the spurious evidence pack arrived.

19. 21st April 2017; flawed investigation No 1.

20. 7th July 2017; first disciplinary hearing.

21. 19th July 2017; 1st disciplinary concludes with none of the allegations being proved.

22. 20th August 2017; fraudulent letters are used to frame me and a second disciplinary process is initiated.

23. 18th September 2017; flawed investigation No 2

24. 8th December 2017; second disciplinary hearing.

25. Wednesday 20th December 2017; emergency meeting with legal counsel.

26. Thursday 21st December 2017; 2nd disciplinary concludes with the allegation not being proved.

......The more I researched the more evidence I assembled of how much of a fool I had been. The actions and inactions of all the organisations and individuals in my story demonstrate that the claims being made about supporting whistleblowers amount to lip service and nothing more. Incompetence concealing cronyism is still the predominant force across the whole board and it's well and truly alive and kicking.

In the period after my suspension and before my dismissal I had made 5 written requests to the Chairman of the council; Dr Magoo, for a grievance. He declined them all. I'd made two requests to the CEO of the NHS trust; she redirected me back to the Icon, informing me that my grievance was not an issue for the NHS or her. She excused the NHS's responsibilities on the grounds that I only held an honorary NHS contract. Sounds like a solid excuse.

On **21st December 2017** I received the outcome for my second disciplinary hearing. The allegation had not been proven, so there was no case of misconduct, but nevertheless my suspension remained active. I was informed by the panel that they were seriously concerned of a 'potential breakdown in my relationships' with my colleagues and how they needed more time to give it further consideration. My experience had become a near permanent suspension of time with a draining feeling of helplessness and inexplicably SHAME. Why the fuck was I felling shame? What had I done wrong? It was clear to me the disciplinary process was being used to exhaust me; which it did to near destruction and in some ways I suspect beyond repair.

After the New Year celebrations I submitted what would be my final request for a grievance to Dr Magoo and here it is (unchanged):

Dear Mr Magoo.

Further to previous correspondence please can you invoke a formal grievance procedure into:-

1. The Dental Institutes (DI) poor handling of my protected disclosures.

2. The organised campaign of victimisation, bullying & intimidation levied against me for having made the protected disclosures.

3. The failings in the university's investigation into my wrongful suspension.

Two years ago I noticed some dangerous and illegal practices at the DI. I did the right thing and made some protected disclosures to help the DI recognise and improve patient safety and student learning. Those protected disclosures are the reason why I was suspended. Over the last 2 years everything I have done has been entirely correct, entirely professional and entirely in the open. The same cannot be said of the DI or its agents.

Several other staff members had also written letters to the DI detailing exactly the same concerns that I had raised. Since raising my protected disclosures it has come to light that the DI was criticised by the regulator for exactly the same failings as I described just 2 years before my disclosures. As a result of my protected disclosures the regulator is actively investigating individual staff members for professional failings including 4 members of the leadership team. The regulator has already written a statement that it has found failings within the DI in the areas that I highlighted and that the DI has admitted the failings and agreed to necessary improvements.

At a previous disciplinary hearing in July 2017 Pinocchio stood in front of the committee representing the DI and said 'Dr Ahmed's concerns are not valid and not shared by anyone else at the institute' That statement was a lie. At that point the DI (headed by Pinocchio) had already admitted the failings to the regulator and had already agreed to make improvements. Pinocchio told the committee that it was not possible for me to return to the DI because they had spent the last 2 years fighting with me. His choice of words said it all. Instead of properly investigating the protected disclosures I raised to them the DI has instead been fighting me personally. It is still fighting with me because of my protected disclosures.

When I first raised my concerns they ignored them. Next they invited me into an office and shouted at me. They openly told my colleagues I am a liability and that they need to get rid of me. They emailed each other discussing their plan to suspend me knowing that they had no evidence of wrong doing. They emailed each other agreeing to delay suspending me whilst they found some evidence of wrong doing. They made allegations against me which have been addressed by 2 disciplinary committees (July 2017 & December 2017). The allegations were unproven.

The leadership team at the DI has waged their continued vendetta against me, blocked me from contacting professional colleagues, students and patients to build my evidence and defence and blocked me from calling witnesses from the above groups. The leadership team at the DI has behaved appallingly towards me. They have failed to provide any evidence whatsoever of any wrong doing on my part. There is copious evidence of extensive wrong doing on the part of the leadership team. The wrong doing has been at individual level and at team level. There is only one possible explanation for me being suspended and that is that my protected disclosures embarrassed the DI and its leadership. As a result the DI wants to silence and get rid of me, there is no other plausible explanation.

The most appropriate and correct course of action is to return me to my post and invoke a full and formal grievance procedure into the DI's handling of my protected disclosures, the subsequent bullying and victimization and the failings in the university's investigation into my wrongful suspension. You have been either complicit with me being victimised and bullied or you and the disciplinary process has been used as a weapon by others to victimise and bully me. This needs to stop now as if you were not complicit before you certainly become complicit if you continue to allow yourself to be misused in this fashion.

On the matter of a breakdown of working relationships, my position is unchanged. I love my job and I see no professional breakdown. Obviously, there must be a proper investigation and a proper grievance process which will identify failings, malpractice and bullying. None of those failings will be mine. I have every faith in the process and its ability to identify areas where the DI needs to improve, staff that need retraining, staff that need to be disciplined and appropriate disciplinary outcomes for those staff. The process will identify areas where the DI and its staff owe me an apology. Once the process is complete I will happily put this whole matter behind me and get on with working with whoever remains in post. I love my teaching job at the DI and I am very good at it. In time we will all look back on this sequence of events and agree that it was a positive catalyst for necessary improvements.

Kind regards

Dr Hafeez Ahmed

Dr Magoo responded by dismissing me on **16th January 2018**. It was hard for me to convince myself that it had actually happened; it was a surreal moment. I couldn't see any goodness in the badness. In a lot of ways this may have been and probably was my greatest loss but it still remained light years behind my lowest point; that remained the moment I received the evidence pack back in chapter 7.

I had dodged my last bullet and was dismissed me on the ostensible grounds of 'breakdown of relationships' with colleagues. I suspect they meant colleagues in the leadership team. Even though I'd prepared myself for this moment by imagining it over and over, the prep didn't help much. Dr Magoo denied me the opportunity of conciliation and the right to appeal his decision. He also maintained his denial of my grievance thus avoiding an investigating into the leadership team's poor handling of my disclosures. Eliminating my right to appeal gave the leadership the safety and comfort of knowing that their accountability would never be tested, not by *The Machine* anyway. Whilst this was calamitous for me and yet another rusty nail to rot in my brain it was a roaring success for them. The leadership were the most qualified to describe a breakdown as they had caused it, but its irretrievability was a supposition which I was not allowed to question. If Dr Magoo had indeed (which I doubt) based his decisions on discussions with the leadership team (of which there is no evidence) then he had most certainly been lied to.

During **January 2018** the GDC concluded its investigations into 3 members of the teaching staff (2 periodontal specialists & one consultant). In each of the cases they described: the level of some of the care to be below the expected; before concluding: the standard of practice was not unsatisfactory to the extent that the overall care was below a reasonable standard.

During **February 2018** the GDC raised some allegations against Dr Dastardly, one of which was that his conduct towards me constituted bullying. They completed their investigations by describing the bullying as an isolated event prior to concluding that as an isolated event his conduct was insufficient grounds to find his fitness to practice impaired.

During **March 2018** the GDC raised some allegations against Professor Pinocchio. They alleged that his conduct towards me constituted bullying, harassment and victimization. They also alleged that his conduct had been dishonest and misleading. They completed their investigations with a decision to close the case on the assertion that there was a real prospect of one of the allegations being proved by a Practice Committee but no real prospect of a finding of misconduct.

During **August 2018** the GDC raised some allegations of professional misconduct against Perfidious in respect to his patient care and allegations of bullying and harassment for his conduct towards me. Their consistently subjective investigation staggered this way and that way making a string of excuses like patients notes are not required to be 'perfect' or 'gold standard'. They concluded that aspects of his conduct were 'below the requisite standard rather than far below it'. Each one of his fallings was washed away as minor and insignificant allowing them to conclude that his failings were insufficient to consider his fitness to practice impaired.

I was advised by the GDC that their role was not to punish their Registrants for past conduct, but rather to consider whether the Registrant's fitness to practice may be impaired because of the issues alleged. It was clear to me that the GDC were not congratulating it's registrants for their fine work but the bumbling nature of their actions failed to address the concerns I had raised to them. Anyhow I had never sought punishment for any of the individuals involved I just wanted them to be honest. Just as Otto Ambros, the third Reich scientist should have been a bit more honest in 1957 about his drug Thalidomide, had he been honest thousands of babies would have avoided deformity and disability. Just as Thomas Midgley, the American scientist, should have been honest in 1923 instead of irreversibly poisoning the planet and its inhabitants with his leaded petrol.

The GDC also informed me that their fitness to practice process is very different from civil law. They explained that civil law looks at the relationship between the parties, whether there was fault, and whether compensation should be paid. By contrast, the fitness to practice process is not to assign blame, obtain financial redress for a party or determine who is responsible for a particular outcome. In order for the GDC to take a case further, the information held in relation to a registrant must be capable of forming an allegation that their fitness to practice is impaired within the meaning of the Dentists Act 1984. If a case does not meet this threshold the GDC does not have any powers to take a case further. I was more than a little surprised when they informed me that within the confines of the fitness to practice process, they don't have the power to look at organisations. They only had the powers to look at each of the registrants individually and were prevented from doing any joined-up thinking. I asked them several times what each of the patients (who had raised their concerns to me) had said to them but was never told. I'm certain the patients were never asked.

They advised me that the correct forum for addressing the relationships and responsibilities between the parties at an organisational level would be an employment tribunal. So for me if I made an application to an employment tribunal I'd have taken part in a total of Six pantomimes: (so far)

Panto one: Investigation for First disciplinary;   (botched)
Panto two: First disciplinary hearing;   (no allegations proven)
Panto Three: Investigation for second disciplinary;   (botched)
Panto four: Second disciplinary hearing;   (no allegations proven)
Panto five: GDC and CQC investigations;   (botched)
Panto six: Employment Tribunal;   (claim accepted)

And Four further potential Panto's

Panto Seven: Professional Standards Authority; (done & ongoing)
Panto Eight: Raise a compliant with my local MP;   (done & ongoing)
Panto Eight: Parliamentary Health Service Ombudsman;   (an option)
Panto nine: Health Select Committee;   (remains an option)

Thank god for efficient systems.

My immediate task was to learn enough to enable myself to submit an application to an employment tribunal. My (tedious) research informed me that beyond the administrative tasks of completing the appropriate form (ET1) in the appropriate way (correctly) in the appropriate time (3 months from the effective date of the termination of my employment; which was different to my dismissal date) I had two broad options:

1. Submit a claim against my employer (the Icon) as the sole respondent.
2. Submit a claim against my employer and add as independent respondents a list of the individual's responsible for the wrong doing.

The University and College Union (**UCU**) who were very good to me throughout encouraged me to opt for option 1. Citizens

Advice Bureau, who offer home visits, advised me during mine that I should opt for option 1. In addressing my queries UCU implied they would only continue to support me if I opted for option 1. Their reasoning was simple, option 1 is almost always accepted as a claim by the courts and option 2 is almost always rejected. The basis for their reasoning was just as simple but a tad worrying. They explained that the courts decisions were taken by Judges and they (being human) preferred option 1 as they didn't mind pointing their finger at organisations (bricks and mortar) and they rejected option 2 because they did mind pointing their finger at individuals (might upset them). The only downside was, if I were to opt for option 1, the wrong doers would continue to play the same denial games they had already been playing and rattle around irresponsibly behind the employer's brand. They had continued to maintain the pretence by pushing the plate of turds round the table. They had continued to express their innocence and ascribe failings to other members of their team by using job titles, (which by virtue of design; are conveniently transient); done very carefully so as not to accidently point the finger at a named individual. They had continued to engage in acts of calumny in order to damage my reputation. If I opted for option 1 the most likely outcome would be that there would be insufficient evidence to establish from which arse the sun rose and in which it set.

The point was laboured; I mustn't opt for option 2. UCU described option 2 as a circus and their preference was to avoid it. The advice on the tinternet was consistent; opt for option 1, avoid option 2. It was clear to me that opting for option 2 was only an option for the stupid and even they were encouraged to keep the number of named individual respondents minimal. The larger the number the more it would look (to a judge) that the claim was an act of revenge or neurotic behaviour (never mind justice). The upside was that if an option 2 claim was accepted then each respondent would have to attend court for cross examination. Making it more likely they might be held accountable and responsible for their actions or the lack of them.

The life I was living had become lonelier as my only adviser, UCU, wasn't responding to my e-mails in a timely fashion. When they did they apologised and explained that they were busy helping other members fighting their battles. I couldn't afford independent legal representation. In addition to which I had been personally responsible for all the administration required for the 9 GDC fitness to practice investigations; I was not represented by any indemnity company whilst those under investigation were. My professional indemnity company apologised and explained that they could not provide any support because my claim was an employment matter not a professional one. A friend explained that I could get legal advice through my house insurance; only the house insurance had been cancelled due to lack of funds.

On **2nd April 2018** during one of the long pauses in which UCU remained silent I completed and submitted my claim to the employment tribunal. Having taken on board all the advice to date it was clear to me that there was only one viable option; so I took it. I opted for option 2 and named the Icon as my employer and listed the five individuals below as independent respondents:

Dean of Education	Professor Pinocchio
Head of Department	Dr Perfidious
Clinical Director	Dr Dick Dastardly
Dean of Education	Dr Delphic
Chairman of Council	Dr Magoo

My claim was rejected on the **22nd May 2018** as I had made some mistakes with the application. I had not included an ACAS early conciliation certificate for each of the respondents. It remained a necessity despite Dr Magoo informing me that he had dismissed any possibility of conciliation. I was given the opportunity to rectify my mistakes, which I did, subsequent to which on **18th June 2018** my claim was accepted with a preliminary hearing scheduled for **3rd August 2018**.

I was informed by the court that the respondents would have **28** days to respond to my claim. The respondents informed the court that they would defend the claim. Incidentally, within six weeks of my claim being accepted Professor Pinocchio stepped down as Dean of Education. I was informed by my colleagues at the Icon that he was redeployed by The Machine to market the machine and its courses in the Middle East.

The Inspiration.

My inspiration has come from observing my teachers, myself, my students, my children and a small number of professional commentators. In 2014 whilst attending a teacher training day at the Icon I had a chance meeting with a former student (FS) in the coffee break and the conversation went like this:

FS: Dr Ahmed, you don't recognise me?

Me: no

FS: you taught me oral surgery in 1995

Me: oh, how did that work out for you?

FS: you changed my life

Me: that's nice.

FS: it started out a bit strange, immediately before I met you I'd been to a meeting with the Dean of Primary Care, he wanted to discuss his new initiative with me.

Me: oh

FS: he said it was really easy to identify good students and just as easy to identify the bad ones. And that previously the institute had mixed the bad students in with the good ones in the faint hope that the some goodness would rub off on to the bad ones.

Me: and?

FS: His new initiative was to put all the bad students in one group and match them to an appropriate teacher.

Me: and ?

FS: that's when I met you.

Me: and?

FS: You pushed me hard and I didn't like you much when you were pushing me but about five years after I qualified I realised what you'd done for me. I was not getting into as much bother or dealing with as many complaints as some of my colleagues. I understood dentistry and what I was doing. With the benefit of hindsight it's obvious that I needed to be pushed. I can remember back in 1995 when some of those same colleagues were ploughing ahead whilst you held us back and made us get the simple stuff right. I work as a teacher now, because of you.

Me: I'm glad it all worked out for you. I needed pushing when I was that age too.

At about the same time I had another chance meeting with another former student (FS), again at a teacher training event. Only this time it was in the gent's toilets. The conversation went like this:

FS: Dr Ahmed, is that you?

Me: nope

FS: you taught me when I was in my fourth year

Me: how did that work out for you?

FS: you took me into the stairwell and shouted: 'you are clearly very intelligent, but if you don't stop acting like a wanker, you won't get anywhere.'

Me: and?

FS: it changed me, I learnt that to get things finished I needed the help of a much firmer hand and you provided it.

Me: and?

FS: I got the educational buzz from you and I am now doing my second masters degree.

Me: Do you know why I took you into the stairwell?

FS: why?

Me: my teacher did the same to me and he said the exact same thing. In my own time I realised that I needed a firmer hand and he supplied it.

Over the years I have met lots of my former students and it generally takes them approximately 5 years after qualifying to realise how things are playing out and the vast majority reach a very similar conclusion. That they needed to be squeezed and pushed and with hindsight have greater respect for those teachers who pushed them than the passive ones. In my experience the vast majority of students I meet in the fourth year of the dental course have no idea of their personality and have no idea of what drives them to be there. Sadly the corruptions of higher education use their insecurities to suppress them into submissive compliance with ease. For me it doesn't matter what one chooses to do with one's life one can never get away from oneself. What one becomes is the sum total of every single day of one's life from birth onwards. Even earlier than birth in the opinion of Esther and Jerry Hicks as they explain in their book: **The Vortex, Where the Law of Attraction Assembles All Cooperative Relationships.** In essence their theory is that your soul exists before your material being and for complete mental health the material you needs to align with the non-material you (your soul).

As a specialist clinical teacher at *the Icon* I used the feedback I received to push the students (as necessary). I'd often say to them: 'if you can't deal with me pushing you in this protected environment how are you going to cope out in the real world; it's far harsher than me'.

Every so often my teaching was assessed and I would like to share part of the most recent assessment with you as it contains my insights into elements of the education was involved in. It was completed in June 2015. As part of the assessment process I prepared and submitted a pre-assessment statement, the purpose of which was to give the assessor an insight and understanding of the aims and objects of my teaching sessions. The rest of the assessment consisted of the assessor observing two of my teaching sessions approximately 6 weeks apart. The assessor then compiled her assessment report and the excerpt below is my response to it:

It was uplifting to read that my pre-observation statement was the most detailed pre-observation statement you have ever received, in your 27 year career. For my part I thought I was just working to the same standard all the others teachers have told me they are working to.

I have taken onboard your comments about the scripted feel of my pre-observation statements and will consider them carefully. I would like to explain my rational behind its development and use. Clinical dentistry is a vocation and requires large components of hands-on skill development. This didactic training needs to be supplemented with activities which allow reflection to realise deeper learning. In the 3rd and 4th year it is necessary to impart, didactically, the skills we want the trainees to develop in the clinical setting. The reflective cycle of learning activity can only occur when they have some clinical experiences to reflect upon. The trainees do not have any clinical periodontal experiences at the start of their 3rd year. The 4th year trainees have a little more clinical experience. The didactic training is delivered using the structured script.

During the previous 3 years the 4th year trainees have not demonstrated any teamwork between the student treating the patient and the student who was assisting. On discussing this point with the trainees they told me that they do not get any guidance on the role of the assistant in any of their other clinics. I have worked with the trainees to address this failing and their response has been enthusiastic. One way to resolve this issue would be to ensure that all 2nd and 3rd year teachers are trained on how to supply the guidance of the role of the assisting trainee to the trainees.

The scripted approach of my teaching was initiated and developed in response to the element you mention in section 5 of your feedback (Maximising the learning of the student acting as assistant). I treat all the trainees as adults with a view to develop a relationship based on trust. The trainees, often, not always fail to reciprocate. Prior to the introduction of the scripted approach discipline was low. On discussing this point with the trainees they told me that whilst standards of discipline are discussed in principle the standards are not demonstrated by their other teachers. The trainees told me that this is due to staff shortages and busy clinics. In response to this I have learnt that I have needed to be more structured and organised than I originally felt was intuitively right. I am confident that one of the reasons for this is caused by how the trainees have been managed at earlier stages of the training programme. On the up side the scripted approach has been successful in engaging both the treating student and the assisting student. I recognise, appreciate, and agree that young people flourish if they grow in a culture which offers them the opportunity to take the lead. The scripted approach has allowed me to present to them, definitively, the skills they need to develop. I monitor and assess that the trainees have taken the opportunity to acknowledge what the parameters of the required clinical activity are. This often takes more effort than I would anticipate as intuitively necessary, the extra effort being necessary due to the trainee's lack of enthusiasm to engage in the learning process. It became apparent to me that the trainees had been completely passive during earlier stages of the training programme. Once I have set the boundaries and parameters of the required skills I encourage the trainees to run their own show. Towards the second half of the module the trainees are given a greater degree of autonomy. It takes a lot of encouragement from me to persuade the trainees to take full responsibility of their cases. The failure to take full responsibility is rarely due to lack of enthusiasm, it is largely due to the fact that they do not know what is expected from them. When they are able to show the initiative to take the lead the confidence they gain is remarkable. The scripted approach gives them the support to reach out more confidently. The scripted approach allows me to be more consistent in an otherwise busy treatment clinic. The consistency results in a fair approach and the trainees have responded to it very well. I have learned that consistency and fairness is very important to the trainees. One reason for this is that the feedback sessions occur on the clinic often in front of their colleagues. The trainees are particularly concerned about how their colleagues see them. The scripted structured nature of my approach allows perfect impartiality. I have observed that the competitive trainees listen carefully to the feedback I give to their colleagues. I have observed that when the trainees experience a fair and consistent approach this increases their competitiveness. In my teaching career, so far, it has been a fascinating experience to observe how the trainees negotiate the myriad of complexities to create a stable and integrated group. I have observed that the structure of the session alongside the fair and consistent approach it allows the teacher play a very important role in this process. In an integrated group relationships develop between the trainees. These relationships lead to opportunities for the trainees to explore within the group. This results in them becoming more adept at negotiating challenges in the clinical environment. I have worked hard to create a learning environment in which the trainees can develop themselves. The structure provides a sort of mesh to ensure no individual trainee is allowed to be left behind in the busy environment. The trainees have told me that they prefer my scripted approach above the teaching styles they have experienced on some of their other clinics. The script that I have devised has been carefully put together to ensure the most robust and successful outcome for both the trainees and the patients that they treat. It has been recognised that the trainee's life is a phase of storm and stress. Some of this is attributable to their adolescence and some of it due to the complexities of *The Machine*. The machine needs to provide a more coherent structure and I am hopeful that my feedback will help in its development.

I agree with you that it is not ideal to have a single plan for both 3rd and 4th year groups but it needs to be considered that ultimately they need to develop the same clinical skills. I would be happy to consider the plans prepared by the others teachers if those plans better suit the needs to the trainees. The variation between the 2 year groups is largely clinical exposure, clinical experience and knowledge. I moderate for this variation by adapting the clinical interaction and feedback I give to the trainees at the chair side. It is not ideal for me to be responsible for both year groups on the same clinical at the same time. I am aware and have alerted the course organisers that the 3rd year trainees do not get the attention that they require. The script that I have prepared gives the 3rd years trainees a point of reference when I am busy with the 4th year trainees. The 4th year students do get more of my attention as the treatments they provide are more complex. It is not ideal to have 14 students to supervise at the same time on the same treatment clinic. The script and the summaries that I have given to the students have made the clinic more manageable. A significant problem occurs when patients need to have a consultation activity on a treatment clinic. The trainees do not have the experience, knowledge or responsibility to establish an informed consent with the patients that they treat. The informed consent needs to be established by me as the supervising clinician. On a treatment clinic the teaching staff to patient ratio does not allow me the time to have detailed discussions with the patients and it disrupts the flow of the treatment clinics. When I have to repeat aspects of the consultation or need to establish an informed consent I do not have the time to supervise or teach other students who are providing treatments for their patients. I am aware and have alerted the course organisers that the trainees do not get the correct level of attention that they require for their learning activities. On discussing this point with the trainees they have told me that the teacher to student ratios in the earlier parts of their course were less favourable. The trainees have confided in me that the have been told that this is due to staff shortages. The trainees have told me that the quality of the teaching is less than they had anticipated from the course literature and that the course literature was misleading as they have been advised by older colleagues that the problems had been a issue for some years.

The success of the training I provide depends upon both the robustness and sensitivity of the buffers. Trainees can and, indeed, must kick against the training structures and rules but these in turn need to be devised with clear boundaries based on an understanding of what drives the trainee's behaviours. The trainees in my group have not felt the need to kick against the structure I have devised. They have responded well to it and have shown a preference for it. As we approach the end of this module the trainees are able to undertake aspects of reflection and this was one of the principle desired outcomes of the module. In my teaching career, so far, I have relied on intuition and common sense in dealing with trainees. Whilst the educational science is developing the current infrastructure of *The Machine* and the undergraduate course do not allow any of it to be practiced. Time is a rare commodity. The infra structure at *The Machine* is complicated when really it needs to be complex. My teaching module was largely developed by me without the assistance, support or guidance of the senior staff at the machine. I have been able to do this due to the self confidence and self belief that I have developed over a 23 year career. Some of the senior staff at *The Machine* have confided in me that its relationship with its young teaching staff is very weak. I am hopeful that some of my comments will help them develop more coherent structures to better engage with and support their teaching staff. For example, currently, the periodontal department does not offer its teaching staff any training, guidance, structure or framework. This makes it very difficult when teachers have to provide cover for colleagues who are on annual leave.

I take on board your concern about my use of the phrase "rubbish student". It seems odd that for all our supposed sophistication in the measurement of academic achievement, all too often the behaviour of the trainees we are trying to help is ignored. To this end I explain to my trainees what the ideal learning behaviours are and how they are far removed from what they have previously developed at GCSE and A-level. I will continue to demonstrate this point to them using better selected phrases like "a good trainee" and "a bad trainee". The schooling system has allowed these trainees to believe that passing an exam is equivalent to learning. Without coherent guidance the trainees revert back to only engaging in activities that they perceive will help them to pass an exam. The trainees are undergoing a process the purpose of which is to help them seek out new roles and identities for themselves. Some of their emerging personality profiles and explorations of behaviour work and are stable, but the vast majority are not and are transient flashes. It is a time for them to understand and appreciate what is required from them so they can engage in "lifelong learning", it is a time for them to understand and appreciate the necessities of "character and discipline". These are activities that require the ability to focus attention and exert control over behaviour; a structured approach helps a lot.

We recently had a presentation given by Pinocchio and he advised us that it has been observed that today's trainees have a greater narcissistic trait. I feel that one of the reasons for this is that the trainees feel isolated in their learning environment. I have spoken to a lot of the teachers and they feel as isolated as the trainees. In the case of the trainees they are venturing away from the safe protection of their parents. They are venturing away from an environment in which they feel safe and secure. This is the very time when they need guidance on and experience of "good" and "bad" feedback. The current culture in teaching favours an unhealthy bias towards "good" feedback. "Bad" feedback is circumnavigated as *The Machine* is fragile and wishes to avoid complaints from trainees. The culture that has developed is one in which trainees are always given "good" feedback on the assumption that this will reduce complaints. The trainees need to develop healthy copying strategies around good and bad feedback. If we continue to give them "good" and "positive" and "sandwiched" feedback they will not be able to develop coping strategies for the adult world. Pinocchio advised us that it has been observed that mental health problems amongst the trainees is at an epidemic high. I suggest that the aetiology for this is the same as that described above, it occurs out of isolation and a failure in giving the trainees fair, consistent, balanced, feedback. The trainees have told me enthusiastically that they prefer being told where they are going wrong alongside methods of improvement. My structured approach allows me to give measured, aligned feedback which in turn allows the trainees to develop the ability to delay gratification of immediate reward in order to follow the rules, make appropriate choices and maintain goals. A successful dentist needs to be a "natural psychologist" with an ability to decide in an instant how to proceed in a social situation. Dentistry is the bad news industry and a dentist is required to break "bad news" to patients all day long. During the training more emphasis needs to be placed on the psychology of giving and receiving bad news. As we know that trainees today experience great difficulty processing negative feedback, we need to help these trainees to better process all facets of feedback, good and bad. It is not helpful in, the longer term, to shy away from "bad news". They also need help to develop a healthy appreciation that sometimes the treatments they provide produce favourable responses and sometimes they do not. Using a structured approach allows them to take the lead. It allows them the essential experience of making mistakes. It allows them a safe environment in which to get things wrong and learn from the experience. The structure allows the mistakes to be identified with consistency and allows for fair feedback.

It often feels as if *The Machine* has give up on the notion of achievement. The age of achievement has not passed.

Achievement is our principle driving force. Achievement results in enjoyment. Enjoyment encourages us towards further progression. Mediocrity is the killer of human spirit. We need to help our trainees achieve bigger and better things than we did. This requires some bold leadership. There has always been a conflict between NHS austerity and the creativity with which we encourage our trainees. We must not allow NHS austerity to negatively impact upon those who chosen dentistry as a career.

I anticipate that I will continue to assess and alter my approach to situations to allow the learning environment to be the most effective. It appears to be fashionable to suggest that much of what we do as teachers will be replaced by clever interactive computer programmes. This I fear reduces situations to the lowest possible denominator for measurement and entirely misses the point of training. Training is at its most effective when it is transmitted with human social contact.

In my experience is there is a fundamental mistake we all make when we are younger. We somehow assume teaching is the same as learning. We misguide ourselves (or are misguided by others) that the act of listening to a teacher (standing at the front of class) is equal to learning or that passing exams is equal to learning. The reality is that listening to a teacher only allows you to collect the information required for you to do some learning; the learning is dependent on what you do with the information. Passing exams measures how good you are at memorising information. Learning is dependent on what you do with the information you memorised.

In my experience far too much expectation is placed on the school to provide the learning; especially since they can only provide the teaching. I'd say:

LEARNING = CHILD + PARENT.+.SCHOOL.+EFFORT

To keep the equation balanced if one of its elements changes then the others need to be adjusted. The greatest variable is the child whose traits and personality influence their ability to learn.

Wretchedly, back when Imani was 3 years old, Zahida believed (as do almost all parents I've met) that the nursery we sent her to was going to be the moment that defined her life; period. She behaved as if Imani's whole life depended on it. I've watched so many parents get neurotic and do the nursery school chicken dance. They all deny it after the event has passed, but that's just another crappy part of the human condition.

So we needed to pick a nursery. Zahida and I argued – proper argued - about this for approximately six months. Our lives became a simmering war zone, with the sense of aromatic Bedouin camp fires burning just past the horizon. We lived in Zone 2 on the London underground which both of us used, sweaty sardine like, to get to and from work. When it came to selecting the nursery I did it carefully (in 3 seconds) without a blip of doubt, I picked the one conveniently located between our house and the tube station; perfect for drop off and pick up. Job-done; feet up, smouldering leathery cigar. Zahida disagreed. She'd become passionate about a different nursery (a Montessori one) after conducting the highest level of scientific research; namely listening to the other mothers at Imani's foot-odour themed play centre. I was as interested in that tripe as I would have been about a wart on Donald Trump's damp porn star. I explained to Zahida (as much as the moon can explain to the oceans) that the other mother's decisions were based on circumstances that weren't the same as ours. I explained (as much as a black-hole explains to the stars) that if the other mothers wanted to send their iddlings to Timbuktu it didn't mean we were compelled to make the same cross boundary trek. Oh I was wrong. Zahida needed desperately to do the same as the others; sheep don't moo. Unless they've accidently got their head stuck up the flea ridden dung smudged fragrant arse of a vegan cow. I banged my head on that particular wall for months. My suppurating blistered bleeding head confirmed that ignorance wasn't a war I was about to win.

The golden temple she'd picked was a 15 minute drive way. Not just any old 15 minutes; but 15 minutes in the opposite direction to the tube station. That's 15 minutes extra for the drop-off, 15 minutes extra for the pick-up in the clang-clang of rush hour London with all its beep-beep; honk-honk and the dog turd size spaces available for parking. As much as I protested (less than peacefully) on grounds of a 'bonkers' decision Zahida politely and respectfully disagreed as if being convivial.

In the end I stamped my feet so hard that I shook the dandruff off China and I was prepared to stamp them even harder; eventually the glistening lice would surface. In my experience men and woman are supposed to attend the parenting party in different fancy dress regalia. Fathers dress to impress offering logic and reason whilst mothers dress to flatter by offering love and emotion. The mothers love and supple emotions are essential for the development of the same aspects in the child and its best delivered in the home just behind its closed door. The father's logic and reasoning (delivered with a kind firmness but without weakness) is necessary to prepare the child for life in a world that hasn't ever been an easy place to survive; so I don't apologise for stamping when negotiating was no longer possible. In the end once my brain was lurching out of my head like a frenetic Swiss cuckoo at high noon, armistice took place in a windswept field as the wild grass lashed at unprotected body parts leaving invisible paper cuts. Wounds started to heal slowly after Imani was enrolled at the nursery between our house and the tube station.

Since that day my view has remained the same and we have sent all three of our children to the school closest to our home. My firm belief is if they're going to do well anywhere they'll do well there. My belief is and was that it isn't all about the school.

I've met tons lot of parents and they were – almost all of them - neurotic about their choice of school. They somehow manage to ignore the 'their bit' and they somehow manage to ignore 'the their child' bit. They only focus on the 'school bit'. They see themselves are far too important and far too busy. You see, it's very important for them to be busy because being busy is what makes them important.

It's difficult to agree with everything **Sir Chris Woodhead** said or did when he was chief inspector of schools but his description of education is the best one I've seen:

'Education is a process designed to help the individual become what they were meant to be and to hinder them from becoming what they were not meant to be'

His statement complements the thoughts and stories of Sir Ken Robinson in his book: **The Element, How finding your passion changes everything.** In which he explains his experience and opinions using succinct statements like: 'if you like rabbits consider working on a rabbit farm'. The theme is further supported by Tony Little in his book **An intelligent Person's guide to education.** The book authentically captures the rich personal experience of the author who is the former headmaster of Eton College. He covers a broad spectrum of themes to include parents, personality, moderated firmness and the undesirability of unfettered independence.

It seems right to me that it's the parent's responsibility to help their child work out: what he or she is. It's sits clearly in my mind that teachers can't do it (but can help); doctors can't do it (but can help); therapist can't do it (but can help). The hub and nerve centre which holds the educational enterprise together is the parent. I didn't find the responsibility difficult to accept but that's not the same as saying it wasn't without challenge. One of the greatest challenges a parent faces is their children's peer group, but by far the most powerful destructive damp squib of all was social media. Social media is comparable to a transparent toilet bowl which acts indiscriminately (exhibition centre like) to showcase the half digested sweet corn laden turds laid by a population whose destiny cannot be know (warning signs have sounded many times; only to be disarmed).

I could clearly recognise the traits, behaviours, likes, dislikes and personality of each of our three children. It didn't take too much time or thought to understand which one's had been inherited from me and which ones from Zahida. It seemed obvious that as I'd had my whole life, so far, to understand the same traits I was (one of two individuals) best placed to help my children understand their inheritance and assist them as they built their lives around them. If we were to avoid falling into the parent trap (see 'This be the verse' by Philip Larkin) we'd have to help them cope with the traits we'd lovingly bestowed upon them. Actually, I would go further than saying all their strengths lie in those traits, I would say everything they are lies in those traits. I believe that genius and talent (as well as madness and oddness) are entirely inherited, and that a person's success comes from the inner nature alone, rather than fortune or circumstance.

Here's a story I used to explain 'parents and personality' to Reyaan (son number one) when he was about 12 years old. I've always been, by my own admission, what others call OCD: Obsessive Compulsive Disorder (and what I call well organised). OCD, despite my detractor's claims, is the wrong description as it seems right to me that it's a foible and not a disorder; it's a trait, and in my experience a particularly favourable one for those blessed with it. I've found it's excellent for planning, organising, structuring, visualising, executing, concentrating and imparts as, a bonus, a twangy edginess which makes it awkward for others to stamp on my head, at will.

The event took place on a daffodil yellow bunny rabbit Sunday in April when the BBC was still running Top Gear at 7pm in the evenings. You know the one, the Clarkson show; it does it for me and I always looked forward to watching the animal's chimping around. My days are planned with a degree of formal casualness and flexibility; 3 days ahead. This particular Sunday had been planned as a Top Gear one. Zahida was away. She'd taken the kids to Yorkshire to rub noses with her parents.

Top Gear Sunday was up and running, shit, shaved and showered I'd left the front door wide open so I could smell the daffodils laced with rabbit fart. I already knew how the day was going to play out.

We live in a south facing house (circa 1832) the front of which sits in the delicate morning rays. The birds provide pitchy twinkling's from the towering lime trees whilst the constipated pigeons vibrate the base notes down the chimney stacks. As the afternoon plays in, it starts to gather a dense musty heat as the lime trees slowly load the air with treacle like sap causing the jasmine in the front garden to lose its light citric note and replace it with a deep sticky sweetness. Then in the evenings the same jasmine starts to sing in the light breeze playing a tribute to a French perfumery (unless the neighbour's cat's trespassed a dump into the gravel; then it's a more of a deeper 'did it really happen' ming-mong note).

Top gear Sunday always started with me perched at the breakfast bar in the Kitchen, 2 metre's left and inside of the front door; I scanned the style section of the Sunday Times. Next, with an apathetic attitude I cleaned the kitchen with military precision in a careless but precise choreographed order. True to my 'got to keep moving' style, I sat down in the corner of the same kitchen under a 2 metre tall white Georgian sash window; in a chocolate brown leather club chair and read the Culture section of the

Sunday Times; I'm a big fan of Camilla Long and love soaking up the book reviews. I'd transformed the gloss finish light oak floor into a uniform sheet of wet; ready to dry. I tend to mop the floor in the same way a decorator might varnish it; along the full length of 2 boards at a time. Time for the Sunday Times magazine. Best enjoyed in the shade, at the patio table, in the front garden next to the jasmine. By about 6pm I had cleaned the whole house and only had the business and money section left to read. I'd read all the other sections of the paper in the same order as I always did: home, travel, news review. I rarely read the main paper and if I do its usually on Wednesday. My Sunday plan is to get the headlines scanned so as to identify the articles for reading later in the week.

The countdown was on as I fluffed up the cushions on the sofa in front of the television. Laid out and fluffed my duvet before placing the business and money section next to the remote controls. Top Gear here I come. I returned to the lounge in my clean t-shirt and shorts having had a slightly too hot shower. I got under the duvet and rolled its edges under my elbows for support and tucked it into my armpits (for security). I picked up the business and money section and switched on the TV.

My eyes almost watered when I learnt that Top Gear had been postponed to allow live footage of Wimbledon to continue. I stared into the abyss in disbelief unable to move and after I don't know how many minutes I found myself counting my blinks. Closing my eyes became easier than thinking about blinking so I kept them closed. Fuuuucccckk; I was having a Melvin Udall moment. The disbelief lifted slower than evaporating dew as memories of my favourite movie character of all time phased in. Melvin Udall, a fictional character, was portrayed by Jack Nicholson in the film 'As good as it gets' Melvin was either an exact replica of me or I was an exact replica of him; minus the misanthropy. In the movie, which is my second favourite of all time, Melvin has a near nervous breakdown if he's asked to do something without being given any 'thinking time'; at short notice. Melvin's OCD meant that he required prior warning so he could plan things; get himself ready. If he was landed with a request at short notice he'd break out in a sweat requiring him to take some deep breathes to settle his mind.

Sat on the sofa, cocooned in my duvet, I'd broken out in a sweat. I slowed the pace of my heavy breathing by holding my breath and said to myself: 'it's only a show about cars, I'm sure you'll live' and what the fuck? Momentarily, I couldn't convince myself that I would live beyond this moment. The problem was that somehow subconsciously I'd promised myself that watching Top Gear was my reward for cleaning the house. Injustice.

Reyaan had sat quietly listening when I asked him: 'do you know why I told you the story son'. He was quick to respond with 'No I don't dad'; 'Because you're just like me son' I told him (see Spike and Tyke, the father and son cartoon characters in Tom and Jerry). 'I am not' he protested, 'I am nothing like you'. I reminded him of the near nervous breakdown's he has when he finds food has gone missing from the fridge . Especially food that catches his eye in the mornings, which he promises himself he'll be eating after school and then dreams about all day long. Right on cue he said: 'shit, I'm just like you dad'. Over the weeks I explained all the dodgy traits he got from me and I continue to do so.

Almost all parents I've met didn't seem to get that it's their responsibility to help their children work out what he or she is and how crucial this is for them, if they are to find their passion. They seem to think (or hope) that school is going to do it for them. They act surprised when their kids can't work out, for themselves, what their passion in life is. Why? The process starts at birth and needs to be nurtured into full function by the age of 16-17 so they are ready to make the more weighty life decisions. The norm seems to be that parents start talking to their kids about how decisions are made at the same time as they start to help them select GCSE topics; approximately 12 years too late. One possible reason for this is that parents are just repeating what their parents did and they certainly didn't encourage any considerations of personality, decision making or passion finding. Another possible reason is that they have never bothered to understand their own traits, personality or passion. Insecurity.

An example of how personality and professional passion are inextricably linked can be found in the legal industry. The word Barrister is derived from the old broken French and means failed actor. Therefore it can be understood that the preferable traits for being a barrister are those of someone who likes to put on a show, a performance but is not good enough to work in the movies. Being a good barrister requires someone who is flamboyant, showy, someone who feels comfortable posturing and pea-cocking in the limelight. The barrister is usually the attention seeking front man putting on a good presentation. But what is it that he's presenting? Usually the hard work of the solicitor who sits somewhere behind him. The traits of a good solicitor are different to those of the barrister and the solicitor tends to be a quieter more focused work horse. It seems right to me that to be a good barrister one has to first be born with the prerequisite traits, the traits need to be identified and nurtured prior to being finished off with the topic specific training. This does not mean that there are no exceptions, there are; but they are small in number.

It seems right to me that the individual's traits should be pointed out to them by parents and teachers alike and their traits should be mentioned in the end of term school reports throughout the schooling process. Career advisers should be involved from an early stage to help the individual appreciate the desirable traits required by the different professions and compare those traits with the ones the individual possesses.

If I were to have the conversation with Reyaan it might go a bit like this:

'Son, what would like to be when you grow up?'

'Superman'.

'Great, son, can you tell me one trait that you'll need to be superman?'

'Yes dad, I'll need to be able to fly'.

'Can you fly, son?

'No dad'.

'In that case son I would pick a different superhero to be, maybe one that doesn't fly'

It's really not difficult to spot the traits or appreciate that those traits are an outward reflection of how the individual's brain is wired and works. What's the point in hammering square pegs through round holes?

All three of our children share a trait with a good number of my students; they have difficulty concentrating. My kids tell me they are great at doing jobs. Yet I rarely see them taking one from inception to completion. On the odd occasion that I challenge them to do one, shortly after they start all that can be heard is 'how am I meant to this' and 'how am I meant to that' and then the job can only be finished if I stand with them and give them short curt instructions. Upon completion I'll be told that they didn't really need the instructions. This isn't a modern problem, it's as old as time. I know for sure I'm not in denial over it. I have as many issues with concentration as the next person. I vividly remember whenever it came to revising for exams I suffered with CDS; constant distraction syndrome. My pattern was always that I'd go through a thirty minute cycle of avoidance before I could sit down to revise. The avoidance was a direct avoidance of revision and crossed over with my other passionate OCD which, if you haven't worked out, is cleaning. First I would clean my desk then I would tidy my books then I would hoover my room eventually I would sit down and study and even then I could only manage fifty minutes at a time. More recently I have noticed that if I have to concentrate on anything, I do best by avoiding glossy magazines (like Hello and OK) and the internet and social media. They all spin my brain off the planet like an unsteady gyroscope.

If you think that's bad listen to this one, it tops them all. I've worked out that when I'm concentrating on being an 'active listener' (which requires me to fully concentrate, understand, respond and then remember what is being said); I don't get much listening done. Meaning that as soon as I've (subconsciously) guessed the point the other person is attempting to make I no longer hear a word of what they continue to say. My brain (subconsciously) concentrates on constructing my response. To manage my professional commitments I've learnt to, flick the switch and, force myself to 'reflectively listen'; you know, slowly repeat back to the other person what they've just said, I hear a lot more that way. I do 'reflective listening' (first coined by Carl Rogers and Richard Farson in 1957) because I have to, and not because I'm pretending sincerity to get the double glazing sold. Essentially, in the listening domain I'm an archetypal extrovert; meaning my preference is to be (yak-yak) talking and not listening. However I am not an archetypal narcissist as I do not surround myself with individuals who pluck the violin strings as I speak. My close friends apply their intellectual foot to my carotid effectively emptying the shimmering pool each time I get too showy.

I've worked out that I can't listen whilst operating a computer and looking at its screen; I can't operate a computer whilst talking, either. Not without making massive mistakes. Whilst I'm listing the things I can't do I'd like to tell you about one I can't understand. I can't understand what is meant when someone is described as autistic. The word autism and the condition it attempts to describe remains as elusive and confusing to me as the words 'human condition'. In an attempt to make more sense of it I have studied many of the presentations given by **Professor Temple Grandin** and what I've taken away from her is that the word autism appears to be the modern fashionable characterisation of what was previously termed the human condition. She also feels that the word autism is being used to attempt to describe too broad a set of characteristics and in doing so it becomes confusing. It appears to me that it is attempting to describe characteristics that have been with the race since the dawn of time, characteristics that make individuals different in how they interact with others. I have become one of her fans and if I was to accept her deconstruction of how brains 'think'; I think, I'd almost be convinced that I think mainly in words. But I'm confident that my thinking involves words, pictures and imagination simultaneously. So, if I have understood her properly I'm likely to be neurotypical.

One of my other invaluable traits is that if I have a project, which is likely to take ten days to complete, I can only sit down and concentrate when I have exactly less than four days remaining. This is just how it works in me; I've tried other ways of doing it but always end up doing it the same way; its how my brain is wired. It is how I was born. I encourage my children to look at their own habits and start to understand them. I encourage them not to attempt to change their traits because that's how they were born and is how they'll naturally remain. It seems right to me that the wisdom in learning our traits and habits is what is necessary for us to use them in the best possible way. Traits, habits and passion are intertwined. I tell my Children that passion is their driver, it's directly linked to their nature, and it's what gets them out of bed in the morning and keeps them going. Sticking close to their nature will allow them to keep going for longer. Those individuals who find their passion do not need to force themselves to concentrate as it comes naturally. I find it's really easy to identify those students who are on the dental course for all the right reasons and it's just as easy to identify those who are there for all the wrong ones. It's not rocket science.

I accept the notion that children can be trained and nurtured to do jobs that are at odds with their traits and that this has resulted in great success for some. That said, I believe those individuals are the exception. It's not how it worked for me and is not holding true for my children either.

Poor concentration wasn't created by the internet or social media, only exacerbated by it. I've noticed the change in myself; everything is a 'click' away. No real concentration or endurance required. That's why it's so addictive, because it appeals to our nature of laziness. I don't do social media as it stops me living; plus my definition of a friend is someone who'll give me five thousand pounds when I'm desperate. My students often protest and say 'but Dr Ahmed, if I ask Google, Google gives me a thousand answers' to which I almost always reply: 'when you've finished reading those, come to me I'll give you one right answer'. Google gives my children telekinetic power. They use what they see on it to criticise others far too readily without having any experience of having done it themselves. In reality the technology is preventing them from having real-time experiences and is liquefying their brains. I tell my kids that it's a good practice to:

'Never judge someone until you've walked a mile in his shoes. That way, when you do judge him, you're a mile away and you have his shoes'
Emo Phillips

Criticizing others in the absence of personal experience is not the same as starting something new and then leaving it unfinished. Nothing wrong with that; as long as it's not a frequent pattern which starts to cause you distress. I've started Italian lessons and then dropped out. I started writing a book: the ultimate chair side assistant; never finished. I have started more than 15 diets and exercise regimes; never finished. But in all fairness I have finished many more things than I have left unfinished. Probably, because going after and achieving those goals was more worth it. Belief.

Children seem to be born knowing it best and often act as if no one has lived before them. This one time one of my nurses was in a huff and a puff. It was clear she was frustrated and we hadn't even started the day's work. Concerned that her distraction might ruin my day I asked her. 'What?' She explained that the day before she had been looking after her granddaughter who was 18 months old. 'It's really painful' she explained. 'Is your granddaughter a baby crocodile?' I asked. 'No' she corrected me 'it's my daughter; she behaves as if no other woman has ever had a baby before'. I sympathised by softly saying 'women'. This phenomenon was elegantly described by the classical pianist Charles Wadsworth, who said:

'By the time a man realizes that maybe his father was right, he usually has a son who thinks he's wrong'

This quote always takes me back to when I looked into my father's eyes and makes me reflect, with a dimpled smile, upon my relationship with my son. It depicts three men and its impact on the reader is dependent on which of the three they happen to be. It has a strong influence on my interactions with my patients and students as it provides an insight into how we learn and adapt and the regret and hurt we feel about some of the poor decisions we've made earlier in life. It enables me to rein in my expectations when dealing with people (younger and older); it's improved my relationships with people and has added some bandwidth to my humility.

Whilst my belief is:

EDUCATION = child + parents + school+ effort.

Frank Musgrove started a movement in 1966 at the opposite end of the educational spectrum when he was a professor of education with his proclamation:

"It is the responsibility of education to eliminate the influence of the parents"

And:

"We have decided that children will no longer be at the mercy of their parents and that local education authorities should ensure that they are not"

Like me, the Australian band Pink Floyd weren't in agreement with Mr Musgrove and in their song 'another brick in the wall' perceived it to be the other way round. They saw education as a wall and felt that every brick in it created a bigger barrier to personal development and enlightenment. They asked the teachers: 'to leave that kid alone'.

I'm sure Mr Musgrove was attempting to address the insanely high number of parents out there who are 'thicker than pig shit'. Point to note; I didn't create the 'pig-shit' problem I just don't deny it exists. He does however make the mistake of assuming teachers are less bad humans than are parents. In my experience being 'thicker than pig shit' is ubiquitous across the entire human race, all professions and classes. Shit is ubiquitous in that it has two key characteristics, it either floats of it sinks. This results in a layer of complete shit right at the top of our society and another almost identical layer of complete shit at the bottom of it. Those at the top no longer able to smell theirs whilst those at the bottom unable to ascertain where theirs came from. The topic of pig shit reminds me of a conversation I had with a newly qualified dentist (NQ). He was after my advice on interview techniques and career planning. The conversation went like this:

NQ: I've got a string of interviews lined up, some in practice, some in hospital and a few in corporate practices. How will I know which is the right place for me? I want to make the best choices.
Me: What you will come to realise is that it's all shit out there?
NQ: What?
Me: You'll need to work in each of the sectors prior to deciding which flavour of shit you can palate.
NQ: Oh, you are very funny Dr Ahmed.   And with that he left.

In just less than three years I received a phone call from him. He called to tell me how right I was. In that time he'd had more 'run- ins' than he had anticipated.

It would be very easy to describe Mr Musgrove and his statements as draconian; blame it all on him and move on. But that would be wrong as he had in his time identified the same problem as me in mine, only he advocated a different remedy. Sadly it's a problem that cannot be remedied by any education system; let alone one which is designed for the masses. So it remains a problem. Any education system designed to educate the masses is going to have limitations and the one we currently have treats all children like 'tin cans'. That's what it was designed for; to educate the masses to a certain minimal level. I don't see the problem as insurmountable. The education system needs to continue to load information into children's data banks (brains) and their parents need to help the same children work out how to operate their machinery (brain). Without the parents input the system successfully turns their children into 'tin cans' and this bites them bad later in life.

In keeping with theme that too much is expected of schools, it's been just over a decade since **Martin Stephen**, the former high master of St Paul's School in London observed that:

'We have shifted a whole load of societies conscience onto the curriculum'

I maintain it's the parent's job to help their children understand their traits, personalities, behaviours, likes, dislikes beliefs and passions; only then can they work out:

'How can you stand out when you work so hard to fit in'

Nassim Taleb

The human instinct is to 'fit in' and 'go along' but talent alone is not enough to help them stand out. The only way children can develop their potential capacities is in an atmosphere free of fear with the support of accomplished adults as role models offering vicarious reinforcement. Adults who help them polish their talents and not ones who try to chisel them into the same shape as everyone else.

I tell my children not to make the mistake of thinking that school is getting them ready for life. I tell them that going to school is their life. They are not getting ready for it they are living it. I explain to them they should not view school as a place which is designed to help them pass exams. It is a place where they should be working out who they get on with and who they don't get on with. Who they can talk to and who they can't. What they like, what they dislike. What it feels like to be encouraged by a friend. What it feels like to be let down by a friend. The same for teachers. I tell them that they should not live their lives for passing exams but to view the exams as part of life. I give the very same advice to my students some of whom are twenty when I first meet them. Often they have passed all their exams but they haven't worked out who they are, what they are, or what they want. They struggle massively with the decision making process.

How do they get themselves into this mess? Well it's the sum total of a repetitive cycle of indoctrinated failings. The thought process behind which goes like this:

I'll start my real life after I finish school and as I'm still at school I'll continue to play, endlessly, on my games console.

Followed by the next neat thought process in the sequence:

I'll start my real life after I finish college and as I'm still at college I'll continue to play, endlessly, on my games console.

Followed by the next neat thought process in the sequence:

I'll start my real life after I finish university and as I'm still at university I'll continue to play, endlessly, on my games console.

Followed by the next neat thought process in the sequence:

I'll start my real life after I've learnt to do my job properly and as I'm still learning how to do my job properly I'll continue to play, endlessly, on my games console.

Followed by the neat realisation thought process of:

'Oh fuck I'm an adult and I'm completely useless because I've waited all my life to start my real life.

There really is no rocket science involved at all. I tell my children life started at birth and everyday of it is real life. Get out and go for it. Life shouldn't be limited to what is or isn't being said inside a classroom. Life is about everything, absolutely everything you see out of your own eyes. Don't make the mistake of looking in a book for it, go out and live it; for real. Touch it, play with it, kick-it. That's life. Life is experience and experience is life. Experience trumps everything. Life is not to be found, don't be caught sitting around waiting for it to find you and don't think that you are going to find it either. Life is for the making, go out and make it. If you don't go out to make it, then be more stoic when you turn out to be a useless cabbage.

Here are a few thoughts to consider on the topic of getting jobs finished.

I've observed a pattern that my children go through each time they start a new project. At first they find it exciting, emotionally arousing, infusing them with the natural motivator of novelty. Sometimes they even get obsessive about their new activity. They behave as if it is "all good" and don't pay much attention to the potential obstacles, negatives, or challenges they may soon face. Then, after some time goes by, when the activity or book or lesson have turned into harder work than they'd expected. Perhaps it takes them longer to complete than they had hoped, or there's some tedium and drudgery involved. Or even, they fail to work out what the next step is. Stuck, they grind to a halt and (very readily) decamp to watch You Tube or lead the world on Play station. They don't recognize that they've essentially quit trying. Or, that they have put off the "getting back to it" until such time as they imagine it will be effortless again. This sort of procrastination is fuelled by perfectionism in one of my children and the fear that the next steps may not be excellent enough. Laziness – probably not the right word – is also one small piece of the problem, but few of us are lazy when it comes to doing what we love, what's easy, and what's intrinsically rewarding. Passion.

I tell my children two things to help them keep a realistic expectation and understand the need for endurance. Firstly, if the job you're doing seems to be going too well you're probably doing something wrong, think again. Secondly, if during the completion of a job you're not experiencing a massive arse ache in getting it done you're probably doing something wrong, think again.

If I were to use the information contained in the deep and sincere but relatively informal conversations I've had with parents, students and patients over a 25 year period relating to: a parents' attitude and actual contribution to their children's education, I would describe its distribution to fall under the normal distribution bell curve. Only it would be an upside down bell curve. To understand what an upside down bell curve looks like we first need to look at the normal bell curve or Gaussian distribution (Fig 1).

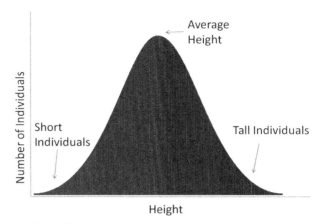

Fig 1. Normal Distribution, Bell Curve using height as an example.

It's used to describe the mathematical concept called normal distribution. Normal Distribution shows how the responses to questions like height, weight, intelligence, blood pressure or susceptibility to disease are distributed when gathered from a random sample. The normal distribution can then be used to project the probability of the distribution of the same feature across the entire population the sample was drawn from.

The important thing to note about the normal distribution curve is that it decreases symmetrically either side of a central average (mean, mode and median) point. This allows the creation of a reasonable prediction for the rest of the population to understand their susceptibility. As demonstrated by the distribution pattern of height for example, the centre depicting the average height with the shorter ones decreasing to the left and the taller ones decrease to the right. Being very tall or very short is rare. A lot of data sets in nature have this shape when compiled and graphed. Let's take gum disease as another example; the vast majority of the population has an average susceptibility to it with the resistant ones decreasing to the left and the highly susceptible ones decreasing to the right. Approximately 1.5% of the population has such a high susceptibility that no amount of intervention succeeds.

Now let's look at parents' attitude and actual contribution to their children's education; it's the vertical flip of the bell curve. (fig 2)

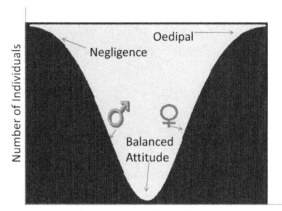

Parents Attitude & Contribution

Fig 2. The distribution of: parents' attitude and their actual contribution to their children's education. The female and male signs signify the overall performance Zahida and I have scored ourselves respectively.

The centre, labeled balanced attitude, signifies a small number of parents taking a balanced approach and showing a 'balanced' attitude. The number of parents failing to provide the correct level of support for their child's needs increasing to the left and those (harming their child) by not allowing them to do anything for themselves increasing on the right.

There's an abundance of research which clearly shows a link between lack of parental support and attitudes to education with, for example, Keys and Fernandes (1993)* showing that 'lack of parental interest and support were related to early leaving and dropout'. I couldn't, however, find any research about what's happening at the other end of the spectrum; with the oedipal parents. I'm sure that if I had found any I'd have viewed it with great scepticism due to the inaccuracy of self reporting especially when considered alongside the nature of oedipal parents. Oedipal parent is the term used to describe a parent or parents who

*Keys, W. and Fernandes, C. 1993 What do students think about school? Research into the Factors Associated with Positive and Negative Attitudes towards Education.   Slough: National Foundation for Educational Research.

overprotect their child and is often associated with a dysfunctional relationship between the parents.

One or both of them deliberately holds their child back to fill the void created by the insecurity and fear of isolation and loneliness. What we do know for sure is that some of the wealthy ones have been blinded by their wealth (and not the light) and they've completely distorted the cherished theme song behind the 1979 advertising campaign 'A finger of fudge is just enough, to give your kids a treat' (another Manfred Mann jingle). They've been lining the pockets of dubious educational psychologist's to falsely report learning difficulties in their lazy children with the standard recommendation that the brats exam essay's should be written by a scribe. Thereafter, equally shady scribes write the cherubs essays for them and pocket the money feigning comfort in not breaking any laws*.

*https://www.thetimes.co.uk/article/confessions-of-an-exam-cheat-tutor-for-3-000-i-will-write-your-childs-a-level-paper-scrm9x3cm

There's no such thing as the perfect parent or parents or parenting; we are all different in the same ways and the same in different ways. But I would say the essentials are discipline, consistency, attention and love; applied in equal measure. Consistency starts at birth and discipline isn't punishment. Children thrive around strict, fair and predictable parents but their immediate responses rarely reflect the dividends paid later in life. It takes a firm hand and one which feels slightly firmer than feels intuitively right but is rewarded with respect and obedience. One of the surest indicators of how a kid is going to turn out is how they behave towards their parents. Self-esteem dispensing should be reserved strictly for accomplishments and compliments should be earned. The easiest way to shortchange your kids is to give them everything they want but nothing they really need. They might be grateful for the moment you give them stuff but that shallow gratitude will turn to resentment as soon as bad things start to happening to them that they're not equipped to handle them. Children need to be raised not just feed.

Zahida and I have certainly burnt each other's flesh with lightsabers over the years; but on the whole feel we've passed the test (our own opinion) and managed to keep near the middle ground. My general approach has been: tell them what to do, tell them how to do it, show them how to do it, but don't do it for them. I've coupled this with: get up, get out and get on with it which has resulted in the odd fractious moment; no deaths, but perhaps what some might call, negligence. Zahida has taken a similar approach to me but often fails to stop short of the 'do it for them' part and tends to get caught in more squabbles over it with them.

Like all parents we coped with the pressures of life by sharing Imani's parenting with Barney the Dinosaur; you know the one, six-foot tall, purple tyrannosaurus rex with a green belly and green spots on his back and his tail and yellow toes. She loved him (as did we) possibly because Barney and Imani almost rhyme. She might not admit it now but she learnt a lot of her basic skills from him; he certainly taught her how to brush her teeth.

On Reyaan's turn we shared the parenting with: Big cook little cook; a television series for nursery school aged children broadcast on the BBC. Ben and Small played by Steve Marsh and Dan Wright respectively kept Reyaan entertained and most probably set his neural pathways towards wanting to be the chef he now wants to be. Anniyah keeps herself entertained with over stimulated, over sugared, screechy screamy creatures (insert long list of synonyms of millennial) on YouTube and it's too early for us to be sure how that will play out.

I was learning……..

I was learning that whether they know it or not most teenager's plans are influenced by the internet, magazines and TV shows, sometimes their direct peers but hardly ever any credible role models. Where have all the role models gone?

I was learning that because today's kids rely so heavily on the internet for their experiences they have very few real ones. In the absence of firsthand ones they are far needier of and demand more feedback. Once they get the feedback they are far less stoic in receiving it or applying it. In respect to experience or inexperience I tell my kids that if they aim to: 'Go as far as you can see and see how far you can go' they'll naturally become more stoic.

I learnt a long time ago a crude but quick and effective way of getting an insight of how an individual's brain is wired and how this insight could be used to understand the general way in which they respond when quizzed or challenged. It's my application of something I leant from one of my teachers. I've used this with my students and in my experience it's worked very well and helped me engage with them much quicker and in a more rewarding way.

How it works is simple. Ask the person if they have a memory of playing with magnets as a child. Almost everybody has a memory and it is rare to find anyone who doesn't. There is almost always only one of two memories. Pushing one magnet using the other and getting the magnets to stick together. As a general rule, individuals who like to watch magnets stick together are the agreeable introverted and soft minded type, the ones who tend to shy away from asking meaningful questions or engaging whole heartedly in discussions. The others are the strong minded disagreeable extrovert types, these are the spirited souls who have character and have a tendency to push right up against the rules. I am from the latter group and I've been called acerbic by those of my teachers who did not like to be questioned.

I accept that the magnet question may not work with everyone but with our brains being as plastic as they are I doubt any assessment tool would suit everyone. Prior to finding the 'magnet question' I had written a thesis as part of my master's degree titled: 'The association between personality dimensions and patient compliance with oral hygiene instructions.' In the study I used the Eysenck personality questionnaire which with its 100 questions can be time consumingly prohibitive. In stark contrast the 'magnet question' is less onerous and readily produced a valuable and workable insight. Perfectly suited for busy student clinics.

I was learning that humans are just not designed for or capable of concentration. They will protest that they are. They are not. They are better at protesting than they are at concentrating. They think they can concentrate, but they cannot. They convince themselves they're concentrating, but they are not. They'll tell you they're concentrating but they are not. They might sit still but they can't stop their brains jumping about. Just look at the lengths the aviation industry has had to go to ensure compliance in its staff. They practically complete a checklist to blow their own noses. One explanation for the low concentration may be a virtue of design. Human being animals are naturally and biologically designed to forage for food, eat the food and then to sleep it off or have a shag. During the foraging they burn an inordinate amount of energy. In the absence of the burn they spoil. Our tendency for low concentration gets masked by the vast array of stimulants we use (and our addictions to them). If you're not convinced just observe your own drivers and moods more carefully (and be honest). How often do you need to stoke yourself up with sugar or coffee? Or have a cigarette? Or shoot yourself full of gin? The rapid rise in the world population and the numbers suffering in the diabetes epidemic tend to support the notion that the two things humans can definitely concentrate on is eating food and shooting loads into each other.

I was learning that the teacher-trainee relationship works best when the discussions between them are uninhibited give-and-take. This allows the necessary rules to be explained and understood easier and quicker. It's long established that we perform better when we have rules to abide by and work to. The better the rules the more they facilitate our goals both professional and personal.

I was learning the majority of my students brains had become conditioned and repressed by the 'parrot' fashion learning required for passing exams. I try to explain to them that vocational learning is less about answers and more about the thinking process. I've attempted to persuade my students to 'speak their mind' or 'show me what was going on in it for them to reach the answer'. I'd made it clear to them that when I asked them a question I was not looking for a right answer or a wrong answer. I was looking to see how they were 'thinking'. I'd tell them that I'd like to see the dialogue they were having with themselves in response to the question. If I could see how they were thinking I could work out how best to help them develop it. But sadly more often than not it wasn't possible as the students were far too accustomed to giving a right answer or no answer. It was exactly the same in my day.

I was learning that sadly by the time I meet the students in their fourth year they had lost most of their confidence in most of the teaching staff. So a fruitful interaction was rare. The young but gullible students just couldn't see that a dentist is required to look simultaneously at the many sides of an issue and then talk the patient through the thinking process of evaluating the problem prior to forming an agreement with the same patient on how they wish to proceed. To help them develop this skill I needed to see how their cogs were whirring as they grappled with the patient's symptoms and the other information they'd collected from the patient. They needed to be able to assimilate the symptoms against the examination to reach a decision on how to proceed. This was not a time for right and wrong answers. I'd often explain to them that dentistry involves using some general rules but beyond that there's very little which is absolutely right and equally little that's absolutely wrong; it's heavily dependent on tons of dialogic processing. A fundamental mistake made by most students is they had convinced themselves the training course would provide them a sequence of lists, tables and formulas with which they go on and treat patients; this is just not the case. It takes a great deal of effort (and is near impossible) to train them away from a mentality suited only to passing exams. It was exactly the same in my day.

I was learning that I hadn't really understood what resilience, tenacity or endurance meant; they had only been words and knowing a word is not the same as having experience of it. Meaning can only be derived through experience. In the absence of a relevant experience the words remain on the page as letters. Now, having had and almost survived the experience I have a more meaningful, practical and tangible understanding of what makes a person resilient and I feel more accomplished for having had the experience. When we are given advice (in the absence of experience) most of it is meaningless but then (after a relevant experience) the very same advice can become helpful in multiple situations. I have always told me kids and students: if I give you my advice and you don't get it and don't understand, it, don't throw it away. Put it on the back shelf of your mind and when you need it, it will speak to you.

I was learning a massive limitation of the educational process, one which had eluded me earlier in life. During the educational process I had only learnt what I'd learnt, I had not learnt what I hadn't learnt. The only way I could have learnt more about what I hadn't learnt required new experiences, experiences which pushed me past my current knowledge. It's the only way it works. As an example, reading about whistle blowing is not the same as understanding what it involves; it was a lot more challenging than I could have ever dreamt. Whistleblowing is a visit to the underbelly of the world where you get to experience the worst in everything and everybody.

I was learning that it's difficult for my kids to understand my advice especially when the majority of the heard around them is engaged in variations of the opposite. Like the time I gave Imani some advice when she was getting a bit stressed in the run up to her 'A' level exams. I told her to aim to get the grades she could get without becoming sick or neurotic. She couldn't understand my advice because all her friends were flaying about with episodes of nausea, sickness and worry. It was the norm. Another example is the time I advised: 'don't panic about going to university; wait till you secure a paid apprenticeship in your chosen field of study; university fees only make a positive difference in some professions' I couldn't get through to her because all her friends were in a frenzy trying to get into a university.

I was learning to give less credence to individuals and organisations who tell me what to do or how to do it and I've subsequently replaced them with selective examples of individuals who I see doing things or those who have done things.

Winning can mean Losing

'All the world's a stage, and all the men and women merely players: they have their exits and their entrances; and one man in his time plays many parts, his acts being seven ages'

William Shakespeare

It's funny how life can work out sometimes and here we are at journeys end, and in the words of T.S Elliott the end of my journey had lead me straight back to the beginning, nothing had changed; well not significantly. But I have a nagging confidence that there's going to be a few more chapters to this story and that it isn't over yet.

This quotation thesped itself to me during a family trip to Stratford-Upon-Avon (Warwickshire) in around **April 2018** when the journey I'd been on was stuck in my mind like a stray fence post. The impasse was an inability to move on with my life and accept defeat. In response to which my mind glitched and often reflected on it almost all day long. I had started to realise how many different roles I had played along the way. I had done the best I could as a husband, a friend, a father, a dentist and a teacher. I had also had to take on the role of human resources expert and employment solicitor.

In this chapter I will explain that my strengths didn't lie in winning and that winning isn't always what it's cracked up to be. More importantly losing isn't a dirty word, its part of a competitive life. The trick is to make it less counterproductive. I wasn't going to develop a losing attitude or let losing make me a loser. My true colours came to my rescue in the way they helped me deal with the loss. The loss had to be turned into something positive and that was made possible by me carefully coming at it in the right way.

The Experience

The cast in this chapter

Leadership team	Given name
New executive Dean	Professor Pinocchio (prone to telling lies)
Head of Department	Dr Perfidious (deceitful & untrustworthy)
Clinical Director	Dick Dastardly (a nasty devious bastard)
Human resources	Horse Rectum ((defecates bullshit on a regular basis)
Dean of Education	Dr Delphic.(deliberately obscure & ambiguous)
Chairman of Council	Dr Magoo (easily blinded and rarely accountable)

The story so far.......

1. 15th September 2015; whistle blown.

2. 2nd October 2015; Nasty Meeting with Dr Dick Dastardly.

3. 16th October 2015; Incognito Meeting with Professor Pinocchio.

4. 19th October 2015; Dick Dastardly's failed attempt to drown me in IT.

5. 1st Week December 2015; Dr Perfidious tells a bunch of staff 'Hafeez is a liability; I'll have to get rid of him'. (ouch my shoulder blades)

6. 7th December 2015; my expression of grievance to Dr Dastardly about the above.

7. 8th December 2015; IT team produces a report which implicates me as uniquely experiencing the concerns I'd reported. (ouch)

8. 17th December 2015; Dr Perfidious produces a report which implicates me as uniquely experiencing the concerns I'd reported. (ouch)

9. 8th April 2016. Professor Pinocchio & Mr Wily failed to re-label my protected disclosures a grievance. (phew)

10. 18th July 2016; Mr high-up concluded the leadership couldn't have known that I had blown the whistle.

11. 4th August 2016; Dr Insightful initiated a formal investigation into my concerns.

12.   30th September 2016; Sinister meeting with Dr Comprehensive.

13. 24th October 2016; I complain to the CEO of the NHS trust.

14. 26th January 2017; I escalate my concerns to the General Dental Council.

15. 31st January 2017; Dr Magoo neutralised my concerns citing Dr Delphic's whiter than white soap-suds report.

16. 2nd February 2017; I informed The Iconic machine that I'd escalated my concerns to the GDC.

17. 17th March 2017; I was suspended on 7 spurious allegations.

18. 12th April 2017; the spurious evidence pack arrived.

19. 21st April 2017; flawed investigation No 1.

20. 7th July 2017; first disciplinary hearing.

21. 19th July 2017; 1st disciplinary concludes with none of the allegations being proved.

22. 20th August 2017; fraudulent letters are used to frame me and a second disciplinary process is initiated.

23. 18th September 2017; flawed investigation No 2

24. 8th December 2017; second disciplinary hearing.

25. Wednesday 20th December 2017; emergency meeting with legal counsel.

26. Thursday 21st December 2017; 2nd disciplinary concludes with the allegation not being proved.

27. 16th January 2018; I am dismissed on the ostensible grounds of 'breakdown in relationship'.

28. Between January and October 2018 the GDC commence 8 'fitness to practice' cases.

29. 18th June 2018; my claim for automatic unfair dismissal, ordinary unfair dismissal and detriment is accepted by the employment tribunal.

30. 3rd August 2018; preliminary employment tribunal hearing.

......By the final bell I'd been handled by 8 hybrid humans each one slightly different than the previous but all members of team Horse Rectum (HR). Each of them had smiled (or e-mailed) charismatically whilst attempting with great care and attention to slip me some nasty sulphur mustard gas which they had falsely labeled as helpful; the fumes from which always burnt my brain for days. I had exchanged over 40 e-mails with them. They had managed to discourage my teaching colleagues from contacting me and blocked me from contacting the patients and students whose complaints I'd escalated.

I had raised my concerns to:

1. The General Dental Council.
2. The Higher Education Funding Council for England.
3. The Care Quality Commission.
4. NHS improvement.
5. The National Guardians Office
6. The Information Commissioners Office
7. Public Concern at Work.
8. The Professional Standards Authority (PSA).
9. My local MP.

The **General Dental Council (GDC)** was quickest to respond. I escalated my concerns and those of approximately 22 patients and over 30 named students to them on **26th January 2017**. I summarised my concerns as ones of:

1. Patient safety

2. Patient harm

3. Negative impact on and compromise to the standards of education of the undergraduate students in respect to integrated restorative care and more specifically periodontal care.

4. Concealment of the above.

The GDC informed me on **1st February 2017** (3 working days) that:

1. They could not investigate all the patients whose concerns I had escalated.

2. The failings I had alleged in respect to the teaching at *The Machine* were not the GDC's remit to investigate and that they would be passing this on to the Quality Assurance Agency for Higher Education separately.

It wasn't the response I had expected but I responded and informed them that it was indeed their responsibility to investigate all the patients whose concerns I had escalated and that it was also their responsibility to investigate the educational failings. They flat refused and remained unconvinced; in a bullish way. I solved the problem by:

1. Going to the GDC website
2. Printing off GDC statements and documents
3. Sending the statements and documents to the GDC with an explanation of how to use them.

Things improved a little but their appetite for mistakes was similar to a bee's appetite for pollen. I waited till they made the Key Stone Cops look like Sherlock Holmes before I wrote 2 letters of complaint in **April 2018**; one to Mr Ian Brack the CEO and another to the Chairman Mr William Moyes. My letters were acknowledged by their personal assistant but neither of them responded to my complaints (not until I had contacted my MP in **July 2019**). I have pasted below the letter which details the concerns that I asked them to address:

My concerns related to educational standards were:

1. The Triage manager at the GDC wrote to me on 01-02-17 stating that "the failings you allege in respect of the standards of learning at KCL are not within the remit of the GDC to investigate. I will be writing to the Quality Assurance Agency for Higher Education separately about your concerns" and continued to insist on this despite repeated communications from me pointing out the GDC's statutory obligations. This is a clear failing which has not been acknowledged, investigated or addressed.

2. I highlighted named students who had expressed to me dissatisfaction, anger, frustration that the failings at *The Machine* were seriously impacting their learning. The machine failed to contact any of these students or conduct any investigations. The GDC has failed to contact any of these students or conduct any investigations.

3. I highlighted 2 previous complaints to the machine from clinical staff along the same lines as my concerns. The machine failed to acknowledge, investigate or address the concerns raised by those staff. The GDC failed to contact those staff or make any investigations into the concerns raised by those staff.

4. My disclosures highlight failings by named members of the leadership team but the sum total of the GDC's investigation was to ask those same leaders to comment on my allegations. This was akin to a judge asking the accused "did you do it then?" and then accepting their word on the matter. The GDC has failed in its obligation to conduct a thorough investigation on educational standards at *The Machine*.

5. I remain in regular contact with my teaching colleagues who tell me nothing has improved and educational standards remain as poor as I described. They are aware that I have raised concerns directly with you and are aware that *The Machine* has terminated my contract for having done so. Many of those registrants have raised their own concerns with the leadership team at *The Machine* but are frightened to pursue the matter further in fear of being victimized as I have been. Those registrants were hoping and expecting that the GDC would contact and interview them directly to give them the opportunity to share their concerns in a safe environment away from the eyes of the leadership team. This is a clear failing in the GDC's responsibility to ensure the quality of educational programs in dentistry.

6. In the outcome letters for the fitness to practice cases CAS-182288; CAS-182469; CAS-182476 the GDC brought my attention to the rule 9 process which enables me to request a legal review of the decision prior to requesting a judicial review. In a letter dated 6th March 2018 you make it clear that in relation to my concerns regarding compromised educational standards at KCLDI you "now consider the matter closed". You have not brought my attention to any mechanisms equivalent to the rule 9 process or made it clear to me how I can request a legal review of your decision prior to escalating to a judicial review.

My concerns related to patient safety were:

1. On 1st March 2017 the triage officer at the GDC instructed me to seek patient consent and supply the GDC with patient's records. This is not something that they should have been asking me to do, they should have been

doing it themselves. This is a clear failing which has not been acknowledged, investigated or addressed.

2.   The document bundle that I provided to the GDC on 26-01-17 included 22 patients whose safety had been compromised by failings at *The Machine*. The GDC failed to investigate all but 6 as they stated that I had not identified the registrants responsible for the failings in the other 16 cases. This is a clear failing in their statutory duties. I made it clear that I had been prevented by *The Machine* from gaining access to the records of the other 16 patients. The GDC has powers to access those records and its failure to recognize the registrants responsible constitutes a clear failing in the GDC's duties to protect patients. If your case workers are findings it difficult to identify the registrants responsible for failings in these 16 cases then I would be happy to assist. Obviously, I would need you to send me a copy of the records.

3.   The senior caseworker at the GDC stated in her letter to me dated 08-02-2018 "these investigations were focused on the care provided to the patients you had named, on the dates you had specified, by the dental professionals you identified as responsible for those periods of treatment". Limiting the investigations in this way is the cause of the GDC's failure in its duties to protect patients and identify failings. What was necessary to protect patients was to have expanded the investigation to include all the care for all the patients I identified and to establish which registrants were responsible for which failings on which date. If your case workers are findings it difficult to identify the registrants responsible for failings, or the dates of those failings, in these 16 cases then I would be happy to assist. Obviously, I would need you to send me a copy of the records.

4.   The senior caseworker at the GDC stated in her letter to me dated 08-02-2018 "We cannot investigate institutions or premises, only the fitness of practice of specific registrants. In my letter to her dated 09-02-18

my final paragraph said "as it is now evident that the GDC cannot investigate institutions and organisations. Please can you tell me who is responsible for investigating institutions?" so far the GDC fails to answer my question.

As the GDC staff maintained their bullish denial I wrote to the Senior Higher Education Policy Adviser of Regulation and Assurance at The Higher Education Funding Council for England (HEFCE). She confirmed that the GDC had indeed escalated something to the Quality Assurance Agency (QAA) but she didn't know what had been escalated. The QAA had in turn passed it on to her office. She then wrote back to the GDC and informed them that it was not HEFCE policy to intervene in ongoing investigations by other organisations and that they would not be taking any further action.

It all got a bit confusing when she informed me that HEFCE had two routes for students, staff or third parties to raise matters of concern with them. She explained them as:

-**The Unsatisfactory Quality Scheme** which is the route for individuals or groups to inform them of systemic quality issues relating to academic standards or the student academic experience within the Higher Education institutes (HEI) that we fund.

-**Public Interest Disclosures (whistleblowing)**: this process allows students, staff or others to report matters relating to financial irregularity, mismanagement, governance, fraud or non-compliance with charity laws by exempt HEIs to us.

I didn't have the time to research further but I anticipated that *The machine* was not one of the HEI's that the HEFCE funded or that the concerns I had raised were not covered under charity laws.

It would be unfair to say the GDC weren't consistent as they were consistently inconsistent. They consistently assessed the patients concerns with subjectivity over objectivity and they were consistently in denial over their errors. Given my experience of the GDC I often ask myself what I consider to be a reasonable question, 'How can the rest of the dental profession or the public be expected to have an accurate understanding of the GDC's standards when their own staff go to such lengths to misunderstand and misrepresent them?' It's against this backdrop of unreliability that the profession has continued to lose confidence in them. They have certainly failed to inspire any confidence in the profession in the eyes of my patients. My experience confirms why dental professionals don't feel invested in them and validates their sceptical and suspicious feelings that the GDC's way of doing things is not balanced, fair or proportionate.

The **Care Quality Commission** CQC responded in a similar way by distancing itself from the concerns by stating: CQC has no legislative powers to settle individual matters of complaint about regulated services. It didn't figure as I had escalated the concerns raised by 22 patients to them

I solved the problem by:

1. Going to the CQC website
2. Printing off CQC statements and documents
3. Sending the statements and documents to the CQC with an explanation of how to use them.

Things improved a little for a while but when they failed to implement their own policies I complained to a manager. I was told: The responsibility for investigating your specific concerns lies with the NHS Trust with recourse to the GDC and the Parliamentary and Health Service Ombudsman (PHSO) as CQC has no legislative powers to settle individual matters of complaint about regulated services.

NHS improvement told me: that their remit relates to how well led NHS Trusts and NHS Foundation Trusts are. Plus they only gather information and they do not have any powers to investigate complaints. They gathered the information from me and sent me a summary of what I had shared with them. They also offered the following advice:

Some of the concerns you have raised relate to the quality of care provided by undergraduate students. Therefore, you may want to raise your concerns with Health Education England as they are a prescribed body and can be contacted about matters that relate to the education and training of healthcare workers. You could pursue concerns about the way the university treated you as an employee with an employment tribunal. Their website is: http://hee.nhs.uk/; you can tell the CQC about any residual concerns you have about patients and they will take them into account when deciding when next to inspect the trust. You will find information about how to contact CQC here. Additional concerns that you have raised relate to the way you have been treated by your employer (the university). Therefore, you may want to pursue claims via an employment tribunal and you will find useful information about how to do that here.

The National Guardians Office acknowledged the concerns I raised and informed me that they would conduct a review for which they placed me on a waiting list. After a year's wait they informed me that I could ask them to review my case before or after the completion of the employment tribunal. The adviser was very helpful and confided in me that I should think very carefully before asking them to investigate my case. He went on to tell me that the outcomes of their investigations were often different to what the facts might lead one to expect. He kindly forwarded me copies of two recent reports they had completed. The reports successfully convinced me not to request an investigation as in both of them they went round and around in circles prior to neutralising all the concerns.

I contacted the **Information Commissioners Office** and informed them that *the machine* had failed to provide me with the personal information I had requested by way of a subject access request. They informed me that they wouldn't look into the matter unless I could provide the evidence that I had already raised it directly with *the machine* first.

Public Concerns at work told me: We offer constructive advice as to how individuals can raise concerns in a way that minimises harm to their position however we are not a reporting body and as such cannot investigate concerns ourselves. They asked me to check and confirm that I had raised my concerns in accordance with their advice. I checked and confirmed that I had done exactly as they advised.

On the **18th May 2019** I had a meeting with my local MP Mr Matt Western to discuss my concerns and I explained to him that the GDC had failed in all of its key responsibilities and asked him for his assistance. Mr Western kindly wrote to the GDC, the PSA and the Secretary of State for Health.

The **Professional Standards Authority** (PSA) informed him on **4th June 2019**: 'The Authority promotes the health, safety and wellbeing of patients, service users and the public by raising standards of regulation and voluntary registration of people working in health and care. We are an independent organisation, accountable to the UK Parliament. We oversee the work of nine statutory organisations, that regulate health professionals in the UK and social workers in England. We review the regulators' performance and audit and scrutinise their decisions about whether people on their registers are fit to practice. We can refer final fitness to practice panel decisions to court where we believe the decision was insufficient to protect the public; maintain public confidence in the profession; and/or maintain proper professional standards. However, we are not able to intervene in the way in which the GDC handles individual cases or on behalf of registrants.'

My comments to my MP were:

'I appreciate the explanation offered by Mr Alan Clamp but feel it is unfair to describe this matter as an individual case, due to the number of patients, students and teachers involved. I would appreciate it if you would ask the PSA to comment in a more detailed way on the value of investigations during which none of the complainants were contacted. I feel this is a reasonable request'. At the time of writing I was still awaiting a response.

Mr Brack from the GDC also wrote to him on **11th July 2019** but remained tight lipped on the failures I had pointed out to him in my **April 2018** letter.

My comments to my MP were:

'I remain dissatisfied because I do not believe the GDC contacted the same patients, students or teachers. If they had they could confirm having done so. I am not surprised that my concerns have not been substantiated as the patients, students and teachers were not contacted or spoken to during the investigations. I would appreciate it if you would ask Mr Brack to appease my concerns by confirming if the GDC contacted the patients, students or teachers cited in my disclosures during their investigations. I feel this is a reasonable request.'

At the time of writing I was still awaiting a response.

A hell of a lot of public money is being spent on regulators yet the greatest thing they deliver with any consistency is ineffectuality. They harbor the same cultures and failings as the organizations they are supposed to be regulating. If you would like to get a more detailed understanding of exactly how ineffectual they are I would recommend that you read; **Joshua's story - Uncovering the Morecambe Bay NHS scandal** by James Titcombe. James described his experience of regulators in great detail and his was a mirror of mine. He presented his story of an experience which lasted seven years and wanted to know the truth behind the death of his son Joshua, who died in hospital 8 days after being born. He exposed poor care at the hospital, failings in the hospital management team and negligence in the broader NHS regulatory systems. He described: 'at almost every turn there was denial, obfuscation and dishonesty.' I admire James for successfully navigating his way around the transparently opaque regulatory framework. I'm from within the industry and found it very difficult at times. I am certain it's not designed to be prohibitive by accident; it's carefully designed to put people off using it. Yet another triumph. James was not reporting the usual margin of error common to all state-delivered services; he reported deliberate acts of collusion, corruption, negligence and dishonesty.

There is no simple or single reason why so many organizations are universally useless but I've managed to narrow it down to three broad ones which compound each other:

- The shortage of basic skills
- A cultural misunderstanding of equality
- Poor leadership

Let me explain what I mean. Individuals use a range of excuses to mask their lacking skill, one of them is equality. I truly believe that we are all born equal and we should all be treated as equals, in our humanity; you know kindness and brotherly love. However I also believe that our right to equality (in our humanity) should not be confused with the status we achieve for ourselves in society in general or more specifically the workplace. Our social and work communities are kept functional by many and varied hierarchical systems. Hierarchies are not the problem; they work very well and are necessary to stimulate our drivers through competition and growth. The problem is misguided individuals demanding equality in a hierarchy which has been abused and corrupted by: 'jobs for the boys' with the granting of jobs for those without the necessary skills or promoting those who happily prostitute themselves to the goals of the greed driven business.

In my experience those who create the greatest waves about equality are often those who've got the greatest skills shortage to conceal. Their motive, the crafty bastards, is to create eruptions to distract the focus away from their inability to perform their duties and to keep the eyes from what they've swept under the carpet. The best workplaces have an established skills hierarchy in place. The hierarchy suppresses the ever present anarchical lazy trait. However, in the absence of good leadership or in the presence of a corrupt one the hierarchy falls apart. Factions of the team start stomping their feet demanding their ill-conceived notion of equality (in the work place). It's an equality which is defined by their wants irrespective of the needs of the employer.

Sadly, the new staff coming into the workplace is becoming poorer and poorer prepared for the task in hand. They often enter an environment where they can be as lazy as they wish and get away with it. The vagueness created by the leadership team at *the machine* caused the teaching staff to float around not knowing what their purpose was, in a state of bafflement and despair. Remember: 'The standard of newly qualified dental graduates – foundation trainer perceptions' in chapter six. I would say what is true for the newly qualified dentists is true for the rest of the team right across dentistry and right across all the other industries to include the regulators.

A poor leadership team fails to encourage its staff to show any initiative or enterprise; after all they don't really want anyone to out-shine them. There's a lot of it about; a lot. If you happen to be in a job with poor leadership my advice would be:

'Don't apologise for not asking for permission, apologise for having shown the initiative; apologise for having made the improvement without asking for permission'

It should sound like this: 'I'm sorry I made the improvement before asking you'.
It should not sound like this: 'I'm sorry that I didn't ask before I made the improvement.'

The Inspiration.

I was left astonished and struggled to accept how all the organisations I encountered seemed to suffer the same syndrome as if it was contagious. It continued to bother and frustrate me to know that it would have been cheaper and far more beneficial for *the machine* to have addressed and resolved the complaints raised by the patients and the students but it appeared that the syndrome was a very old one:

'Nero Fiddled While Rome Burned'

Oliver Cromwell in the 1650's may well have presided over the power shift from the crown to the crowd but now we have to abide by the incompetence of the crowd and not a lot seemed to have changed since **Enoch Powell** was pounding the people with his extraordinary intellect:

'Ones love is for an entire generation that is doomed'

My experience leads me to gravitate towards the views Jonah Goldberg expresses in his book: **Liberal Fascism: The Secret History of the Left from Mussolini to the Politics of Meaning.** My application of his phrase Liberal Fascism attempts to explain the general behaviour of some of the staff at *The Machine.* I appreciate that some people hold the opinion that liberal and fascism are diametrically opposed and as such the phrase liberal fascism is nonsense, but I disagree. Let me explain my view of how it applies to and plays out in the workplace.

Liberal is when people want their opinion to be respected even though they lack the training or experience necessary to be able to form it. An example of this is when my receptionist tells me that she thinks I did the wrong type of treatment for my last patient. **Fascism** traditionally is characterized by dictatorial power or forcible suppression or opposition by one person over another. In the workplace it's when the individual becomes oppressed by their own mind; their mind continues to force them to expect their opinion to be heard. Keeping with the same example, this is what is perceived when I tell my receptionist that if she wasn't so busy creating conspiracy theories about what I might or might not have done right or wrong she wouldn't make so many mistakes of her own at the reception desk. For all the wrong reasons she feels oppressed by me, it's part of the 'no one wants to concentrate and everyone wants to speak' syndrome.

In summary and contrary to the traditional sense, Fascism when it is used in the phrase Liberal fascism is when the staff becomes dictatorially controlled by their own mind. They become controlled in the belief that their every thought needs to be respected. Even though they do not have the experience to form the opinion they want respected. I believe that this is part of a cunning plan and is driven by their subconscious desire not to have to do an honest day's work. It's a slavish extension of their most innate biological passion; to be lazy. If they succeed in their cunning plan they have avoided the alternative which would have required concentration and some actual 'work'. This is one explanation as to why it so difficult to find a well written set of patient's notes at *The Machine*. Workplaces with poor leadership are prone to accepting the liberal views expressed by those who lack the experience to form them and when this happens nothing progressive is achieved or get's done. If only they could see it more like Noel Coward, who felt that:

'Work is more fun that fun'

I would say that if the correct person has been recruited to the job they prefer some tyrannical perfectionism in their leadership, assuming the level of overall staffing is correct. Good staff work best when they are given some rules to work to. Good staff like to feel pushed. Good staff get satisfaction from having worked hard. However, when the level of staffing is inadequate the same approach is bullying. Tyrannical perfectionism creates an environment in which staff can easily identify their objectives, targets and goal. The job gets done.

Some of the inspiration on this occasion was not positive in any way whatsoever. It was a disappointing indictment of my previous experiences of dentists and dentistry most of which had regrettably been poor. It was yet another episode signaling the need for change in the industry. I have met a lot of good honest talented dentists; honest and good and talented until they stepped out from behind their websites. In 25 years of practice I have never met a single dentist who had provided any of the poor quality dentistry which is evident in patient's mouths everyday of the week. Aliens must have done it?

I had responded to an advert in the classified section of the British Dental Journal. One of the larger corporate chains of dental practices, Portman Dental Care, was looking to recruit a periodontal specialist. The group has a professional website which displays the five industry awards of excellence they had achieved. They boast eighty five practices nationwide on their website. I went to one of their practices for an interview. The practice was a forty minute drive northeast of my home and within commutable range but I ended up declining the opportunity to work there. I have pasted below the e-mail I sent on the **1st March 2018** explaining my reasons (names have been changed):

Dear Sarah.

Thank you for organising the meeting at the practice. I really appreciated the opportunity to meet with you all.

You wanted to know what my requirements would be as a visiting periodontal specialist and I advised you that:

1. All patients should be referred to me for specialist periodontal services using a formal letter of referral.

2. That should a patient raise a concern or a complaint I would explain to them that "I am a visiting specialist and I only have access to the notes I am making. Please discuss your concerns with your dentist".

You and Lesley agreed with my requirements and advised me that this was the correct way to proceed and in accordance with the professional standards that the group stands for.

I was pleased but sceptical about your rapid agreement to the above terms. I advised you that in respect to periodontal services there was a trend and a problem in some practices. That problem was that some dentists fail to discuss gum disease with their patients and some dentists fail to record discussions about gum disease in their patient's notes. Gum disease and the lack of its discussion with patients is a big problem and requires a culture change, moving forward. In this respect the letter of referral is a necessary element, as is an agreement that the visiting specialist will not "trawl" though the patients notes.

When we met with the principle dentist Dr Stewart he advised us that he did not feel that above approach would work within the practice patient base. He agreed that not all dentists record all conversations in the notes and it would not be appropriate for a visiting specialist to "trawl" through the notes. However, he did not suggest an alternative. The associate dentist Dr Mostin highlighted to us that the previous dentists (who had now left the practice) had not discussed gum disease with their patients. She told us that it had been a hard struggle for her when she joined the practice to educate some of those patients with gum disease. That the previous periodontist had told her that your practice was the toughest practice he had worked in compared to his other places of employment. That things are better now but patients often expressed dissatisfaction when they moved from one dentist to another within the practice.

Based on what your dentists told me I have decided to decline the opportunity to join your practice on this occasion. I am certain that the group will want to address the highlighted problems and I remain open to discussions about a future role at the practice should it be considered that the conditions we discussed are the right way forward for the practice.

For now, I wish you the very best.

With regards

Dr Hafeez Ahmed

The head of recruitment at Portman Dental Care acknowledged my e-mail and suggested that I consider an alternative practice in the group as he felt it might be more suitable. This one was also forty miles southwest from my home. It too was in commutable range so I visited it for an interview. In the run up to the interview I explained my concerns about the first practice to the practice manager of the second and I sent her a copy of my previous e-mail to the first practice. During the interview we discussed my concerns and the practice manager readily accepted my terms of engagement so I signed a contract and within a week arrived for my first day at the practice. Sadly, the relationship did not last very long. I have pasted below the e-mail I sent to the head of recruitment on **15th March 2018** shortly after my departure which was about 20 minutes after my arrival (names have been changed):

Dear David Green.

I did not like the situation you put me in yesterday.

I have never been treated as deceitfully as you have treated me since I contacted you after my visit to your other practice.

I turns out that the situation at this practice is as bad if not worse than the other one.

I arrived at the practice at 8.25am. I got changed and was about to start reading the patient notes for the day. At 8.40am the practice manager arrived and said to me "We need to have a chat about the situation with Julian. He is struggling a lot. He is finding it really stressful. He has been left in a terrible situation. It's not his fault. The dentist he took over from didn't use to write any notes. Julian is having to work with no notes in lots of cases. It's not his fault but we have to help him sort it out." I asked her to tell me which Julian she was talking about as both of the dentists who had departed recently were also called Julian. She told me she was talking about Julian Gardner. I asked her if the dentist who Julian Gardner took over from had failed to document gum disease or related discussions about gum disease in the patients notes. She told me that the previous dentist was the previous owner of the practice and that he hardly made any notes at all. She gave me an example. If the patient had had a white filling in the lower left first molar the notes would say "Composite filling LL6".

It turns out that you were not honest with me and as a direct result of that I have lost all faith, confidence and trust in everything you had told me about the practice.

The contract I signed is based on deceit and as such null and void, you can tear it up.

It would have been easier and better if you had been honest with me then we could have agreed a way forward. That said the opportunity has been squandered as I have lost all faith, confidence and trust in you.

Please can you confirm that you have destroyed the contract?

Kind regards

Dr Hafeez Ahmed.

At the time of writing, I would say, all things considered, that some of the best NHS practices are providing care which is equal to if not better than their private counterparts. Finding those practices is no easy task though. The future however appears to be capitalist and corporate. When I qualified, a dentist would work in a variety of posts honing skills for approximately 5 years prior to setting up or buying their own dental practice. They would then nurture it and care for its patients with a plan to sell it at the end of their career. The sale of the practice used to, in some ways, be the dentists pension pot. This was all before some super-fast, super-smart, bitch-ness man said to himself: 'I know, I'll borrow lots of money from the honest banks and I'll use it buy up lots of dental practices and then I'll get lots of dentists to work in them like sweat shops. I'll employ the newly qualified dentists because they won't have a clue about what's going on'.

The corporate chain was born and it grew and grew and grew. When a practice came up for sale the corporate chain could always offer more money for it than an independent dentist. Thus pricing out the independent. Similar to when retiring fisherman in the UK sold their fishing rights to the highest bidder with the result being that they ended up in the hands of fishermen from the EU. Sometimes the fee the corporate paid was 'excessive' but that wasn't a problem because the loan was going to be loaded back onto the business. Just like Glazer did at Manchester United football club. Once the loan's been loaded on to the business patients pay higher fees which aren't directly related to a superior service. Just like the banks and their sub-prime mortgage deals. It's a bubble. Before long dental chains became a big thing a bit like Greggs and Pound Stretcher. I even remember when Boots the chemist tried being Boots the dentist. It didn't last long. They got into trouble with the advertising standards agency for misleading marketing. Once the chain's been grown it's often (if not always) offloaded onto the next bitch-ness man. Very similar to banks selling sub-prime mortgage packages to each other. And then one day the bubble pops. I've seen loads of chains change hands with each new owner leaning a bit harder on the dentists to sell sell sell.

In a dog eat dog world the dentist selling his practice to the chain prepares it by inflating the profits by reducing his take home for a few years. The incompetent accountants in the chain don't notice because they just want to add another practice to the gravy train. He also hides all the cases of supervised neglect. The selling dentist is required to stay on (usually for a fixed term of two years) as a condition of the sale. This works out well for him it allows him to continue to conceal his cover up of the negligence cases. Once he departs the new dentists are left to sort out the shit. That's exactly what was happening at the Portman practice I visited and every other chain I've had the misfortune to work at. All of them. The current money spinners are Botox and facial aesthetics. Which makes all the sense in the world, the logic being that because dentists are so good at teeth and gums they should be great at facial aesthetics. The ticking time bomb, however, is dental implants. Sold like hot cakes and performing like soggy buns. It's the gum disease around them that makes them soggy. I have lost count of the number of dentists who have whispered in my ear 'if you tell patients about the gum disease they won't want to pay for the implants'. It's probably because I'm a gum specialist but I've taken more implants out than I've put in.

Portman Dental Care didn't treat me with any great respect or competence but by far the most incompetent individual I've ever met was a practice manager at a multi award winning prestigious private dental practice in Central London. She was a chartered business psychologist with an MSc in occupational psychology. To describe her as incompetent would be an insult to cloddishness. She had so much important stuff in her head that it had pushed out any intelligence or sense she might or might not have had. She just talked shit. Lots of shit. Great big carrier bags of poop purged at will. She had an innate affinity for freakish faeces. I'd say she had been recklessly eating her own. She probably dreamt of pooping on futuristic toilets which delivered it straight on to a plate for her (with ketchup).

I often ask myself 'what is wrong with all these people?' I've always viewed the dental industry as a pond, a very small pond and I've always hated standing in it whilst everyone else continues to piss into it. I have never got used to it. For example, earlier this year I was asked to consult a patient, she presented with active advanced gum disease with many mobile teeth; soon to be lost.

During the consultation she told me how surprised she was when she given the news by her new dentist. When I asked her why, she told me that it had only been six months since she had paid another gum specialist four thousand pounds for gum treatment which he had told her had been successful. She then asked me incredulously: 'don't you think I have the right to be surprised?' 'I don't know' was my reply before I confessed to her that what surprised me was that she wasn't having the conversation with the fella she'd given her four thousand pounds to.

I suppose I should demystify gum disease to allow you to take more responsibility for yourself. About 35% of people are susceptible to it. They are born that way, comparable to being born with asthma; it's in the genes, the individual has no control over it. The best a sufferer can do is to manage it to keep the bone loss minimal. The hygienist is the dental equivalent of the Ventolin inhaler used by the asthmatic individual. She helps the sufferer control the condition but does not eliminate their susceptibility to it; the susceptibility cannot be eliminated. Gum disease irreversibly destroys the bone that holds the teeth in place. No one knows why it happens. It can affect one tooth, multiple teeth or all teeth. Cleaning teeth with regular toothbrushes (electric or manual) doesn't make much of an improvement for those who are susceptible. Improvement requires a detailed clean of the cuff of gum around each tooth; where the tooth emerges from. In my experience this is best achieved with Cocktail sticks, preferably ones without pineapple or cheese on them. The type of cleaning sufferers should consider undertaking is demonstrated in my YouTube video titled 'Oral hygiene instructions with gum specialist Dr Ahmed'.

The British Dental Association published my letter on the benefits of cocktails sticks in Volume 220: No6 of the British Dental Journal in March 2016*.

*https://www.nature.com/articles/sj.bdj.2016.209

As a simple rule of thumb gum disease runs in families so if you want to know if you're likely to have been born with the predisposition to lose the bone around your teeth then just look at your parents. Have they been told they have gum disease? Have they lost any teeth? Do they wear false ones? Did their parents (your grandparents) wear false teeth? If they did you are likely to have inherited a similar susceptibility for bone loss and as such you need to be more proactive to retain your gum health. A word of warning on human denial, I once consulted a female patient in her forties; her mum was in the room as a chaperone. During the consultation I said to the patient: 'gum disease is a story, what's your story?' she told me she told me she'd been persuaded by her dentist to whiten her teeth and during the bleaching process she had 'caught' gum disease. Her overactive imagination left me with an image of the 1974 cartoon Roobarb and Custard in my head. I explained that this wasn't the case and asked her mum if she had her own teeth. Her mum who was sat just behind me gave me a coy smile and softly confirmed that she indeed have her own teeth. From where I was standing my peanuts could only see dentures so I asked mum to flash me another smile, she did and I whispered back; 'those are false teeth'. To which she replied: 'that's right, MY false teeth, you asked me if they were mine and they are mine'. Before I knew it I'd belted: 'god help us'.

To summarise susceptible individuals are born with a predisposition to lose the bone that holds their teeth in place. There's no cure for susceptibility. There is however a way to prevent the bone loss, this requires a dedicated approach to homecare. Something I've witnessed happening successfully in approximately 10% of my patients over a 25 year period. The other 90% are individuals who scrub their teeth a bit harder in the two weeks prior to appointments. This is even after I've explained for the first seventy three times that the professional cleaning that I or any dentist or any hygienist provides is an adjunct to and acts to complement the homecare and is not in itself sufficient to prevent bone loss. What we professionals do is simply remove what shouldn't be on the teeth in the first place, the removal of which is necessary for patients to be able to get to the gum margins (which would otherwise remain buried under it) to clean them.

In respect to the overall experience I had to get some closure and decided to call time on it the day after the employment tribunal accepted my application. Come on, what else could go wrong? Only joking there's no virtue in being unrealistic. Point to note though, I hadn't quit I'd stopped. Quitting is what you do when you can't handle a setback and leave a goal unfulfilled. Stopping is what you do when you've passed the test and are ready to move onto something else. I was comfortable I'd reached inside myself and passed the test and in doing so I was confident that I had also avoided the pitfall described by **Friedrich Nietzsche** who warned that:

'Whoever fights monsters should see to it that in the process he does not become a monster'

What a journey it's been, it's been precious, every minute of it. In my naivety, I had thought I would raise a few concerns and then if necessary muck in to help sort them out. Could I have been any more wrong? Now I'm caught in a dilemma: am I more torn than I am exhilarated? or am I more exhilarated than I am torn?

As things all too often do my claim for unfair dismissal was settled out of court. The settlement agreement became official on 18th July 2019. The details of it were to remain confidential and nobody who was involved was permitted to talk about it. That is until the Icon breached the terms of the agreement exactly 22 days after it was made. In settling out of court the Icon paid me five times what I would have been awarded if the case had gone to court and my dismissal had been proven to be indeed unfair.

One thing's for sure, the memories will always be bittersweet. When I speak to my former teaching colleagues at The Machine and they tell me; nothing has changed, I am definitely more torn. Could I have done more? Could I have done it differently? When I look at the journey I've had, the experience, the exposure, and the fact that I have the material for three more books I am definitely exhilarated. Exhilarated; as in outrunning a tiger in the jungle. I wouldn't change it for the world and am left wondering if I'll be lucky enough to have another equally invigorating experience.

I was learning........

I was learning that even though the odds were set against me I had remained resolute:

'The man who wins is man who thinks he can'

Voltaire

I was learning that although not always possible most of the time I retained my dignity:

'Disagree without being disagreeable'

Zig Zigler

I was learning a lot from a Chinese proverb. The proverb assumes that a man is at the top of a mountain and he needs to get to the sea at the bottom, making his journey by river. The proverb is: 'The man who succeeds is the man who negotiates his canoe with the ebb and flow of the river to his destination' This conveys the message that to get from where you are to where you want to be involves many unpredictable variables in spite of you knowing what your route is. You cannot know what the river will do so you cannot have a rigid plan. Success lies in feeling your way down the river and taking reflexive decisions as necessary. You have to be prepared to be thrown out of the canoe and if you are you only have one option. Get back in. What's the alternative? You wouldn't dream of just giving up, would you?

I was learning that this book wasn't easy to write. If you get the impression that I could say just about anything and really not care. You'd be wrong. It's taken a lot for me to say what I've said and I did it because I care. I had promised the students that I would help them and I had to keep my promise. I had promised the patients that I would escalate their concerns and I had to keep that promise too. If I have given you the impression that standing against my peers was easy. It was not. If the way I have expressed myself in this book makes it look as if it was easy to expose the failings. It was not. But I'm glad I did.

I was learning how painfully difficult it was for me to accept the number of professional organisations and regulators who publish their expectations of a whistleblower and then do the arse end of nothing to uphold their published expectations or to protect the individual who follows them. The truth cannot be denied just misrepresented. At first glance Christopher Columbus is known to be a great explorer, navigator and colonist credited for leading the first expedition to Central and South America. You have to look much much deeper for the raping, slavery and genocide. It's all there.

I was learning that we're all conditioned to believe the law exists to protect us. Yet, in my experience, I was working out that it wasn't. It was incapable of doing such a thing since in the U.K you can't legally make anyone do anything. You can only make them not do things, or you can have things taken away from them. Knowing this made it seem half-witted for me to continue to indiscriminately rely on the say-so of others. Especially since so many had been given the opportunity to uphold standards but had failed. I reconciled (and warn my children) that the law is not designed to protect us. The law is the new secular religion, purposely shrouded in an elusive mystique so the wealthy can continue to exercise possession. It's the modern equivalent of the Tripitaka, the Vedas, the Torah, the Bible, the Quran and any other religious publications you can think of. The law is a collection of rules written by individuals, agreed by groups and worshiped by the foolish (like me). The motive(s) behind the rules may have been honourable (some of the time) and whilst they might have been intended to offer protection, in reality they only provide some encouragement some of the time. They encourage individuals to treat themselves and those around them in a certain moralistic way. When individuals abide by them it's happy days but when they don't the victim is exposed to a pendulous experience comparable to the pirate ship ride at Alton Towers. Their guts wrenched under great force from side to side with the prospect of justice equal to the probability of winning the national lottery. That said, even though the law might not be perfect it's preferable to the other forms of mob rule (sike).

I was learning to deal with knowing that my effort and energy had been wasted and how in our ever-changing world nothing ever changes. My energy had been swallowed up fuelling the monstrous egos pervading those in power, like a pernicious cancer of the brain. The Latin's, Freud and Jung were of very limited help to me as they hadn't offered any guidance on how to apply their abstract scientific theories to yield interpretations of practical everyday situations. I would say the purpose of the healthy ego is to stimulate ambition and incentivise it prior to driving it along with a motivational momentum. To provide us the gradient against which our efforts feel more rewarding and prevent us from falling over flat. Comparable to taking part in competitive sport with the team's position in the league table being a strong incentive to succeed.

I'd describe the ego as a transparent ball (of whatever) mounted in the subconscious mind in the blind spot immediately behind and above the optic chiasm. The imaginary ball takes a quarter-turn clockwise rotation with the achievement of a pre-conditioned goal in life. Crawling, walking and talking in the early years. GCSE's, a kiss and a cuddle, 'A' levels, first job or university degree in the middle years. Promotion, promotion and p-p-p-power in the later years. The imaginary ball has attached to its one side a toothed cog with an integral winding cord (remnants of the gubernacular cord a possibility). The cord is weighed down by the equivalent of a builder's plumb attached to its lower end (testicles or ovaries). At birth the plumb rests with its tip poised on the upper inner surface of the anus (Freudian fixation). With the achievement of each additional conditioned, perceived or preconceived goal in life the ego-ball takes a further rotation; with its overhead clasp preventing it from reverse motion. As the ego-ball turns, the plumb is winched upwards. As the cord shortens and the plumb gets closer to the underside of the ego-ball the mental tension (subconsciously) heightens. The psyche's perception being when the plumb strikes the underside of the ego-ball it's 'golden-buzzer' time. As the chemical tension mounts desperation builds. In the presence of a healthy ego the plumb never strikes the ego-ball, that's not its intended function, there's never meant to be a golden-buzzer moment. Constructive feedback and/or criticism results in the overhead clasp lifting, releasing the ego-ball to spin backwards dropping the plumb for the whole cycle to start again.

I was learning that there is no end to 'man vanity'. Humans struggle to cope with power, power corrupts and the appalling behaviours such as those displayed by the leadership team are a cultural epidemic the world over. It's just one big out-of-control ego-trip. Credential seeking careerist twat types, can't handle the gushing when their egos require a reset as described above; it's below them. Instead their imbalance allows the plumb to strike the ego-ball, sounding the golden-buzzer; oh yeah! Once it sounds they melt in its sweet honey, reminiscent of sugar in diabetics who just can't seem to get enough of it. Its charms as strong as heroin they need to hear it again and again, as the addiction builds the interval between hits diminishes; like a pensioner on a slot machine (ding-ding –ding- ding). It doesn't take too many pomp's of the golden-buzzer before greed engulfs the senses like a match to a gasoline refinery. The whole process is dependent on them first dismantling and/or corrupting any feedback mechanisms that link to their office (as evidenced in chapter 1). If any negative feedback still squishes through it's reviewed with enthusiastic selective amnesia and denial. Once the golden-buzzer sounds its screeching infects the individuals mind and resets the focus of ambition from achievements in life and work to a desire for recognition and adulation. It sets in motion a heavy pendulum which swings erratically between vanity and pride *(as evidenced in the nasty meeting back in **October 2015**)*; the pendulum unnecessarily sucks up a lot of energy.

I learnt a helpful example for enhancing my understanding of egotism, here it is. The Prime Minister of the Tang Dynasty was a national hero for his success as both a statesman and military leader. But despite his fame, power and wealth, he considered himself a humble and devout Buddhist. Often he visited his favourite Zen master to study under him, and they seemed to get along very well. The fact that he was prime minister apparently had no effect on their relationship, which seemed to be simply one of a revered master and respectful student. One day during his usual visit the Prime Minister asked the master, "Your Reverence, what is egotism according to Buddhism?" The master's face turned red and in a very condescending and insulting tone of voice, he shot back, "What kind of stupid question is that!?" This unexpected response so shocked the Prime Minister that he became sullen and angry. The Zen master then smiled and said, "THIS, Your Excellency, is egotism."

I was learning that I have got many personal flaws but I keep them out of my work. Throughout the experience I have changed and evolved and somehow avoided a nervous breakdown. The journey almost 'took me out' but I'm going to breathe better for the rest of my life. The strength was inside me, it was there all along; I just didn't know how to use it. I define nervous breakdown as an event which results in the individual no longer turning up for normal work. Instead they follow in the footsteps of pigeons around the park unable to prevent their elbows from lifting outwards or their head from bobbing forwards and backwards as they recite: 'hello, who's a pretty boy?' (everything else I define as challenge and change). That said, one thing's for sure, I've worked out that I don't like long journeys and in life the reward needs to be close to the effort otherwise the drivers fade away.

I was learning that the leadership team had set the poorest possible example in all of the GDC's four domains of dental training: professionalism, communication, management and leadership. *The Machine* had previously been heavily criticized by the GDC in 2013 and burying my concerns was yet another missed opportunity to put things right. The industry needs a shake up. The starting point should be patients being told the straight truth and allowed to make up their own minds. Patients should grow-up so that when they make the wrong decisions they can learn to live with it. Those who are found to be professionally negligent should be admonished and sanctioned subject to having their negligence judged with consistent objectivity against the GDC's published standards.

I was learning that the evidence points to the fact that the rules need to be rewritten and the system needs a purge. The young students most of whom were serene and easygoing and not yet cynical have a genuine passion and wanting to be good dentists. The patients have demonstrated that they are happy to pay for an ethical service. The nature of the human condition is such that regulation is essential. It baffles me to distraction how and why the students are failing to be trained adequately in spite of them investing so heavily in the training, why patients cannot receive an honest professional service and why the regulator can't ensure the above.

I was learning about some of the things going wrong at the regulators. I found some reports which strip back all the hype and describe the performance of the GDC and CQC. With the hype trimmed back the facts come as a shock and reveal exactly how poor they are. Reading these reports contributed heavily to my earlier statement: 'of all the animals in the animal kingdom none is as stupid as the human'

I learnt that in 2012 The House of Commons Committee of Public Accounts published its report into the Care Quality Commission*: they reported:

1. The Commission is ultimately responsible for the effective regulation of health and adult social care but has not had a grip on what it has been doing.

2. The Commission has been poorly governed and led.

3. The Commission's role was unclear and it does not measure the quality or impact of its own work.

4. The information provided to the public on the quality of care is inadequate and does not engender confidence in the care system.

And so the report rumbled on to fill eighty six pages. I've had several undesirable experiences with the CQC and each time it was evident to me that no improvement has taken place since this report was published. None whatsoever.

*https://publications.parliament.uk/pa/cm201213/cmselect/cm health/592/592we02.htm

I learnt that in 2013 People Opportunities Limited published its report* after exploring bullying and harassment within the CQC. They reported that there were worrying levels of perceived bullying at all levels in the culture of the CQC as reported by the people who self selected to be interviewed. This report only rumbled for 36 pages.

*https://www.cqc.org.uk/sites/default/files/documents/bullyin g_and_harassment_in_cqc_-_full_report.pdf

I learnt that in March 2015 the Parliamentary Health Select Committee held the GDC accountable*. The head of the under-fire GDC Mr William Moyes struck a defiant tone at a Parliamentary inquiry, telling MPs: 'Our prime responsibility is to protect patients.' he repeated it several times 'we are very clear that the GDC's prime responsibility is to protect patients'. When I wrote to the very same head of the GDC with my complaints he never responded. In my experience the GDC failed on all its objectives let alone protecting patients.

*https://www.parliament.uk/business/committees/committees -a-z/commons-select/health-committee/news/27-1-15-2015- accountability-general-dental-council/

I learnt that in December 2015 an investigation committee conducted an investigation into the General Dental Council's handling of a whistleblower from within its own ranks. The whistleblower had raised concerns about corruptions spanning right across its fitness to practice process and Investigating Committee. The report* was 306 pages long and very critical of the culture at the GDC. It bought their entire purpose into question. When I reported my concerns to them several staff got very bullish with me but neither the CEO nor the chairman responded when I wrote to them directly. Helpful. (*I waited over a year before contacting my MP*)

*https://www.professionalstandards.org.uk/publications/detail /report-of-investigation-of-general-dental-council- whistleblower-s-complaint

I learnt to neutralize my spent emotions using the take home message of my story:

'not to question what people do, simply accept that they do it'

Jordan Peterson

I no longer question what people do, I accept that they have done it and I move on.

I was learning to look at it this way, I did not lose my job. I lost a job, I still have my job, and I still have the rest of my life to do my job. Having had the experience I am reassured that I will do my job much better and feel more satisfied doing it.

I'm glad it's all over for now but I am going to leave you with this, if the problem could be solved who'd pay the taxidermy bill.

Final Note

It's not right to cheat readers and I don't want to cheat any of mine, but given the current climate of political correctness-which I rarely agree with- I left two quotes out of my book as I felt they held the potential to attract undeserved negative attention and that it might be too early in life for some younger readers to fully appreciate my application of them. But in the end I resolved that the magic of quotes is that they mean different things to different people at different times, often the same people at different stages of their life.

These two quotes were the glue which held me together and acted as the foundations on which I built the 'Philosophy for my life'

"Fuck' em all"   Ray French

I knew this one helped me but I didn't really understand what it was doing for me. During the experience I got the impression that it acted as a very effective buffer as it stopped any and all self criticism in its tracks by appealing to my inner - animal instincts - human. It created a window of time in which I'd structure and articulate a more considered intellectual philosophy to deal with the event(s) that provoked it. But after the experience was over I realised that it had worked by removing the guilt and shame which I felt throughout it. These emotions were the most difficult to decipher but I came to realise that they came from me absorbing the negative emotions, upset and the hurt of the wrongdoers. It's horrible that it works this way.

"Dr Ahmed, your wife is the most balanced person I have ever met, and you...are not"

Luke Smith

This quote held the attention of my priorities and kept my feet on the ground. Prior to hearing it I had always thought I was perfect, it made me realise that I was being too modest.

BIBLIOGRAPHY

A list of books that "found me"; ones which became the backbone of my journey and development.

1. **The Definitive Book of Body Language**
by Allan and Barbara Pease
Orion: ISBN-13: 978-0752858784

2. **Blink. The power of thinking without thinking**
by Malcolm Gladwell
Penguin: ISBN-10: 0141014598

3. **Max Perutz And The Secret Of Life**
by Georgina Ferry
Pimlico: ISBN-13: 978-1845952198

4. **Outliers**
by Malcolm Gladwell
Penguin: ISBN-13: 978-0141036250

5. **What the Dog Saw**
by Malcolm Gladwell
Penguin: ISBN-13: 978-0141044804

6. **David and Goliath**
by Malcolm Gladwell
Penguin: ISBN-13: 978-0241959596

7. **The Establishment And how they get away with it**.
by Owen Jones
Penguin: ISBN-13: 978-0141974996

8. **The Element. How finding your passion changes everything.**
by Sir Ken Robinson
Penguin: ISBN-13: 978-0141045252

9. **George Orwell: A Life in Letters**
by Peter Davidson
Liveright: ISBN-13: 978-0871404626

10. **An Intelligent Person's Guide to Education.**
by Tony Little
Bloomsbury: ISBN-13: 978-1472913111

11. **Atlas Shrugged**
by Ayn Rand
Penguin Classics: ISBN-13: 978-0141188935

12. **PostCapitalism: A Guide to Our Future**
by Paul Mason
Allen Lane: ISBN-13: 978-1846147388

13. **Talent Code. Greatness isn't born its grown**
by Daniel Coyle
Arrow: ISBN-13: 978-0099519850

14. **Words Can Change Your Brain : 12 Conversation Strategies to Build Trust, Resolve Conflict, and Increase Intimacy**
by Andrew Newberg & Mark Robert Waldman
Penguin: ISBN-13: 978-0142196779

15. **Antifragile: Things that Gain from Disorder**
by Nassim Nicholas Taleb
Penguin: ISBN-13: 978-0141038223

16. **Bully In Sight: How to predict, resist, challenge and combat workplace bullying - Overcoming the silence and denial by which abuse thrives**
by Tim Field
Success Unlimited: ISBN-13: 978-0952912101

17. **Soul of a Butterfly**
by Hana Yasmeen Ali & Muhammad Ali
Bantam: ISBN-13: 978-0553816464

18. **Think Slow Think Fast**
by Daniel Kahneman
Penguin: ISBN-13: 978-0141033570

19. **This Child Will Be Great: Memoir of a Remarkable Life by Africa's First Woman President.**
by Ellen Johnson Sirleaf
Harper Perennial: ISBN-13: 978-0061353482

20. **Catherine Graham A Personal History**
by Catherine Graham
W&N: ISBN-13: 978-1842126202

21. **12 Rules for life: An Antidote to Chaos**
by Jordan Peterson
Allen Lane: ISBN-13: 978-0241351635

22. **Like the Roman. The life of Enoch Powell**
by Simon Heffer
Faber & Faber: ISBN-13: 978-0571246618

23. **The Reason I Jump: one boy's voice from the silence of autism**
by Naoki Higashida
Sceptre: ISBN-10: 9781444776775

24.**Mind of a survivor: What the wild has taught me about survival and success**
by Megan Hind
Coronet: ISBN-13: 978-1473649316

25.**The University of Oxford. A new History**
by G R Evans
I B Tauris & Co Ltd: ISBN-13: 978-1848851146

26.**The Big Questions. How philosophy can change your life**
by Lou Marinoff
Bloomsburypbks: ISBN-13: 978-0-7475-6586-4

27.**The Intimate history of Humanity**
by Theordre Zeldin
Vintage: ISBN-13: 978-0749396237

28.**The Lost Child of Philomena Lee**
by Martin Sixsmith
Pan reprints: ISBN-10: 9780330518369

29.**Liberal Fascism: The Secret History of the Left from Mussolini to the Politics of Meaning**
By Jonah Goldberg
Penguin: ISBN-10: 0141039507

30. **The Father Effect: Hope and Healing from a Dad's Absence.**
by John Finch and Blake Atwood.
FaithWords: ISBN-10: 1478976861

30198363R00210

Printed in Great
Britain
by Amazon